WILD ABOUT **KEW**

The Village by the Thames

For Diana, Sam and Amy (my family) for their unshakable support for what I do and not forgetting Josie of course

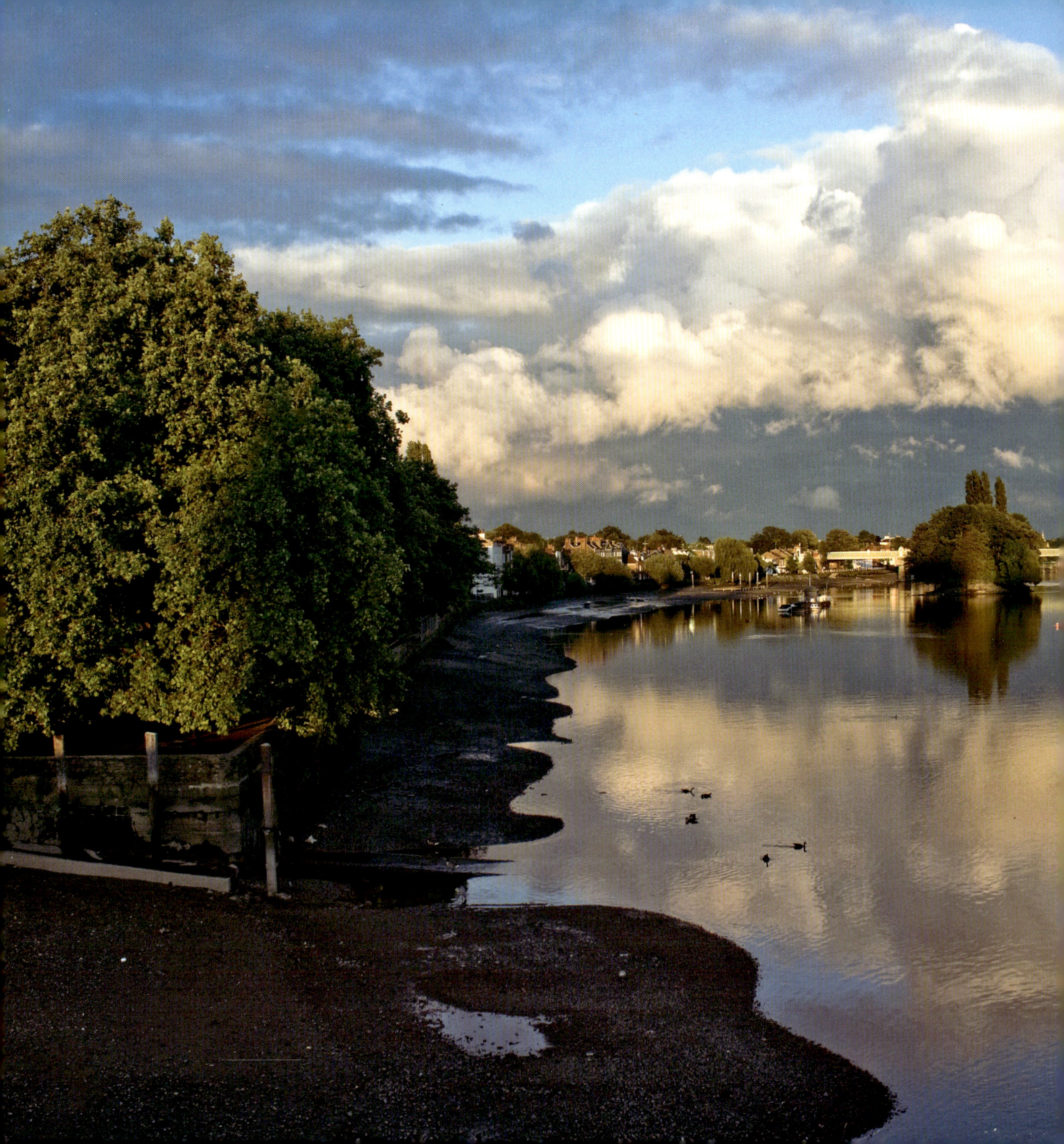

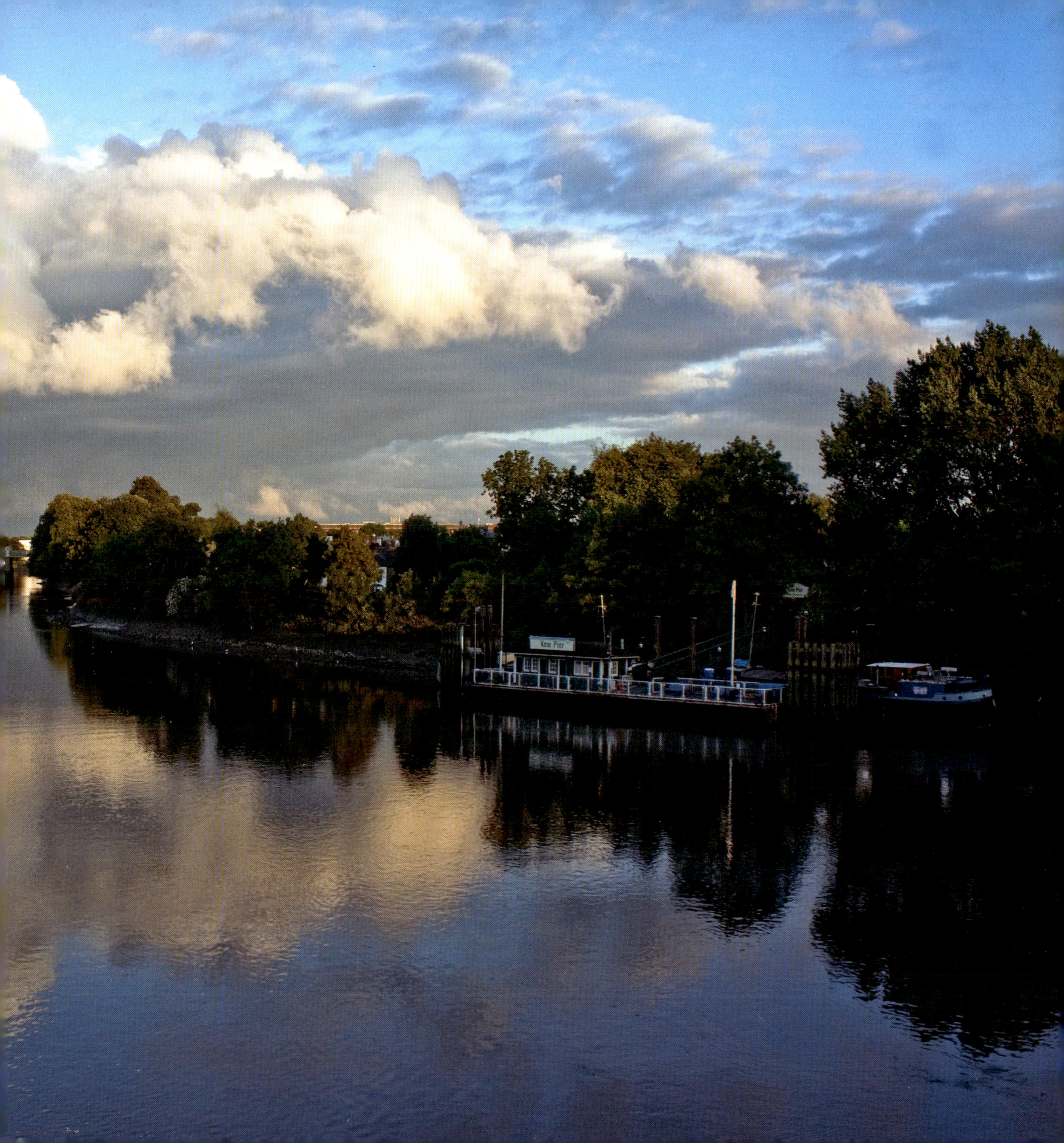
Kew Pier

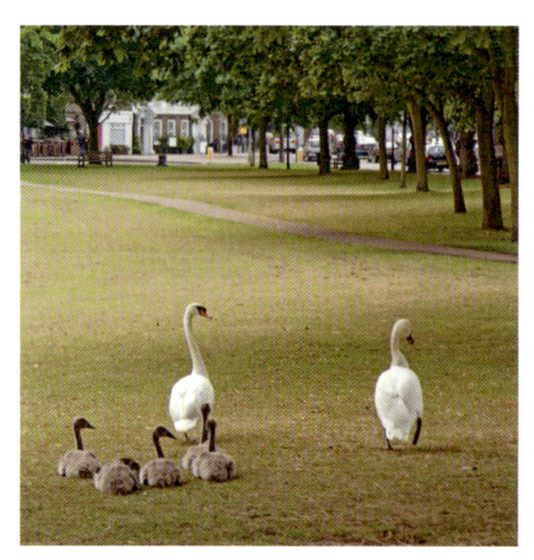

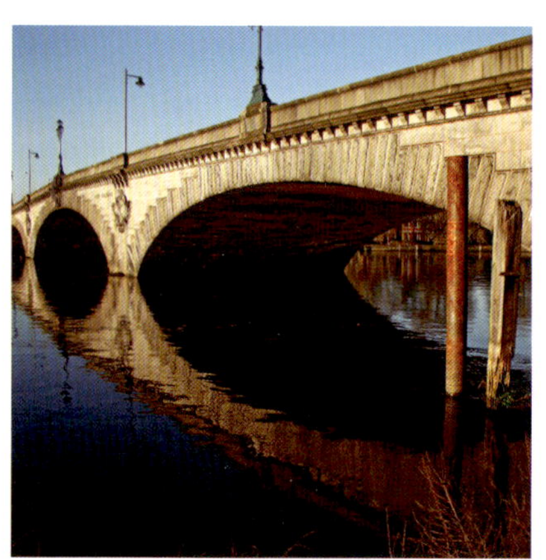

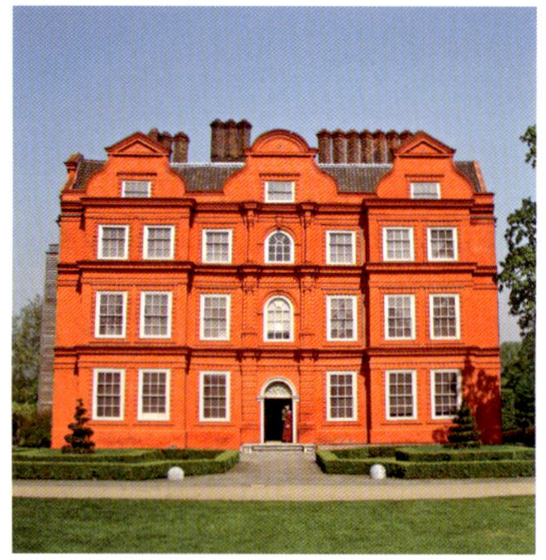

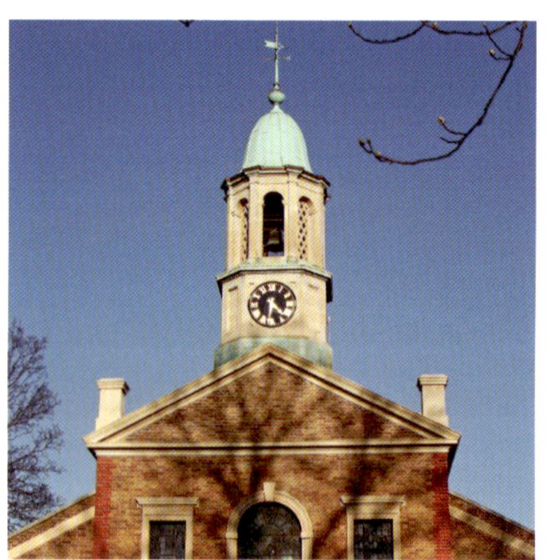

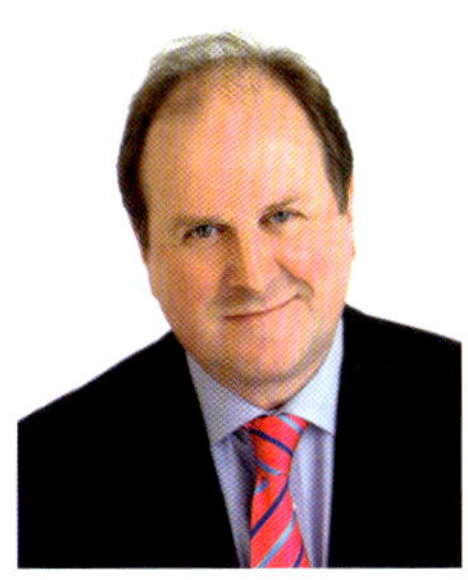

FOREWORD

A Bend in the River

I used to envy my bees. They could take off from our back garden and be in Kew Gardens a minute later, before starting their progress through the lime trees on our street and beginning house-to-house activities in all the gardens as far as Kew Green. It was the patch that gave them succour, and no doubt provided the daily satisfaction that comes to everyone, man or beast, who lives in the shelter of that bend in the river we all know so well.

Such freedom to roam at will in every corner of Kew would be a privilege. I remember once having the joy of a wander through the botanic gardens at dusk, when the gates had closed and the sounds of the night were beginning to rise. The place took on a ghostly but friendly calm, one of its many moods, and it was enchanting. A walk along the river just after dawn is just as memorable, and how many of us have whiled away a summer afternoon around the Green, listening to the sound of bat on ball and contemplating nothing more serious than the choice of watering hole for a refreshment at the close of the day.

The territory between the river and the start of downtown Richmond, which Kew-dwellers sometimes think of as an urban maelstrom, has qualities of intimacy, grandeur and eccentricity that are rarely pulled together in such style. There's history around every corner, vistas that transform themselves magically with the seasons, and a bustle of village life that reinforces the proud message to everyone who crosses the bridge going south: you have left London.

In ten years in Kew, I came to love its avenues and quiet corners, its history and its foliage. All comfortable and civilised dwelling places come under threat from time to time, whether from planners or road-builders or low-flying aircraft, but the good ones know how to defend themselves. Kew always has, and I suspect it always will. These beautiful pictures are testimony to its lure and its sense of itself, the character of a place that people will always find it easy to love.

James Naughtie

WELCOME TO THE WONDER THAT IS **KEW**

Welcome to my latest collection of pictures. My first two books were very much my own creation but I am pleased to say that they were the catalyst for this my latest work. Almost a year ago Mark Brighton, of Kew Bookshop, and his partner Isla Dawes approached me and asked whether I would put together a modern collection of Kew photographs. Several historical books have been produced but nothing up-to-date. Pat Thomas's book is wonderful but again, very much from a historical perspective.

Having encouraged me, I then set about the project with much relish. Kew has so much to offer the photographer; the river, the bridges, the green, two amazing national institutions (The National Archives and The Gardens) and so much more. One of the more exciting aspects was the unknown; delving beneath the surface and discovering places that I didn't know existed. Pensford Field, for instance, was a real gem and getting behind the gates of all our local schools was full of surprises and on the way, I made many new friends.

This project has been a year in the making and terrific fun and I hope that when you are taking a look at my book that some of this magic drifts off the page for you too. To try and give the book some structure and to help you find your way, the content falls into neat sub sections and if you study the contents list opposite I hope that this will be easy to follow. As with my previous books, I have included a simple map to help you place my pictures geographically and I am grateful to my brother, Jeremy Wilson, for again supplying this.

As with all projects of this kind, it is never a one man show and there are numerous people to thank. Firstly, Mark Brighton and his partner Isla Dawes, whose idea it was. David Blomfield, the foremost local historian and his wife Caroline. It was a huge piece of luck to be put in touch with David. Having agreed to help me with an introduction, in the end, he and Caroline, a photographer herself, were kind enough to provide much advice along the way on how best to present my pictures and it is a vastly superior collection because of it. Further, together with my wife, they also helped proof the whole thing, which for a job of this length was a monumental task, so thank you.

I would like to thank James Naughtie, for providing a wonderful scene-setter of a foreword; you can really picture his bees. I would also like to thank all the people whose property I visited to take pictures, from Richmond Council who owns much of it to the lovely lady that owns the oldest house in Kew, West Hall. There is just not enough space to thank everyone but I hope you know that you are not forgotten and that when you see my book you will be pleased with how it's turned out.

As I say, this has been a huge undertaking but brilliant fun and I do hope you enjoy it.

Andrew Wilson, October 2011

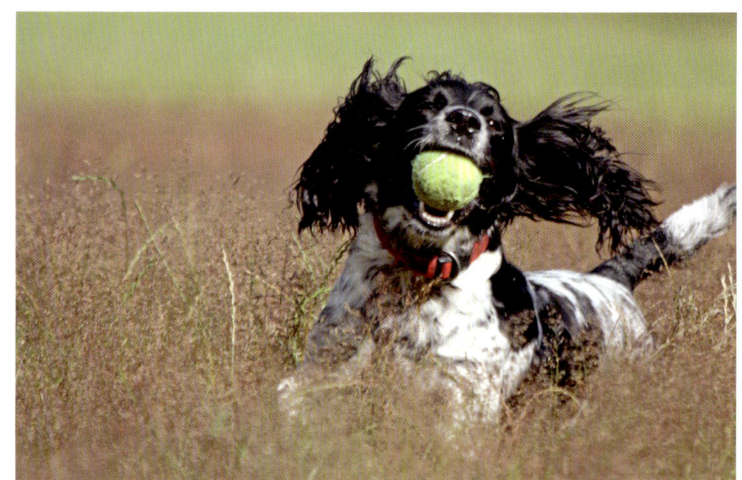

Filmmakers have their 'best boys', I have my best dog, Josie, who I try and take on as many photographic assignments as possible.

CONTENTS

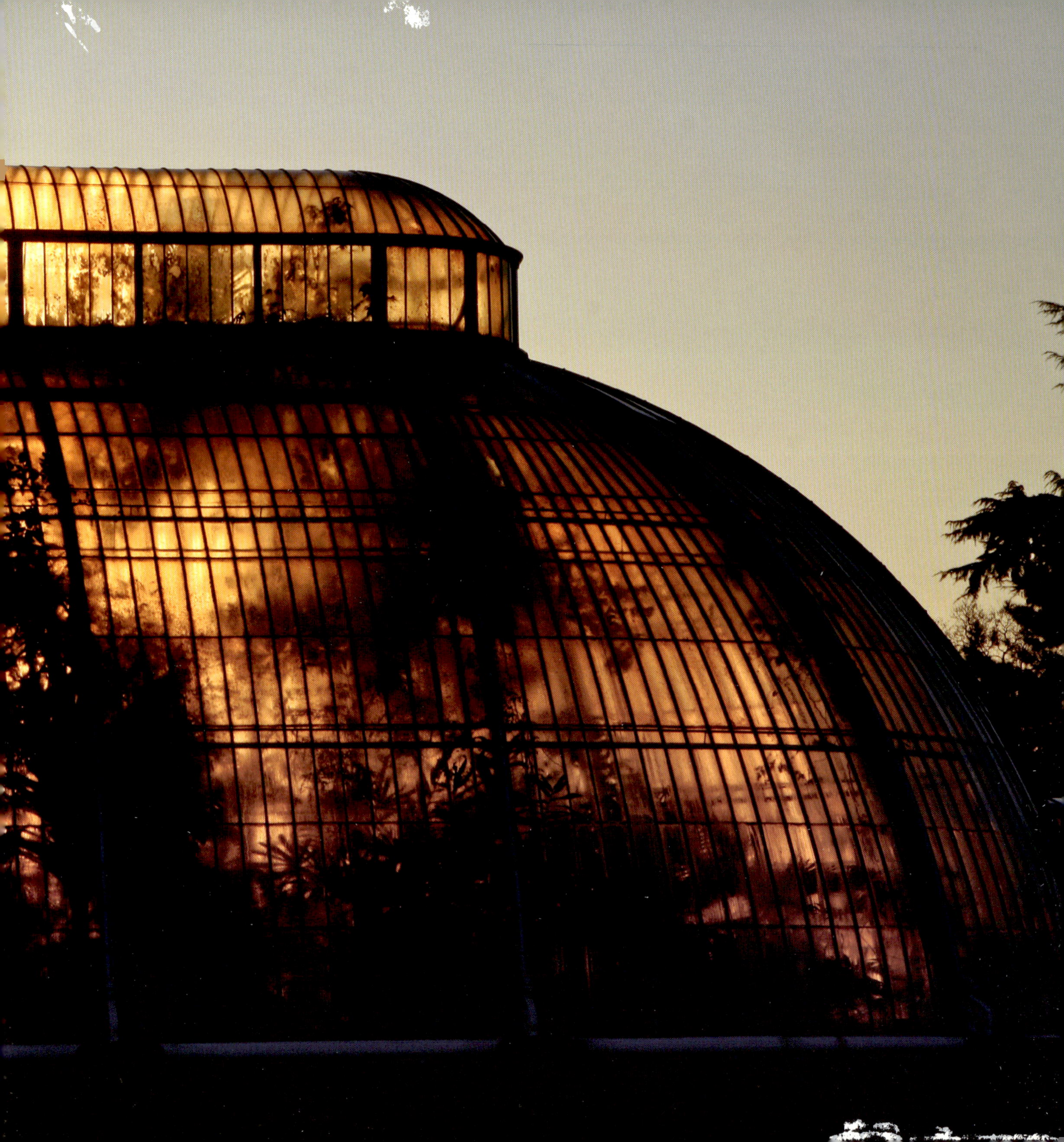

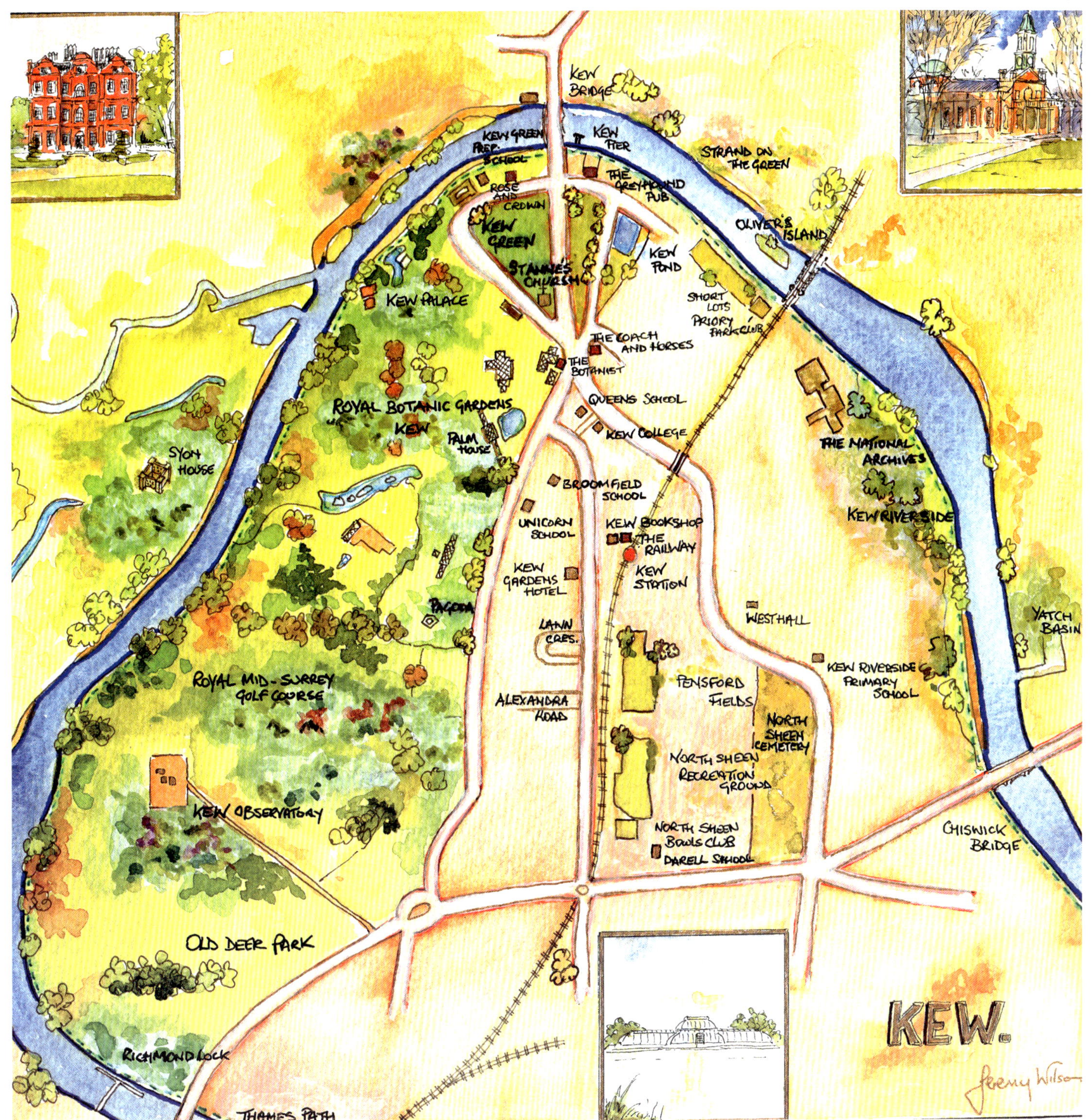

This watercolour map, which has been produced especially for this publication, is not meant to be to scale but purely to act as a guide to Kew and some of the places covered by this book.

There is however even more to the village than the three Rs, as Kew's bounds have long since spread well beyond the community that grew up around the green. Most of our homes, quite literally, are rooted elsewhere. They are built on the acres once farmed by the market gardeners that fed London for three centuries. These gardeners were based mostly at Brick Stables in the hamlet of West Hall. The stables are now replaced by housing, as are the fields on which the market produce was grown, but West Hall itself survives, like Kew Palace an elegant survivor of the seventeenth-century.

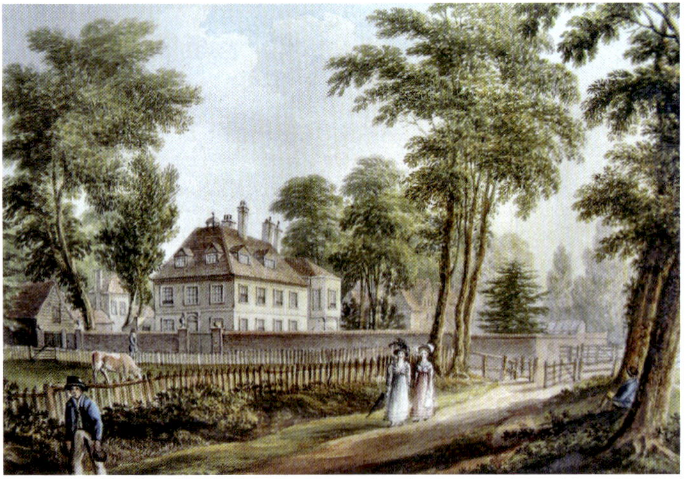

West Hall in 1819, painted by William Harriott. Behind it, to the left, are the farm buildings of Brick Stables, from which the market gardeners worked. The picture is reproduced by kind permission of Ann Thomas.

What also survive are some of the plants those gardeners planted so long ago. Asparagus still stubbornly persists in gardens throughout Kew. So too do apple and walnut trees from the orchards that succeeded the market gardens.

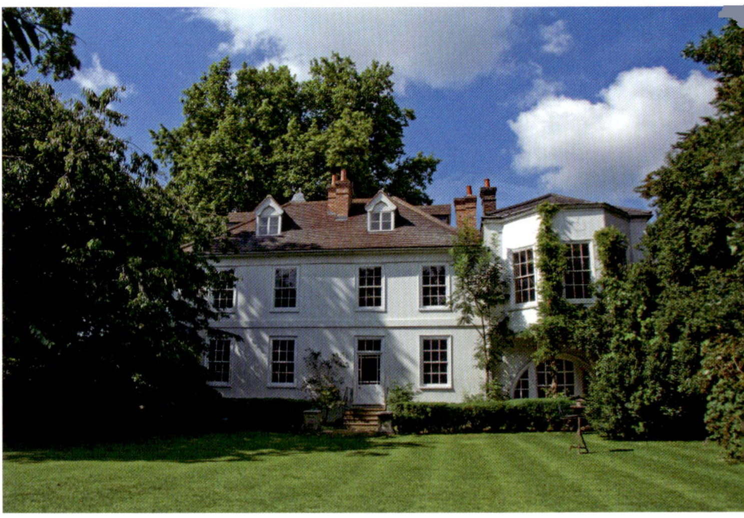

West Hall as it is today; it has hardly changed in hundreds of years.

Our history is thus all around us, to remind us of how the previous generations made their precarious living, and perhaps of how precarious is our own way of life. Now that the boatmen, the fishermen and the market gardeners have gone the way of the noblemen and kings, most Kewites work in London to fund their mortgages.

However, not everyone works elsewhere; for when it comes to local employment Kew is uniquely privileged. It is extraordinarily home to not one but two of the most important of Britain's major institutions, the Royal Botanic Gardens and the National Archives, which are substantial employers of labour, if of a special kind.

The village seems comfortable with this unusual mix of domestic and national buildings, and so of course it should. Over the centuries it has learned to live with princes and palaces. There is no danger of it being overawed by the thirty-nine listed buildings of RBG or the great mass of the National Archives. They are seen rather as an extension of the village recreational amenities, preserving as they do the last of its green acres for the enjoyment – if at a considerable price in the case of the RBG – of residents as well as visitors.

While there is still much to remind us of the past in the existing buildings and landscape of Kew, ironically far fewer pictures have survived than one might expect – after all, the churchyard of St Anne's holds the bones of some of the country's greatest artists. Gainsborough and Zoffany, Meyer and the Englehearts lie there; and later the pre-Raphaelites, Hughes and Deverell, lived in Kew.

However, all of them painted portraits, not landscapes. (The exception was Camille Pissarro, who painted both the green and gardens, but the paintings are now mostly in private hands and lost to public view.) Consequently we are left in the main with just a few prints and engravings of the more important buildings, and with nothing to illustrate the life of the village itself. Happily, thanks to Andrew Wilson, our own generation can be assured that our own lives and the buildings will not be similarly lost to history.

David Blomfield

The author of *The Story of Kew* and *Kew Past*

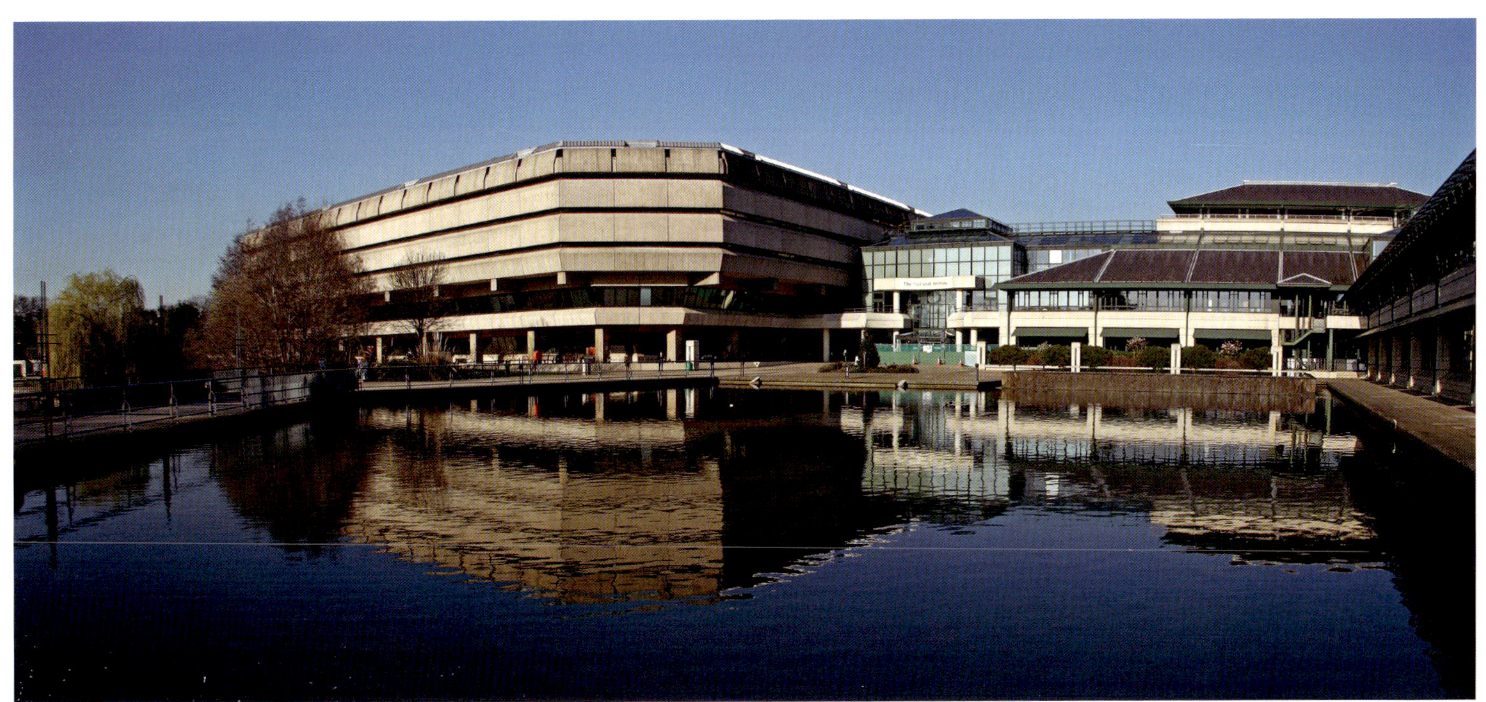

The National Archives in 2011

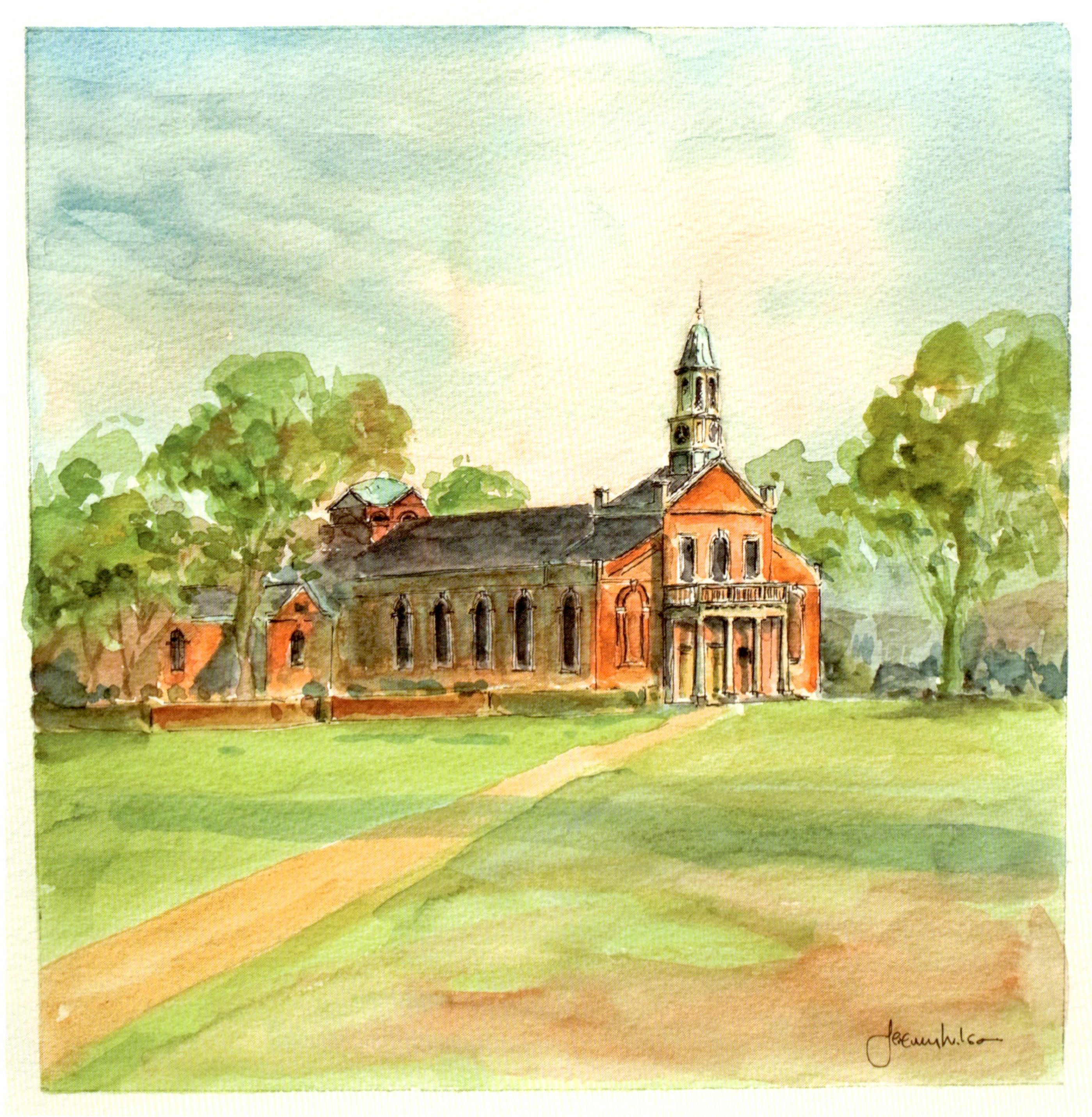

St Anne's on the Green - an original watercolour by Jeremy Wilson produced exclusively for this publication. A limited number of prints will be available for sale after publication, please contact the publisher for more infromation.

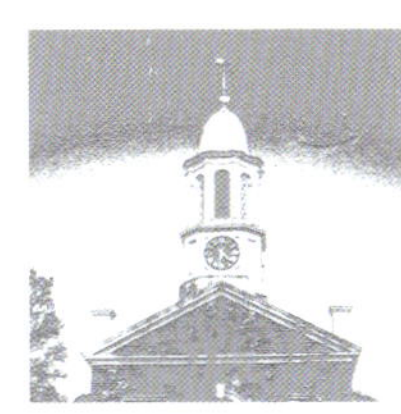

THE VILLAGE GREEN

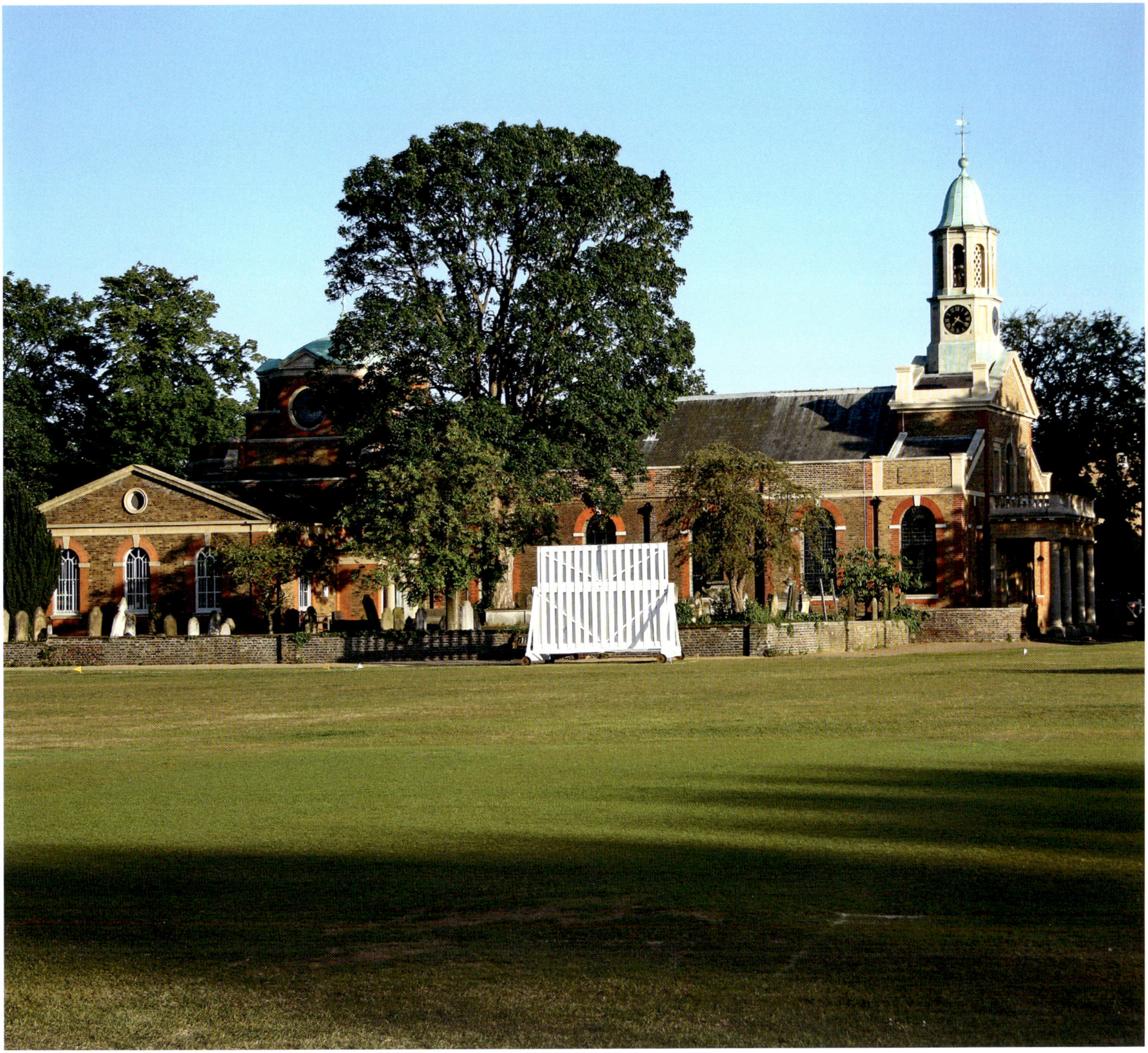

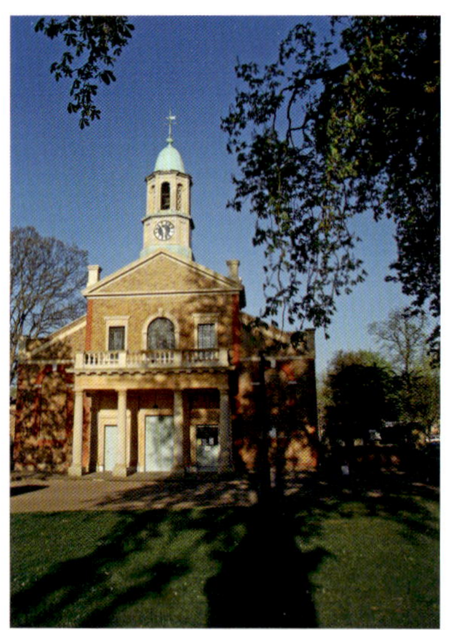

St Anne's dates from the early 1700's when a group of local residents clubbed together to raise sufficient money to build Kew's first place of public worship, a chapel, dedicated to St Anne (after the Queen at the time). Kew, unlike many English villages of its size, did not have a church; this has been put down to a variety of reasons of which the most compelling is that of ownership. Kew from Tudor times did not have a local squire as such but rather a group of powerful nobles, most of whom only spent a small proportion of their time in Kew.

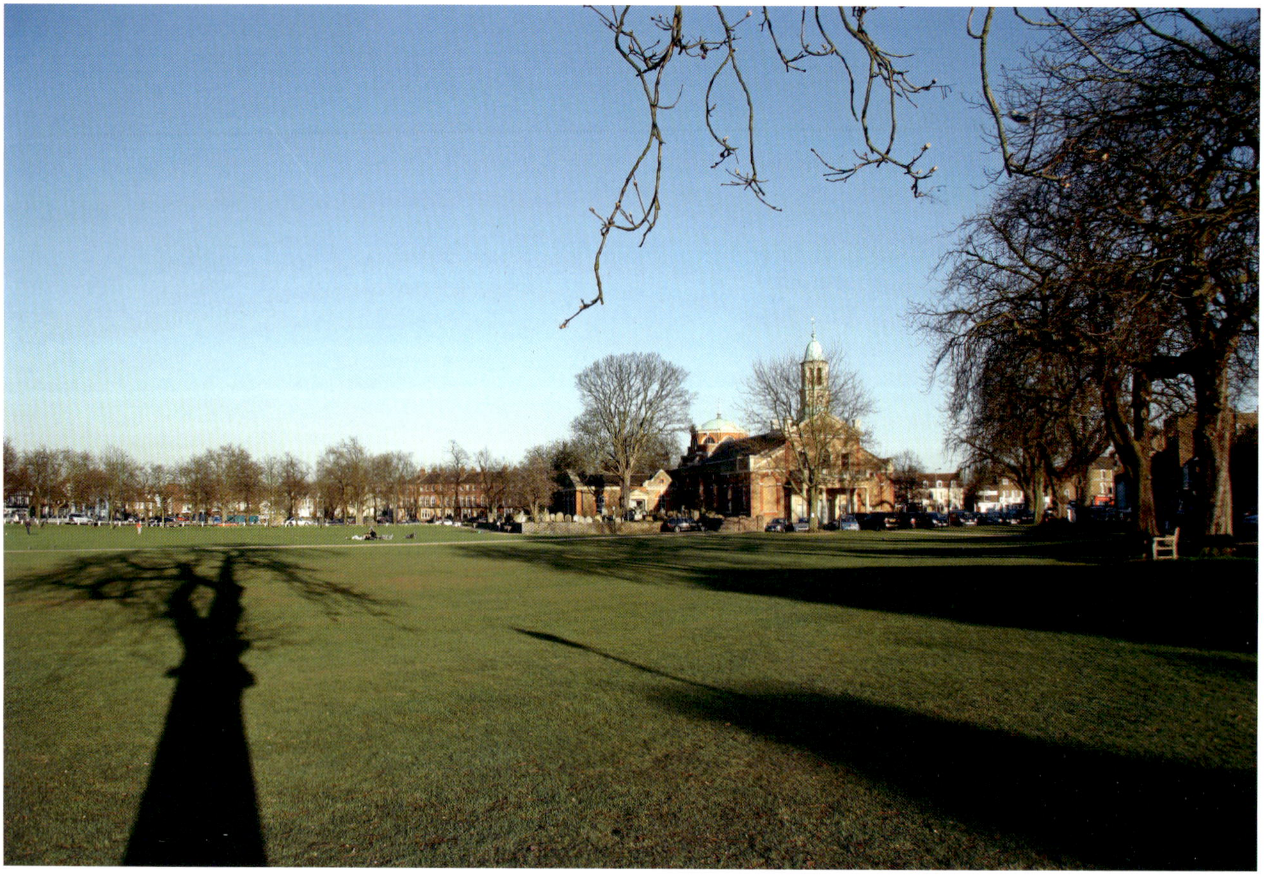

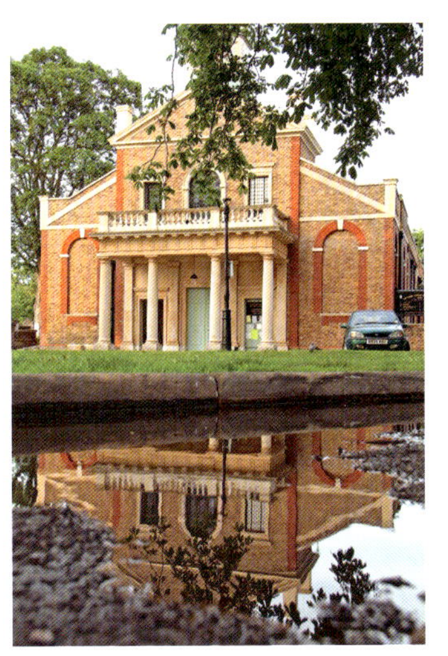

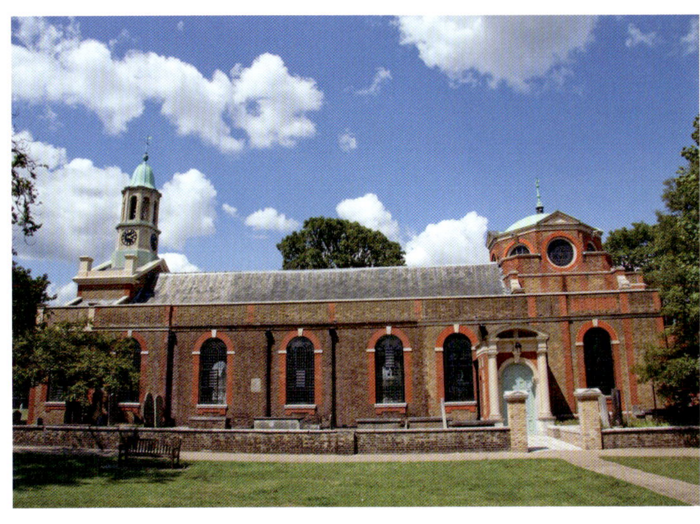

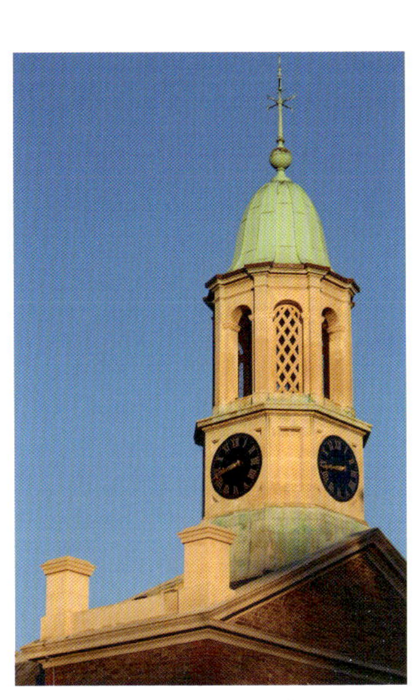

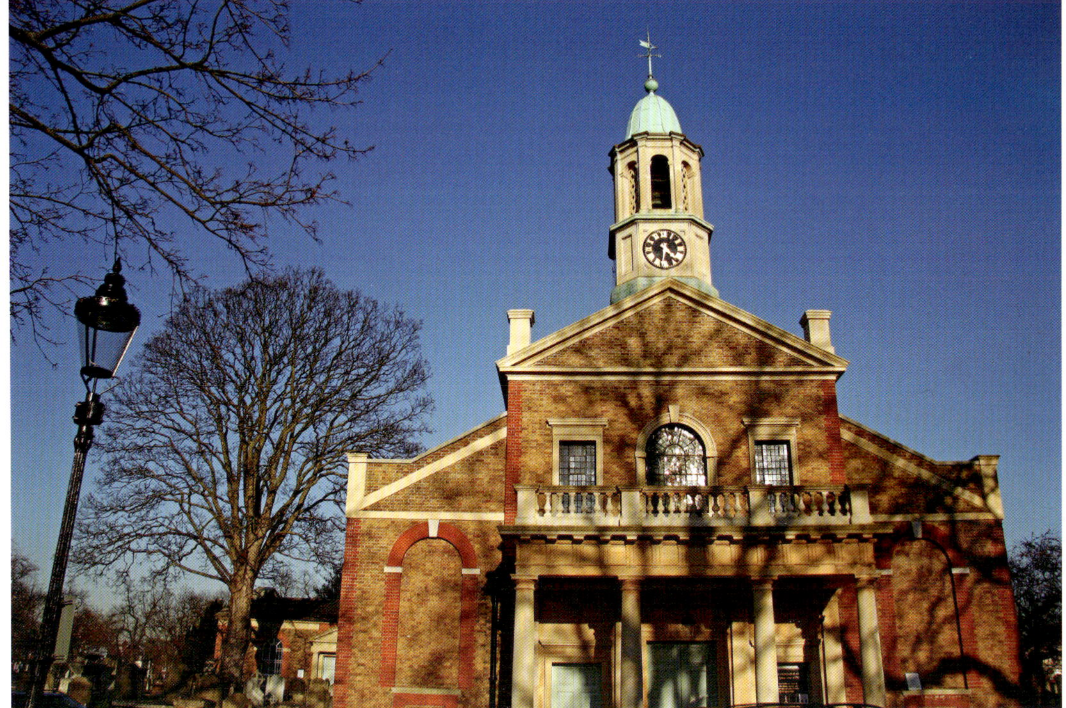

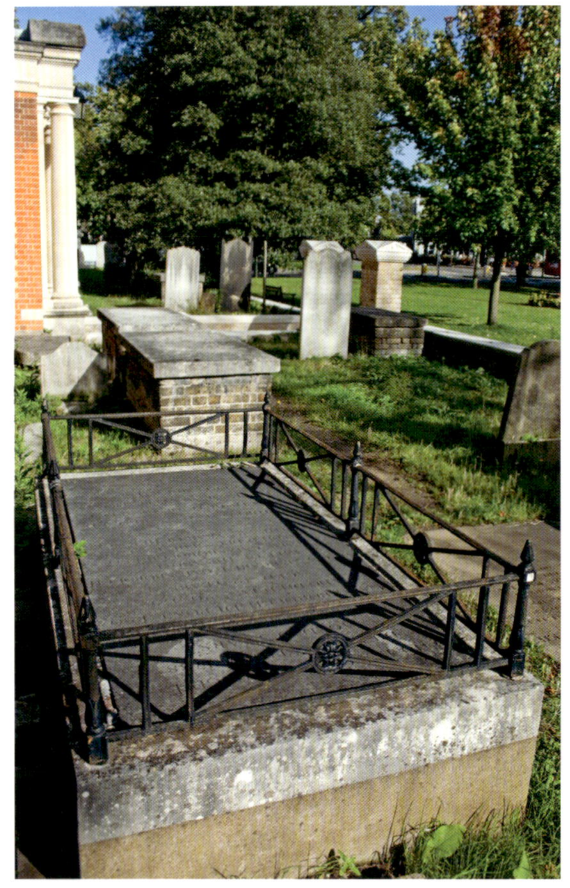

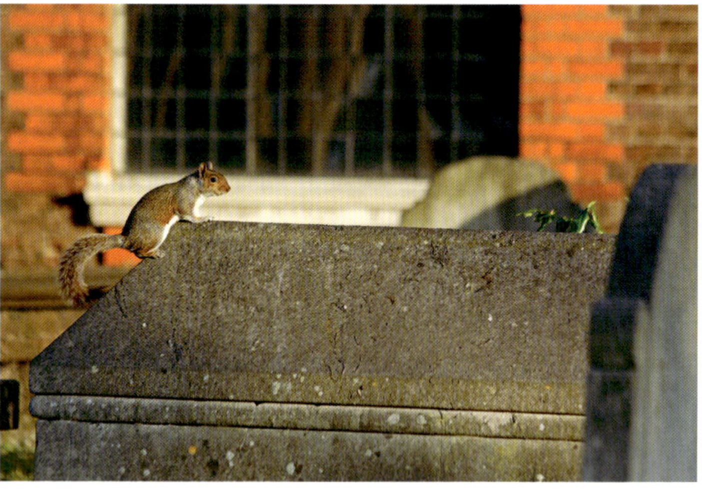

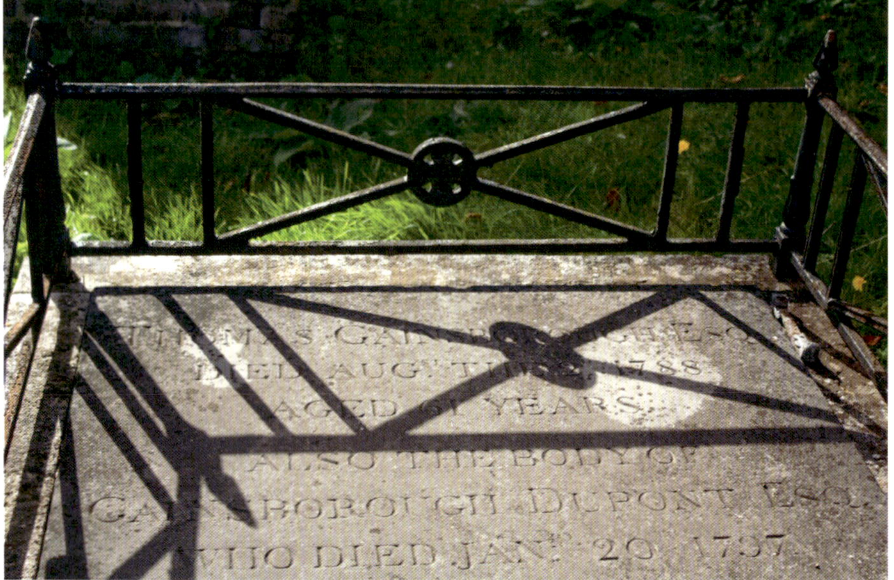

Top left and left: Many famous people are buried within the grounds of St Anne's including Gainsborough, the famous artist.

Page opposite:
Bottom: West side of The Green
Top right: East side of The Green
Top Left: The main A205 that runs through the centre of The Green is often waterlogged after a heavy downpour.

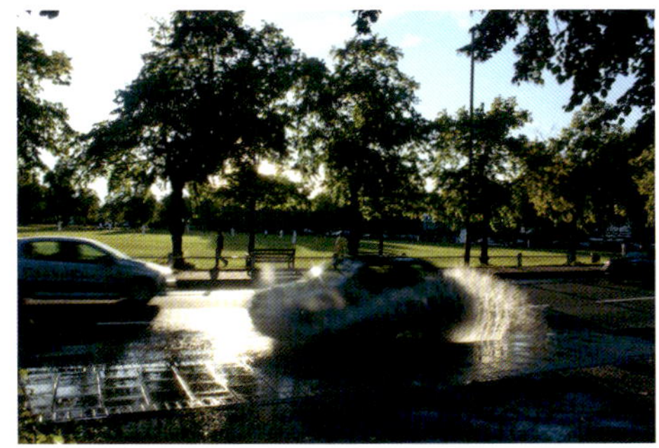

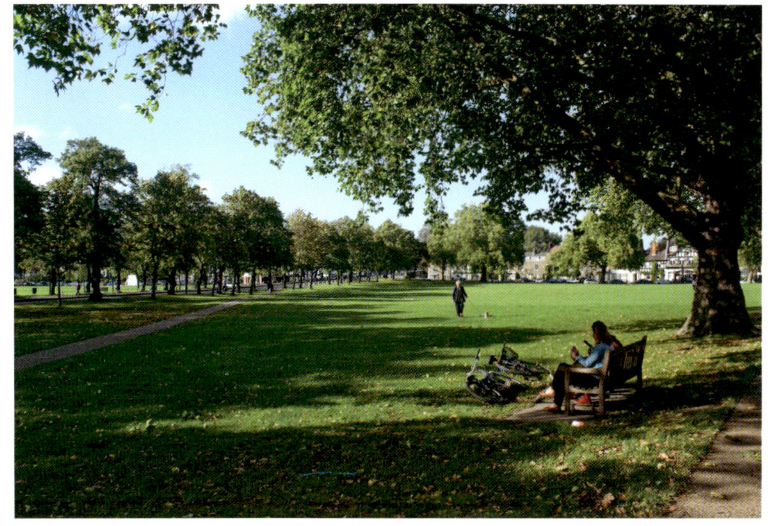

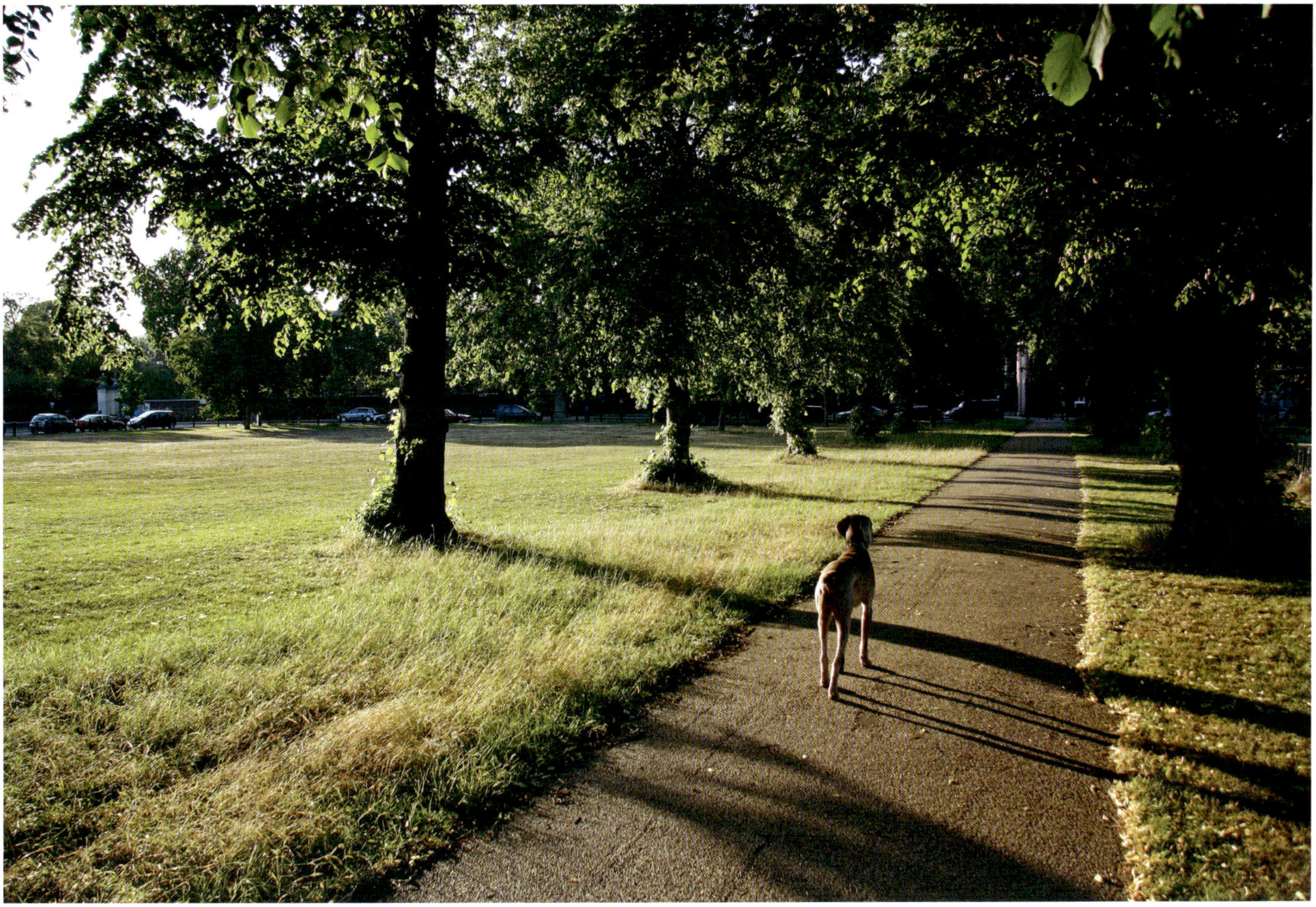

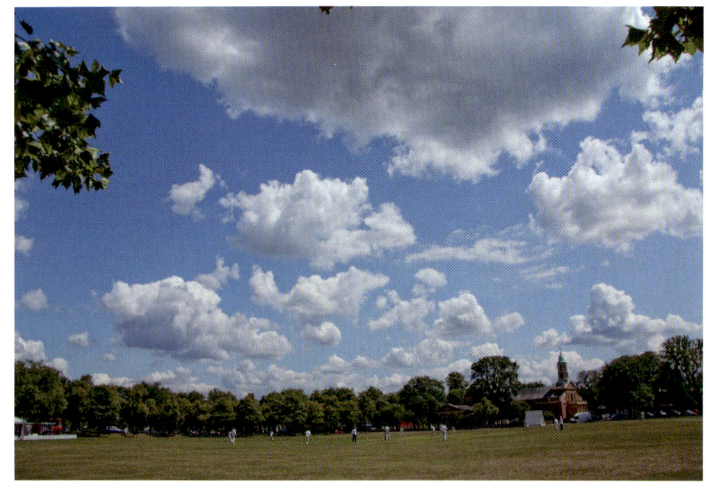

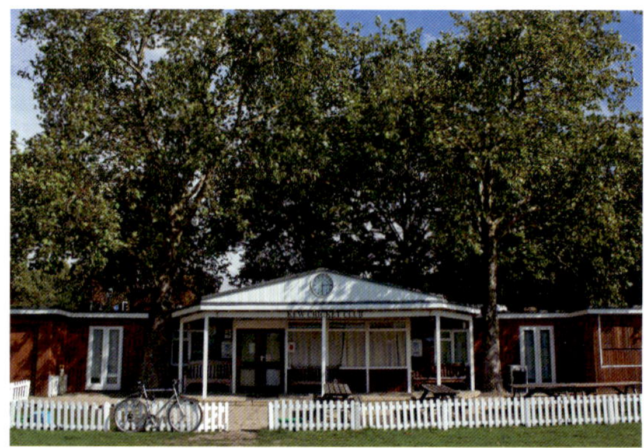

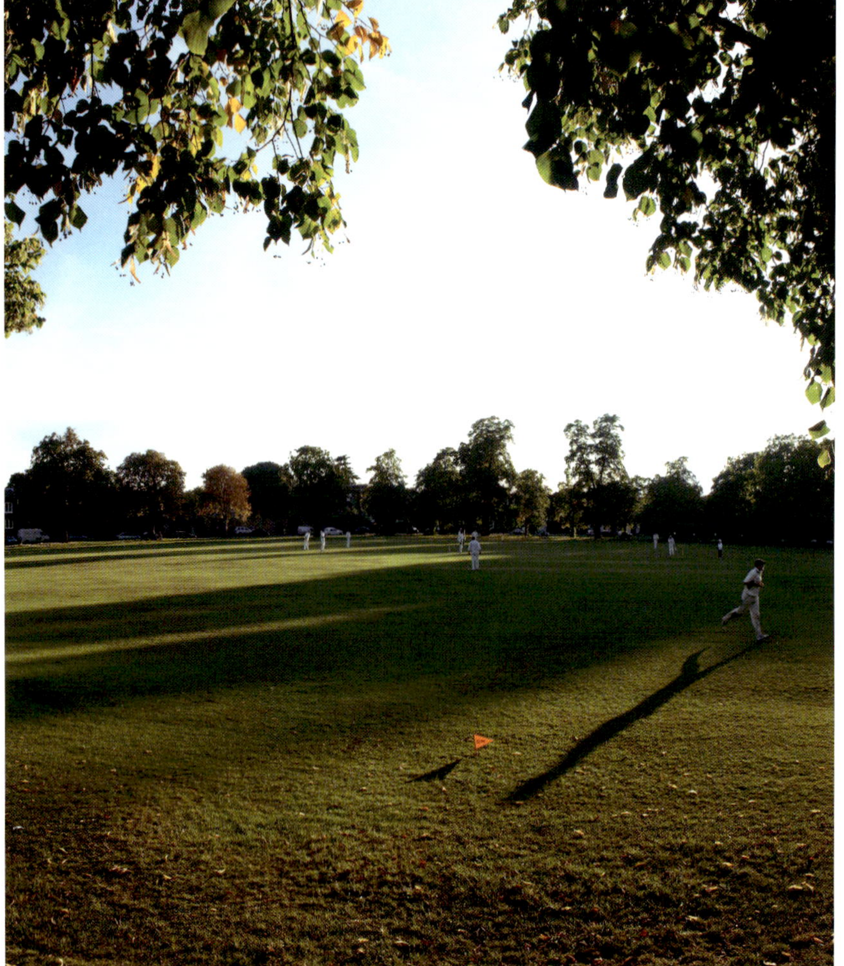

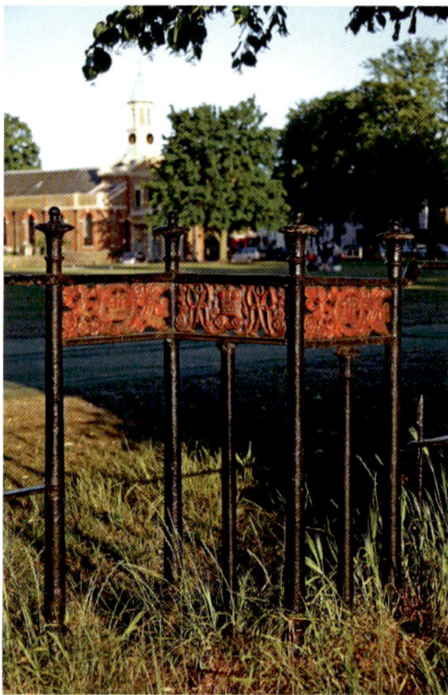

Cricket is played throughout the summer.

The main part of The Green is bisected by a path (see previous page) and by an attractive, very old, small metal fence, with some intricate design work, see picture above.

In the early summer of 2011 the pair of swans from Kew Pond made a dash, or rather waddle, for pastures new. They were tharwted on this occasion, as passers-by considered it too dangerous for them to cross the main road. However, they finally made it away and set up home in Kew Gardens.

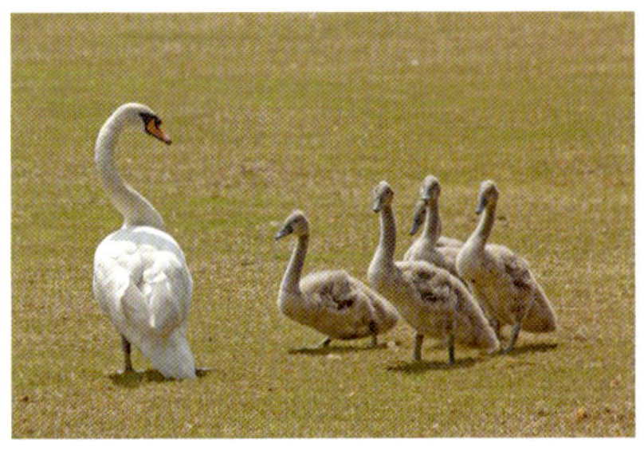

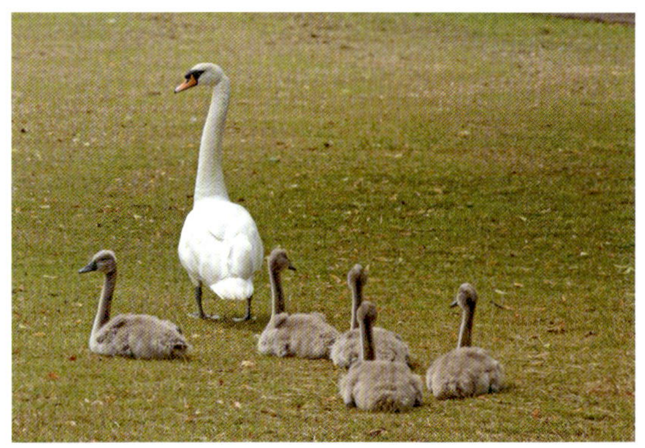

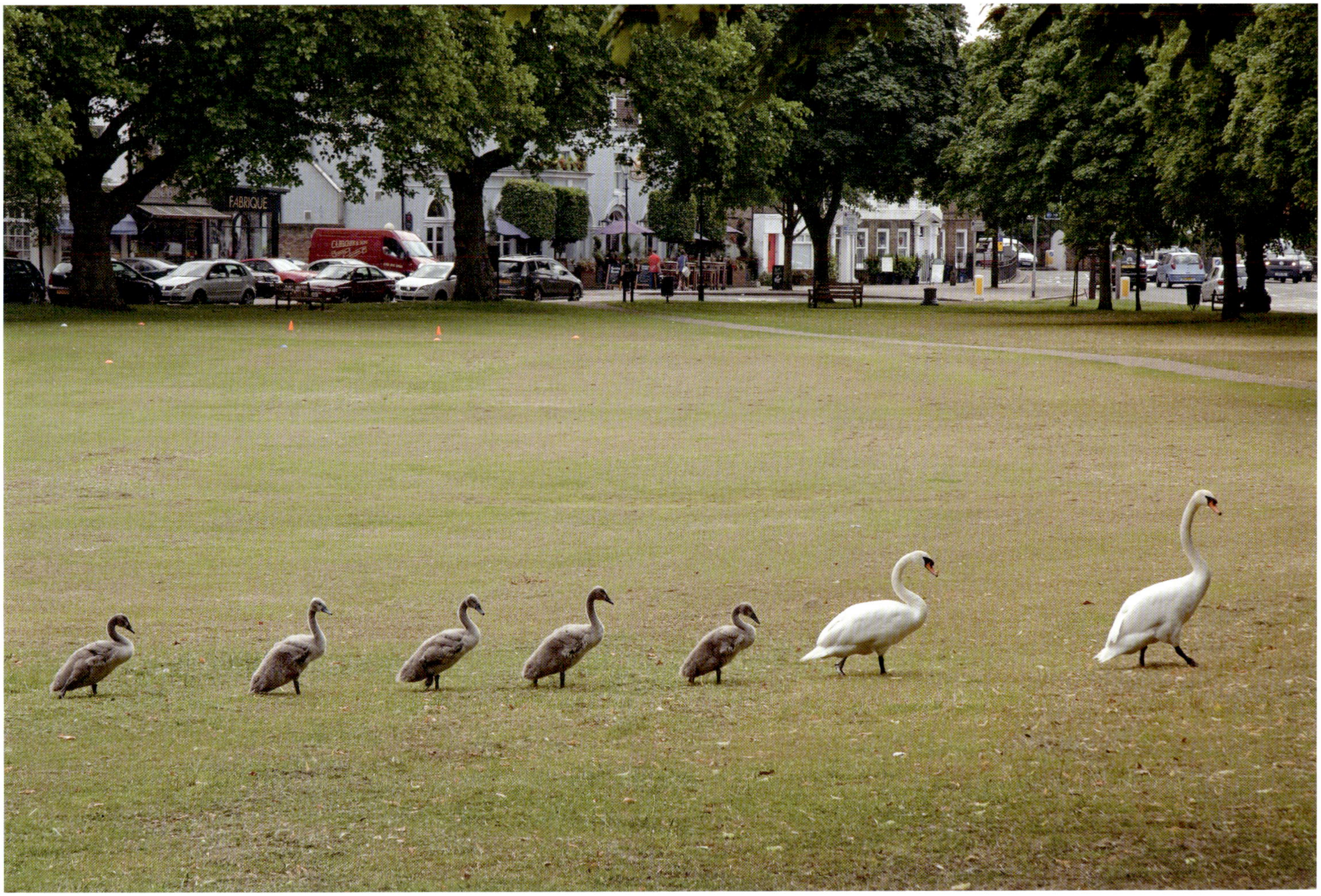

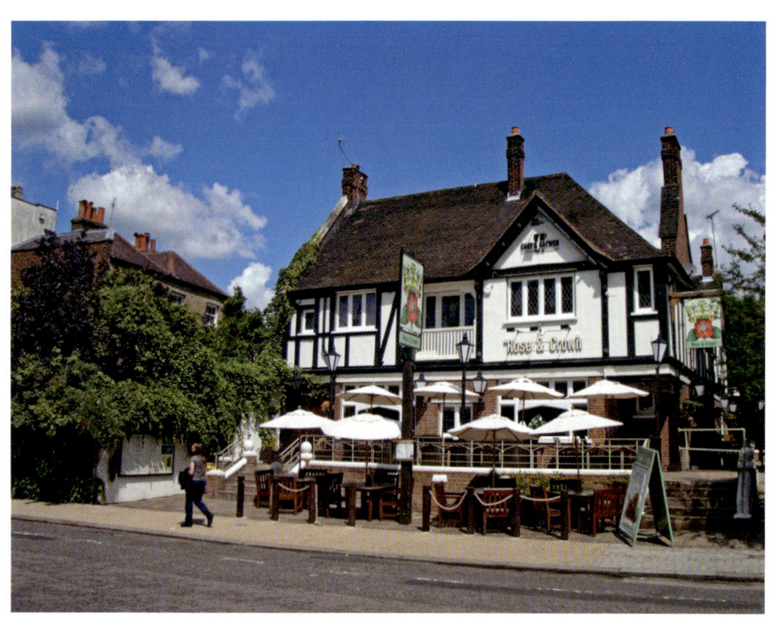

This page and opposite:
The Green is bordered on three sides by some delightful houses, several pubs and even a school and on the fourth, to the west, by the main entrance to Kew Gardens.

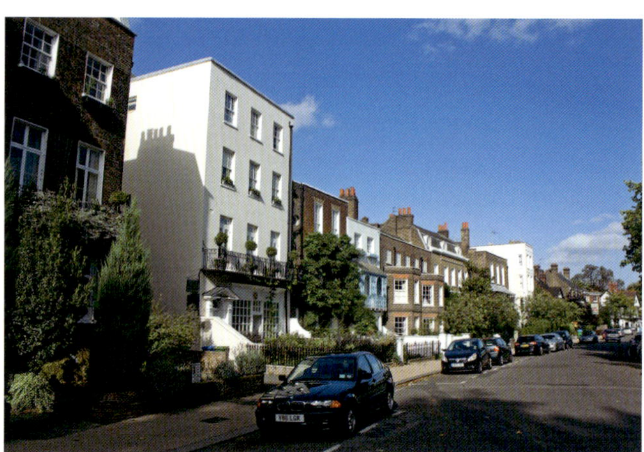

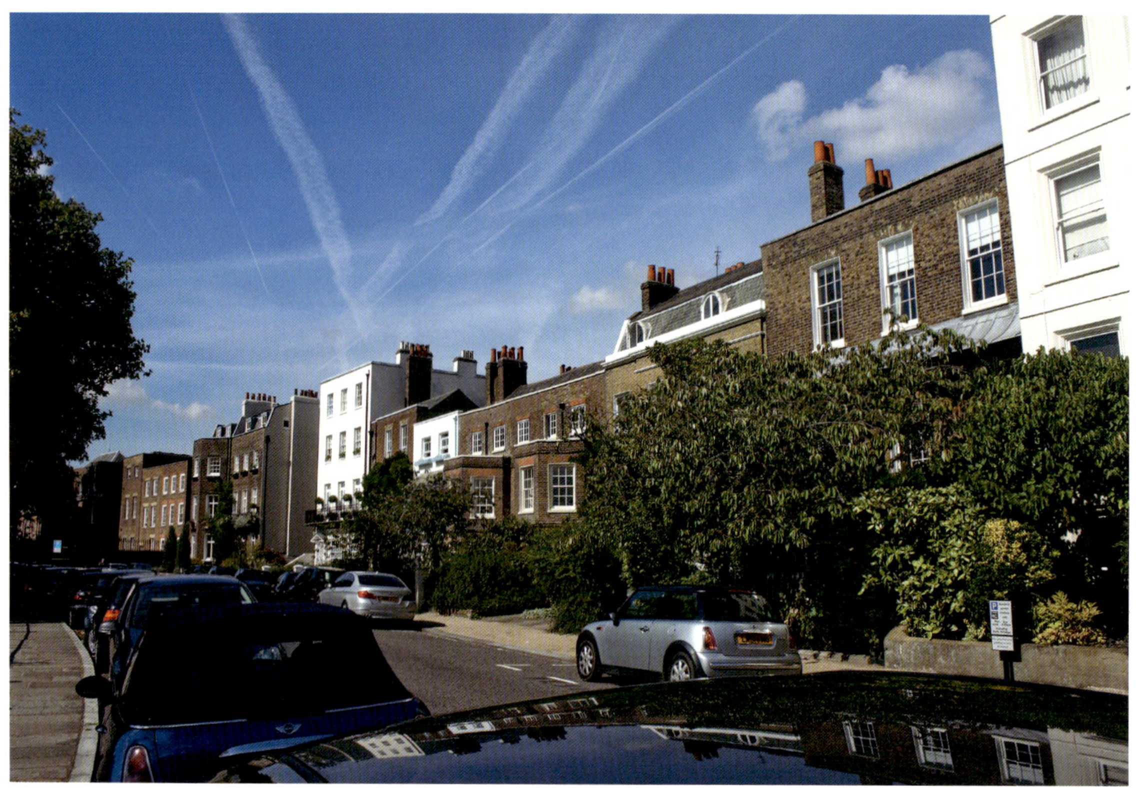

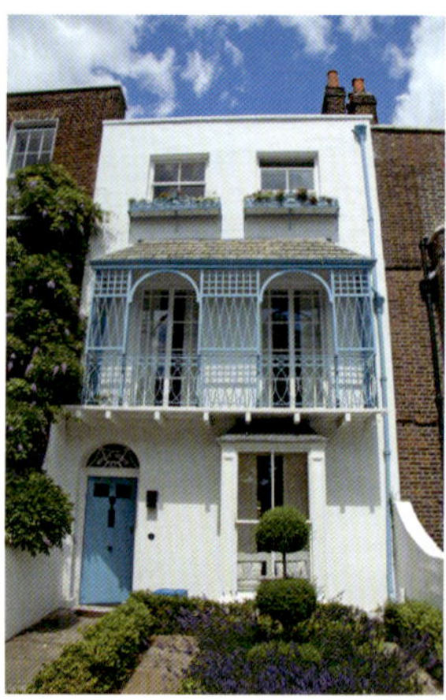

Top left: Rose and Crown

Below: Ask restaurant, by the bridge, used to be The King's Arms.
Below right: The Green from the north east corner looking west.

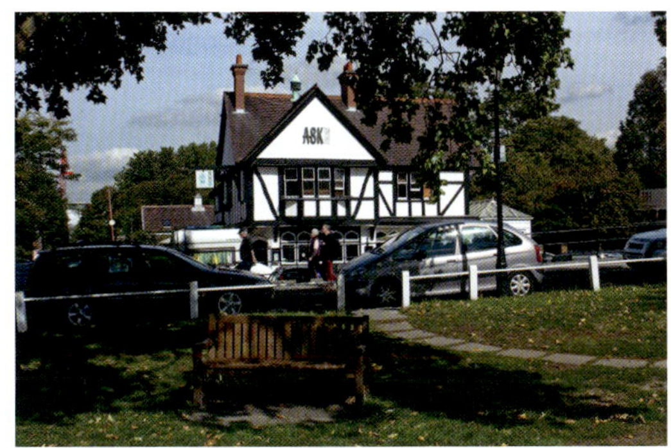

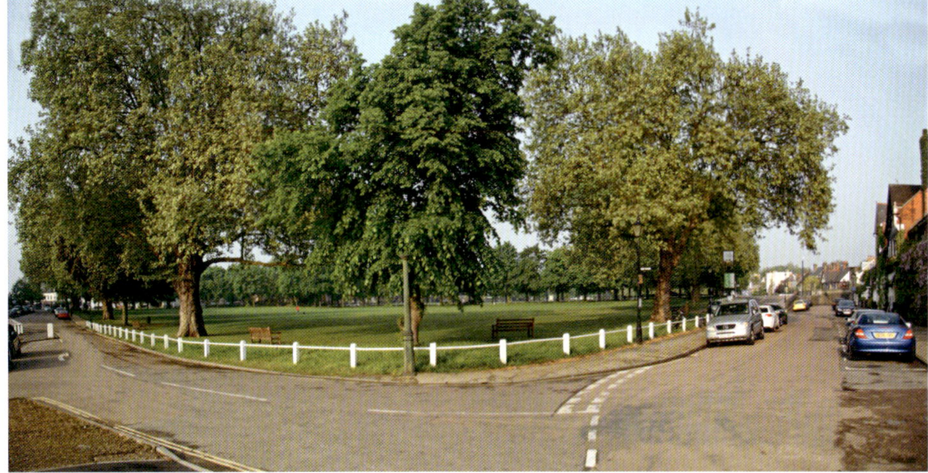

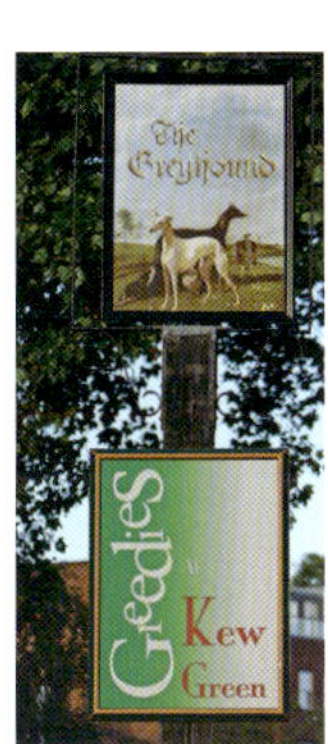

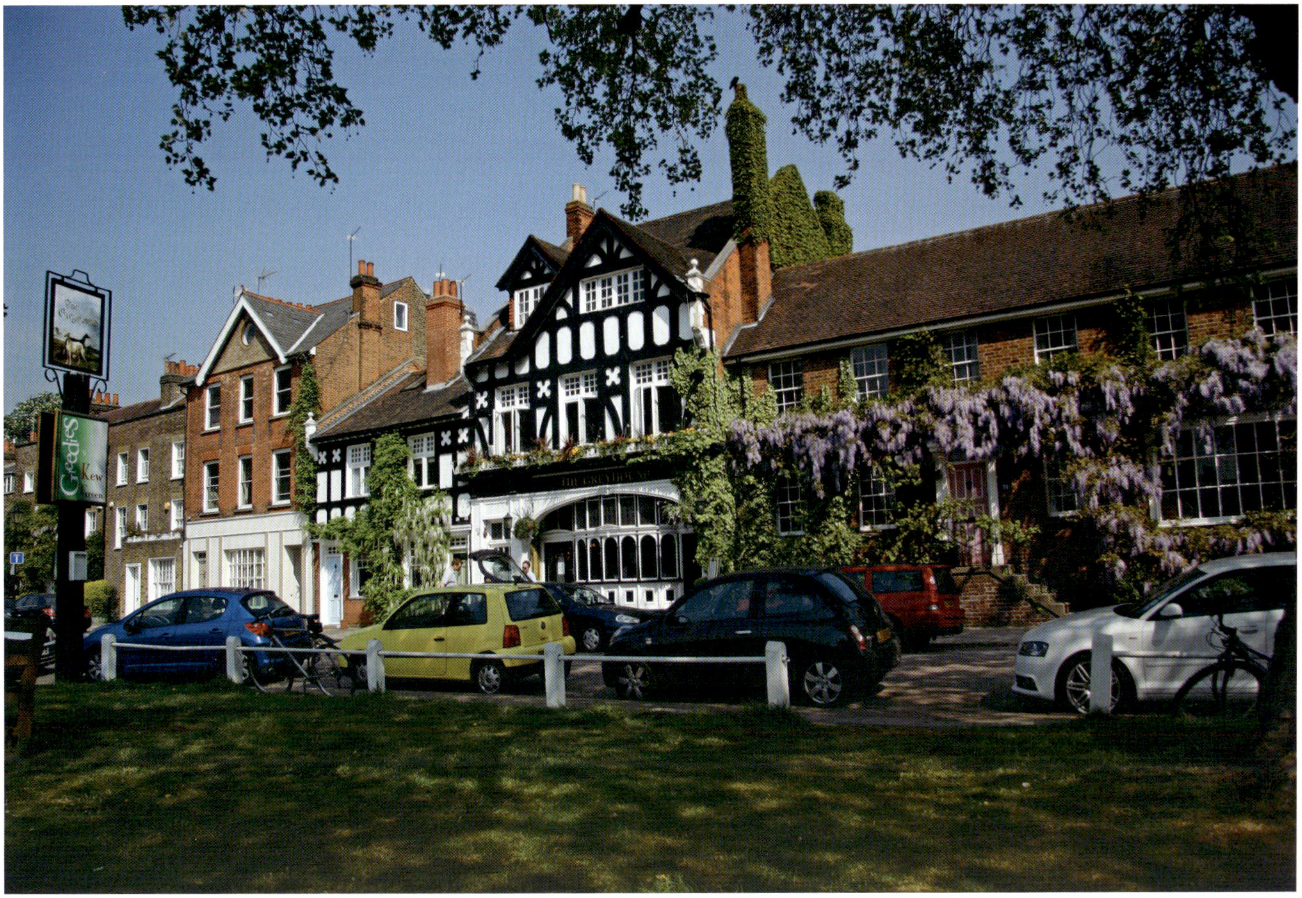

The Greyhound

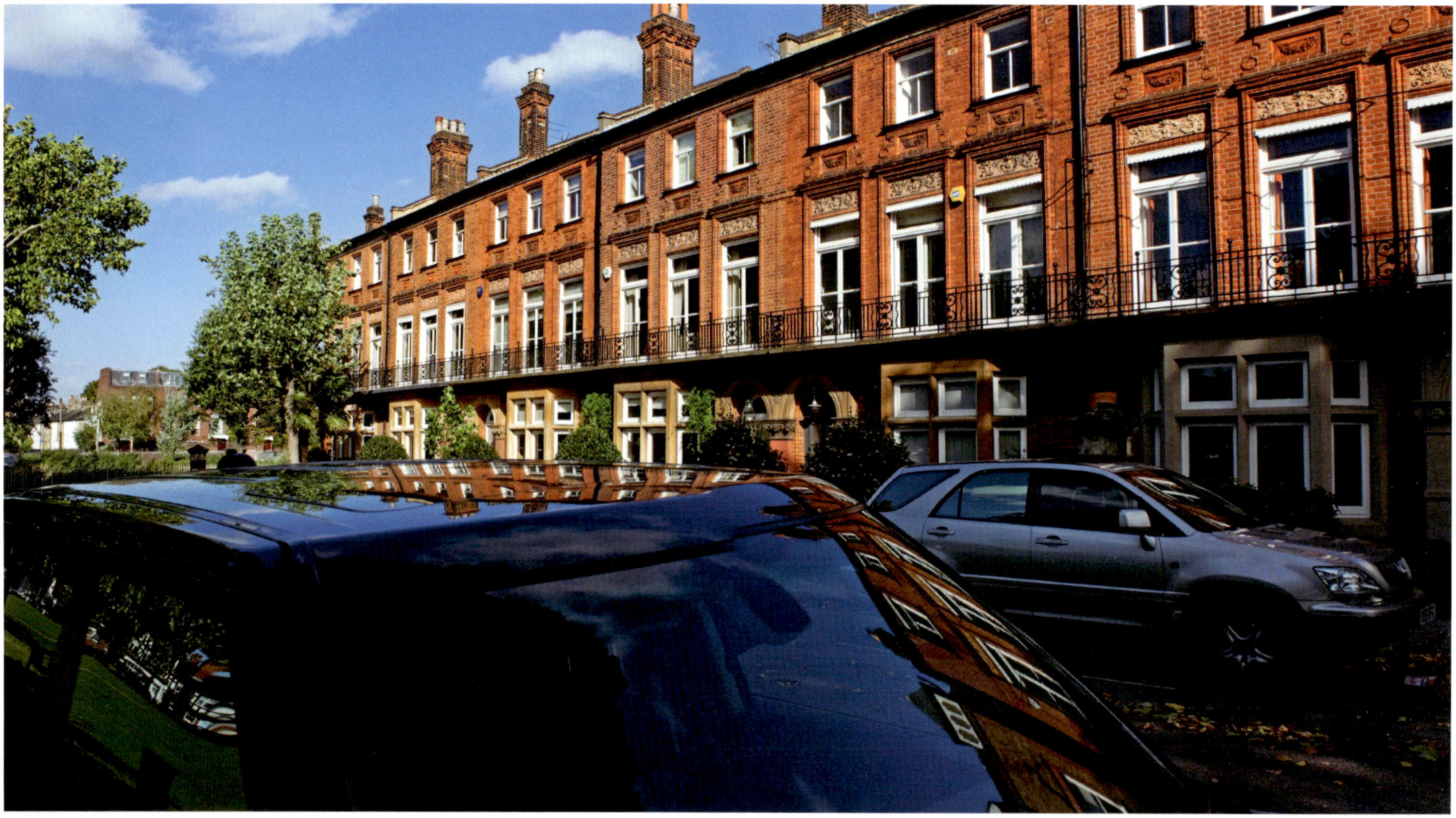

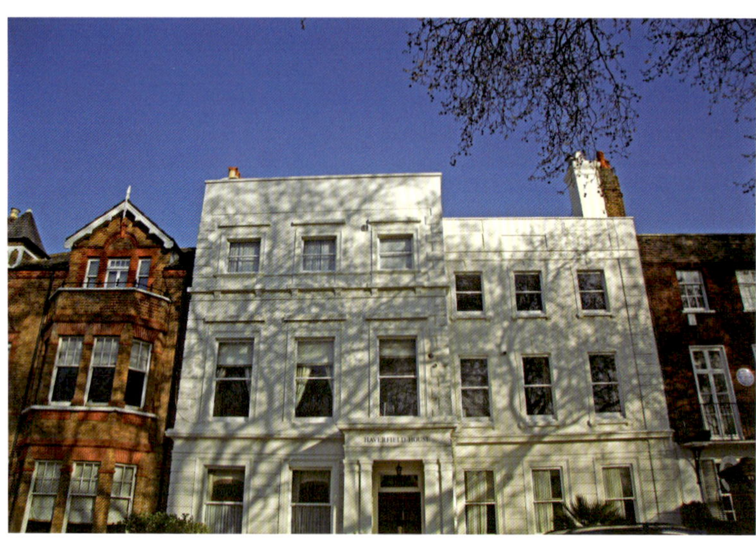

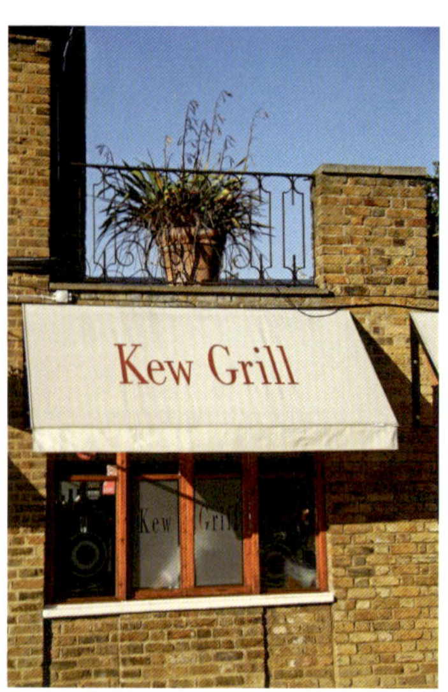
Kew Grill

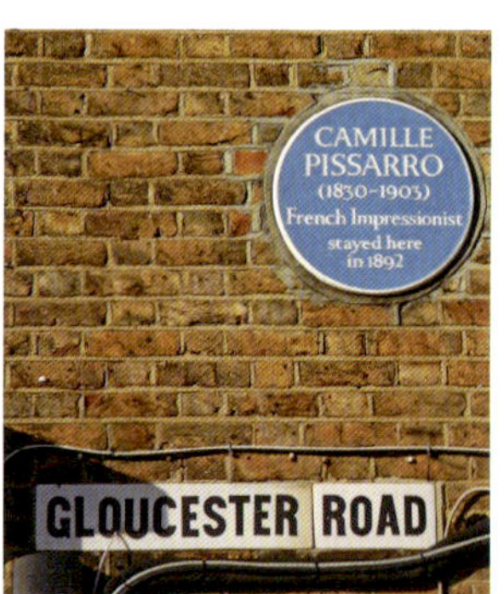
CAMILLE
PISSARRO
(1830–1903)
French Impressionist
stayed here
in 1892
GLOUCESTER ROAD

Opposite Page: The east side of The Green, and just where The Coach and Horses meets Gloucester Road is Kew Grill, one of Antony Worrall Thompson's restaurants.
This Page: The Coach and Horses

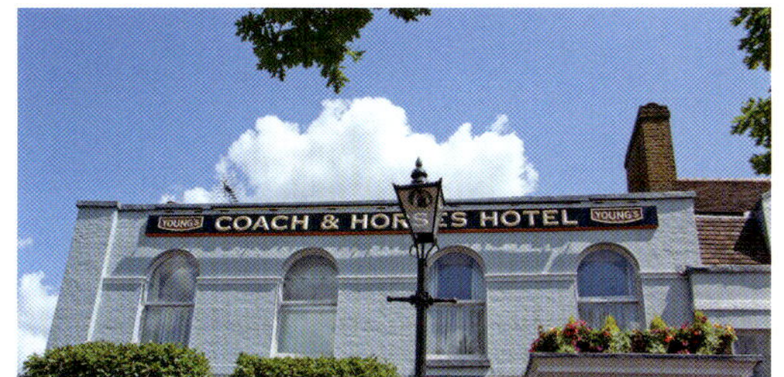

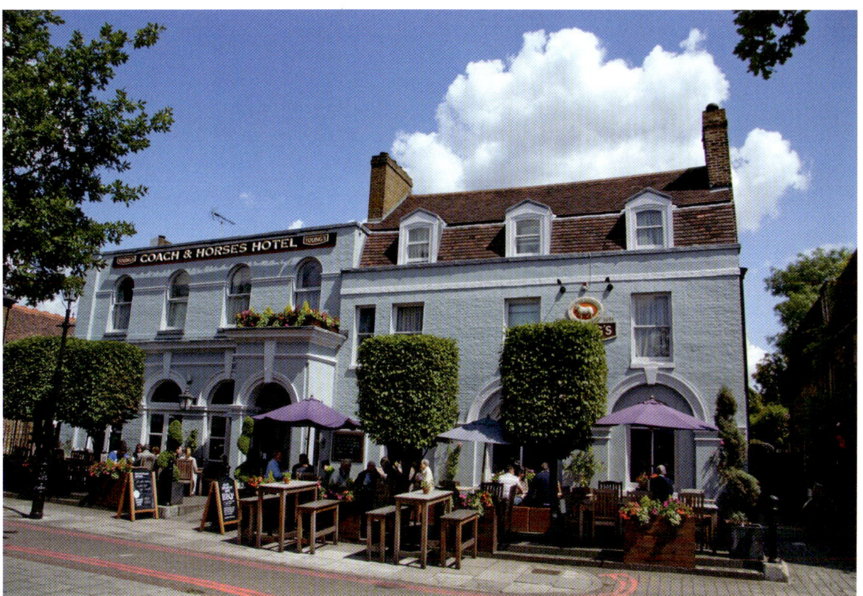

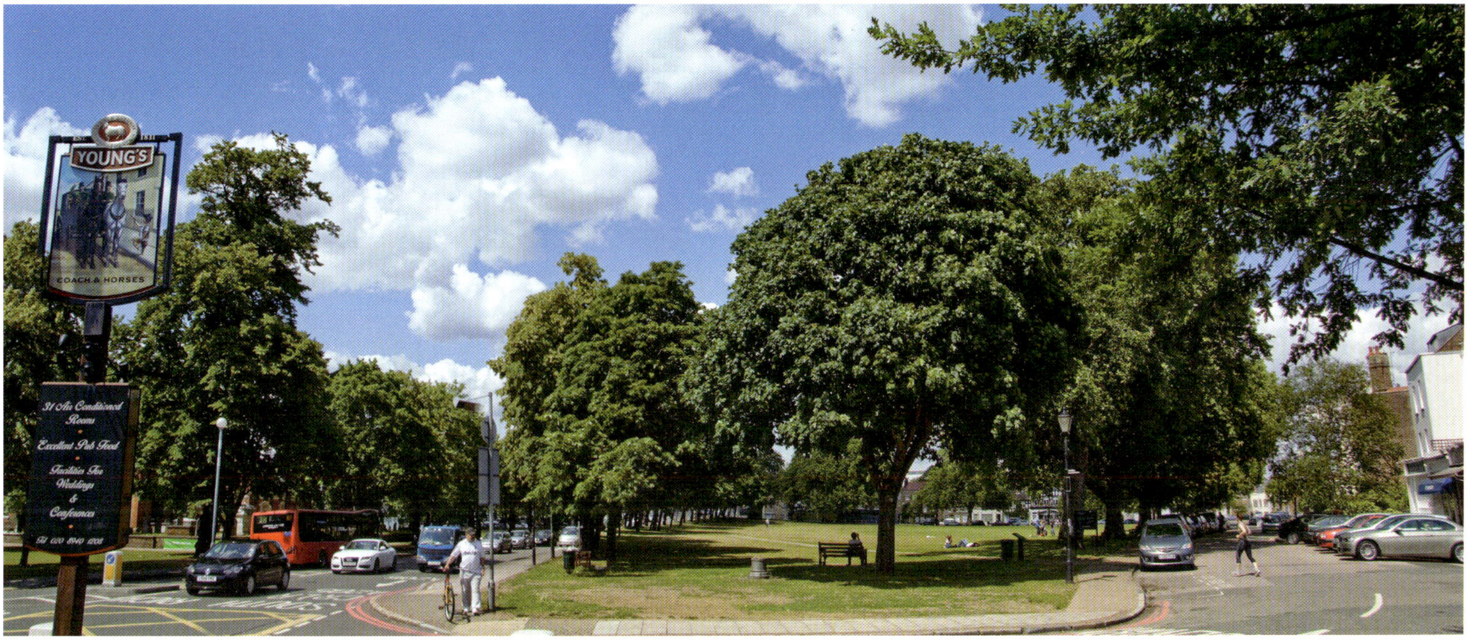

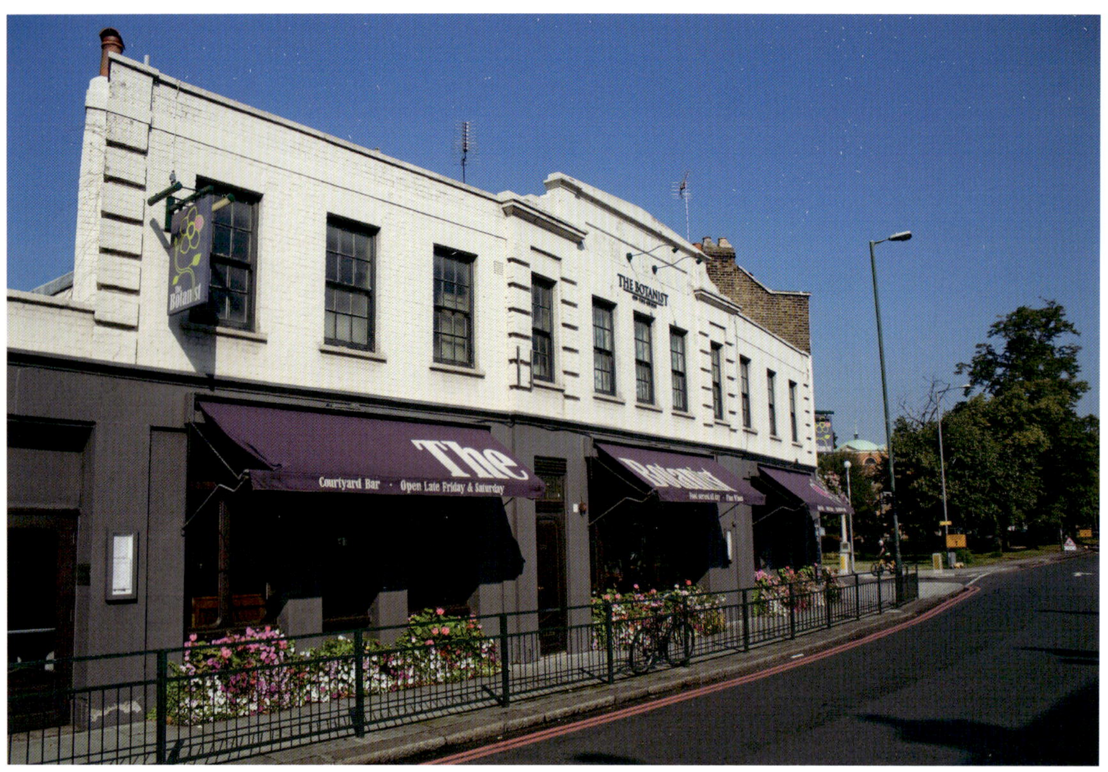

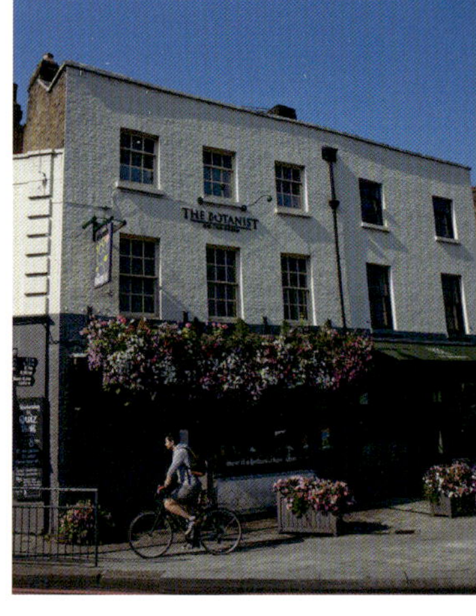

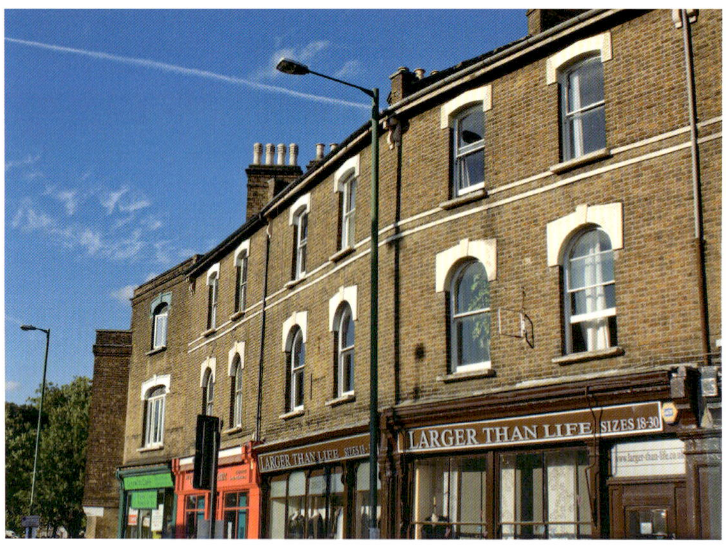

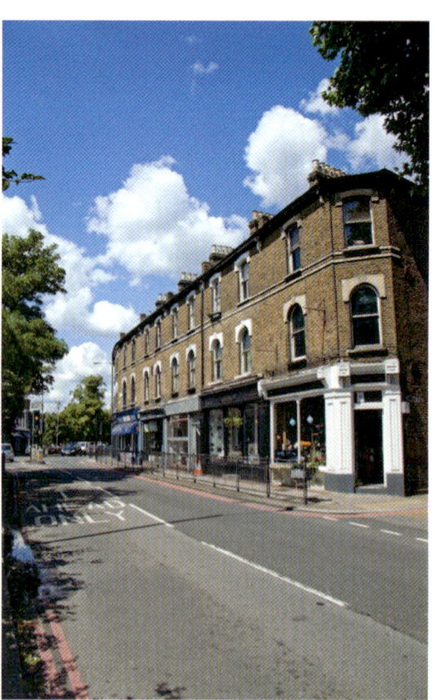

Top and above:
The Botanist on the south side of The Green.

Left and far left:
On the corner of The Green and as you enter from Mortlake Road there is a row of shops, including 'Larger than Life', with its very distinctive sign.

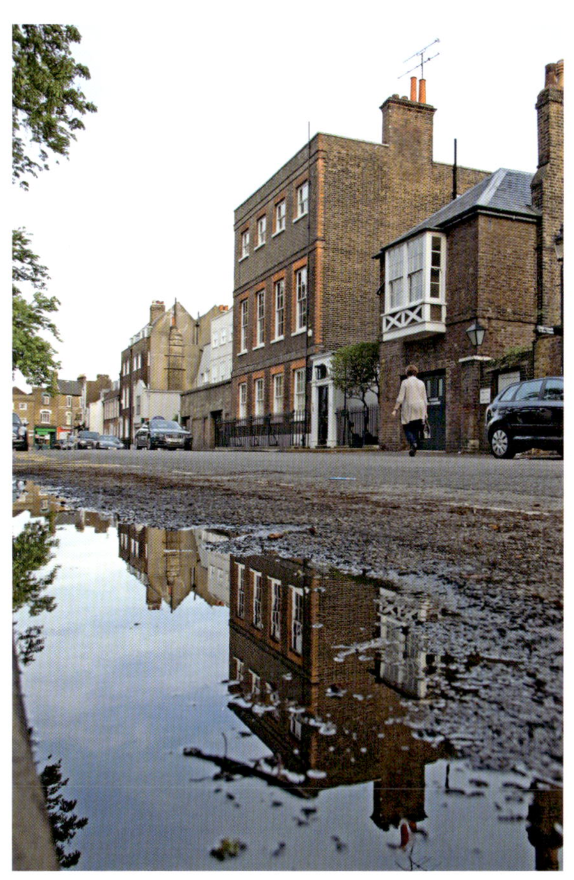

This page: Kew Green, south side

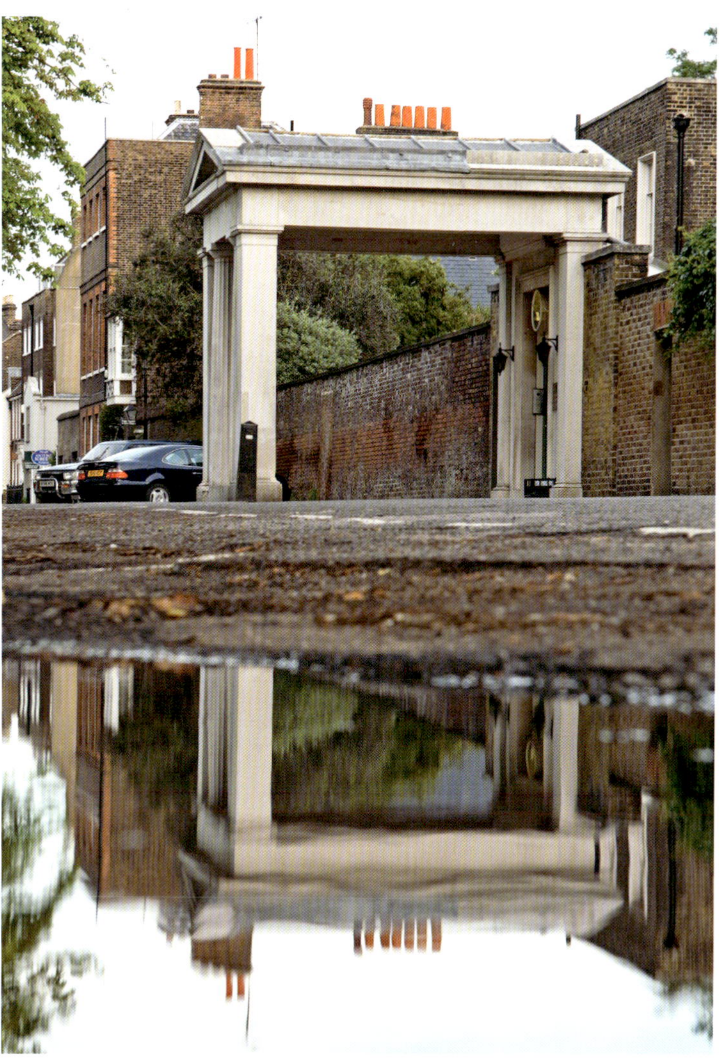

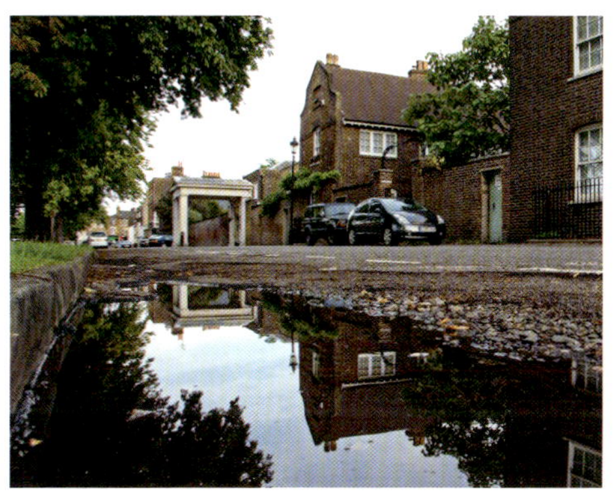

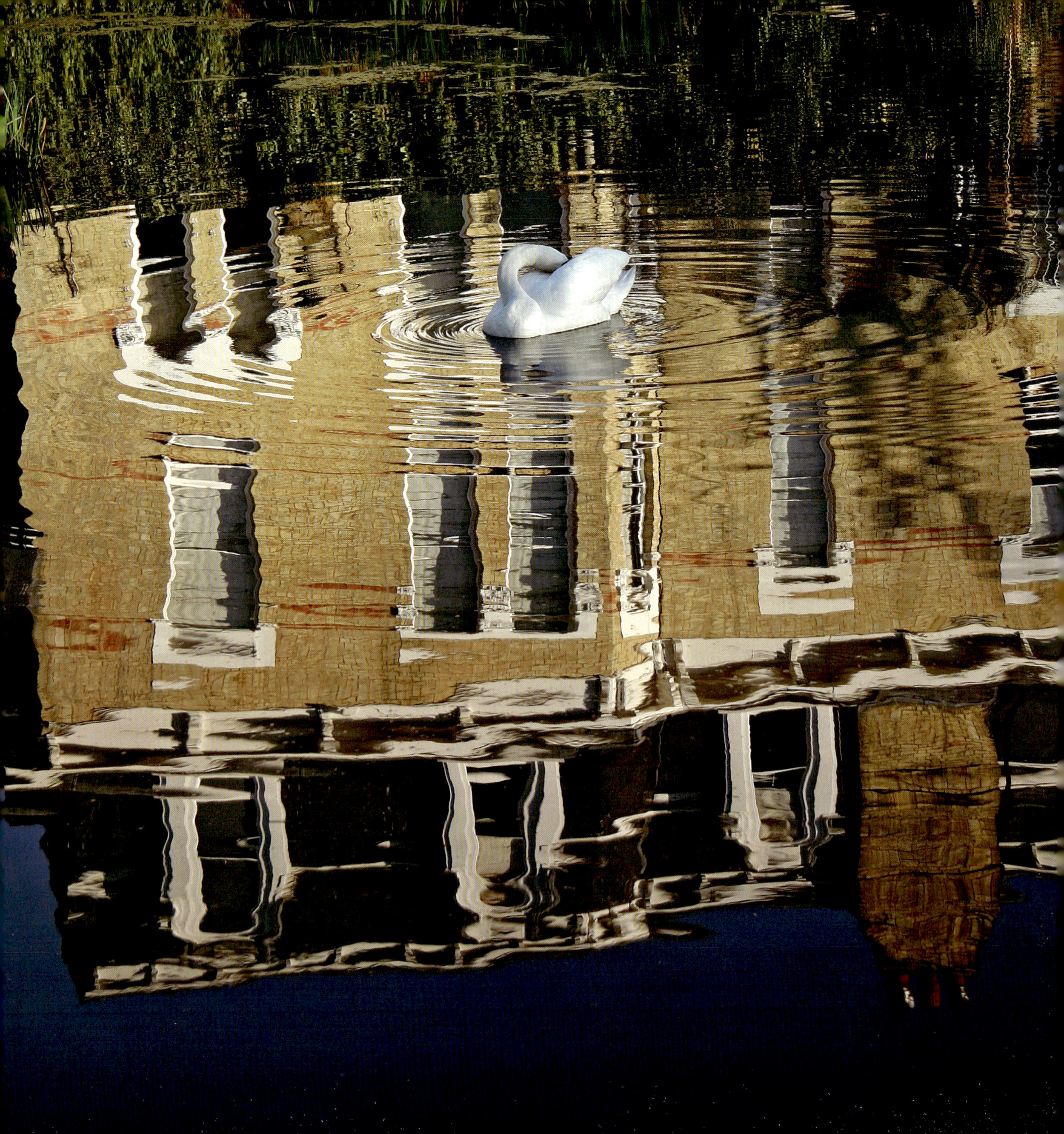

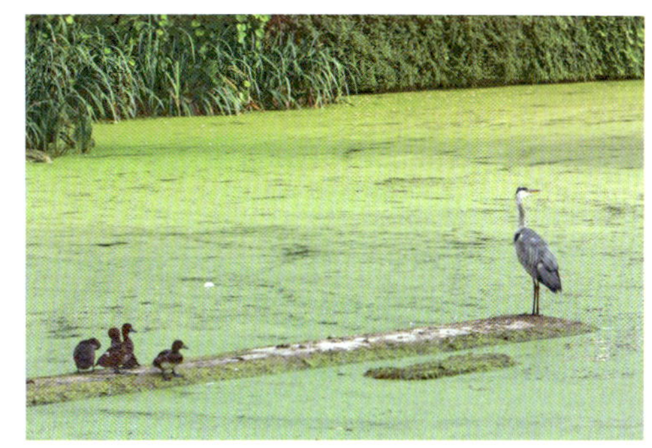

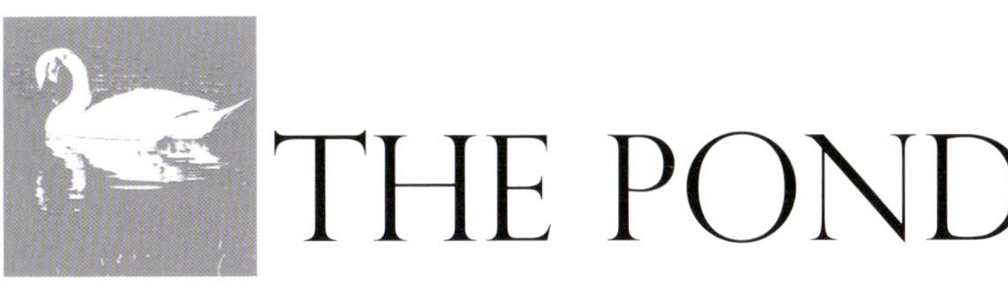

THE POND

The Pond is believed to have once been a medieval fish pond and then a dock for the royal barge. Later it became the Victorian equivalent of a car wash, the ramp on the left (see below) being used by carters for watering their horses, cleaning their carts and soaking the wooden wheels when the iron rims worked loose.

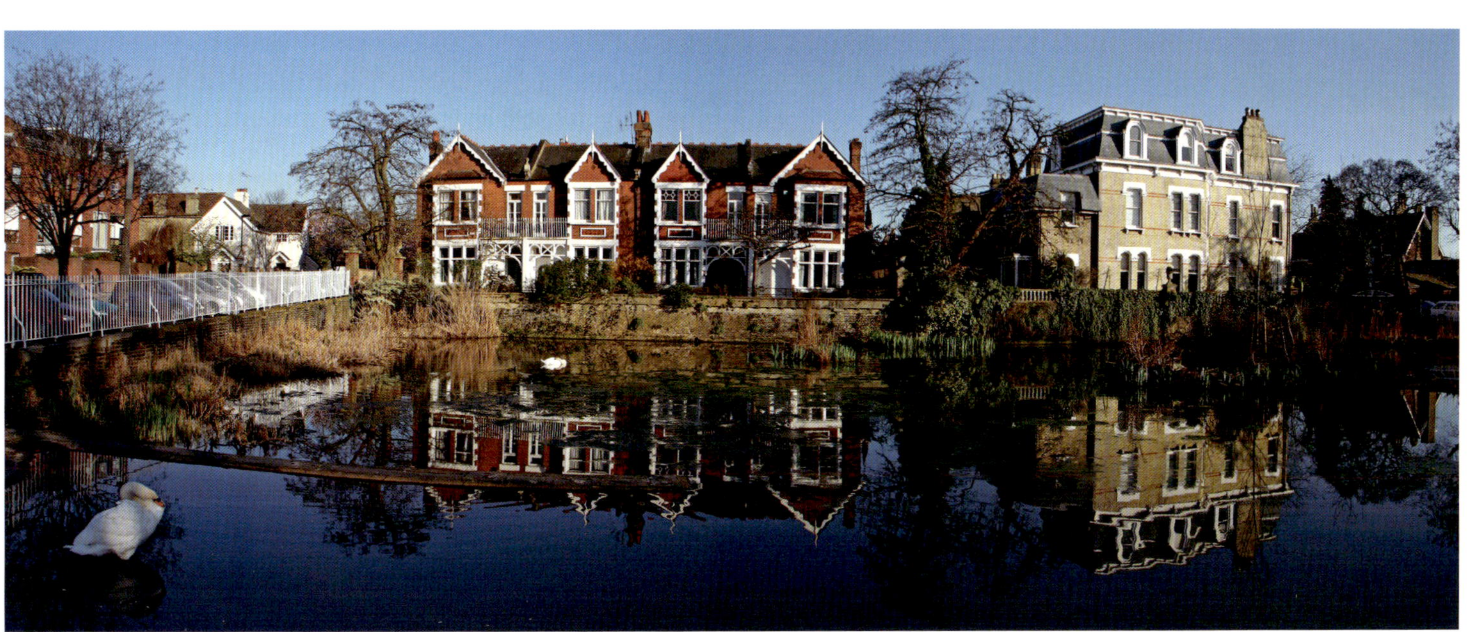

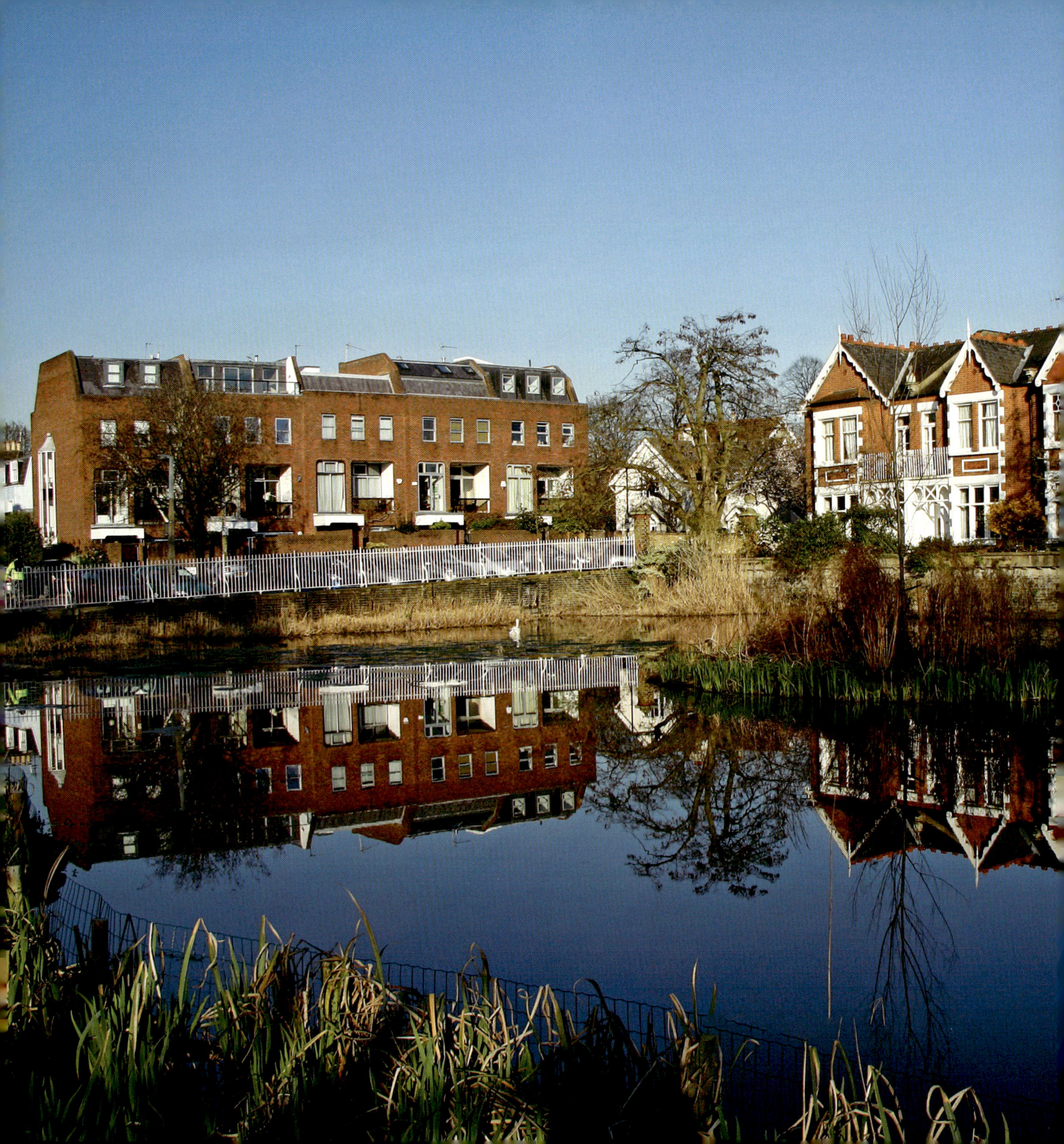

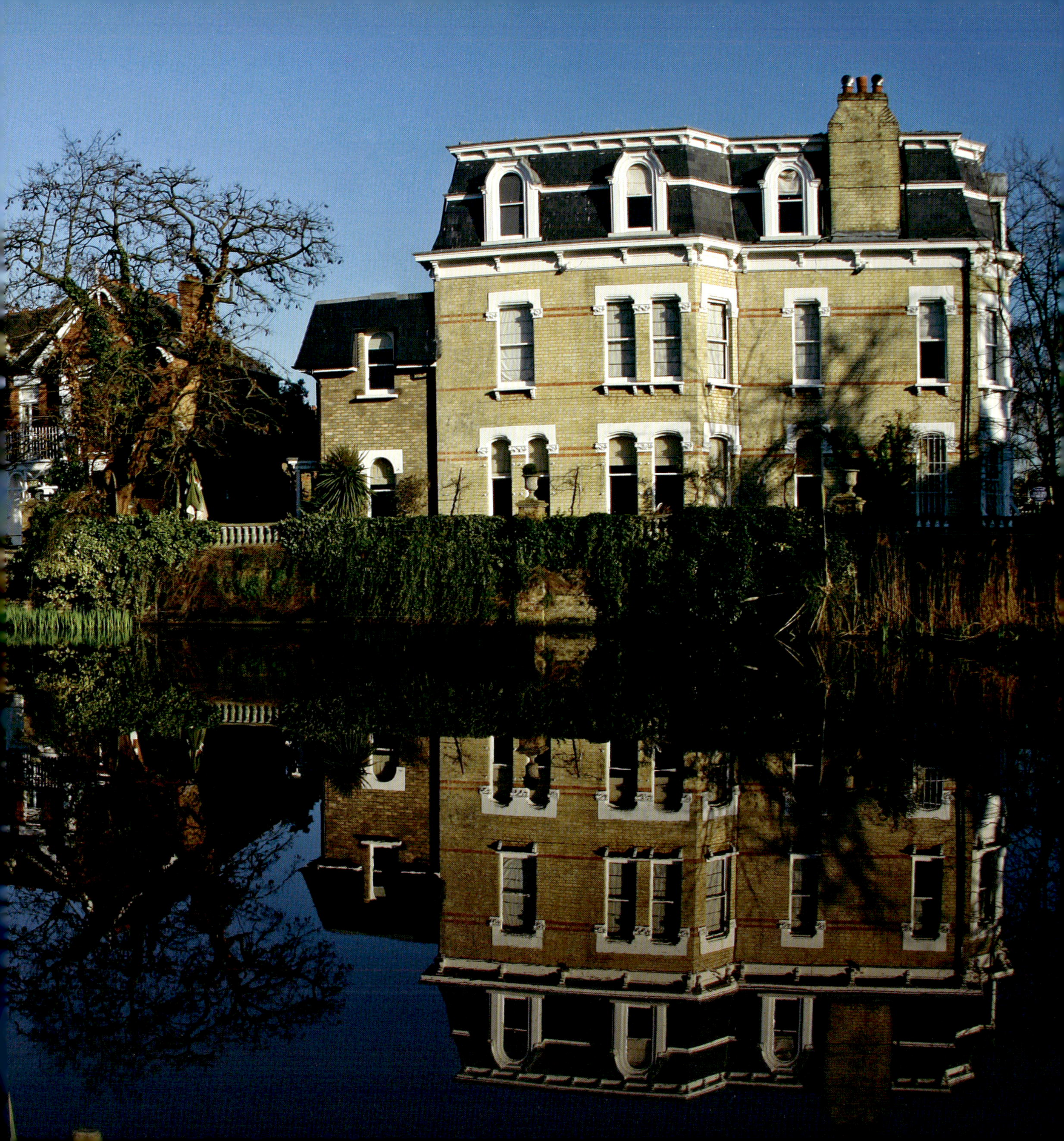

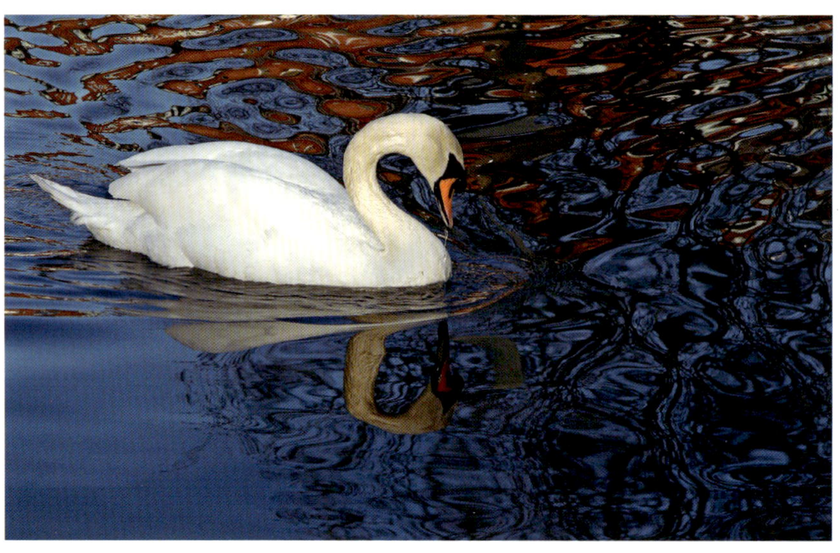

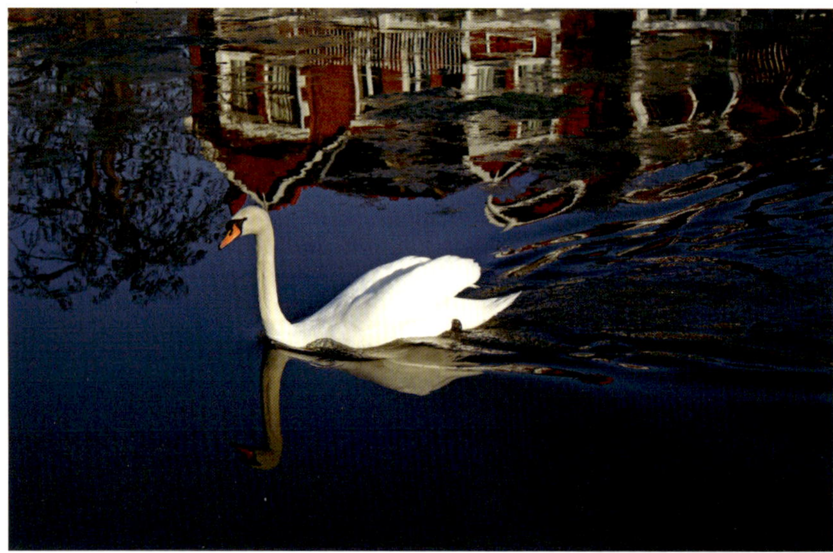

This page and the next: The resident pair of Mute Swans again bred successfully in 2011, eventually leaving in June for the greater freedom offered by Kew Gardens.

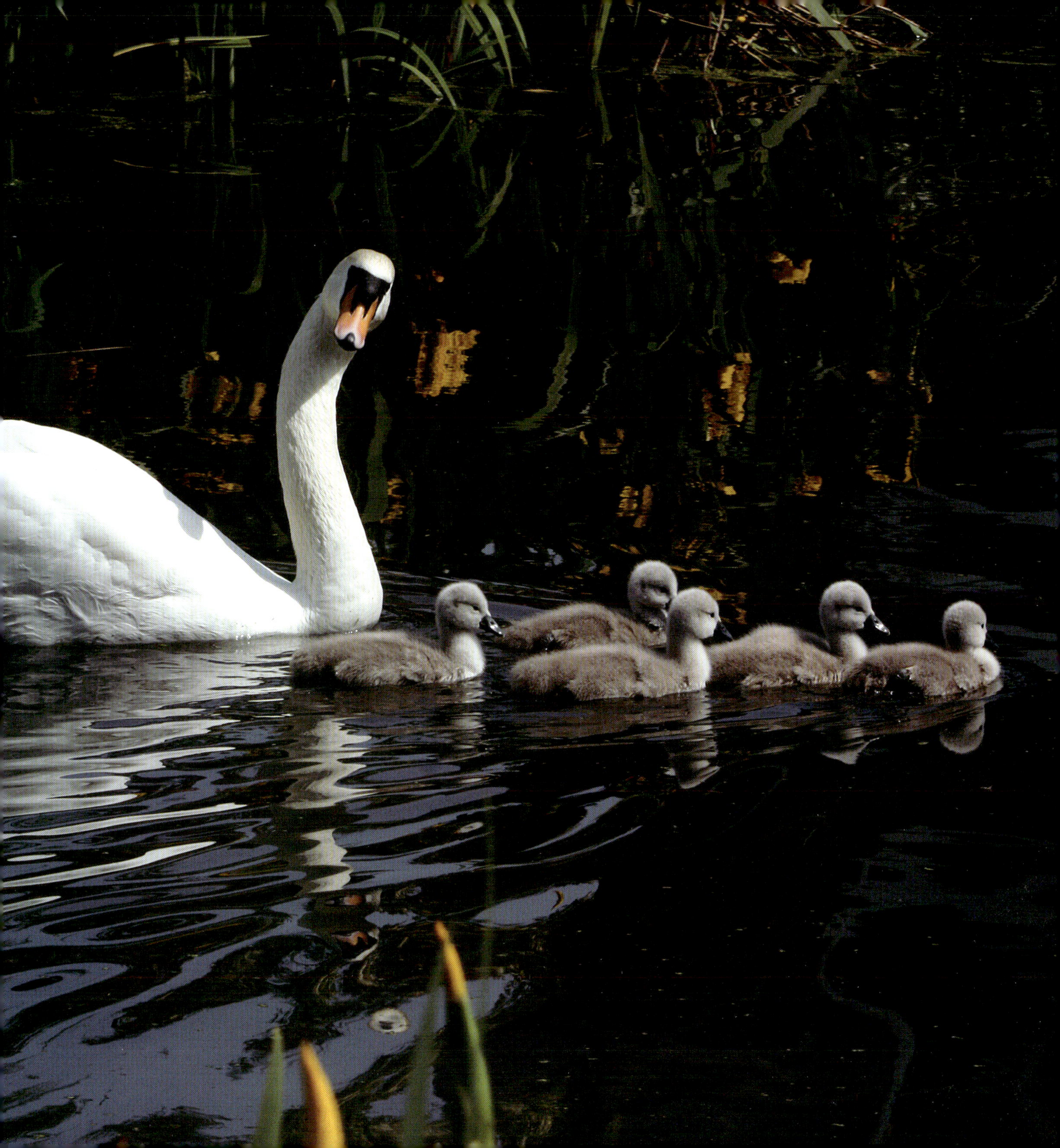

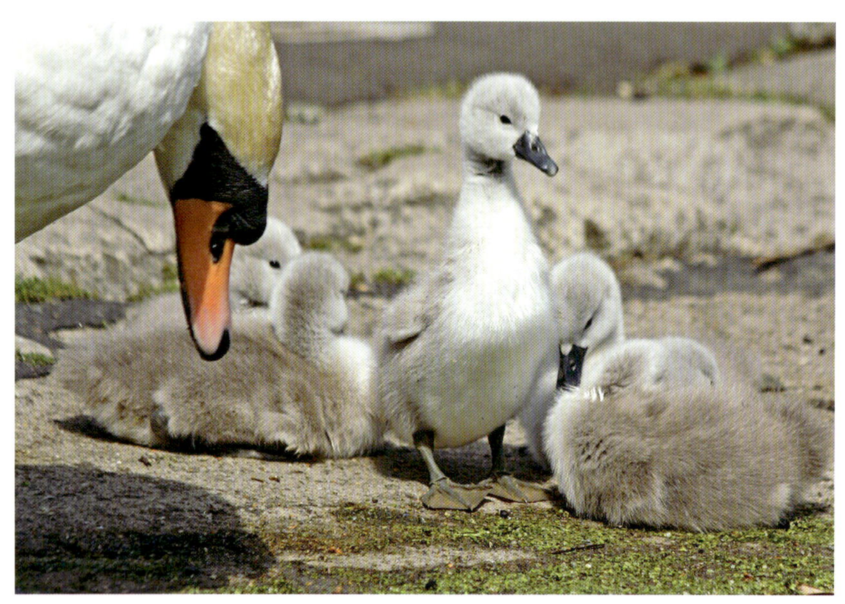

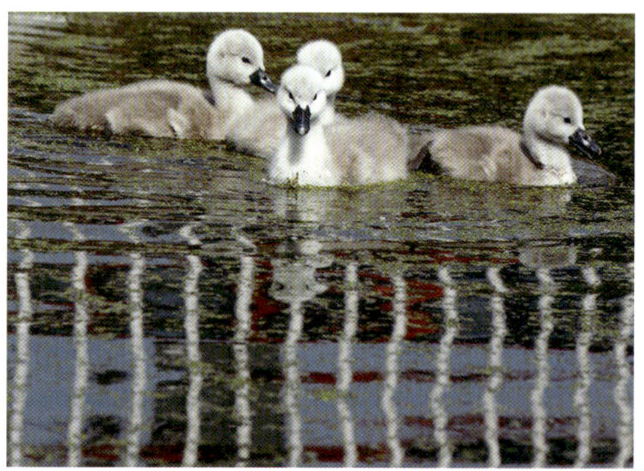

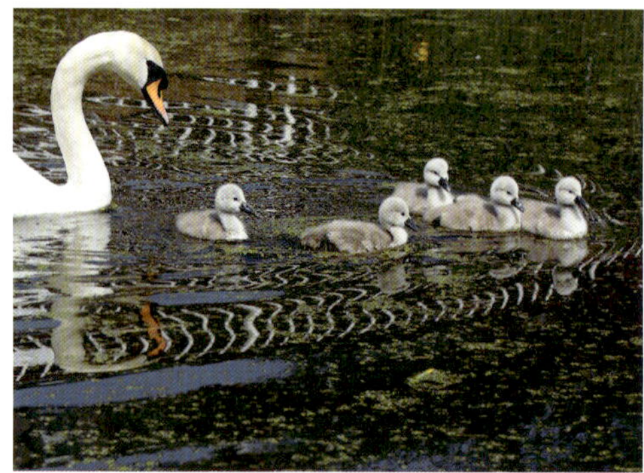

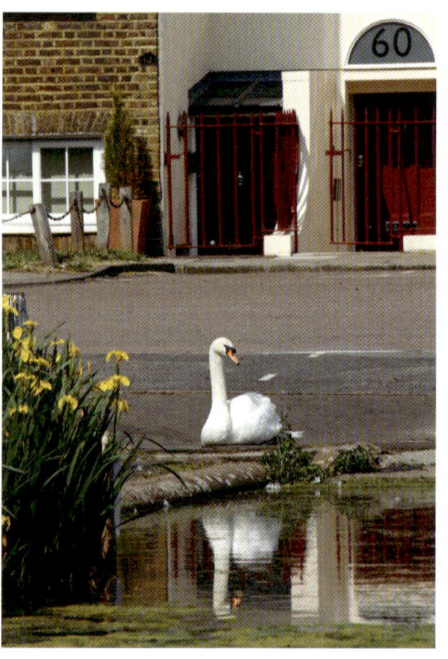
60

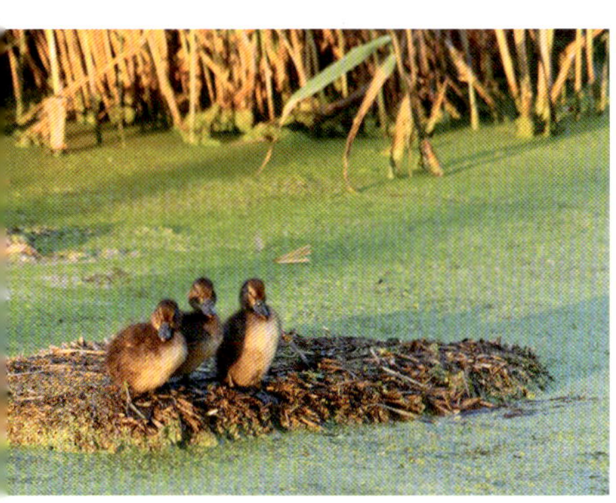

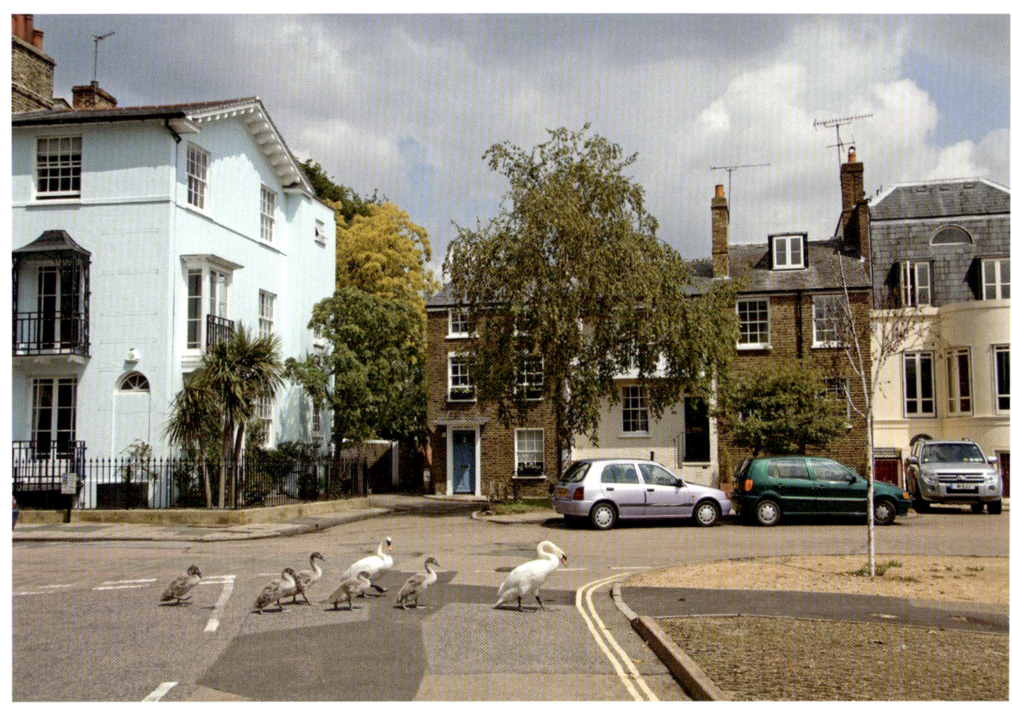

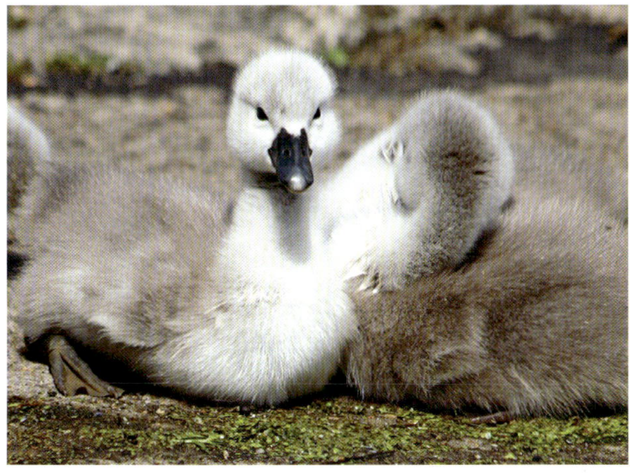

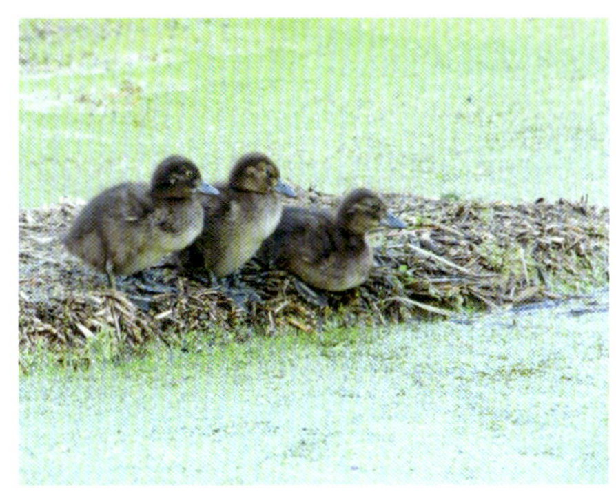

Tufted ducklings

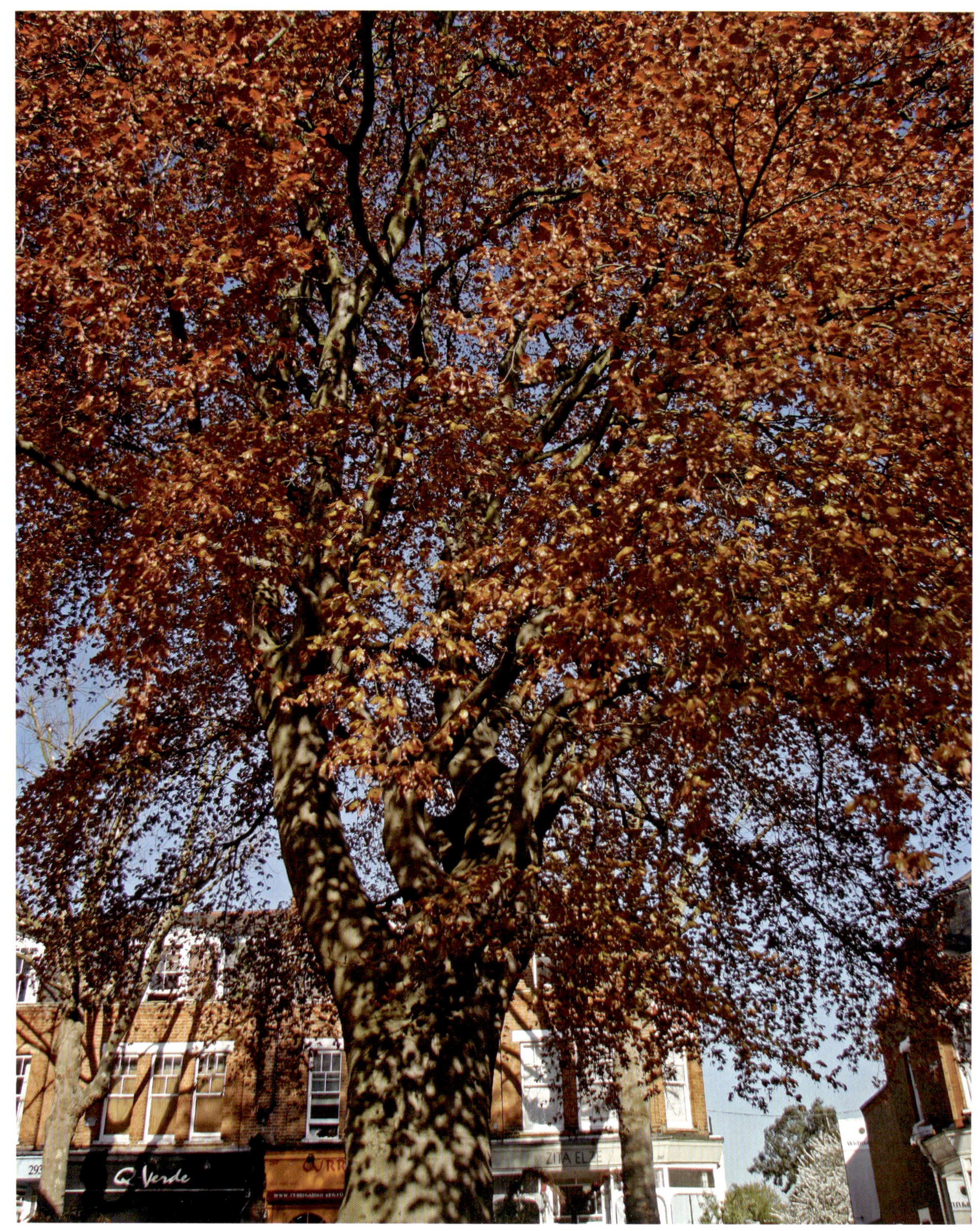

Victoria Parade, Sandycombe Road

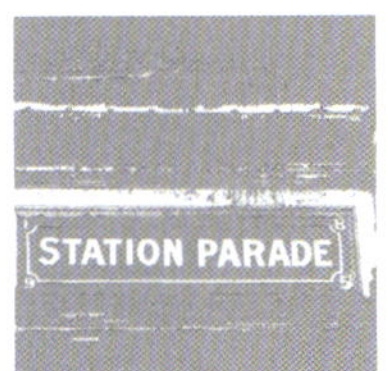

STREET SCENES

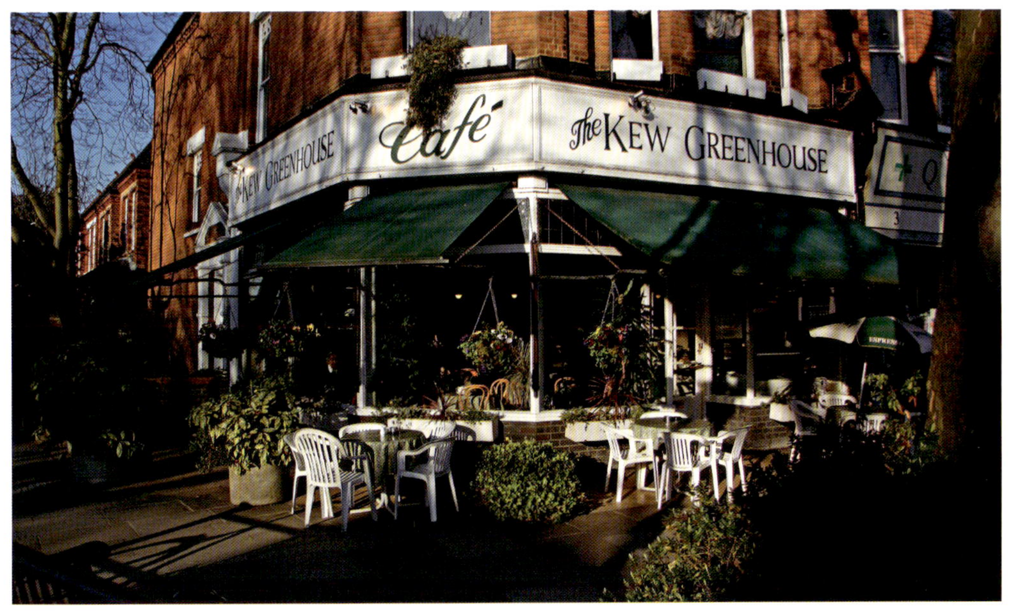

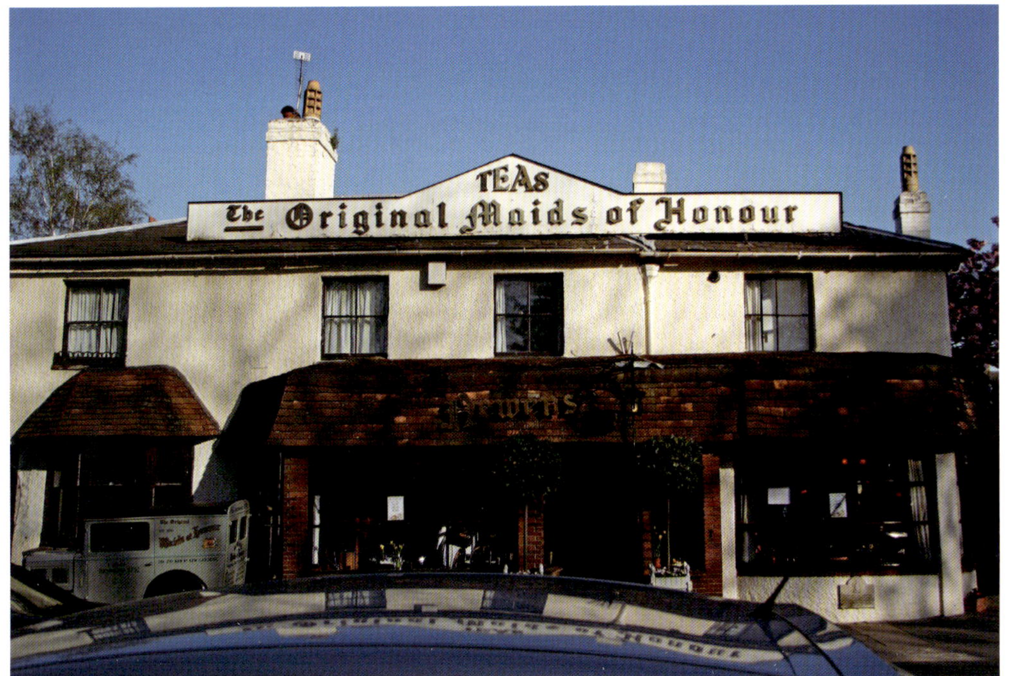

Top: The Kew Greenhouse Café on the corner of Station Parade and Sandycombe Road.
Left: Formerly known as Newens Refreshment Rooms, The Maids of Honour in Kew Road is the most famous of all Kew's tea houses.

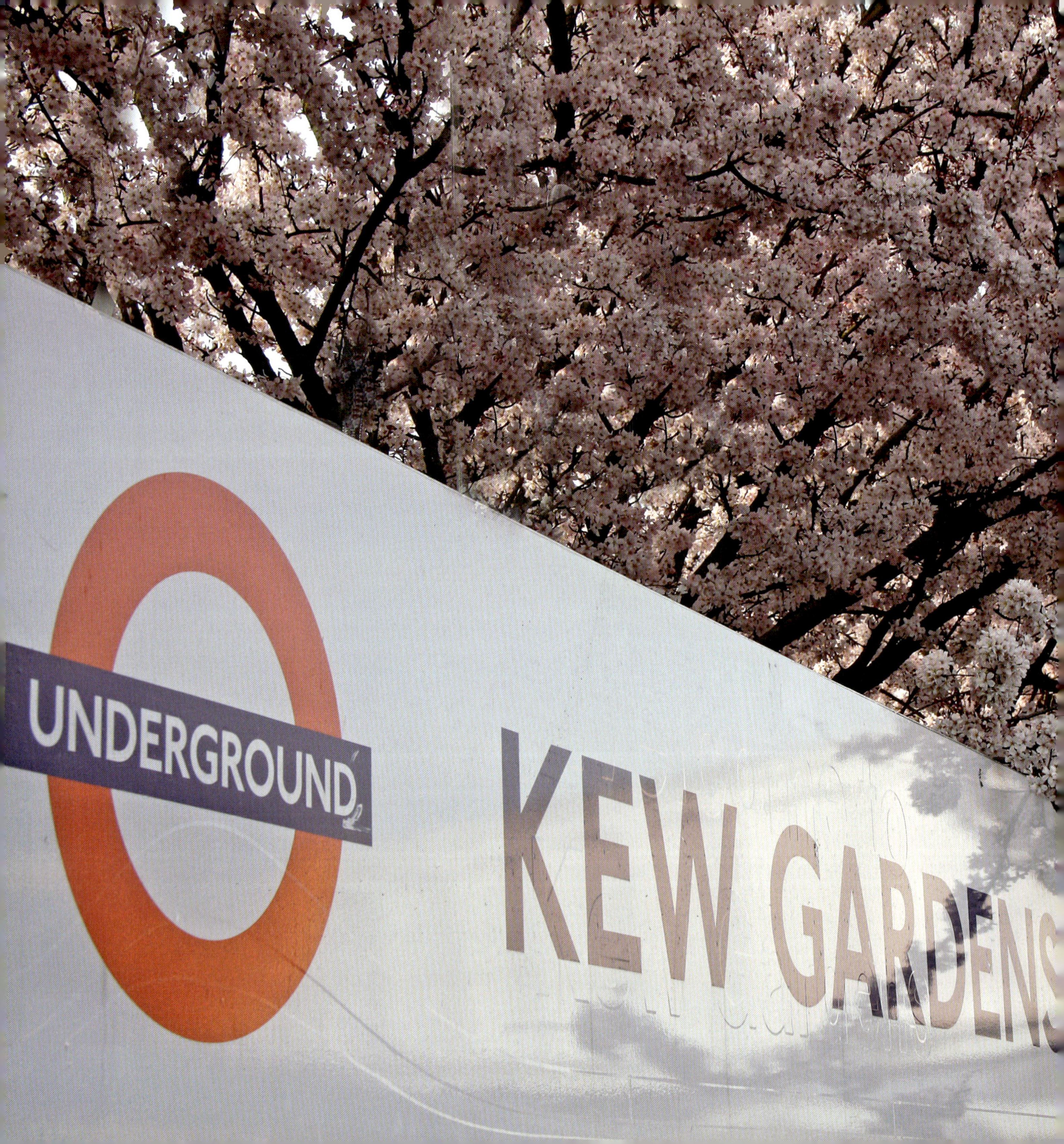
UNDERGROUND
KEW GARDENS

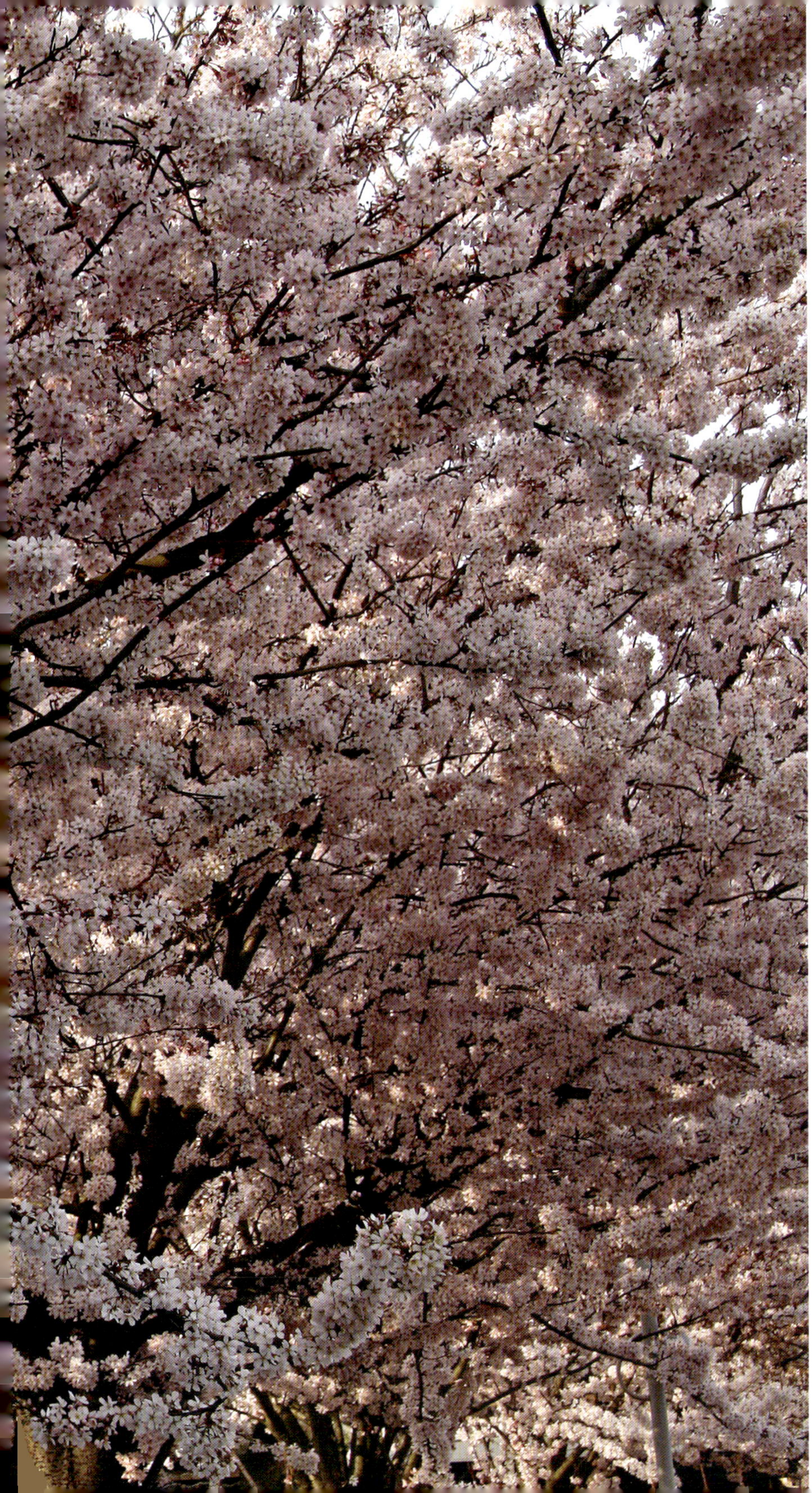

The railway arrived in Kew in 1869, in part encouraged by the people at Kew Gardens, as they knew that this would ensure the crowds required to keep the place going.

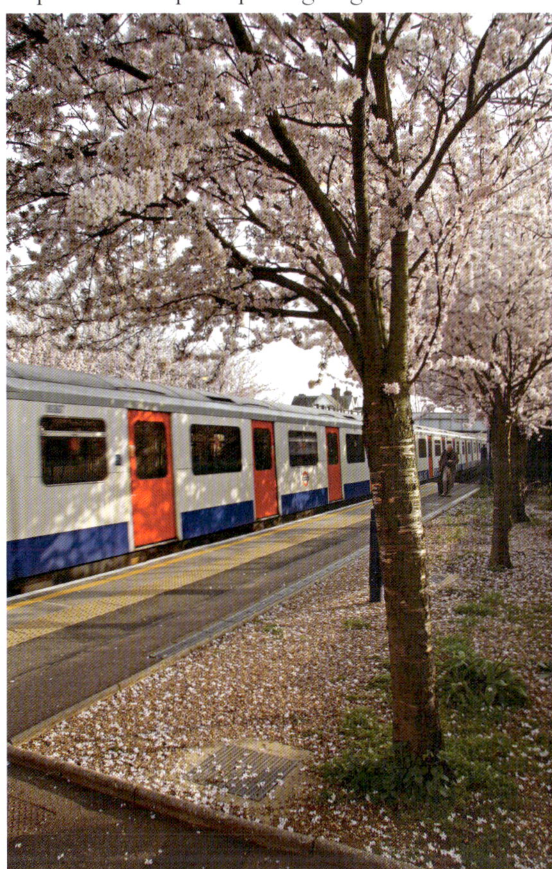

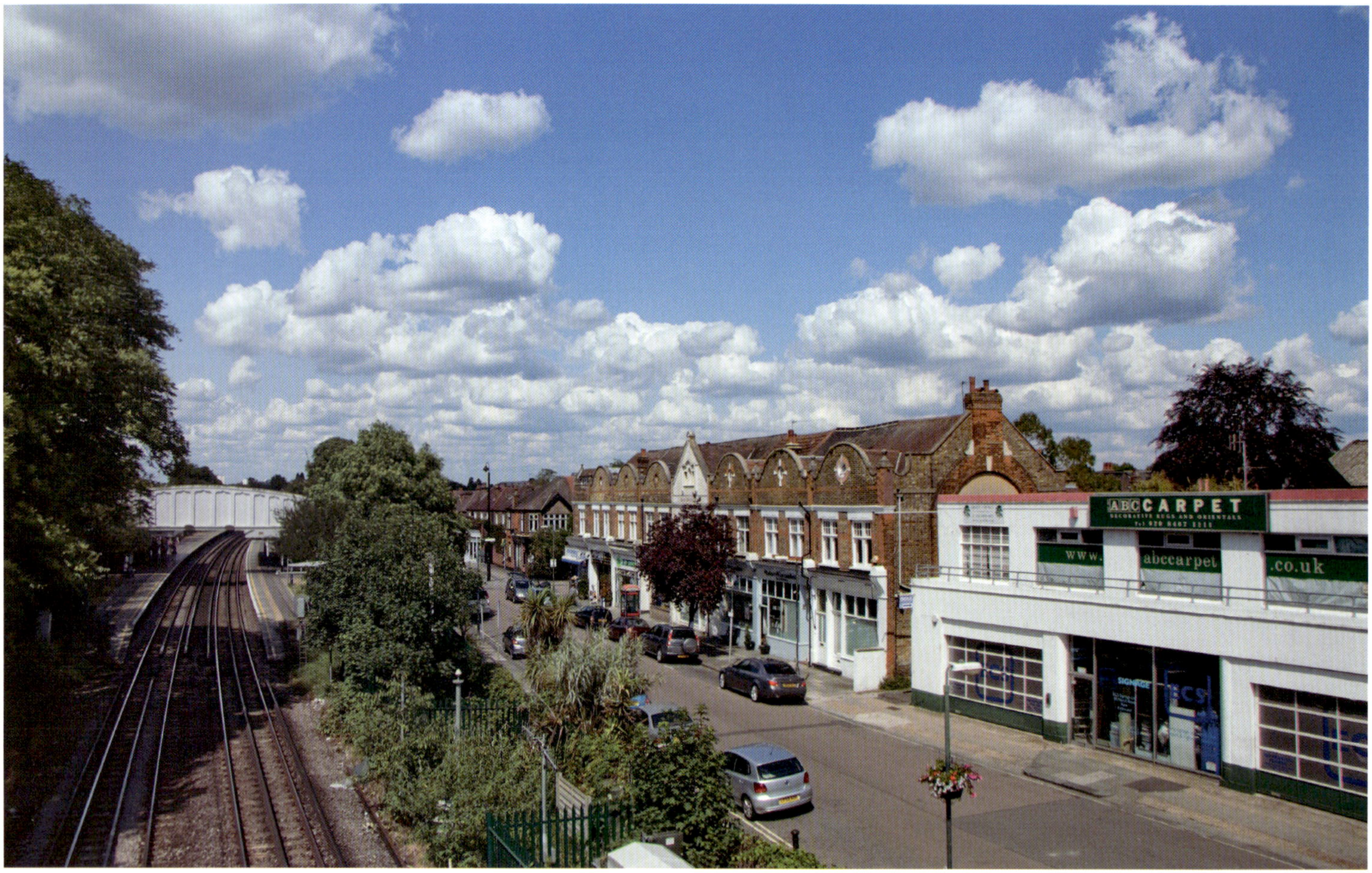

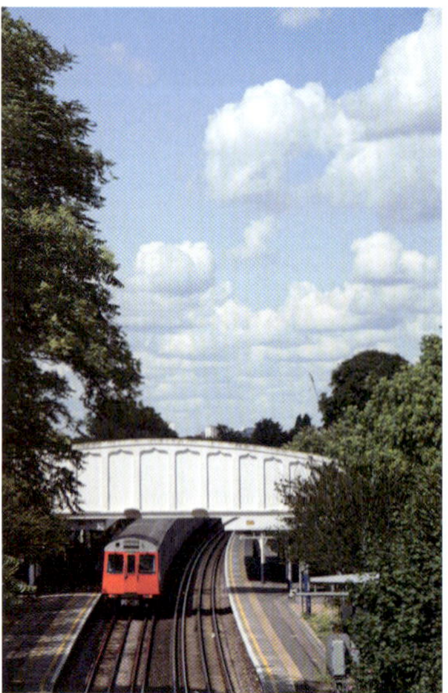

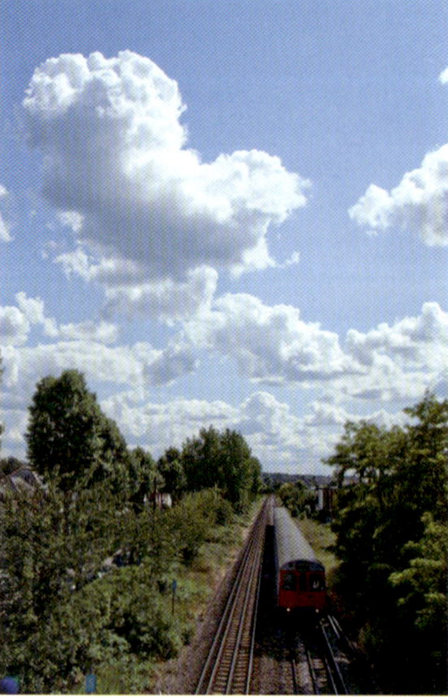

This page and opposite: The shops on either side of the station are connected by a tunnel under the line, a footbridge and a road bridge.

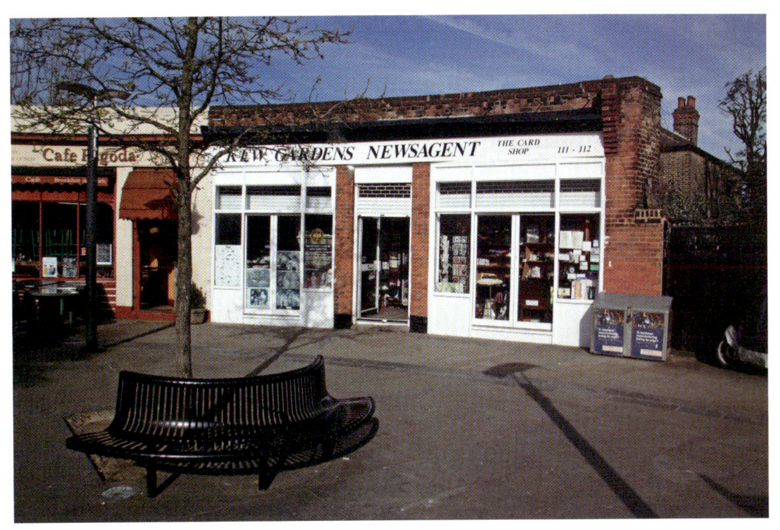
KEW GARDENS NEWSAGENT
THE CARD SHOP
111 - 112

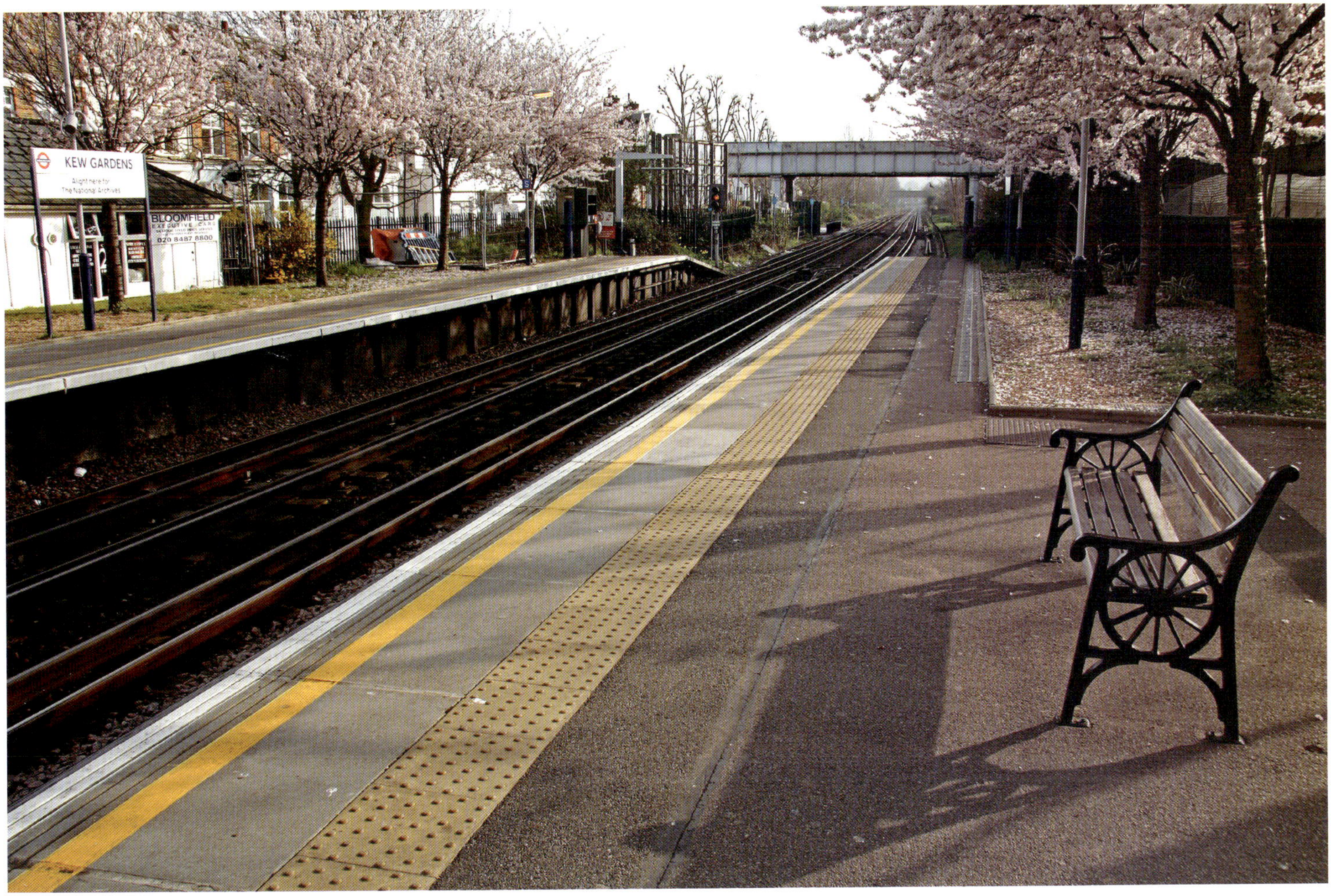

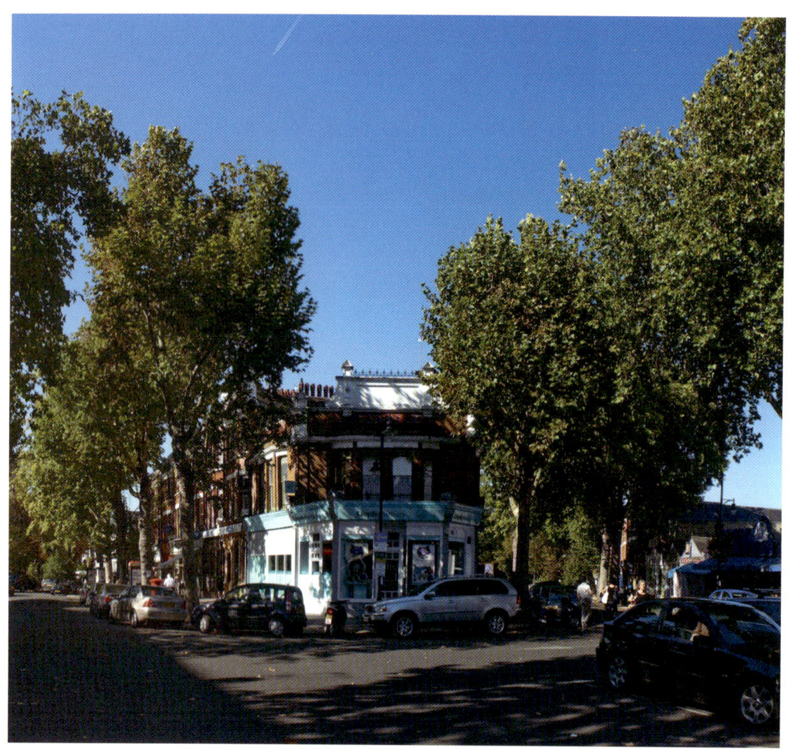

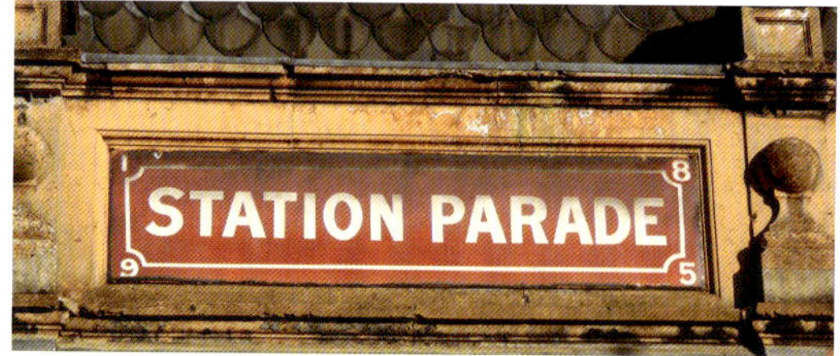

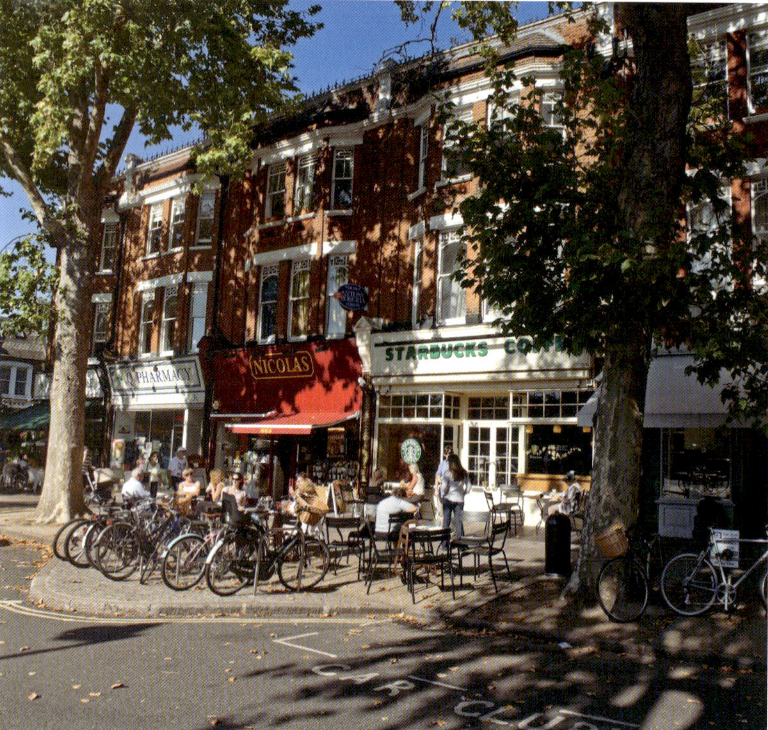

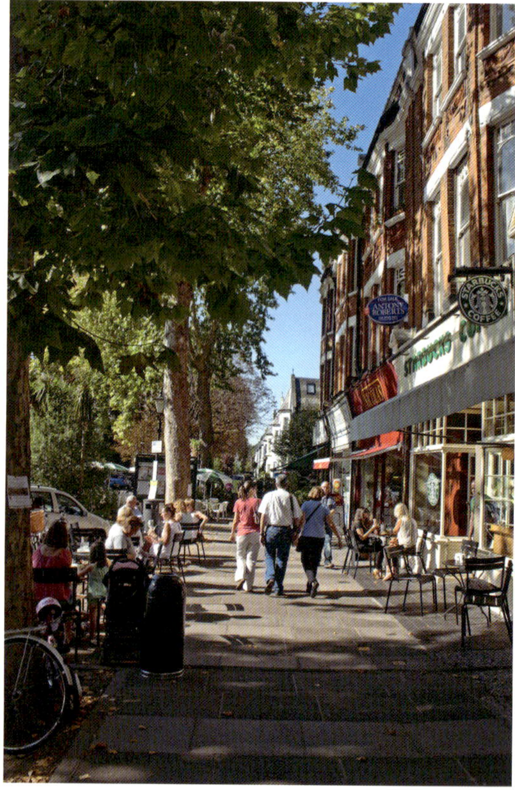

This page and opposite: The area around the station is a fun and lively place with many shops, pavement cafés and The Railway pub.

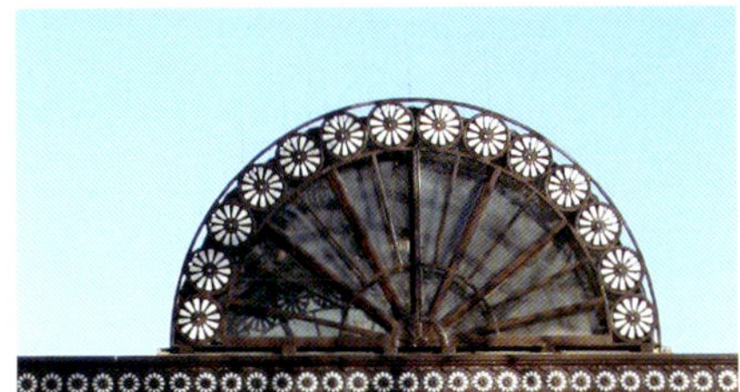

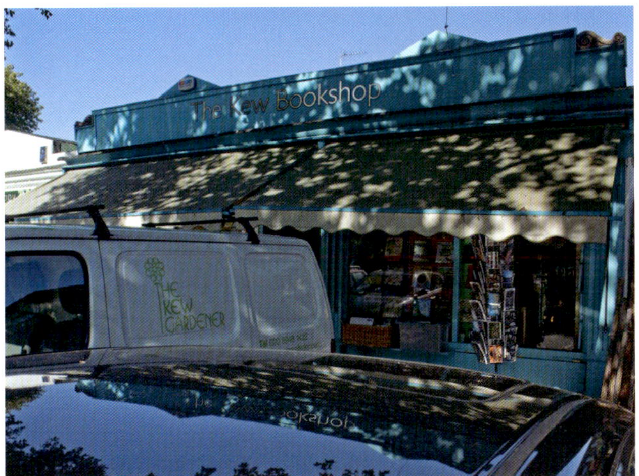
The Kew Bookshop
THE KEW GARDENER

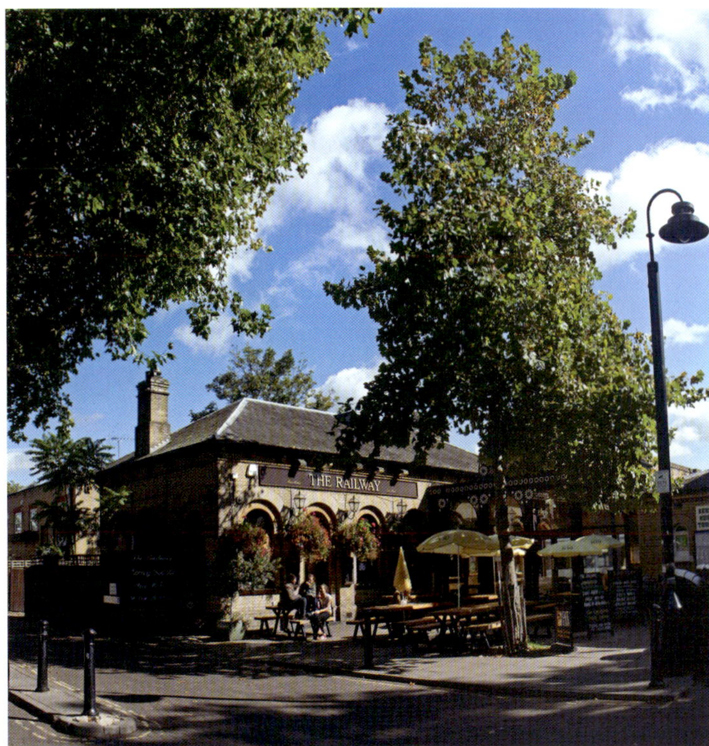
THE RAILWAY

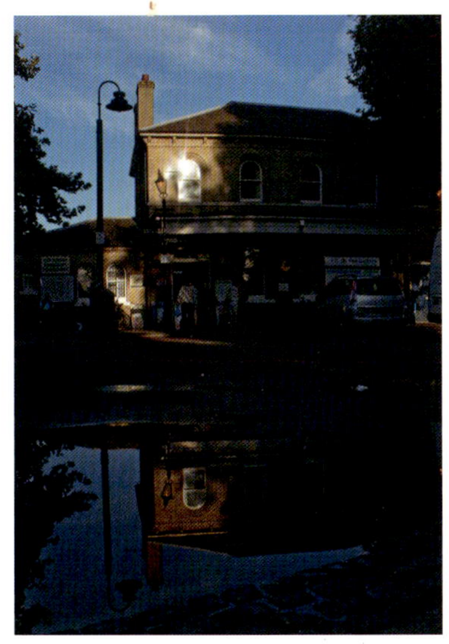

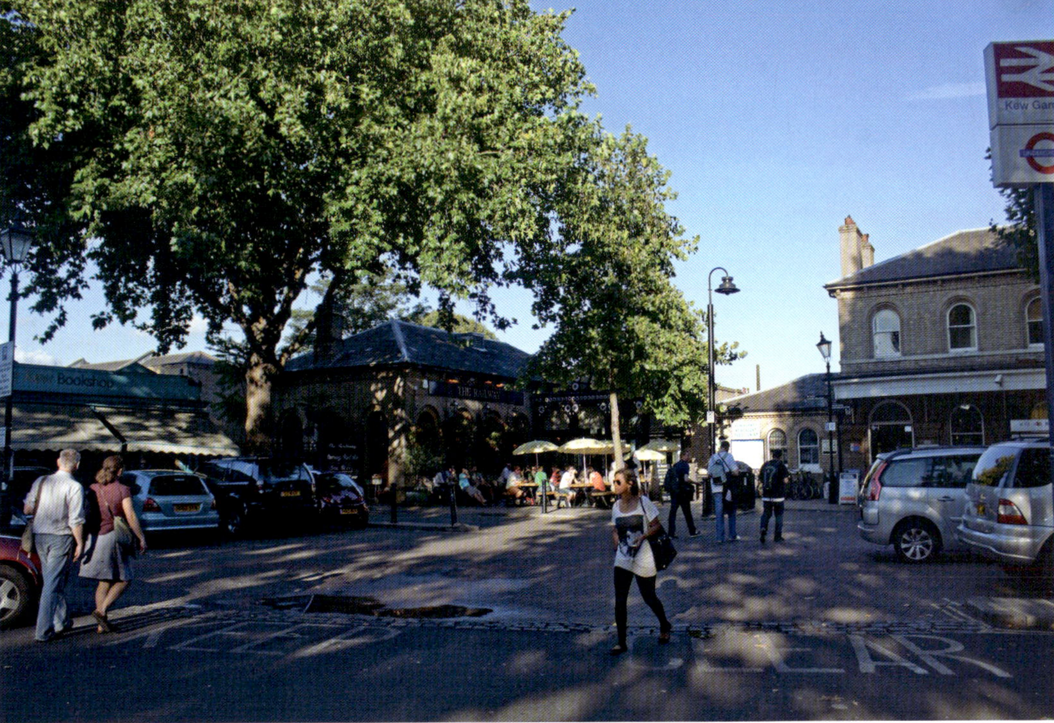

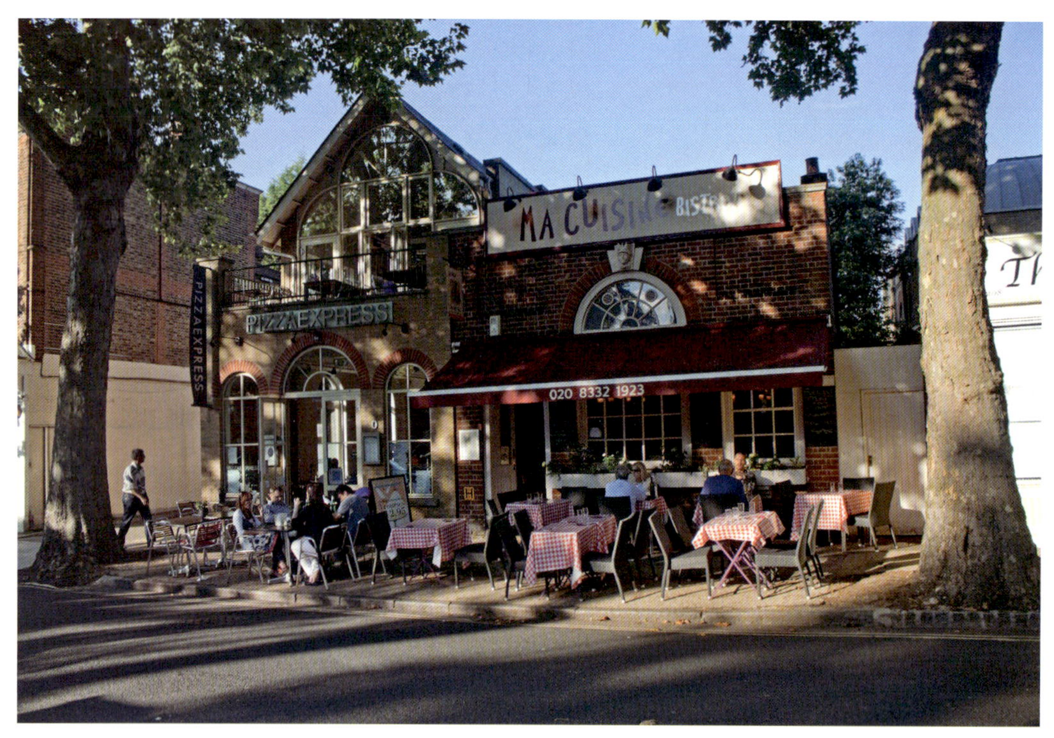

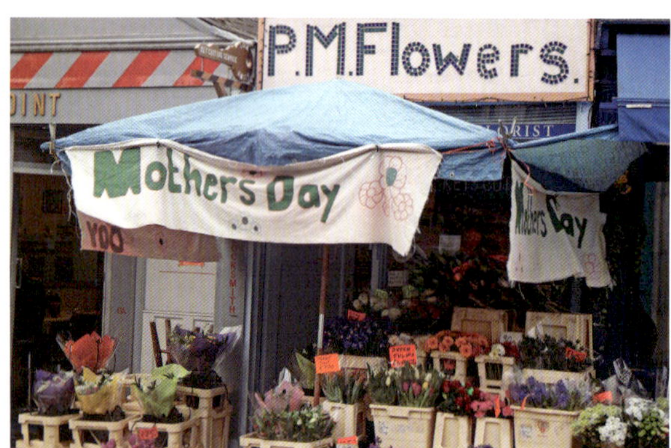

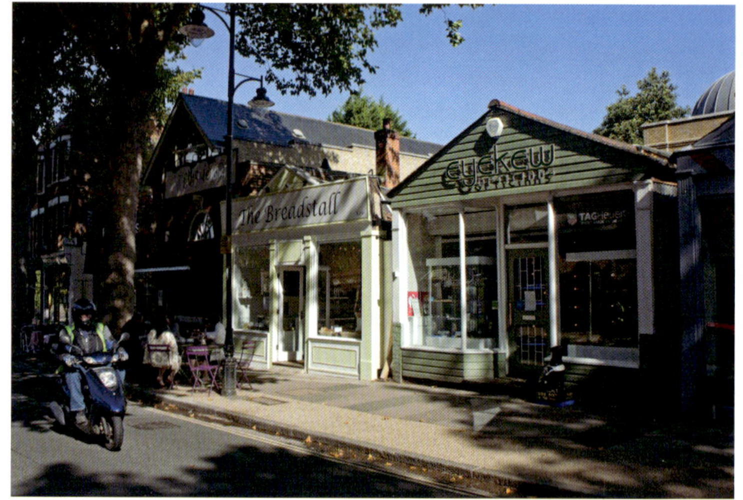

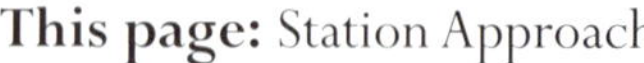
This page: Station Approach

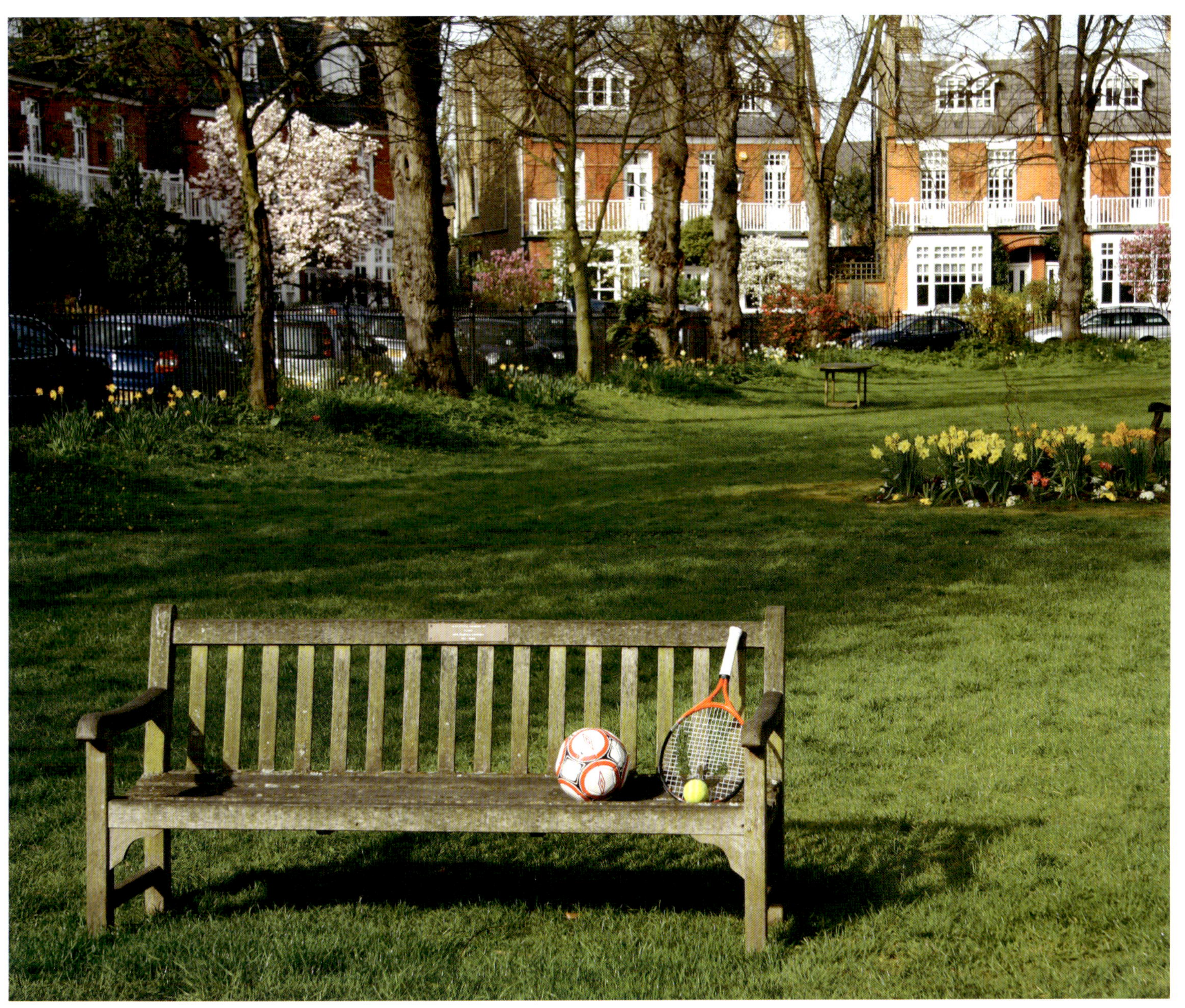

Lawn Crescent, off Sandycombe Road

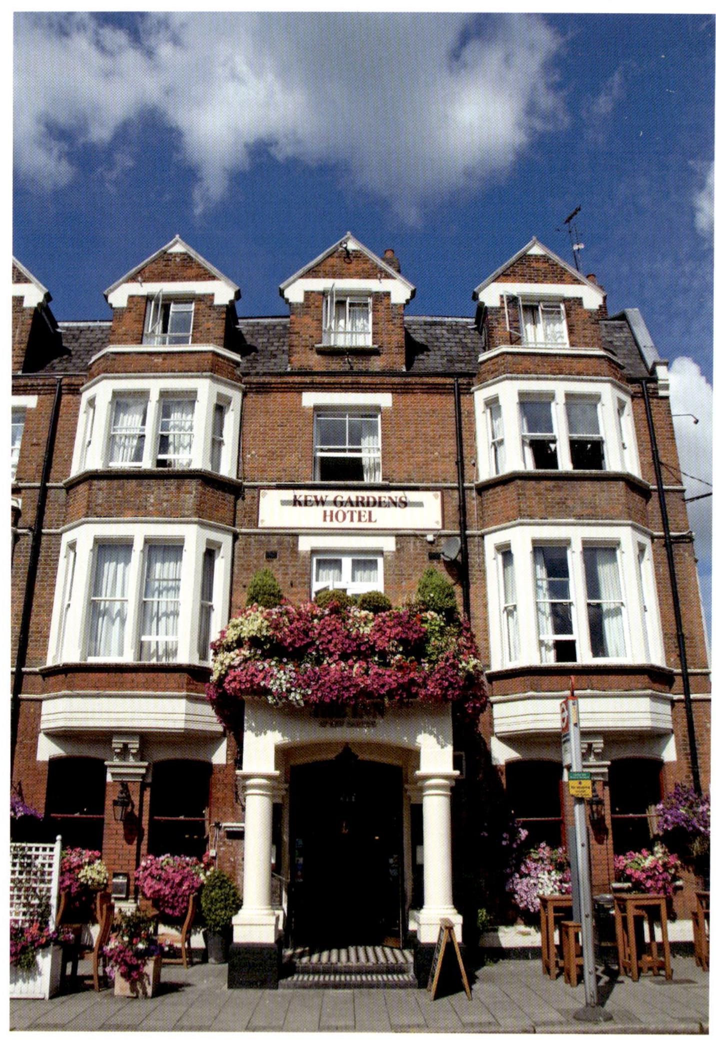

This page and opposite: Sandycombe Road
Below and left:Kew Gardens Hotel, pub and restaurant
Bottom: Windsor Road

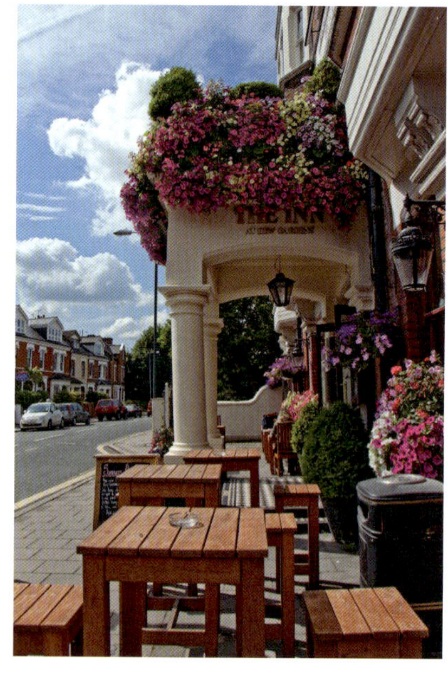

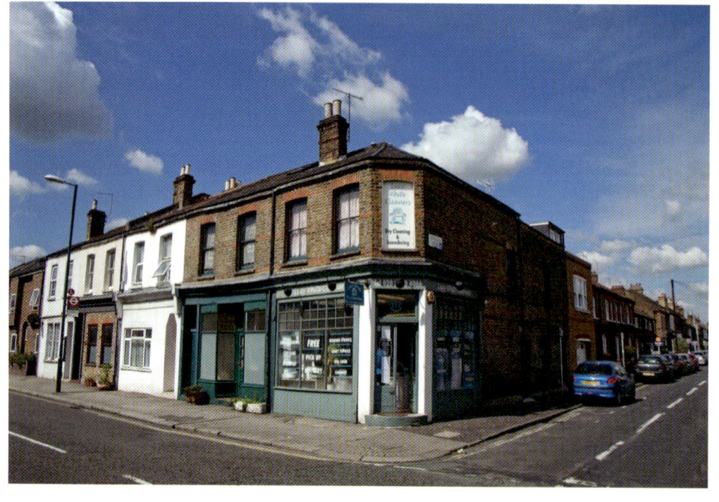

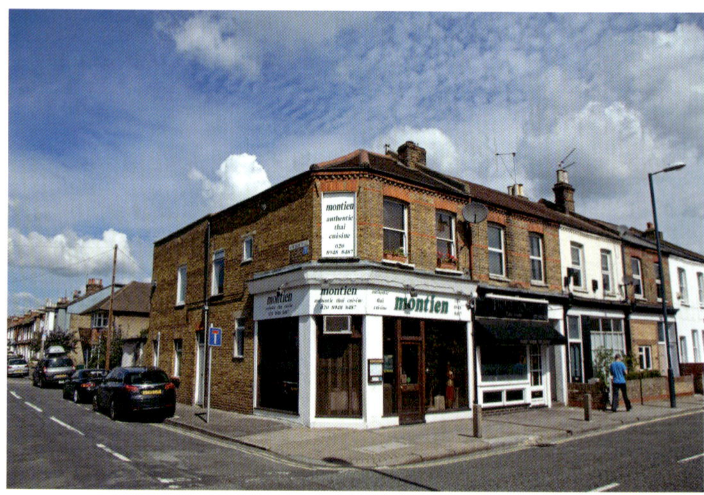

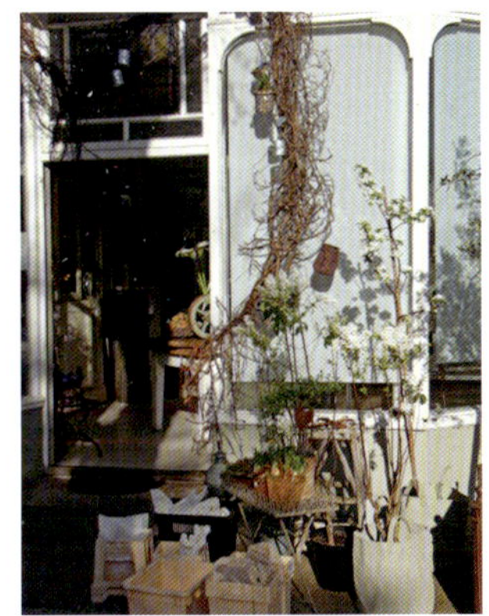

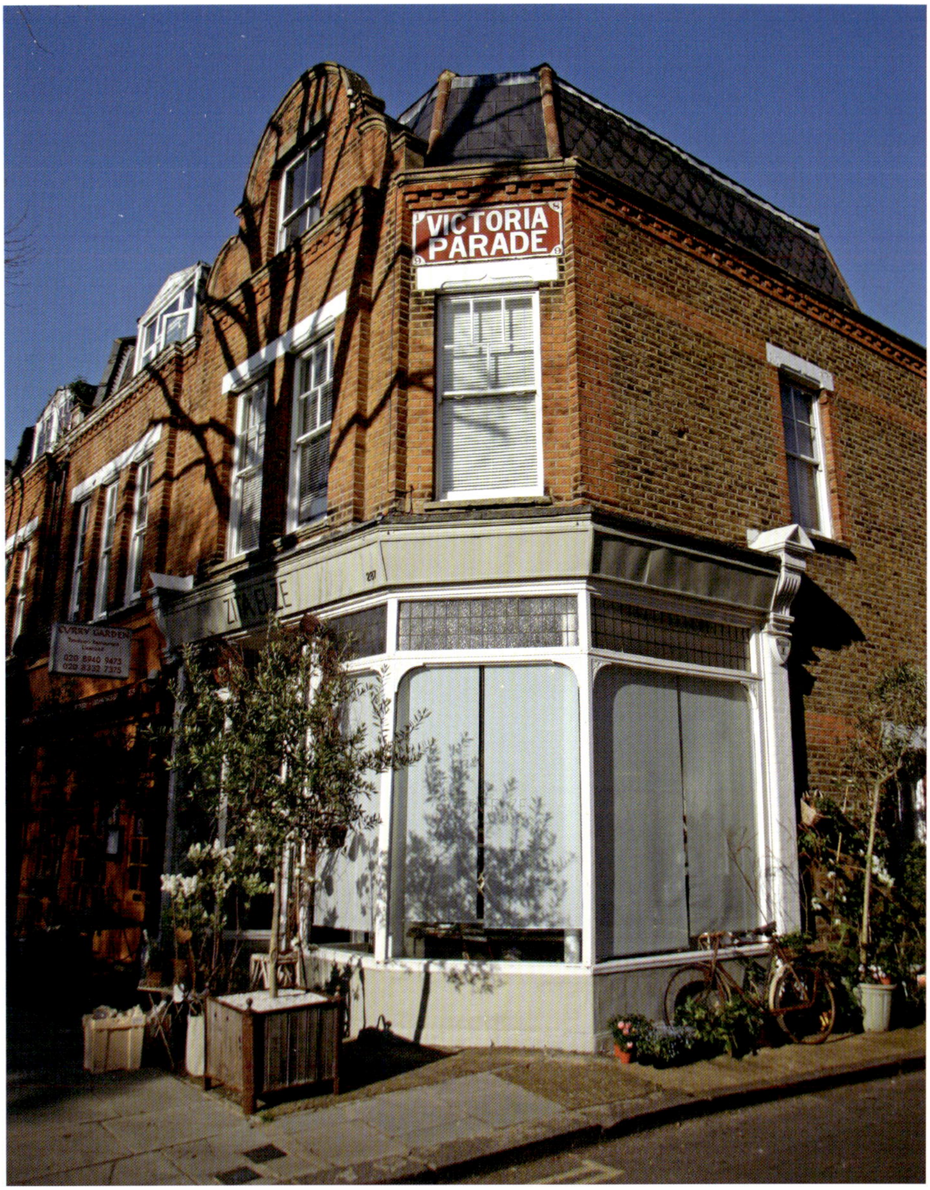

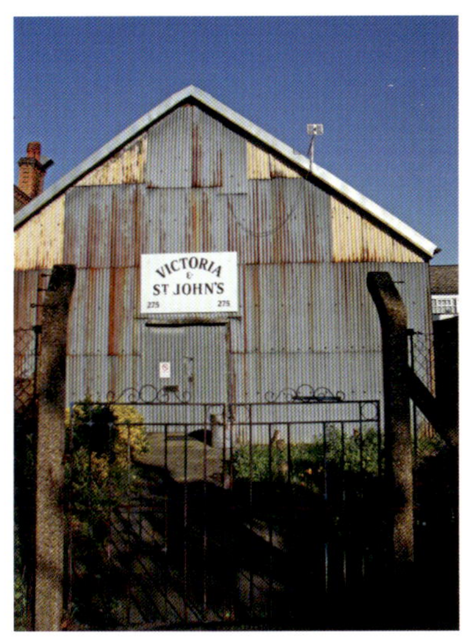

Above: This rather odd looking building has quite a history; at various times being a church during the 1870's, a social club in the 1890's, visited upon by Royalty and Heads of Government in the early 1900's and finally becoming a fitness club.

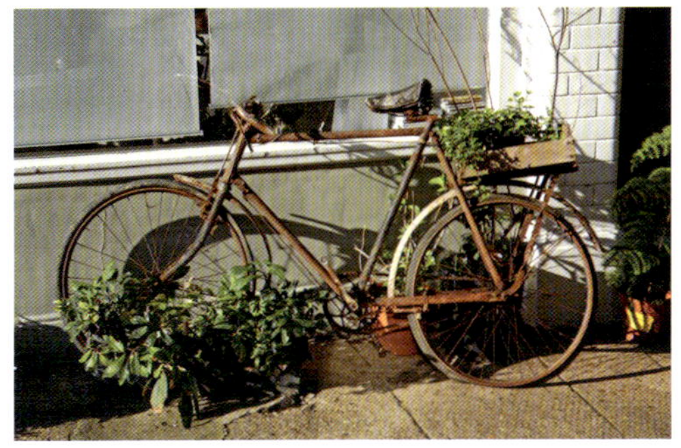

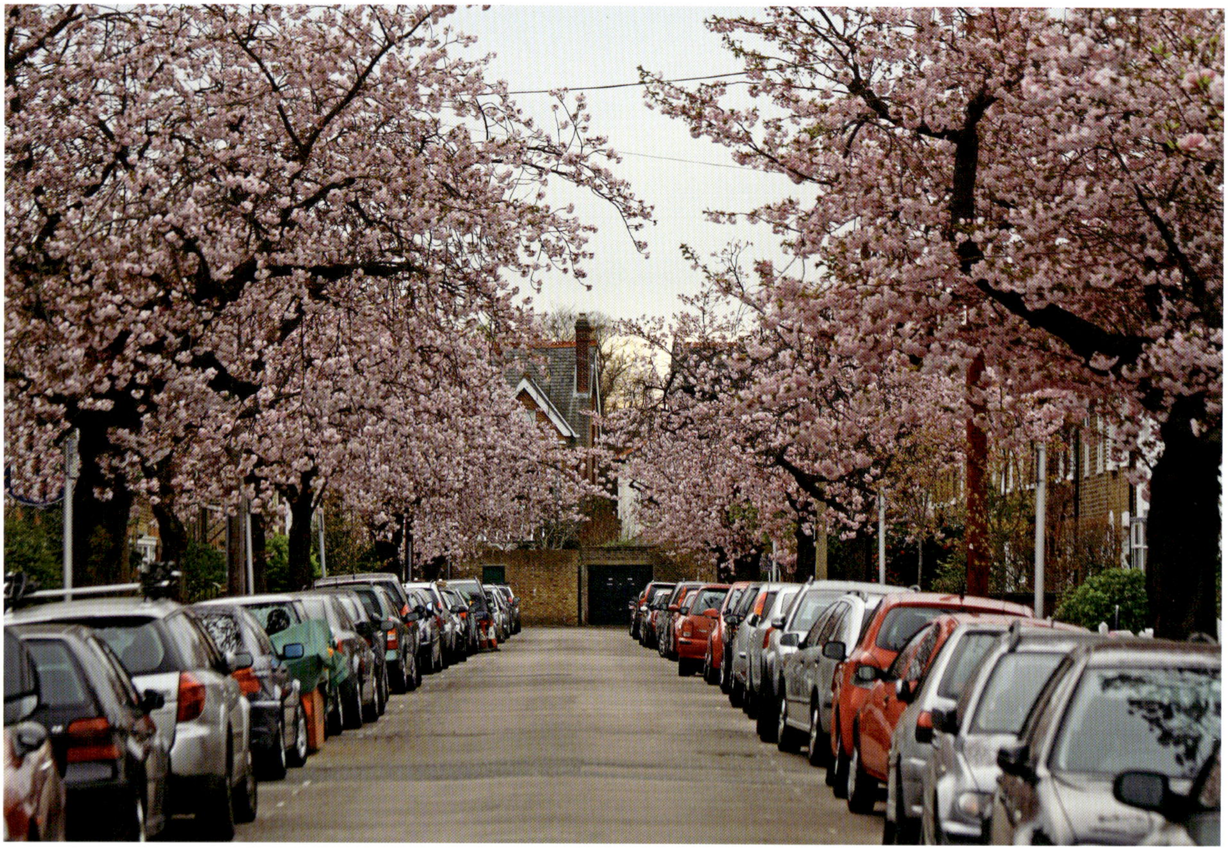

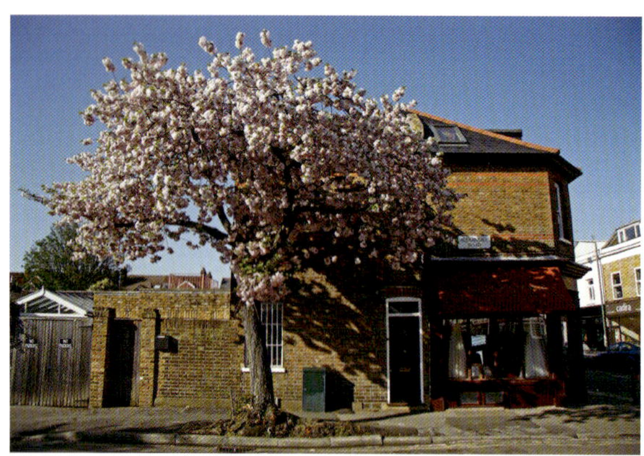

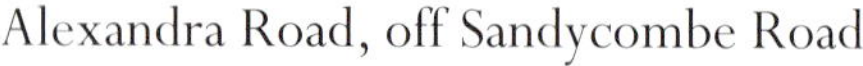

Alexandra Road, off Sandycombe Road

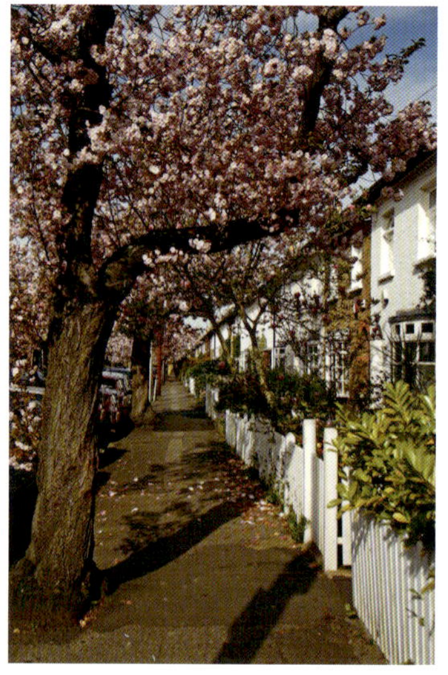

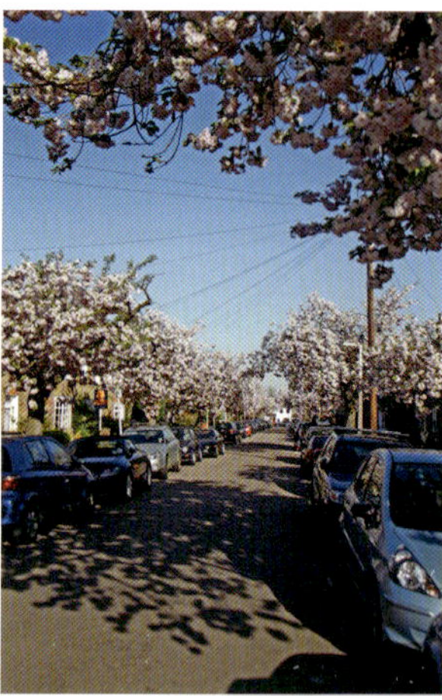

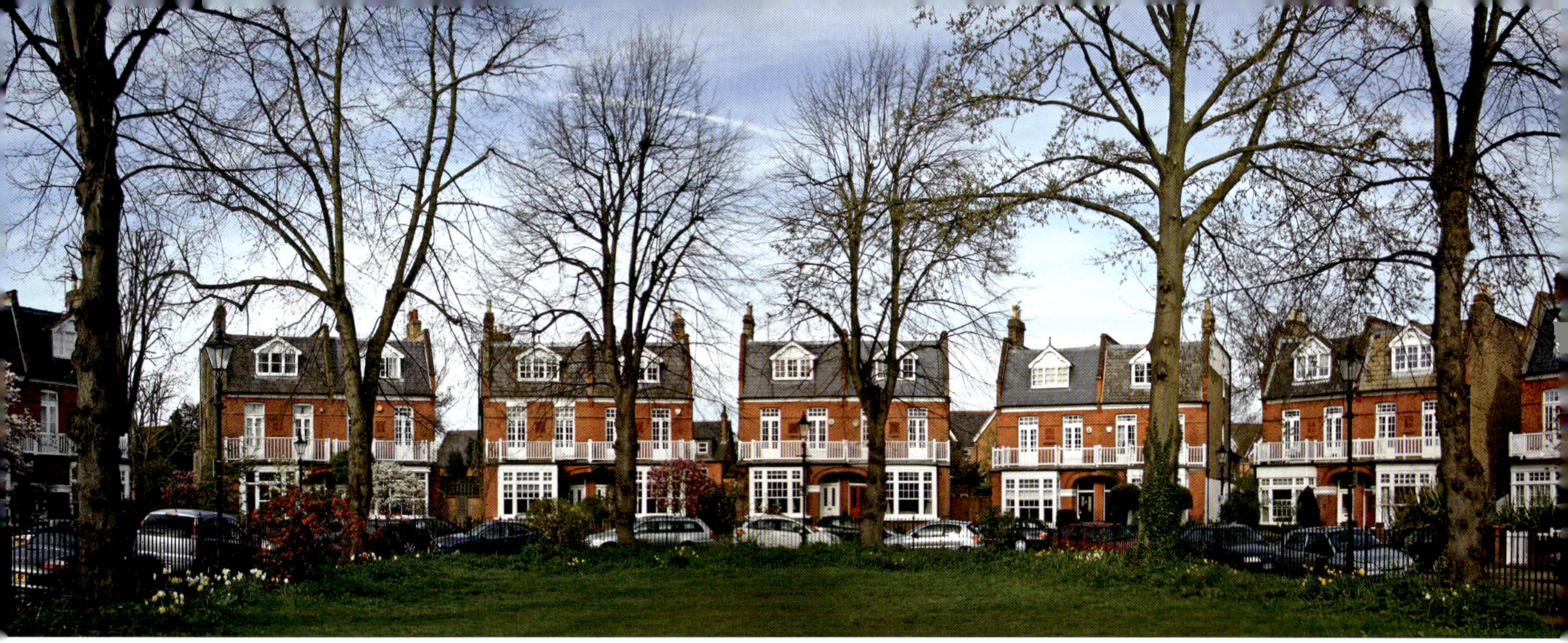

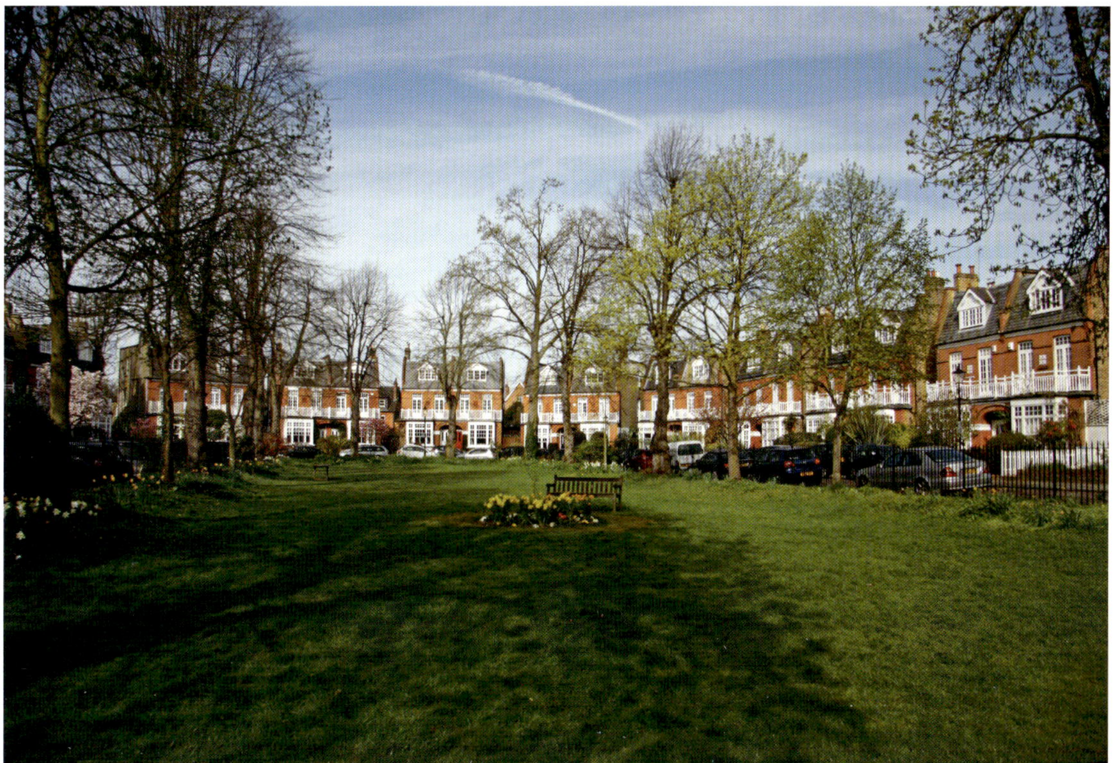

Lawn Crescent, off Sandycombe Road

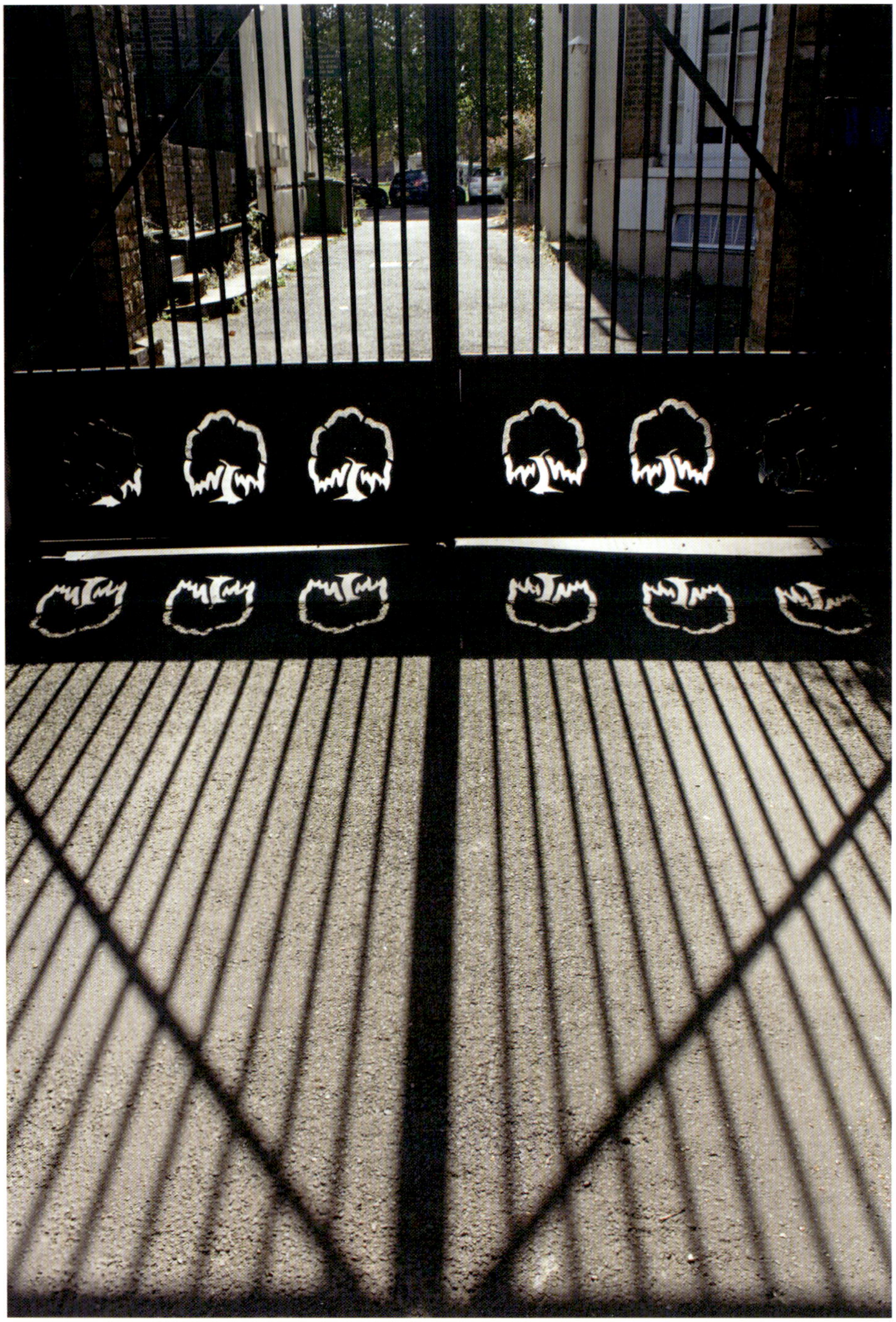

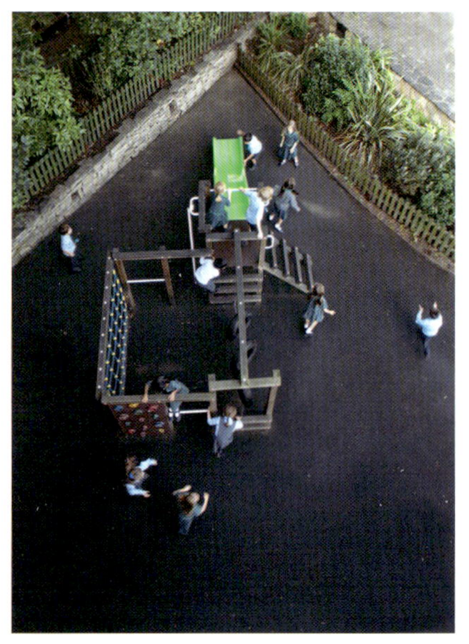

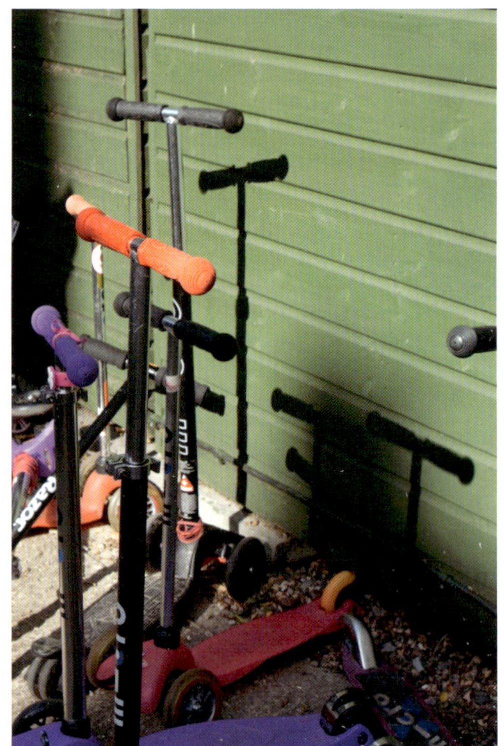

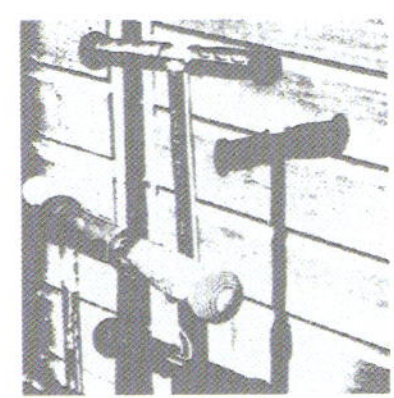

SCHOOLS

Kew Green Preparatory School:
Opened in 2004, this school is hidden away in the north-west corner of The Green. If it wasn't for the odd joyous shriek from one of the kids playing you wouldn't know it was there. Flanked by the Thames, the Green and Kew Gardens, what an enviable setting for a school.

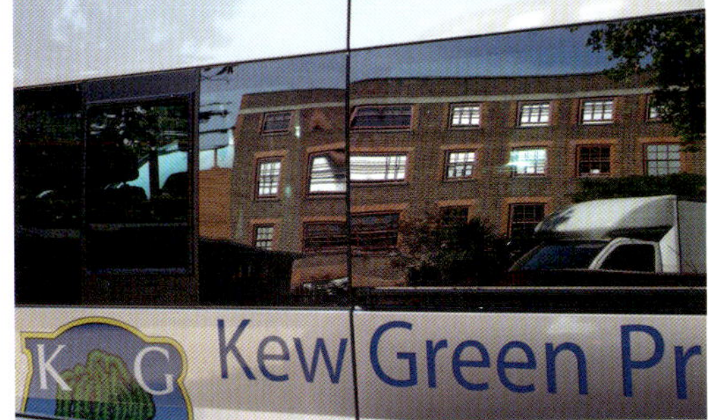

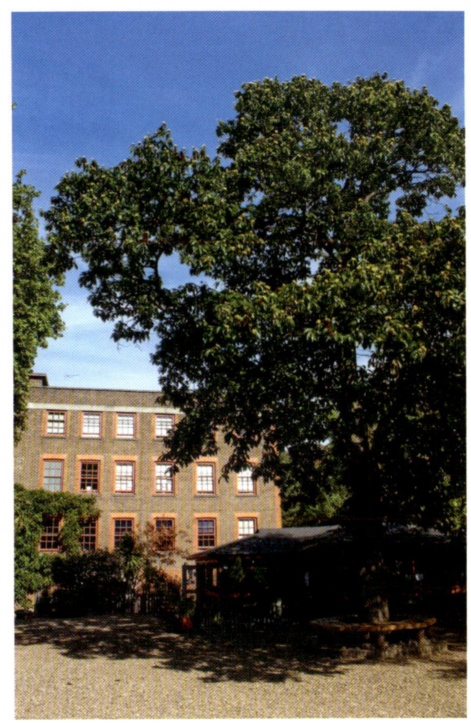

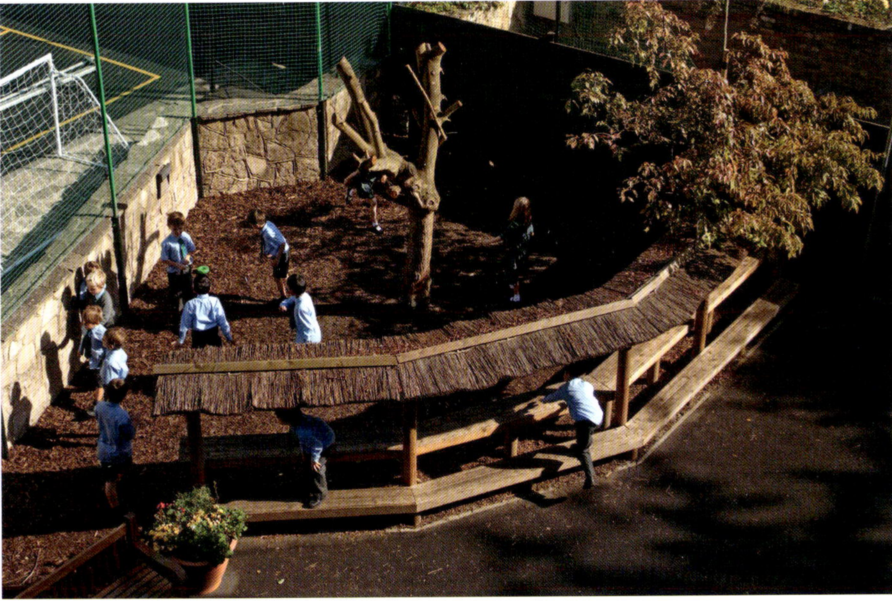

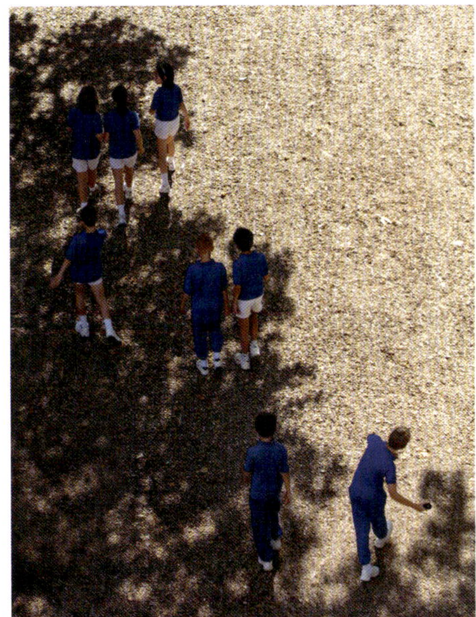

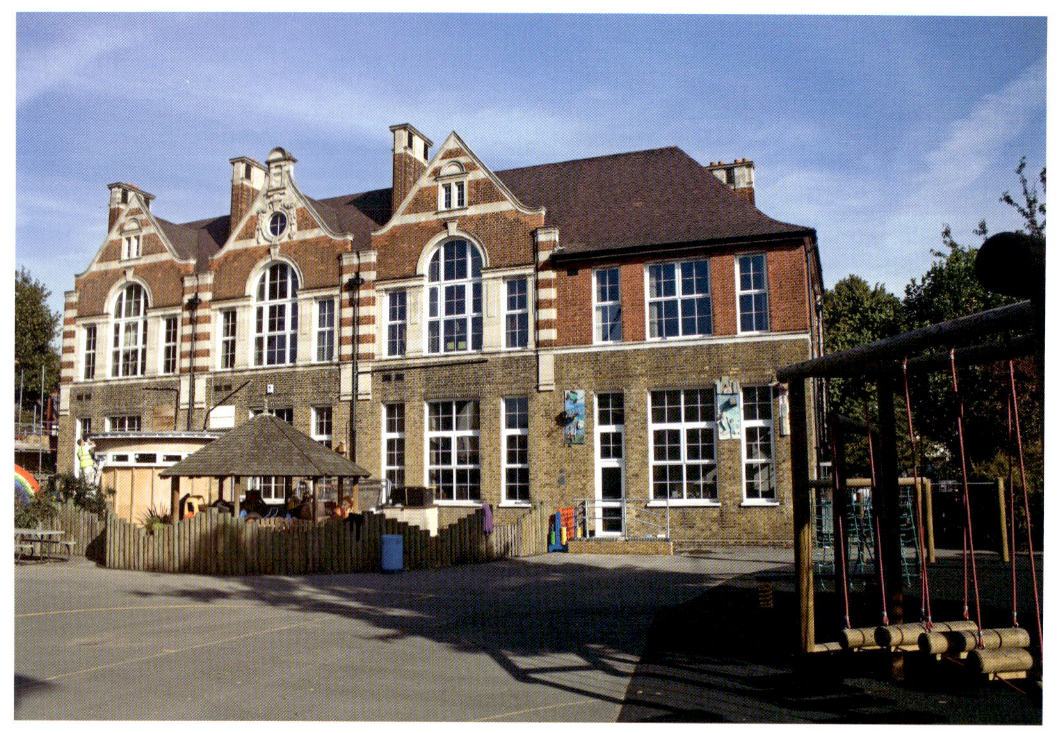

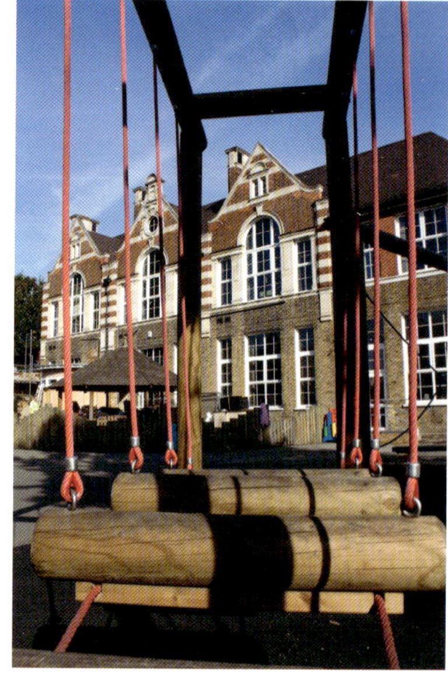

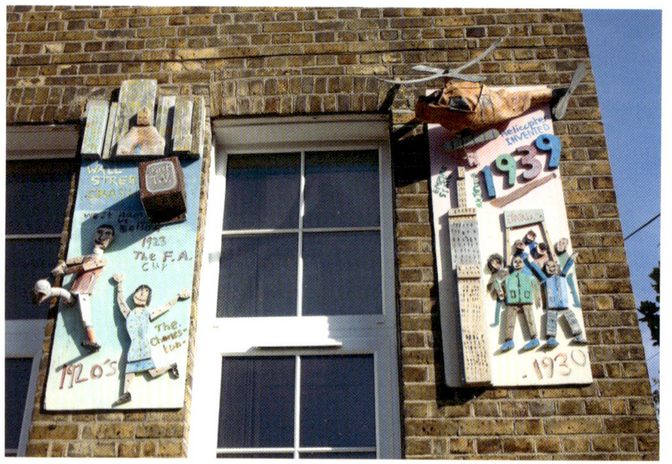

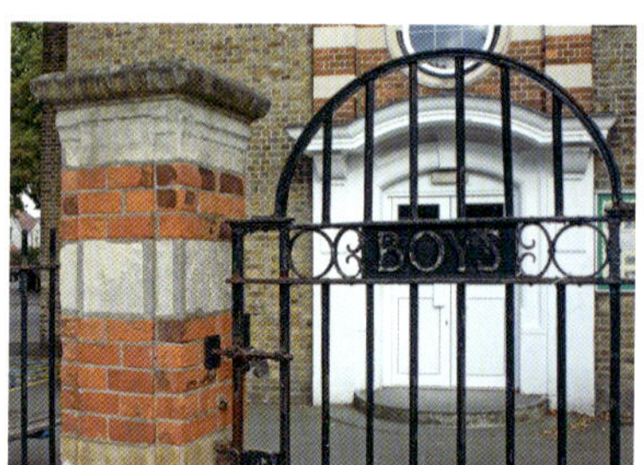

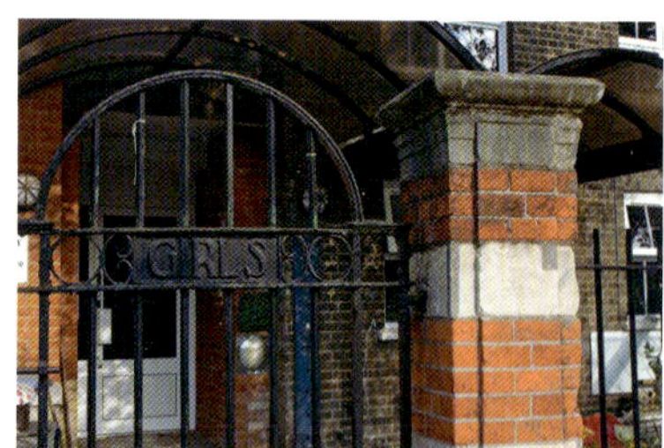

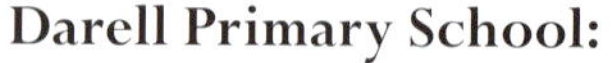

Darell Primary School:

This wonderful building is tucked away in North Sheen. Over 100 years old, this school still keeps its great 'boys' and 'girls' signs, although not used today of course. For the Millennium, the children were encouraged to create some murals for the outer walls and a fine job they did too.

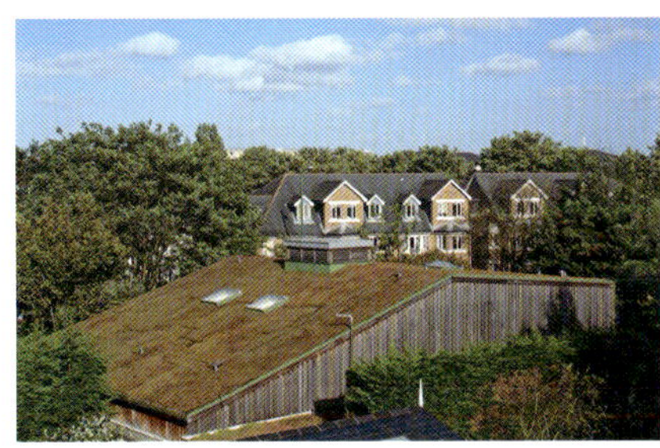

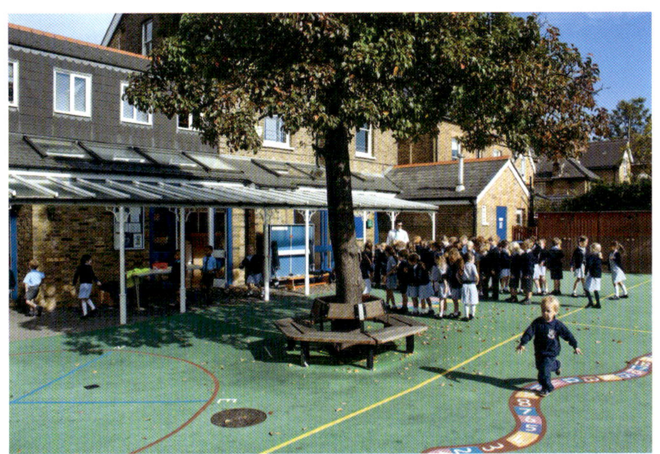

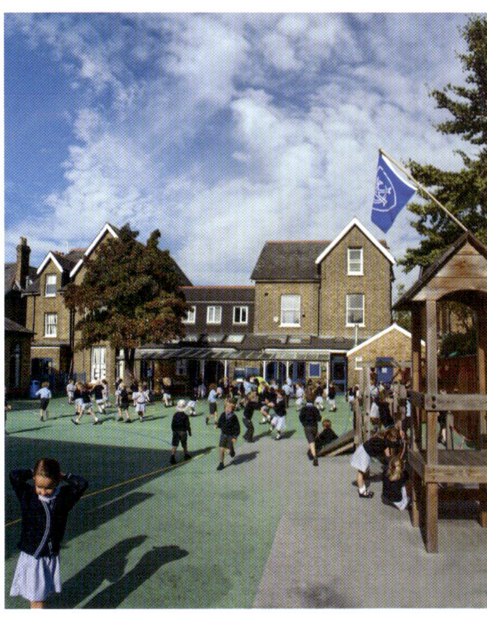

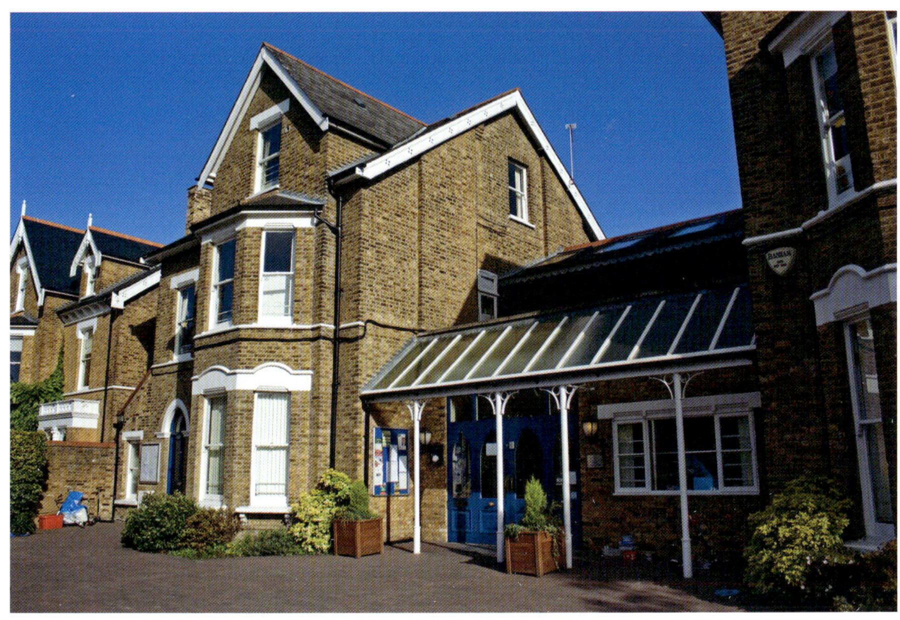

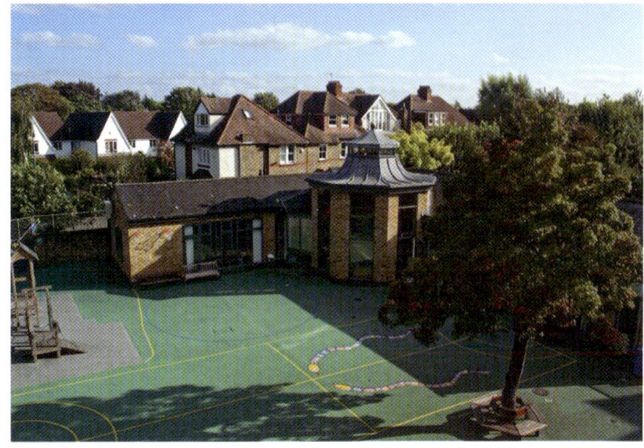

Kew College:
One of two schools in Cumberland Road, Kew College opened in 1927. Started above a shop in Kew, it soon moved to Cumberland Road for more room. Fascinatingly, part of the building boasts a 'green' roof, although the birds will find it hard to nest as it slopes.

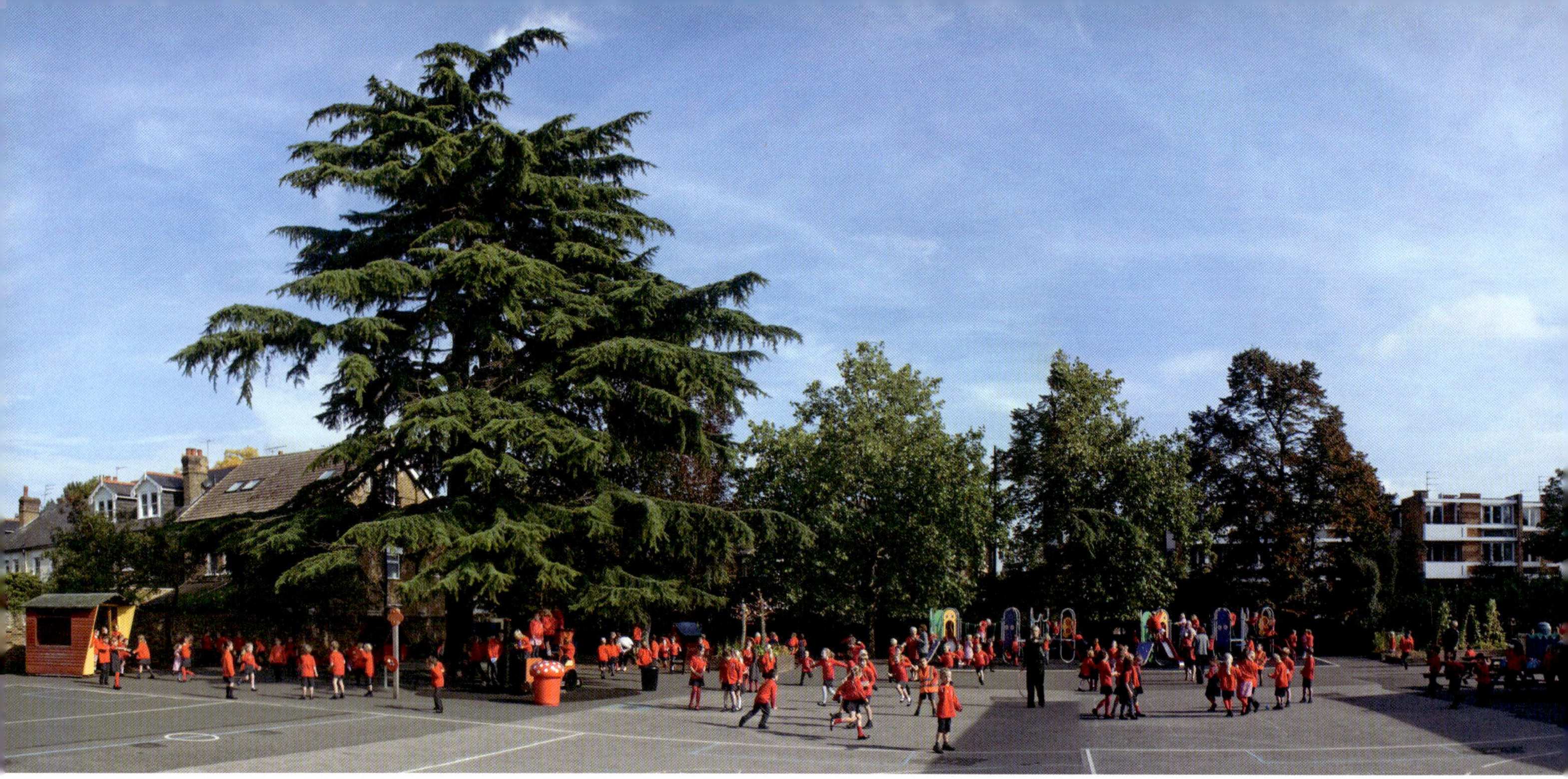

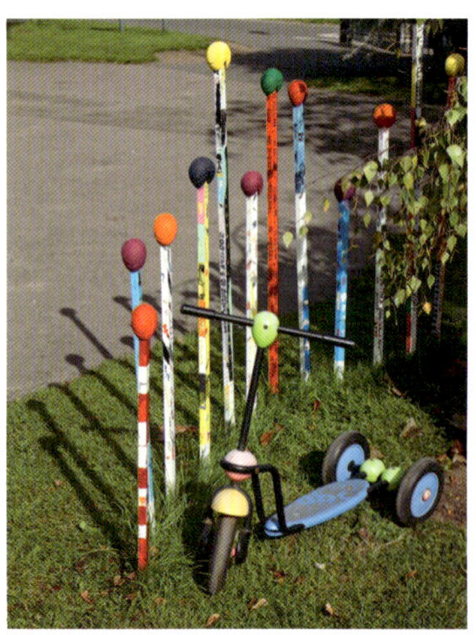

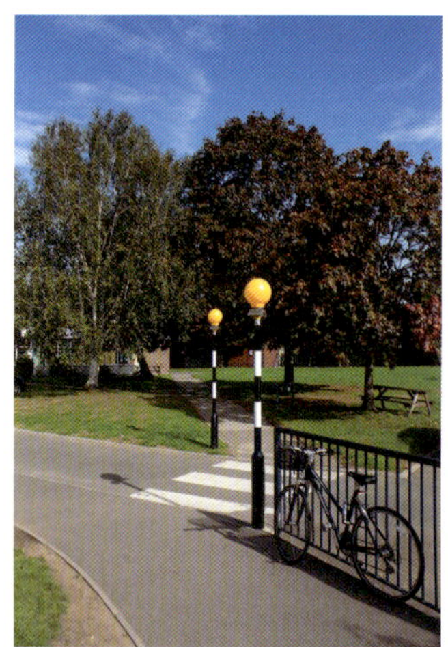

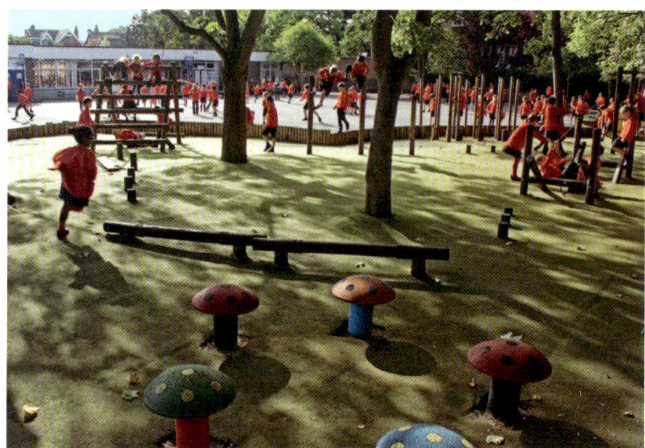

The Queen's School:

Queen's history goes back 250 years to when a school was formed in St Anne's Church. They moved to Cumberland Road in 1969, originally got their name from King George IV, who also decreed that the name should change with the monarch, hence its current name since 1952. Besides the majestic Cedar in their playground that would not be out of place within Kew Gardens, they must also have the shortest Zebra Crossing in London.

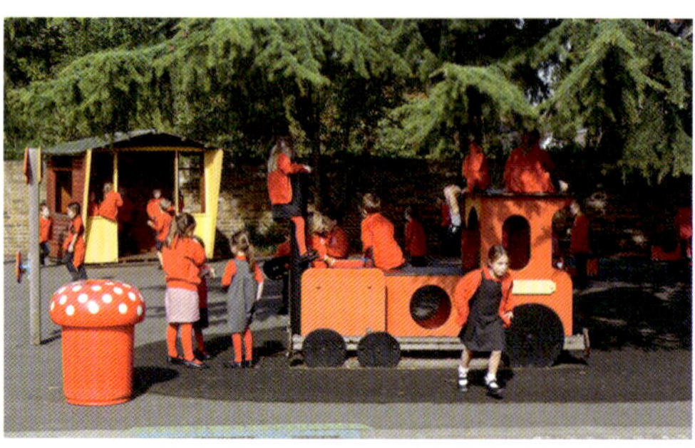

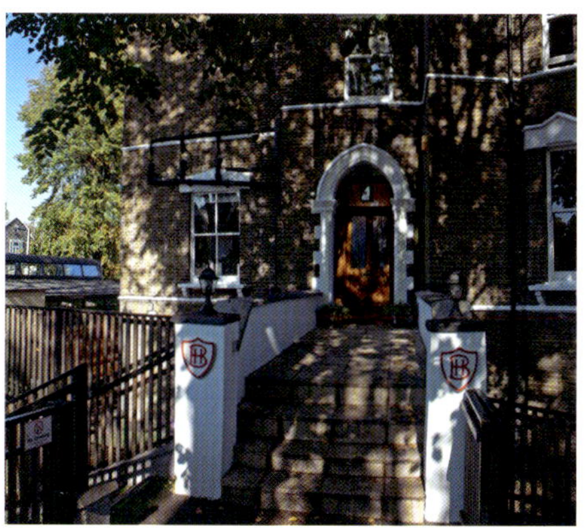

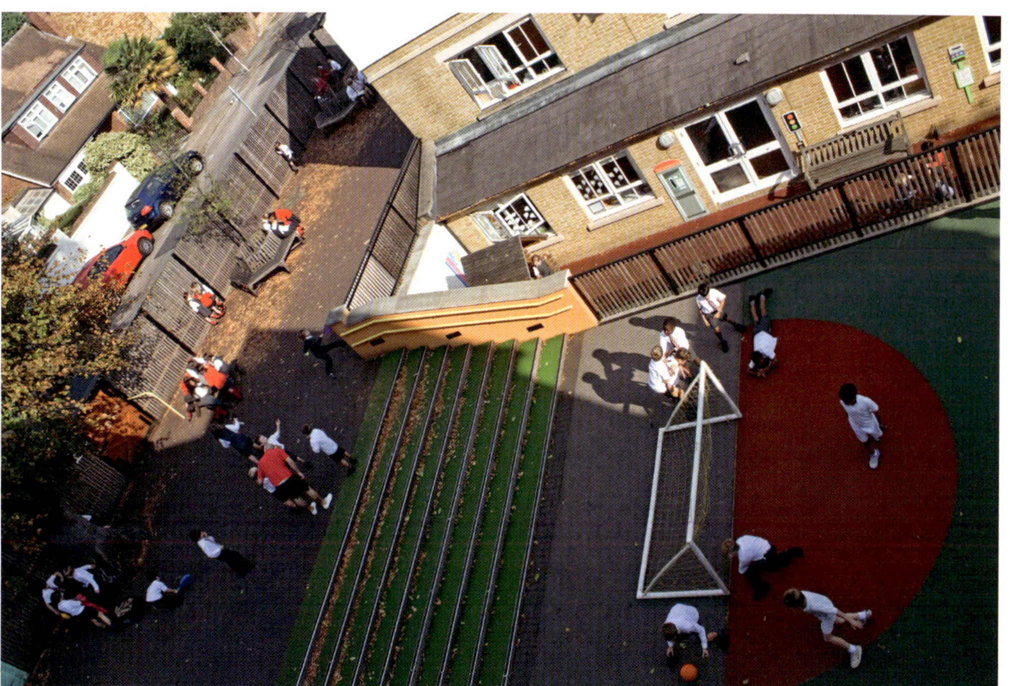

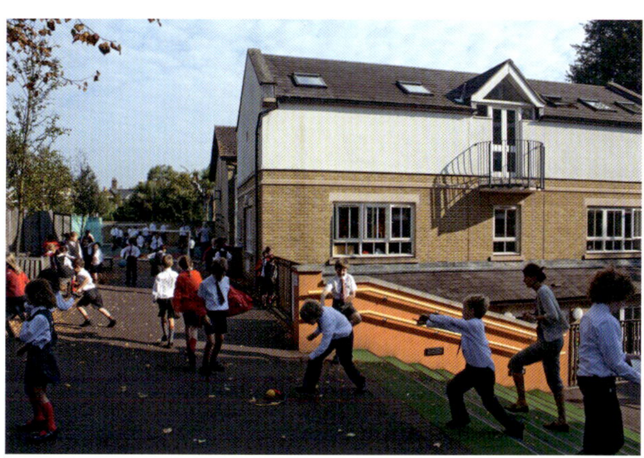

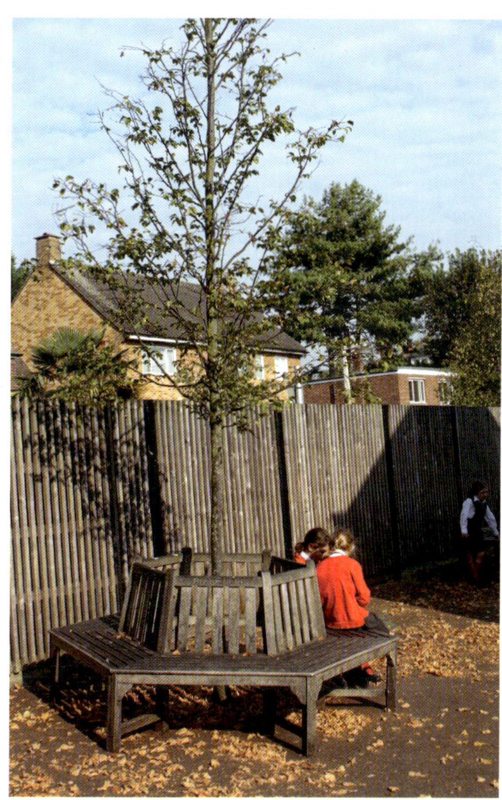

Broomfield House School:

Formed in 1876, Broomfield House is Kew's oldest independent school. Very much a family affair, the current headmaster, Norton York, is the son of the previous headmistress, who bought the school in 1969. Following a trend set by his mother, the school has a rich tradition for the arts and music.

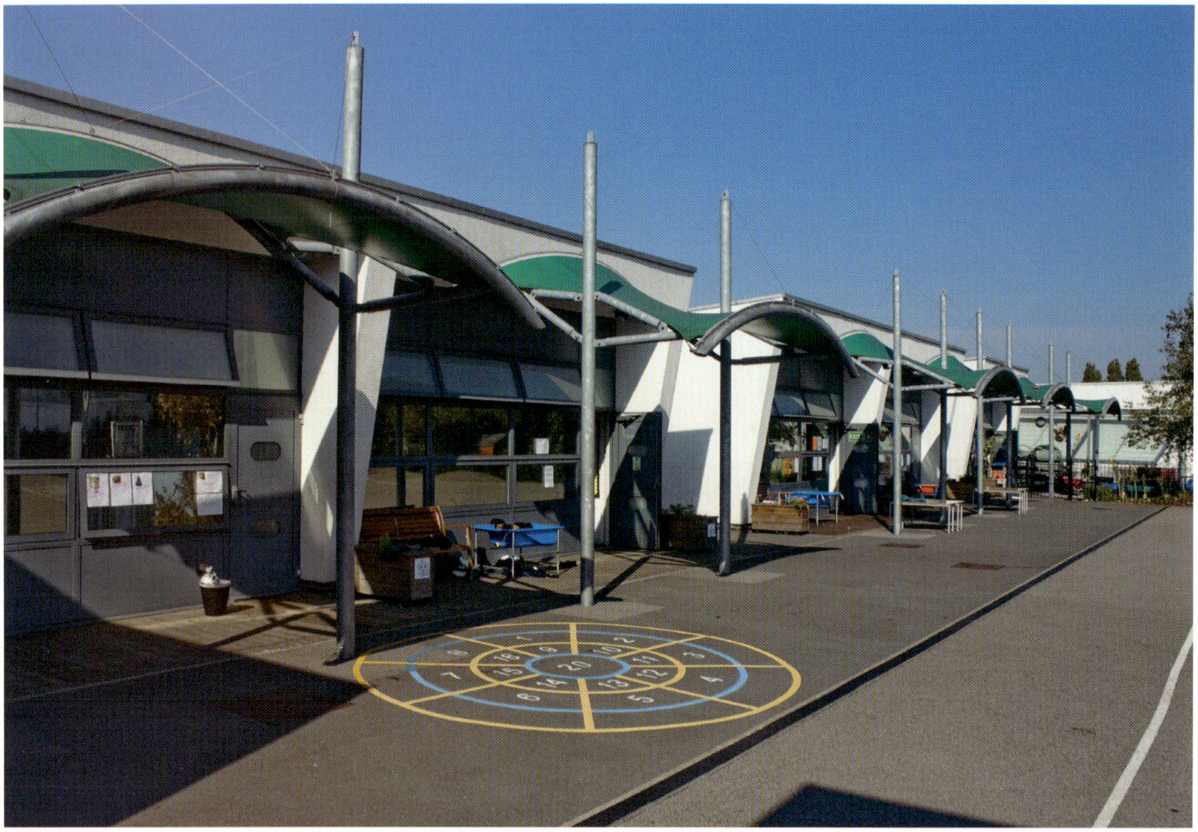

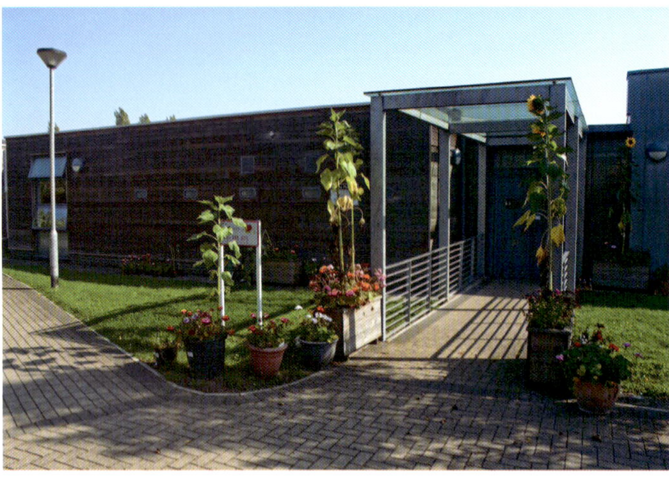

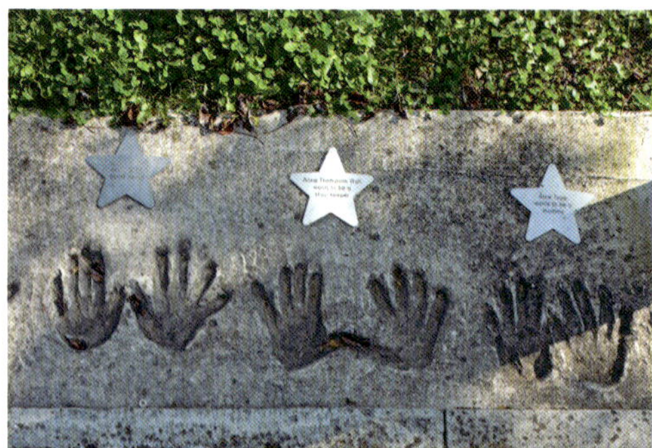

Kew Riverside Primary School:
A community school off Mortlake Road which, according to its prospectus, boasts a bank which opens on a Friday and is operated by all the children. Besides being great fun, this also teaches the children a valuable lesson about saving, very important as the kids also run a shop, so plenty of temptation to spend.

Unicorn School:

Unicorn is unique amongst local schools in so much as it is collectively owned by each set of current parents. This all started in 1970, when a far-sighted group of parents and teachers were inspired to form a school, as they didn't feel that what was then available fulfilled their ambitions. They are lucky amongst Kew Schools to be situated directly opposite Kew Gardens and make full use of this wonderful place for school outings.

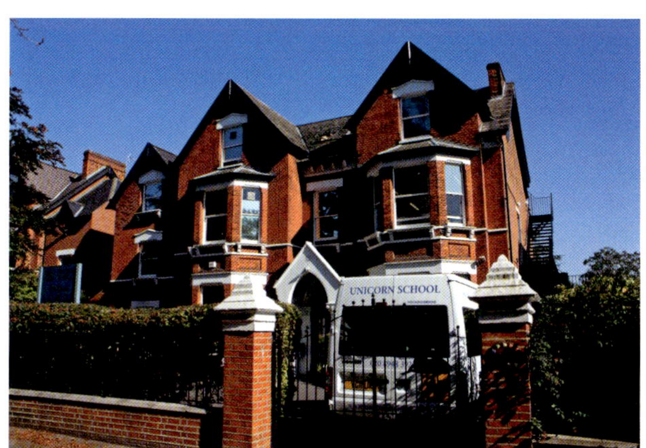

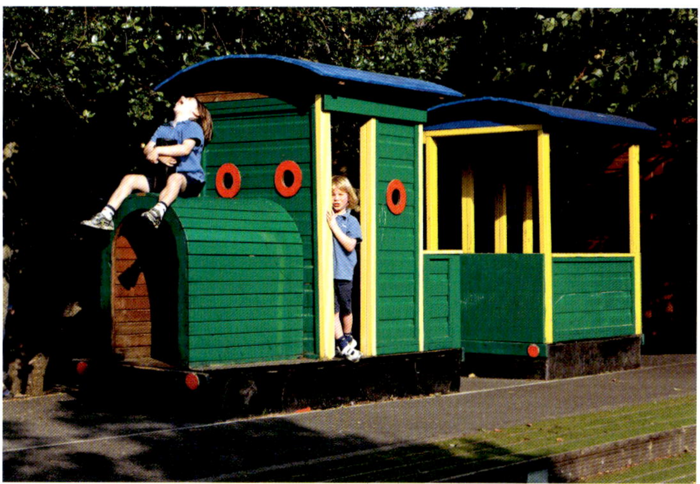

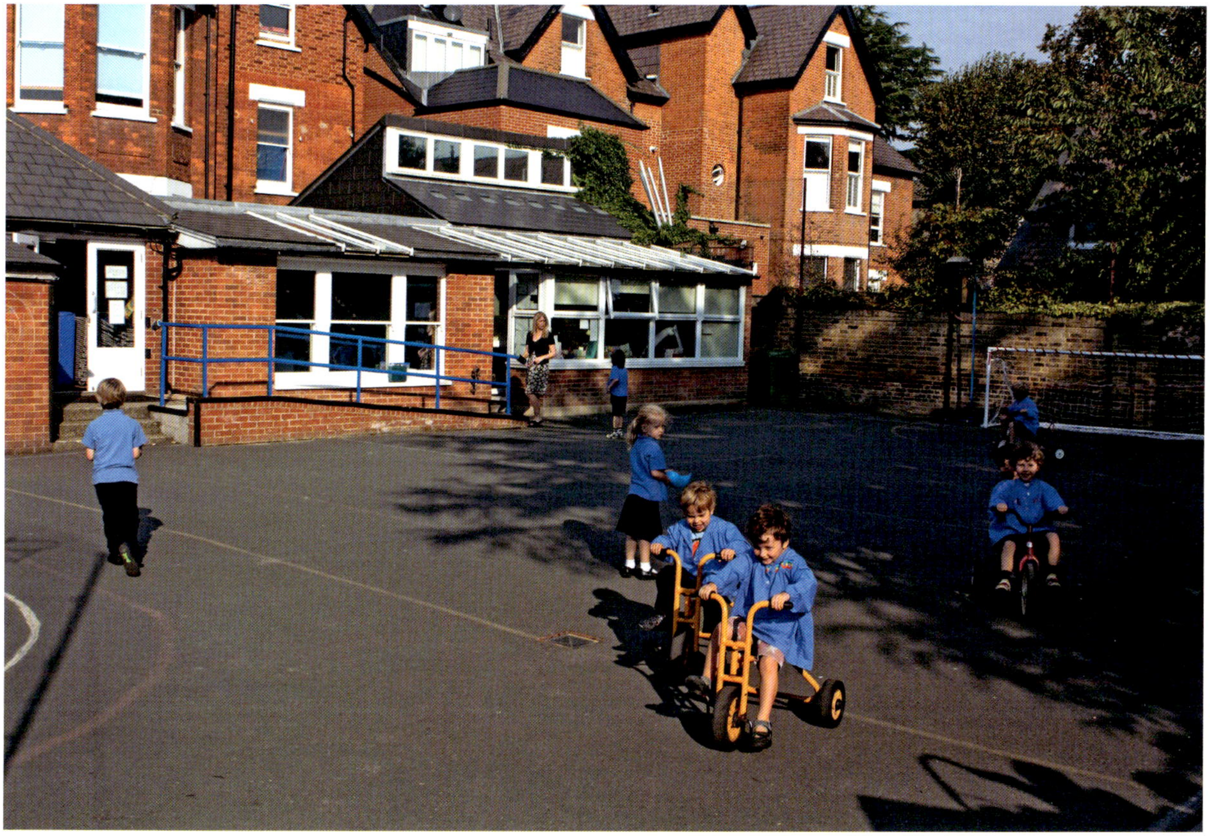

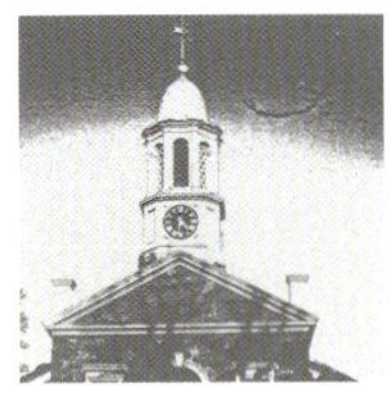

CHURCHES

The Barn Church of St Philip and All Saints:

'The Barn' is a most unusual church with a history to match. It was built as recently as 1929 from the remnants of a barn from Oxted in Surrey. Back then the estate on which it is built lacked a church and although now not unique, at the time it was the only church in the country to have been built in this way. The building is very impressive, particularly the beams inside, which are thought to be at least 400 years old.

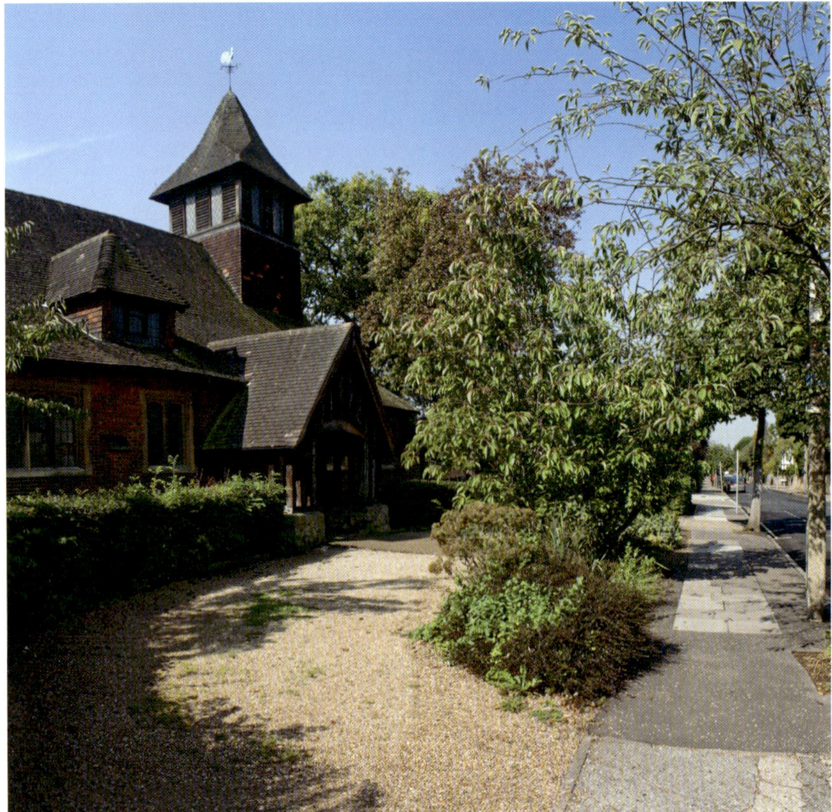

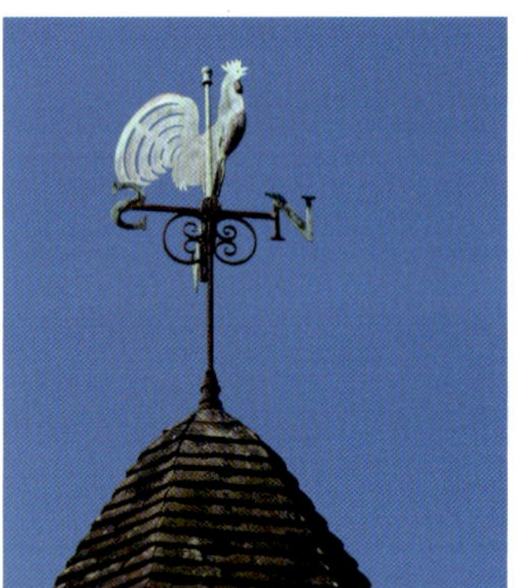

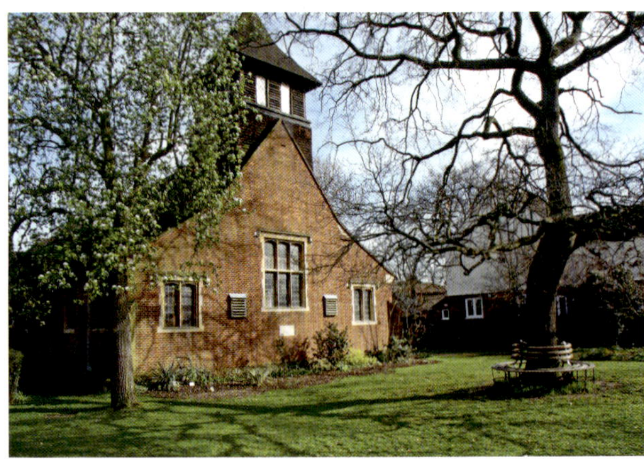

St Luke's:

As with the Barn Church, St Luke's was built to fill the need of the new estates that were being built during the latter part of the 19th century. Completed in 1888, the site is large and currently houses Kew Community Trust and the Avenue Club.

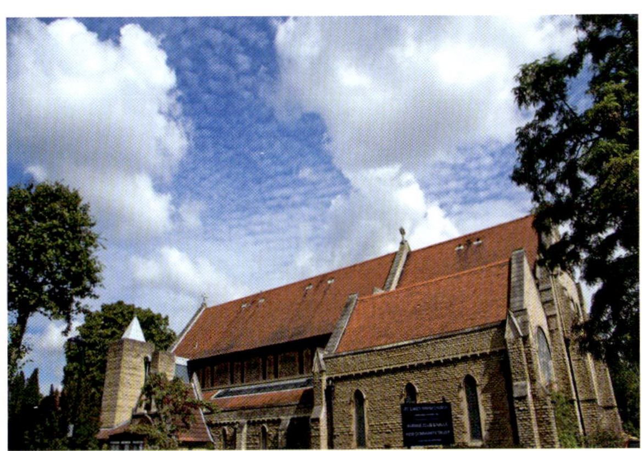

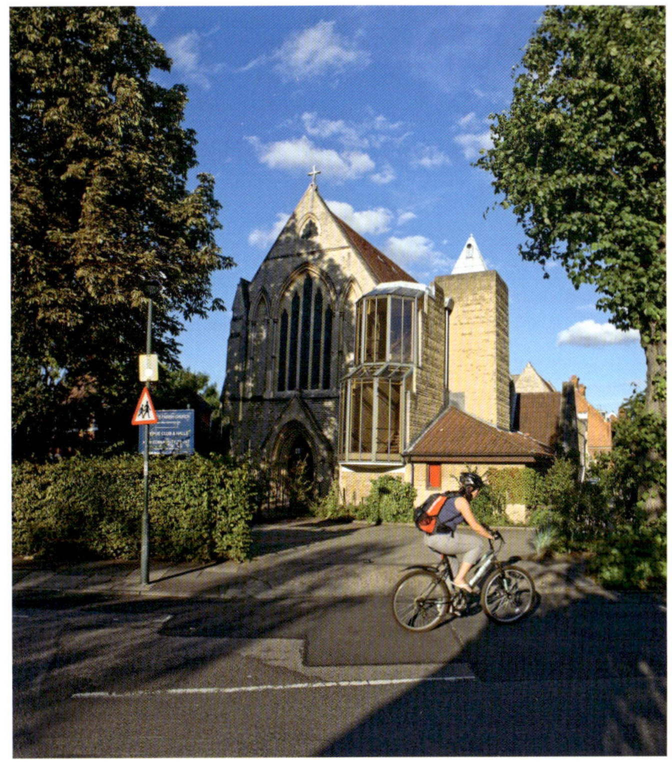

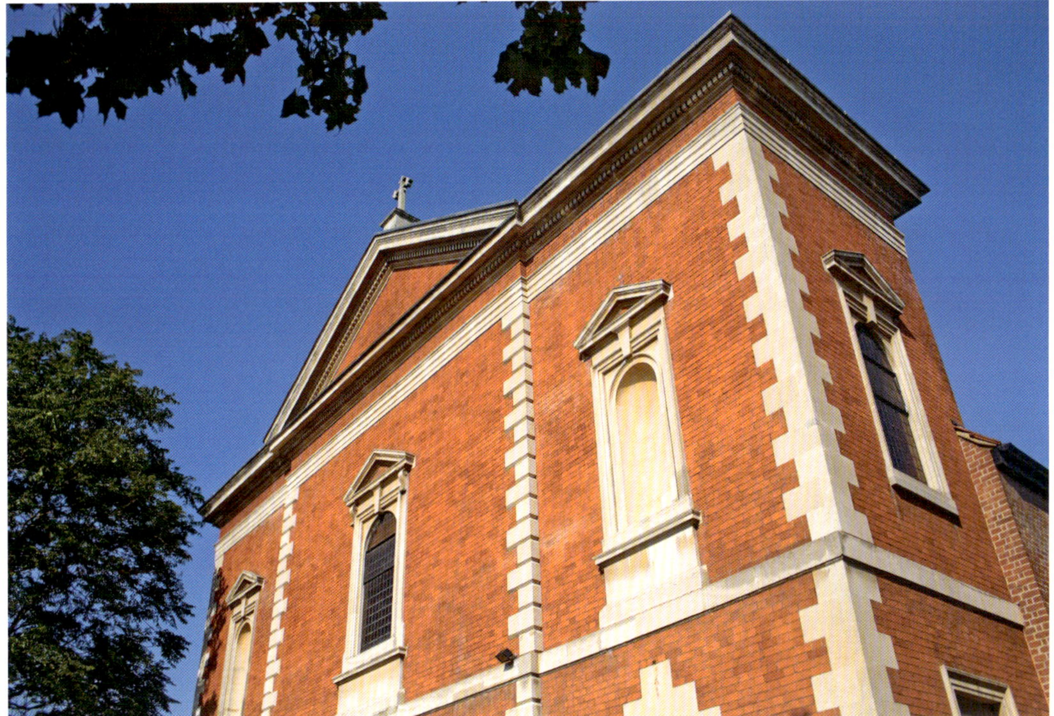

Our Lady of Loreto and St Winefride's:

St Winefride's is an impressive Catholic church, dating from 1906. It was served by the Marist Fathers until 1984. Its double dedication arises because the Founder of the Society of Mary made a pilgrimage to the Loreto shrine in Italy in 1833 immediately after asking for papal approval to establish the Society, and Saint Winefride was the favourite saint of one of this church's principal local benefactors.

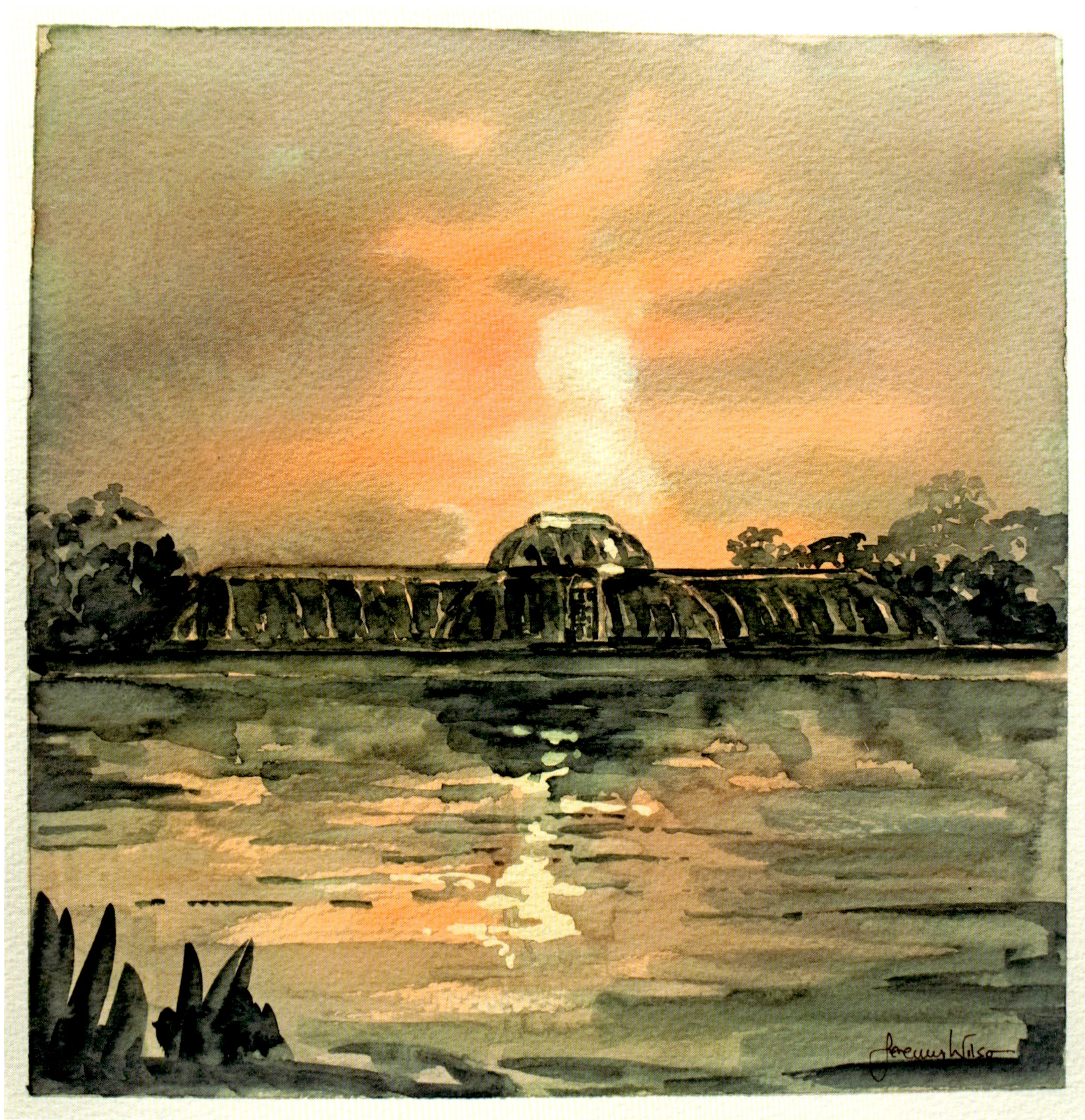

Palm House Fire - this is an original watercolour by Jeremy Wilson produced exclusively for this book. A limited number of prints will be available after publication - please contact the publisher for more information.

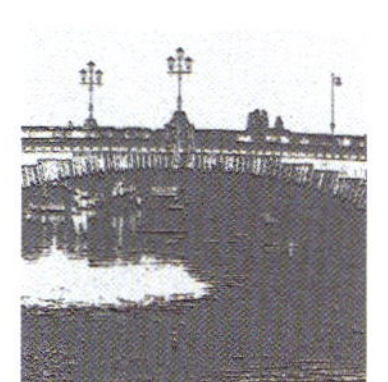

THE RIVERSIDE

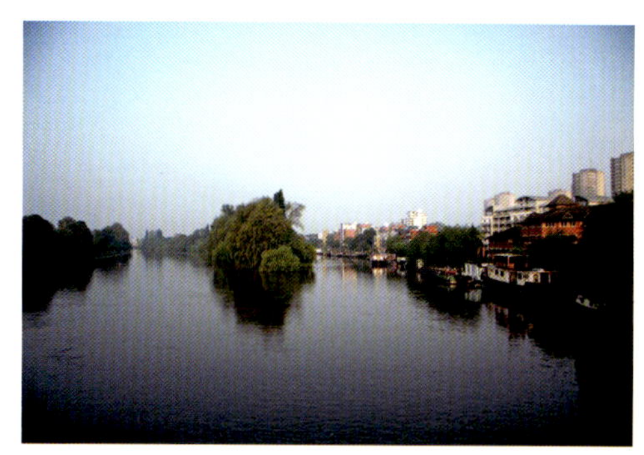

The view of the the Thames looking west, with Brentford Ait in the middle.

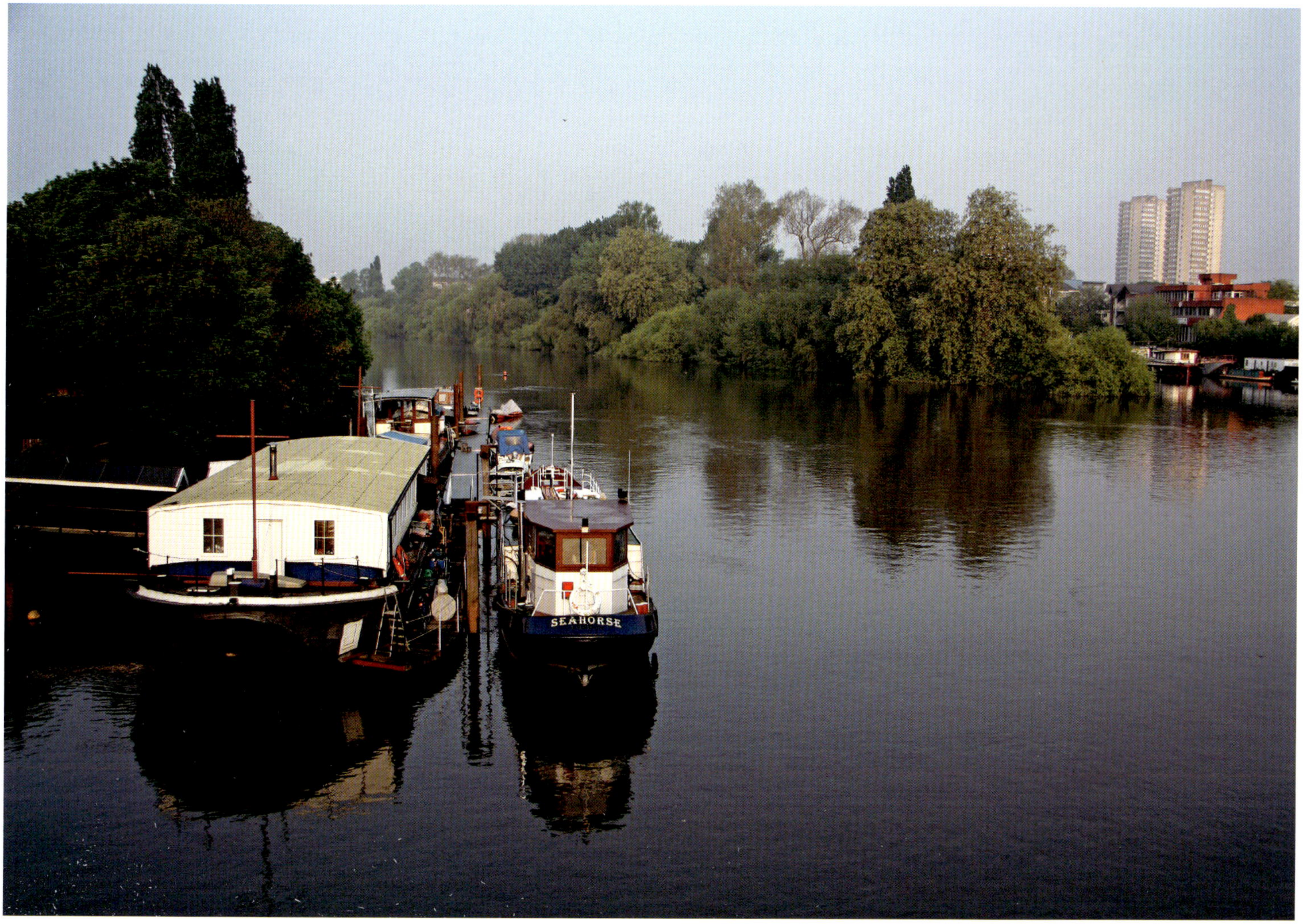

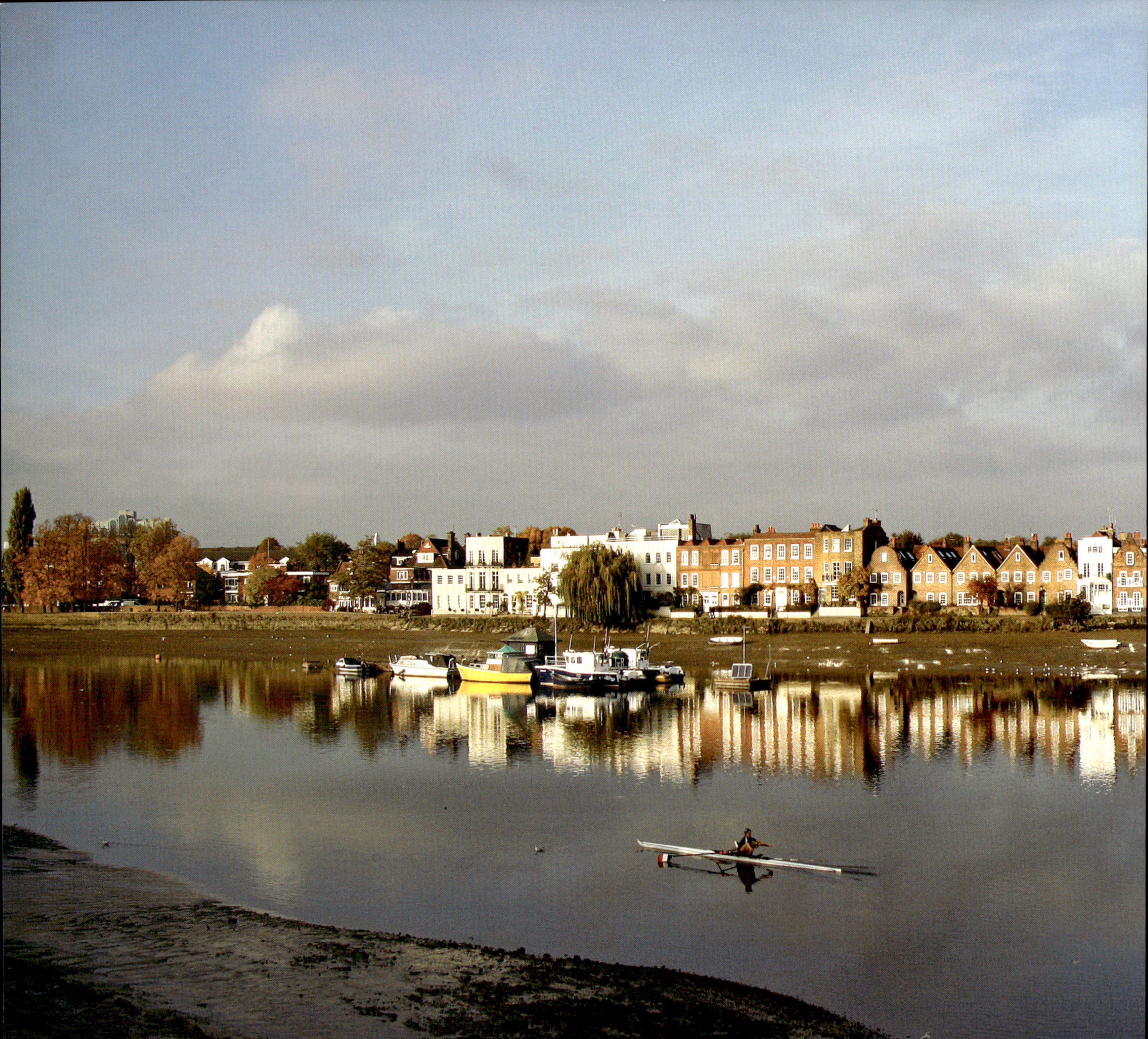

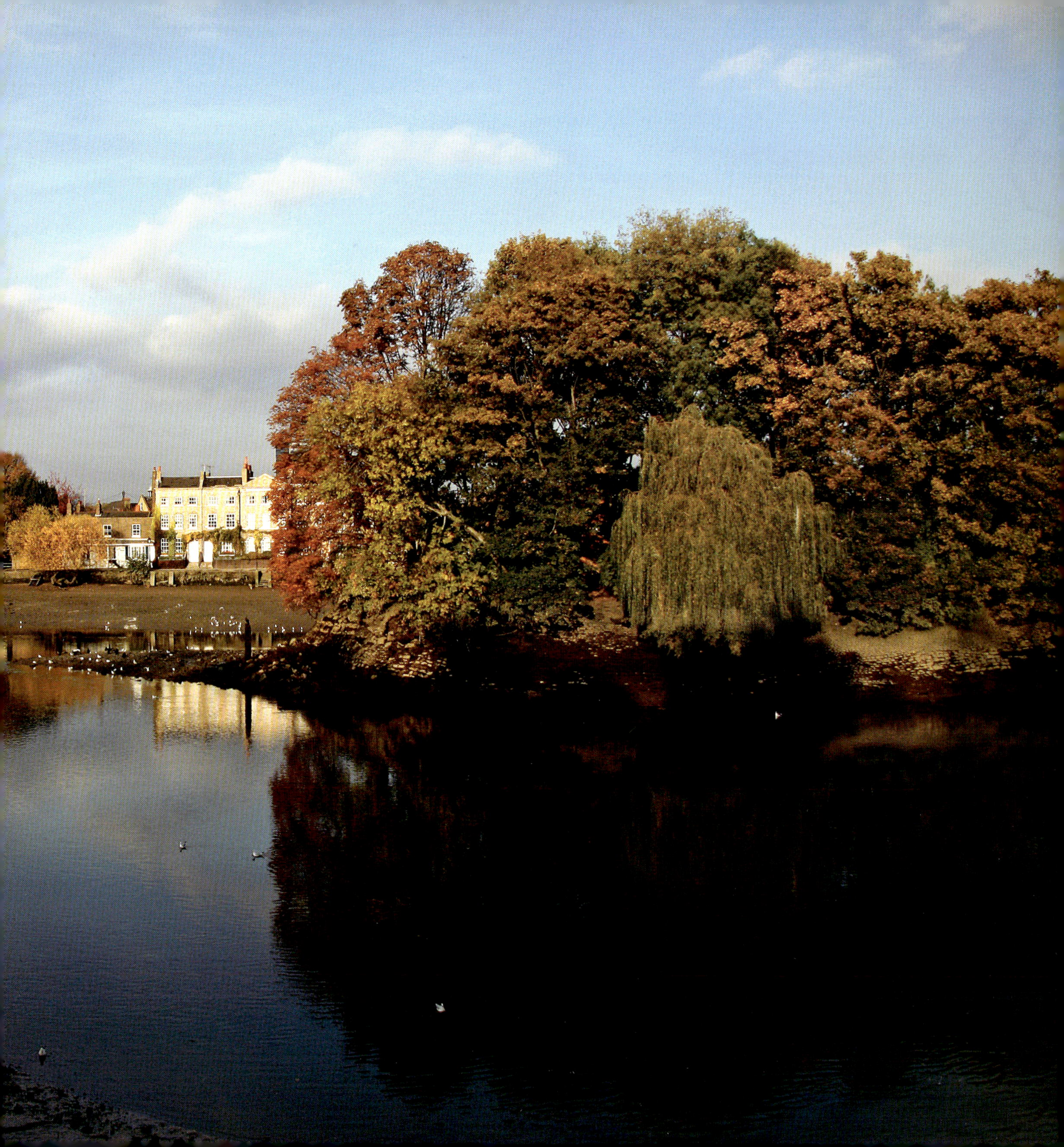

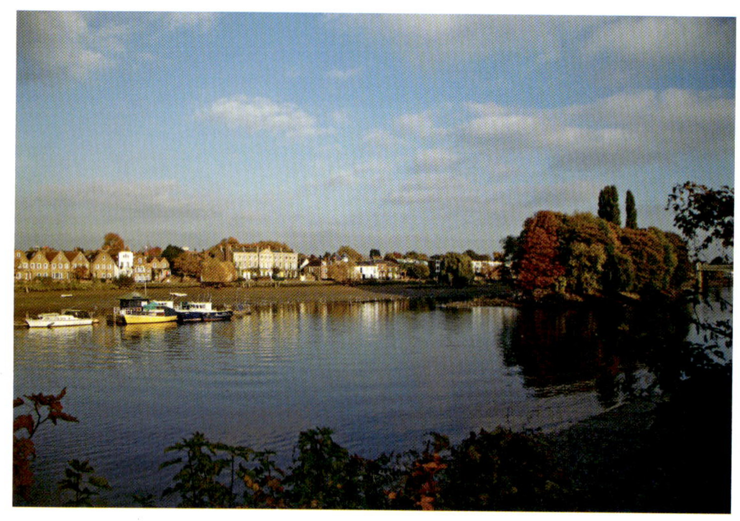

This and the previous page: Views along the river towards Strand-on-the-Green and a display of rich autumn colours.

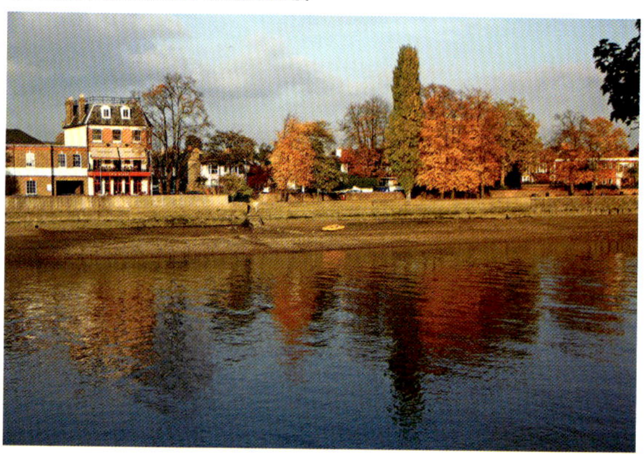

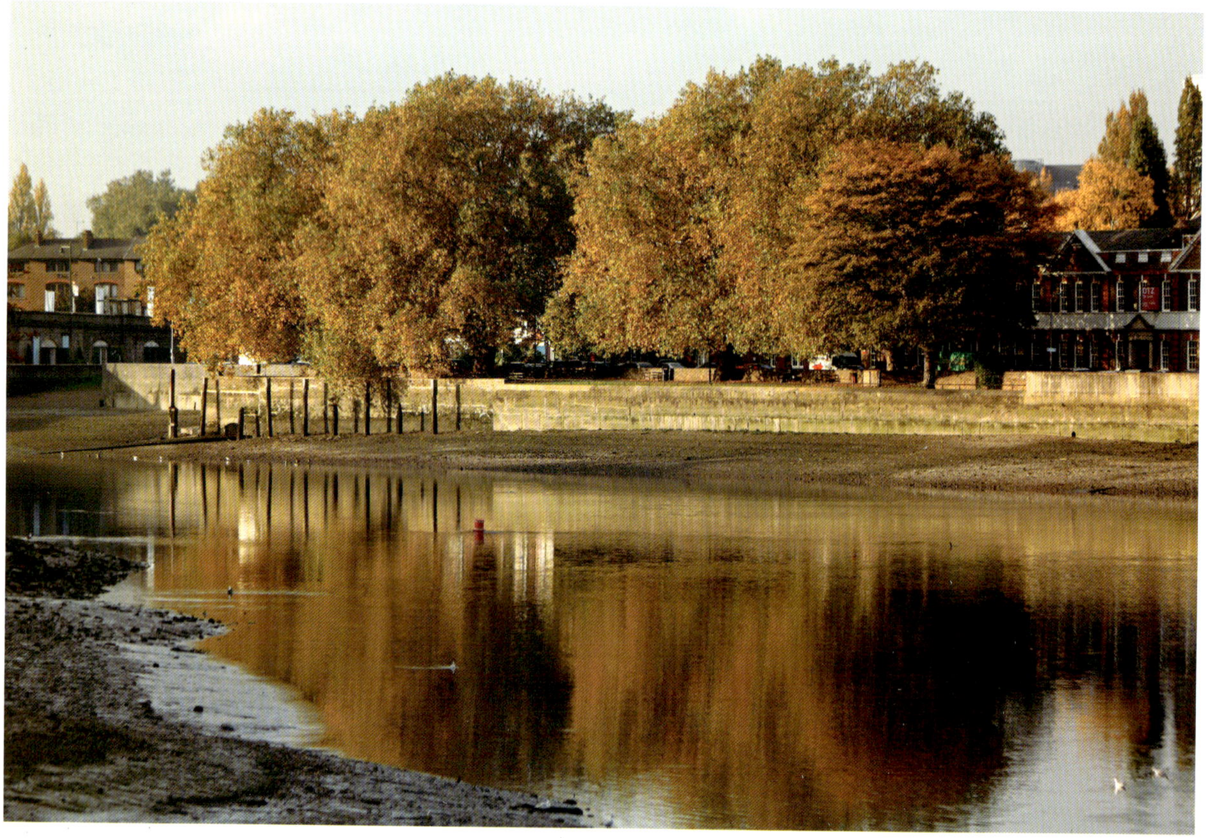

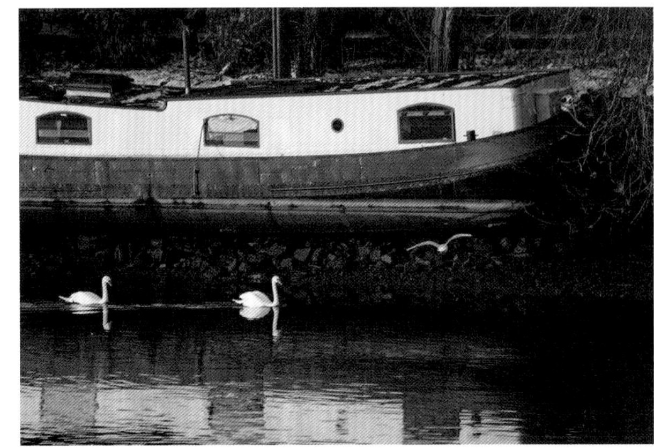

Right and below: A pair of mute swans on the Brentford side under Kew Bridge one autumn evening.

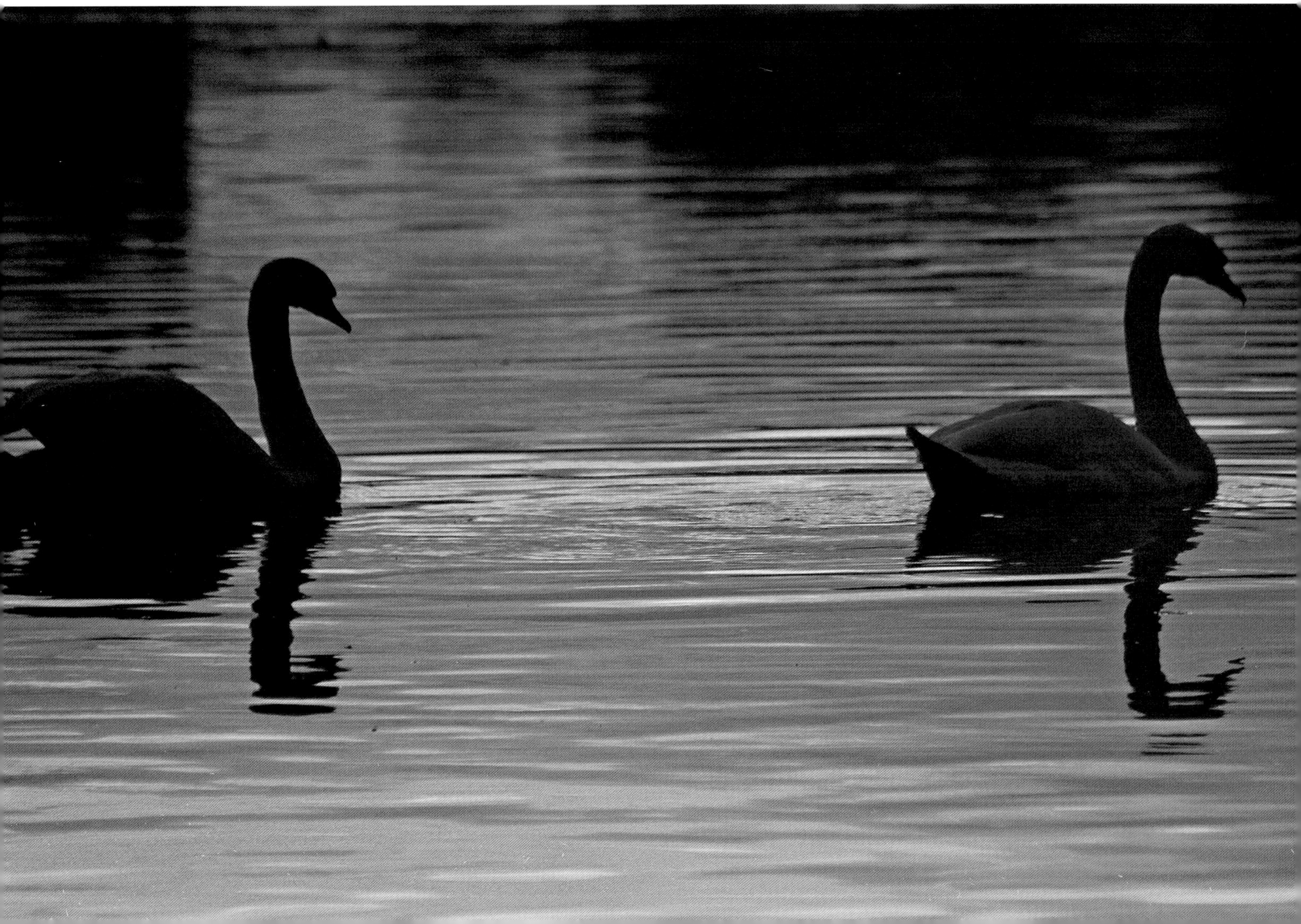

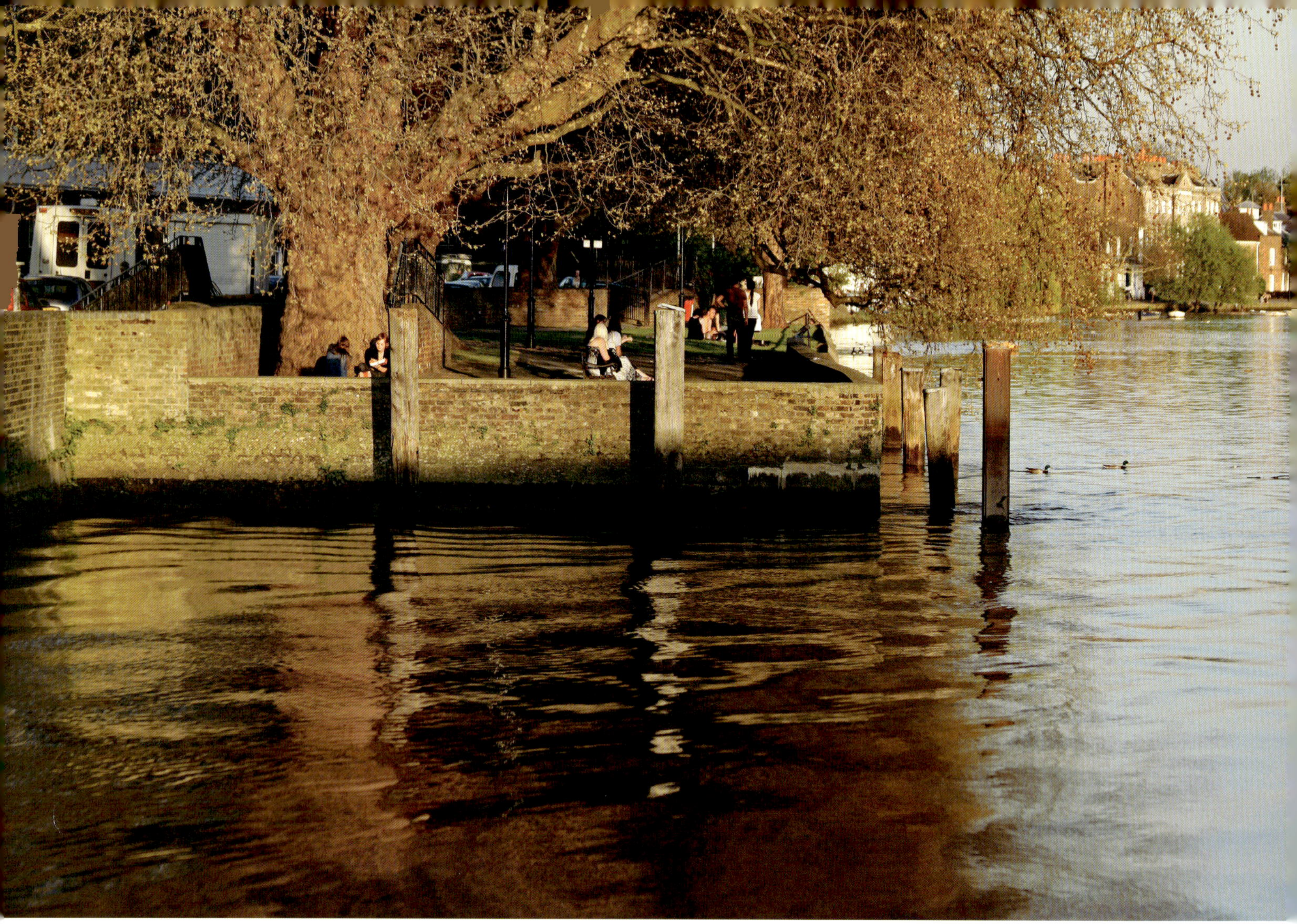

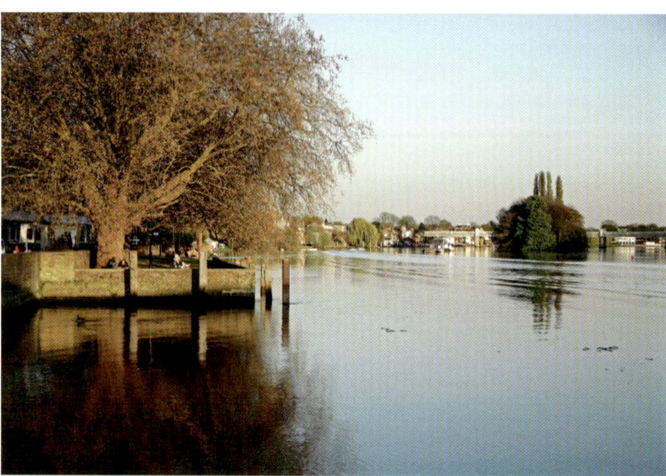

This and the page opposite:
The view across to Strand-on-the-Green.

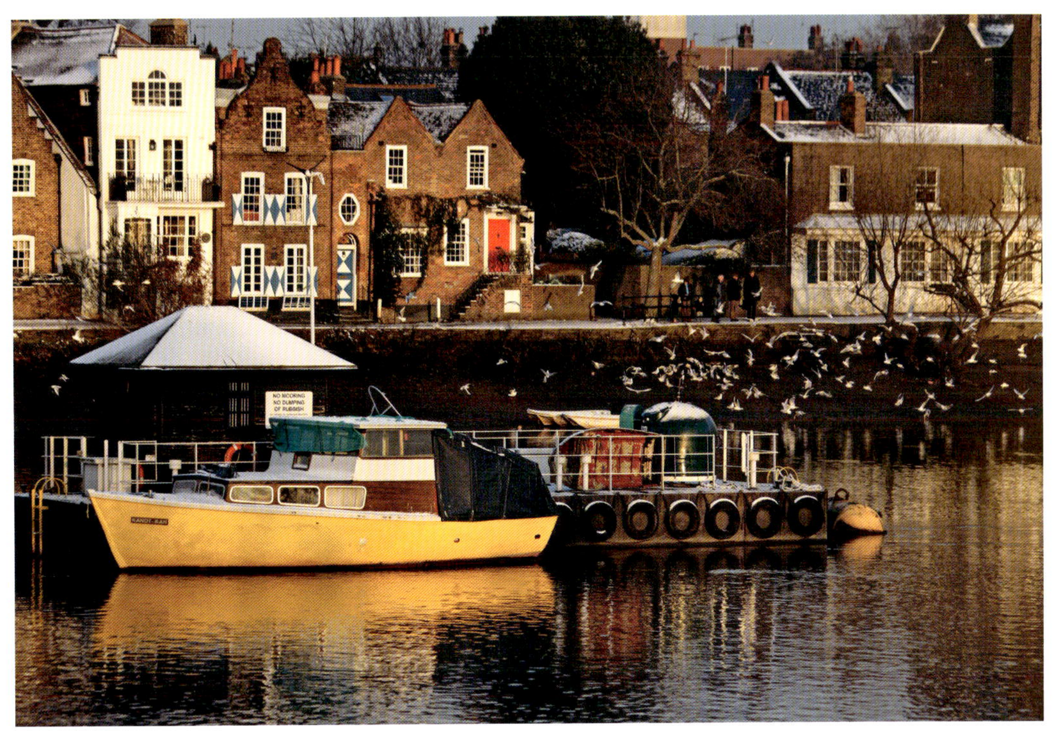
NO MOORING
NO DUMPING
OF RUBBISH

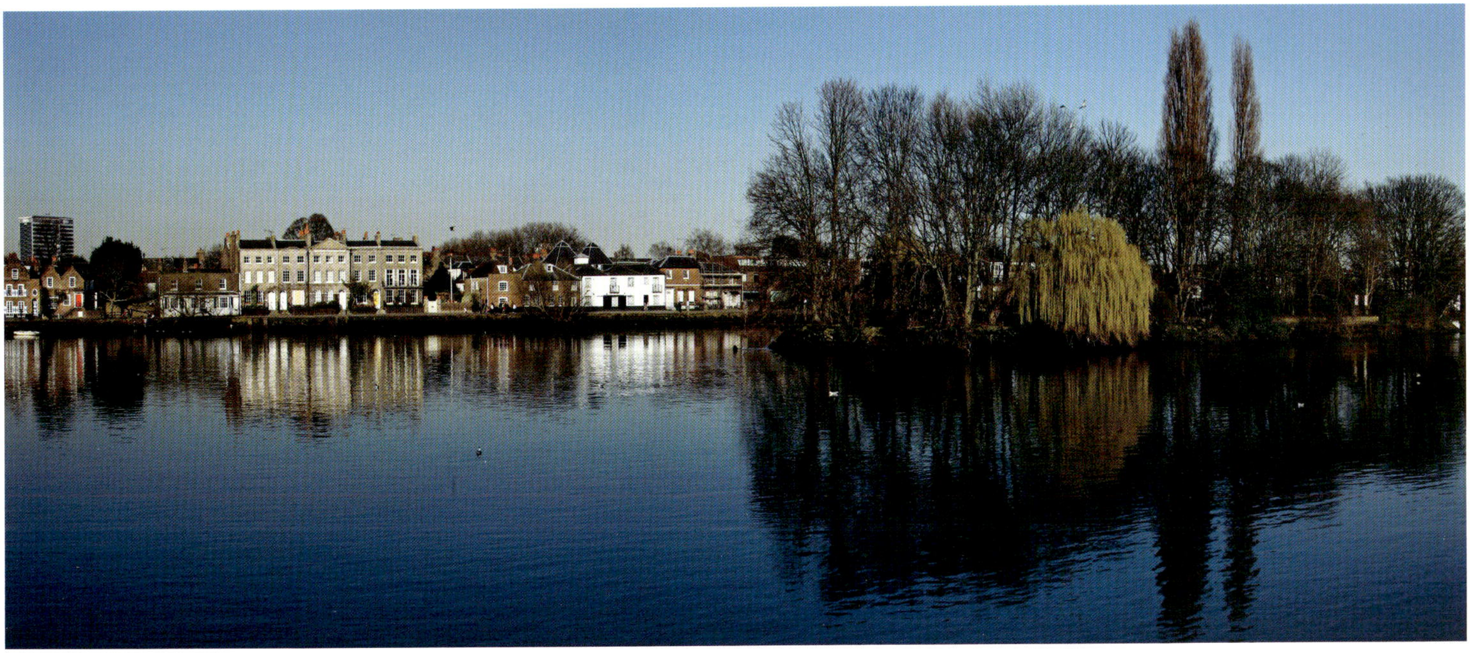

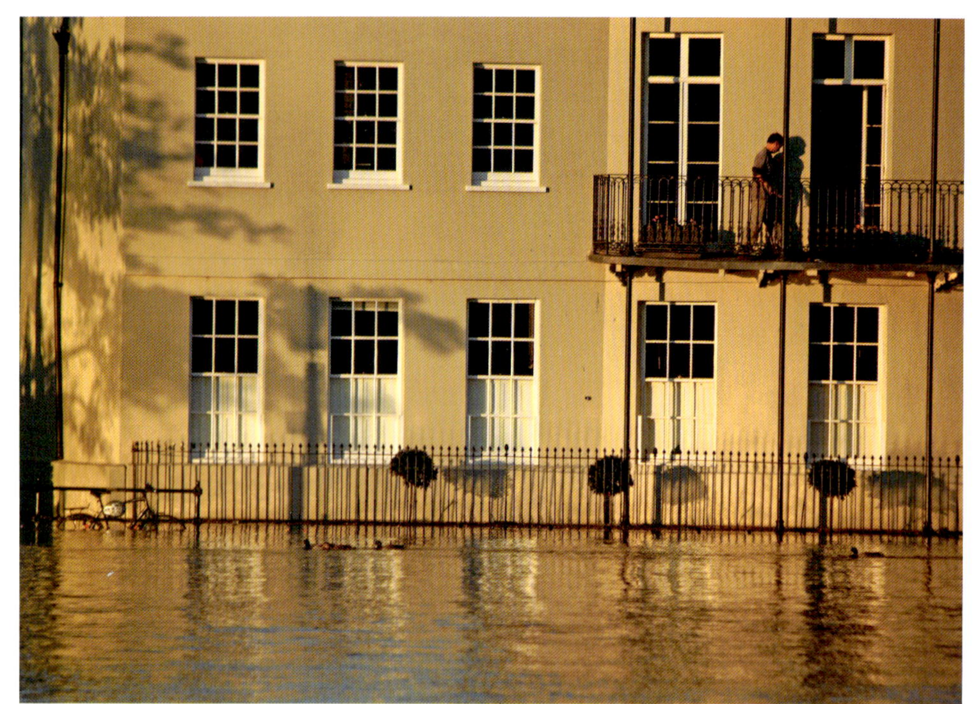

The towpath that follows the river in Strand-on-the-Green regularly floods with high tides; notice the bike far left in the picture on the left.
Page right: The rose coloured house, as viewed from the Kew side, late one spring evening.

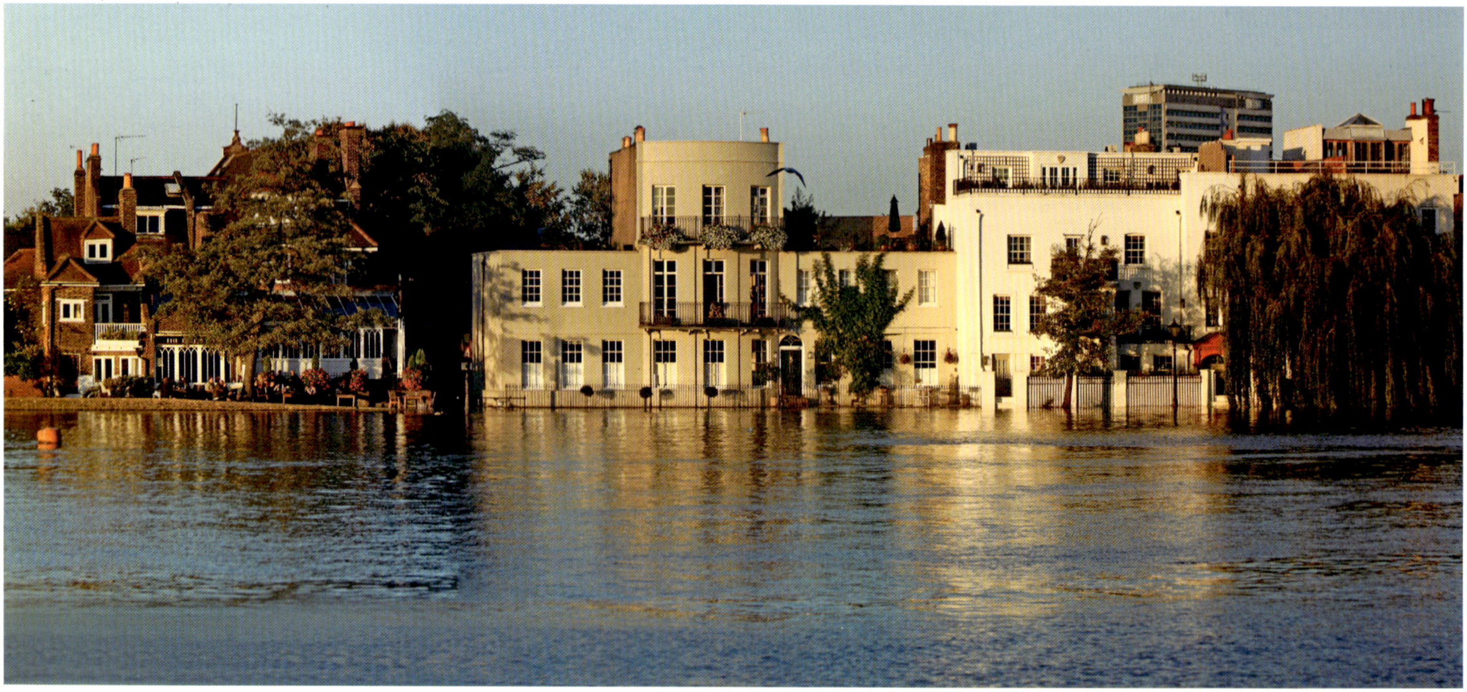

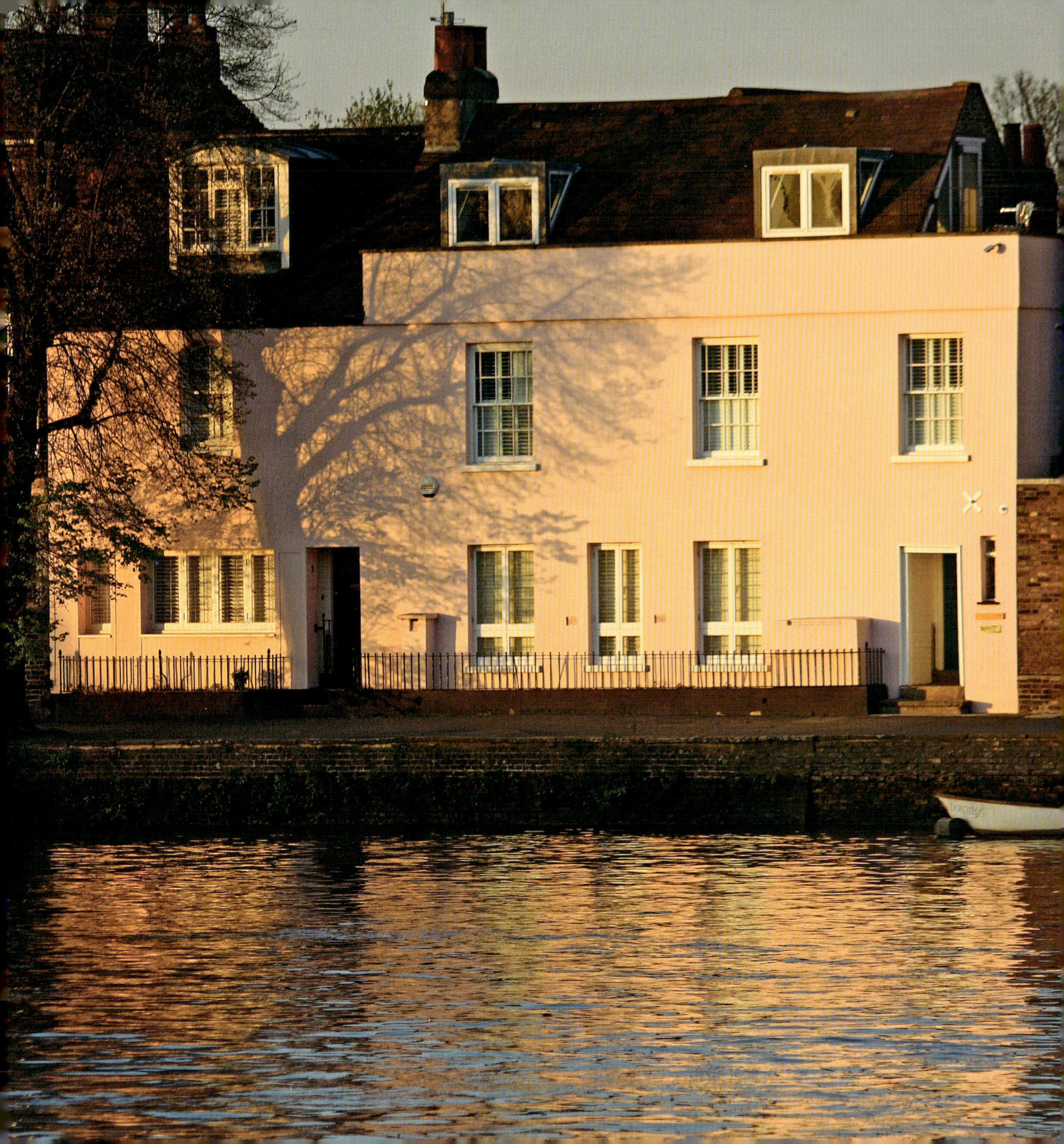

This and the following pages: Kew Railway Bridge

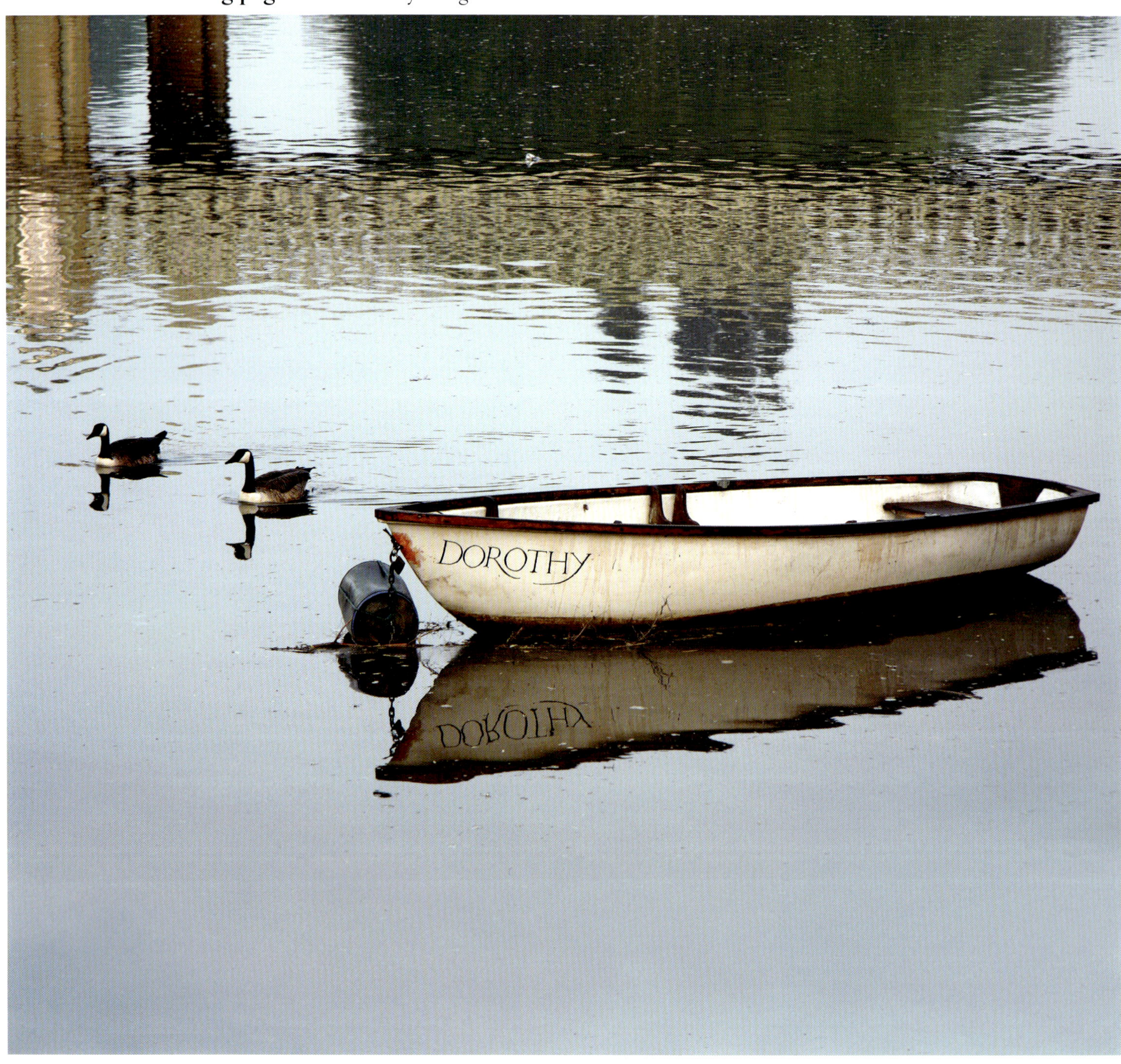

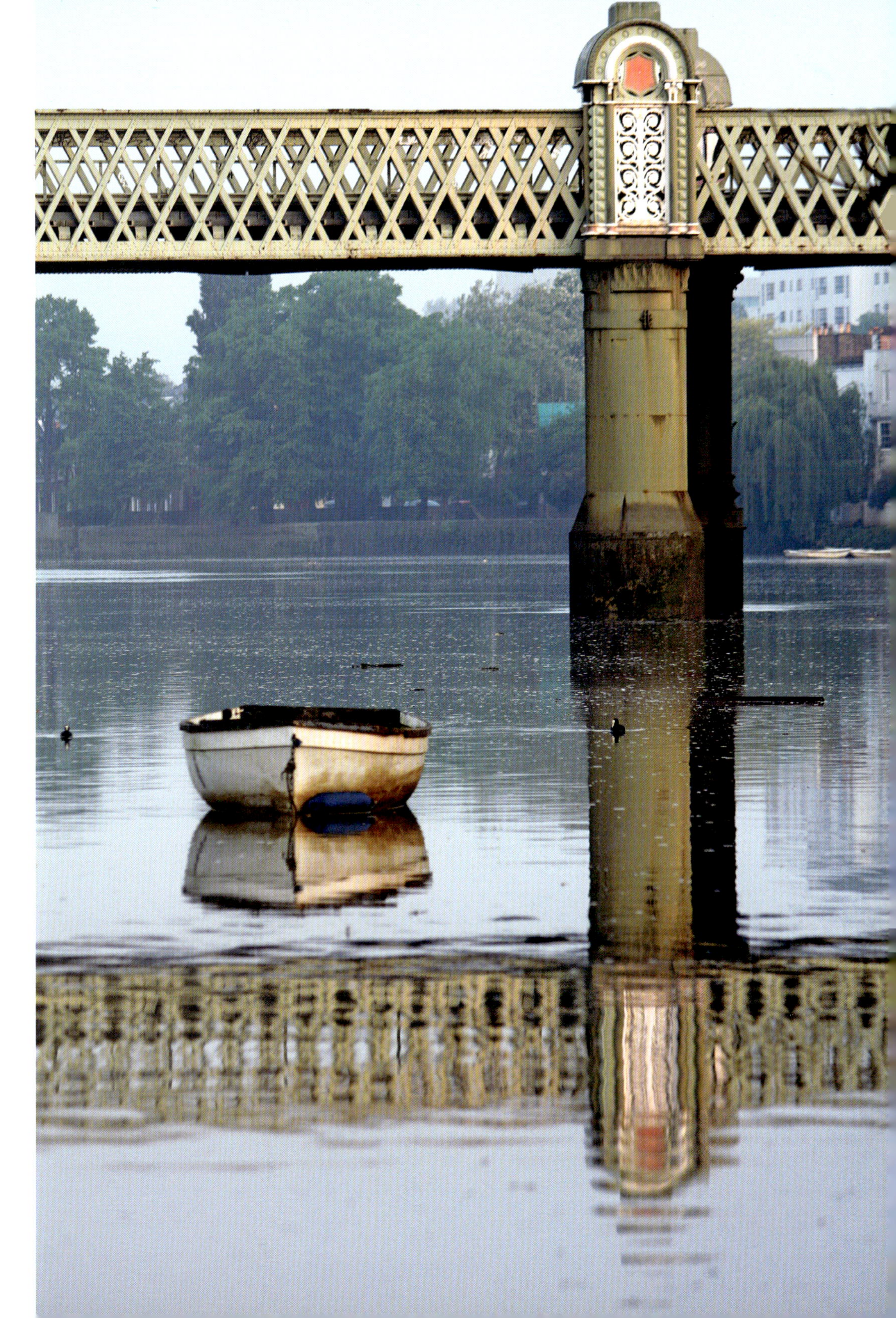

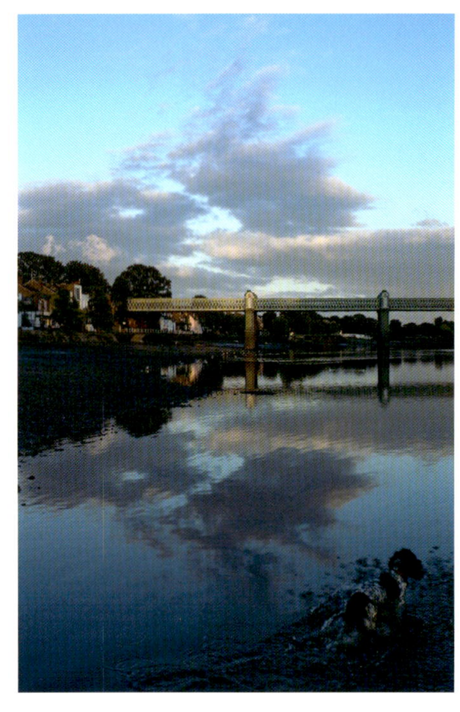

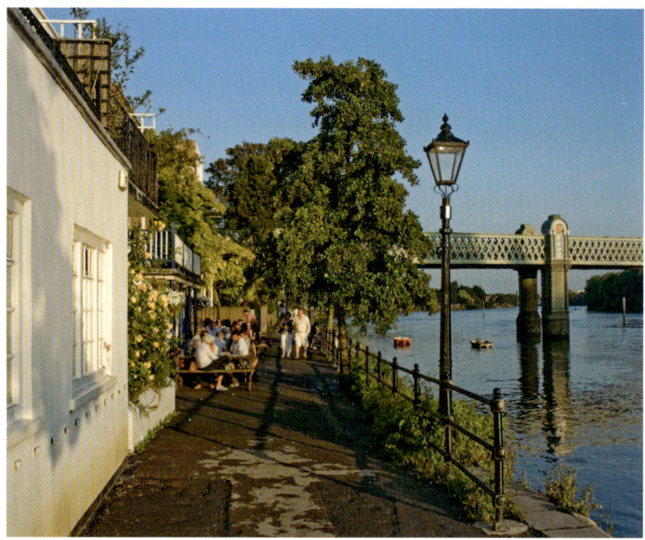

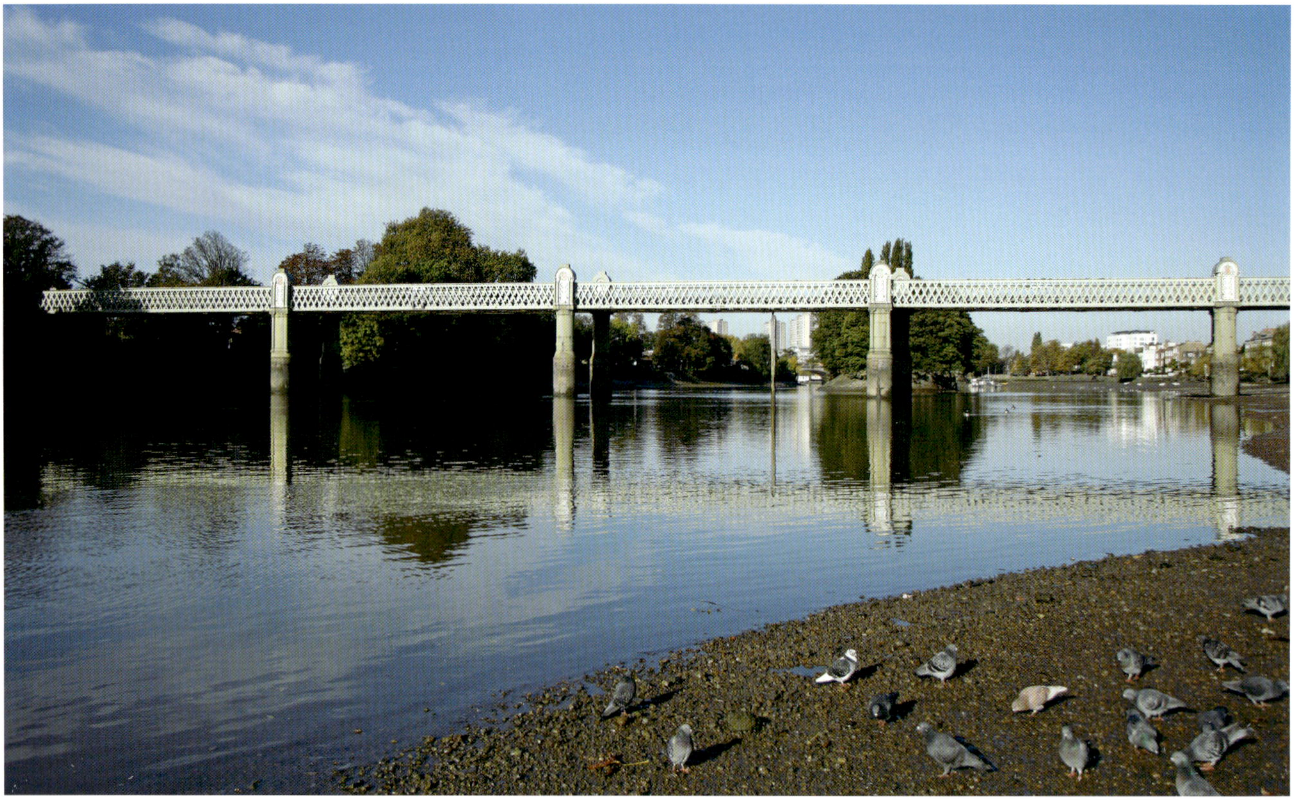

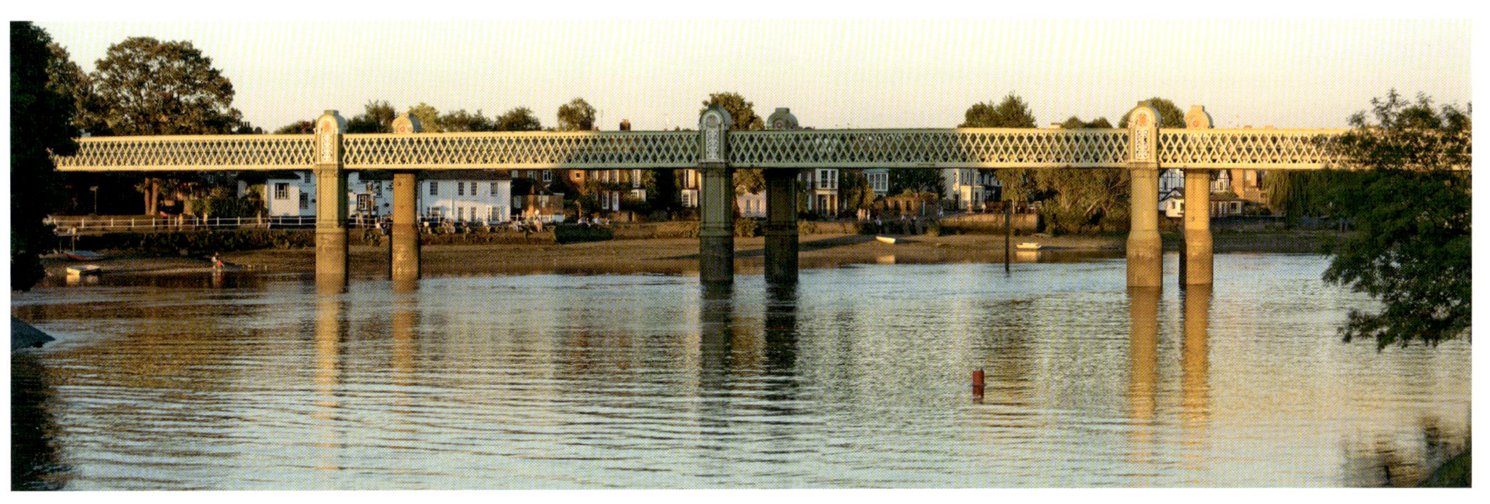

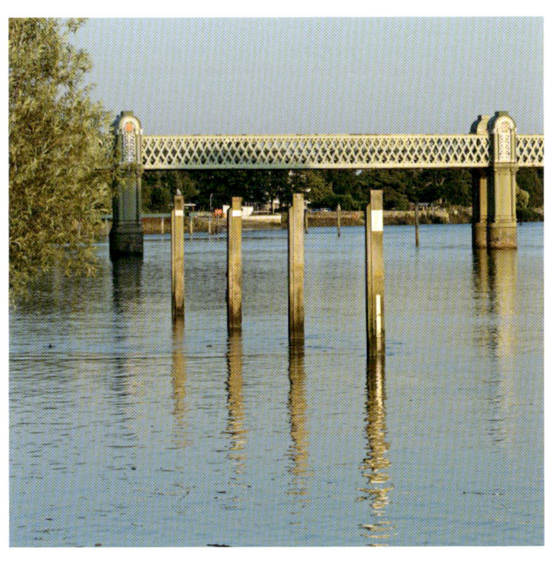

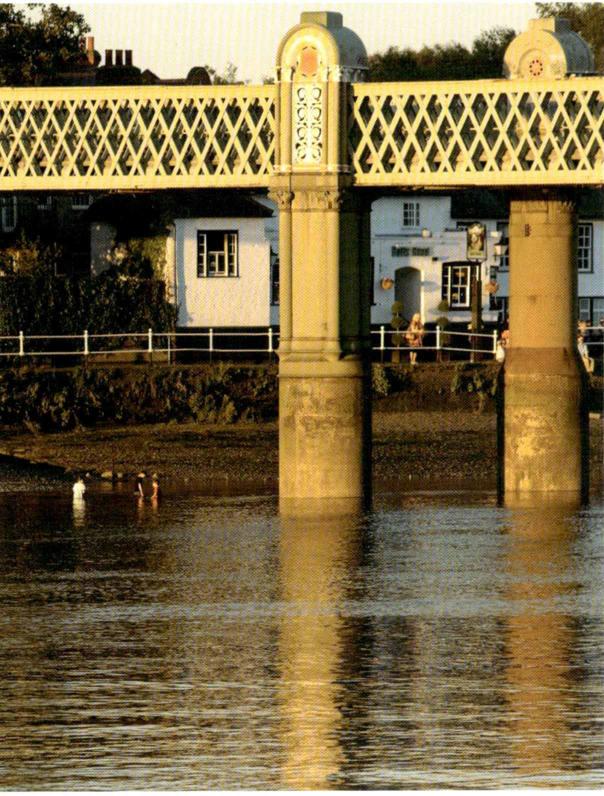

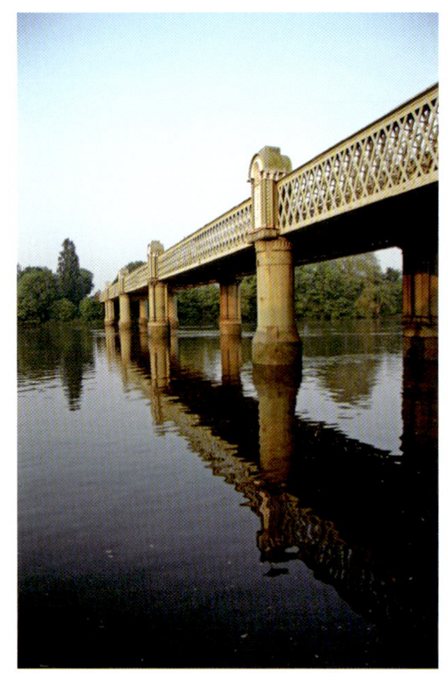

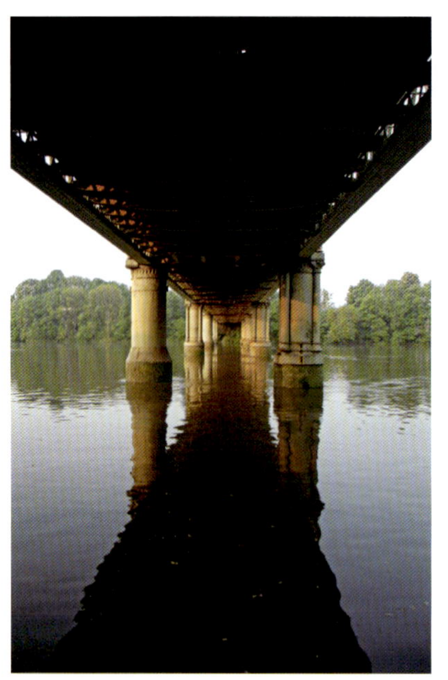

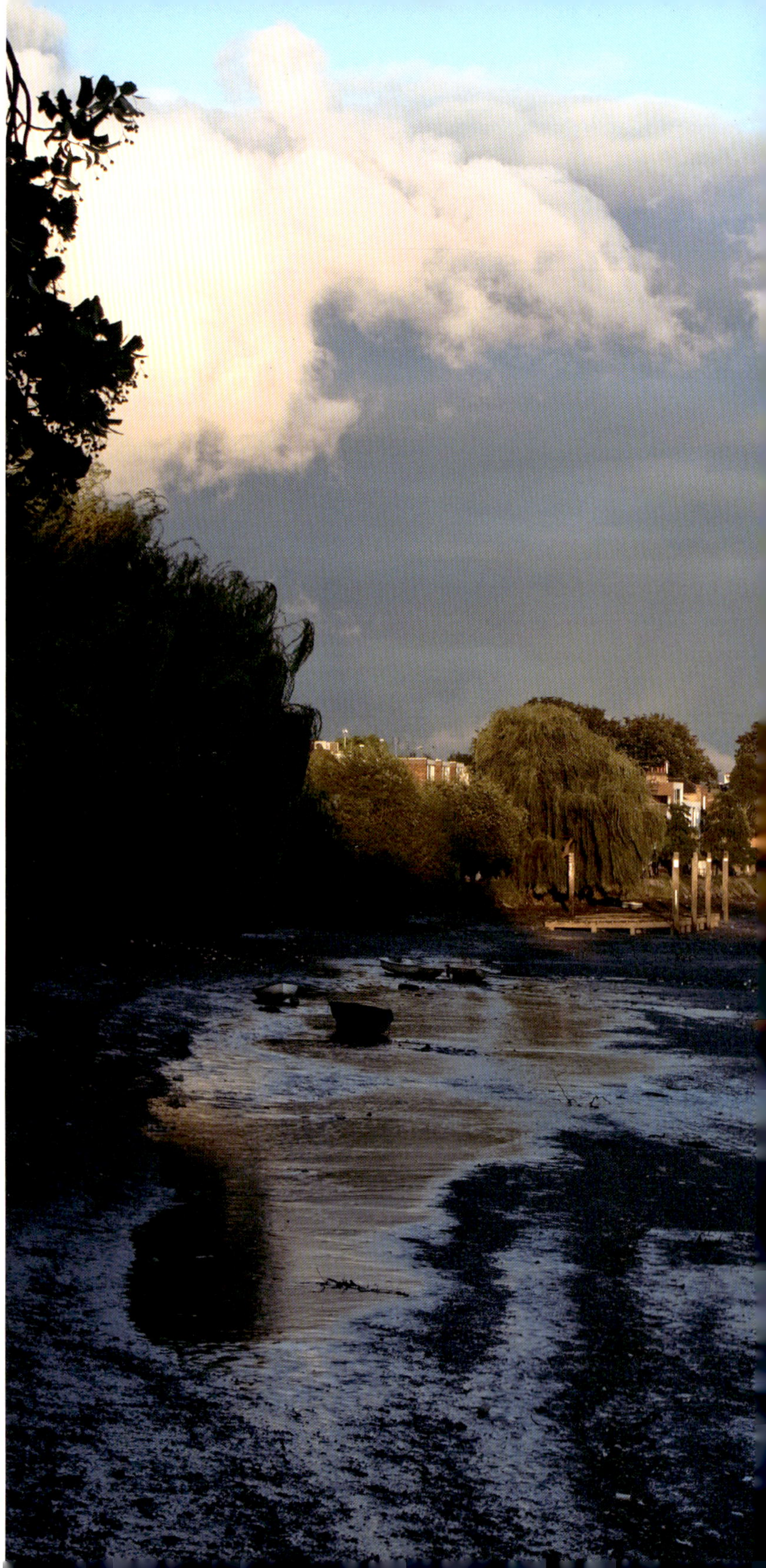

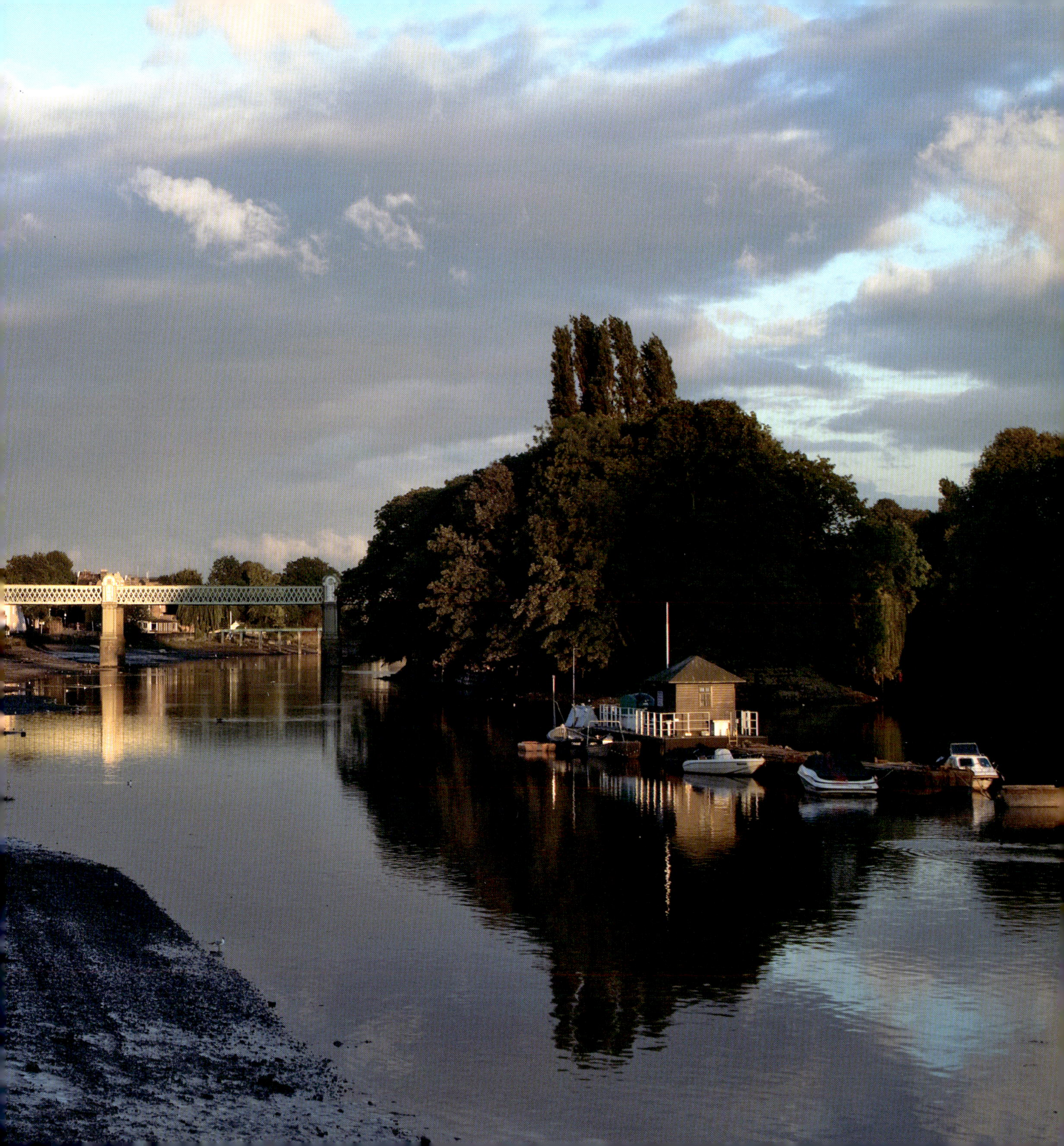

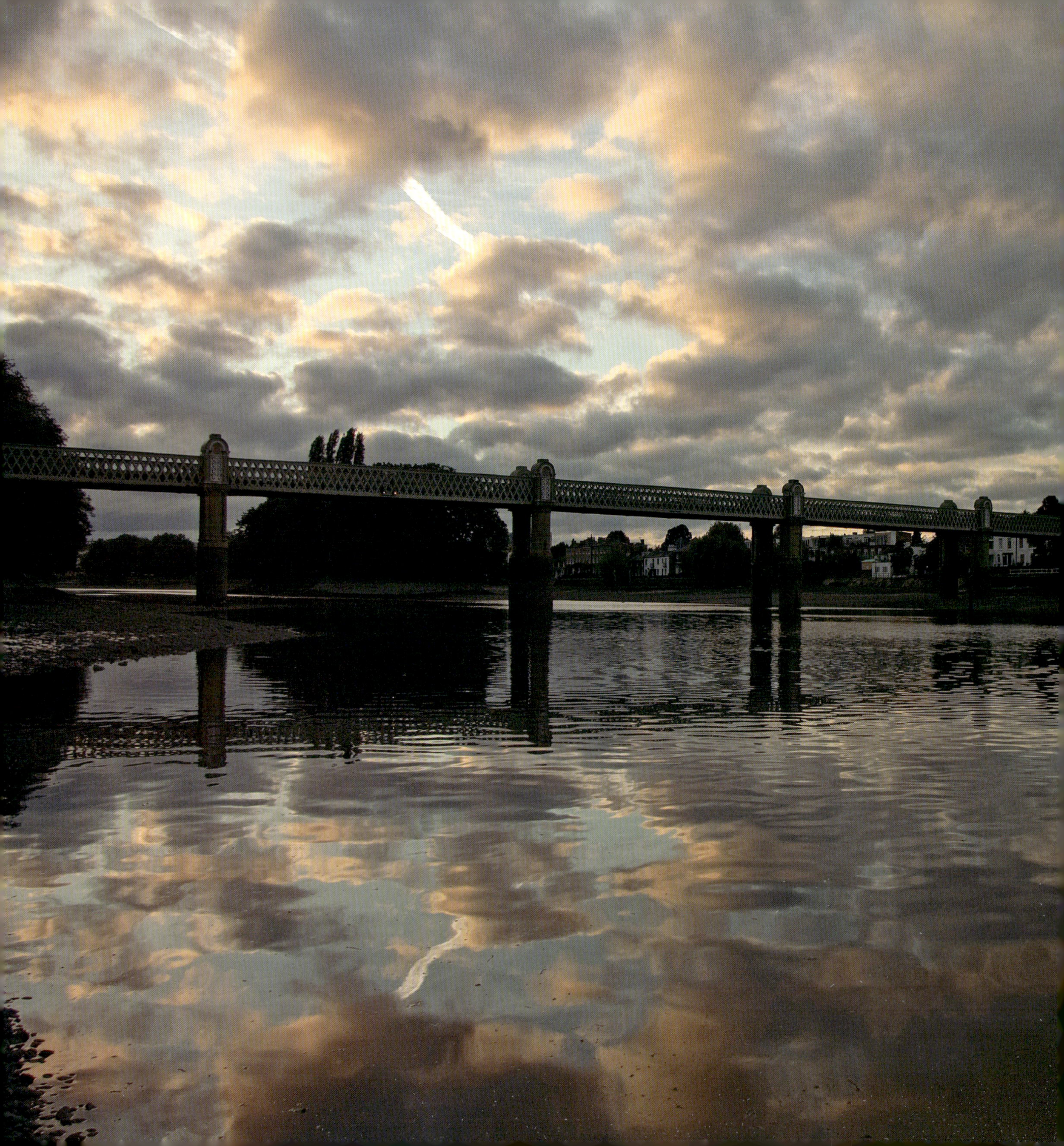

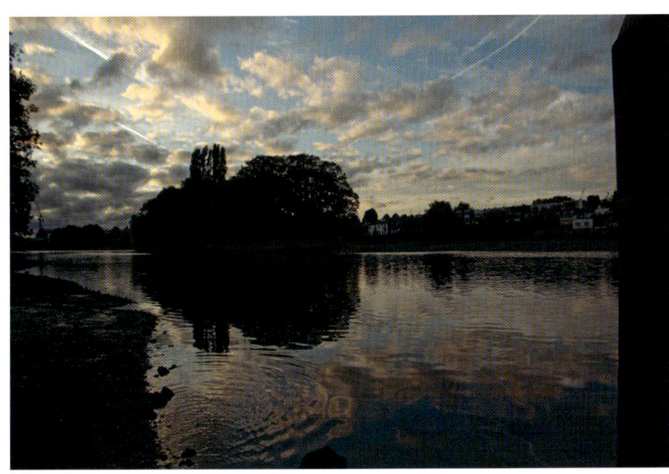

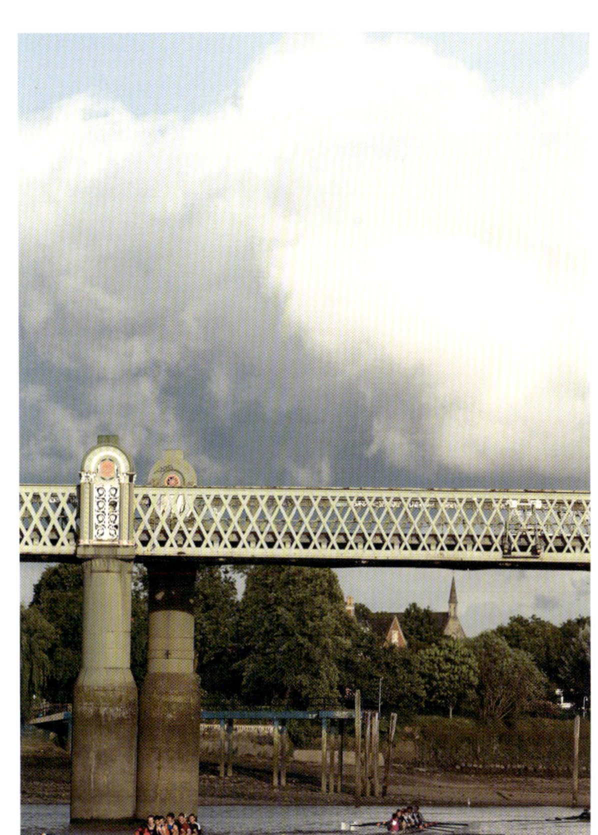

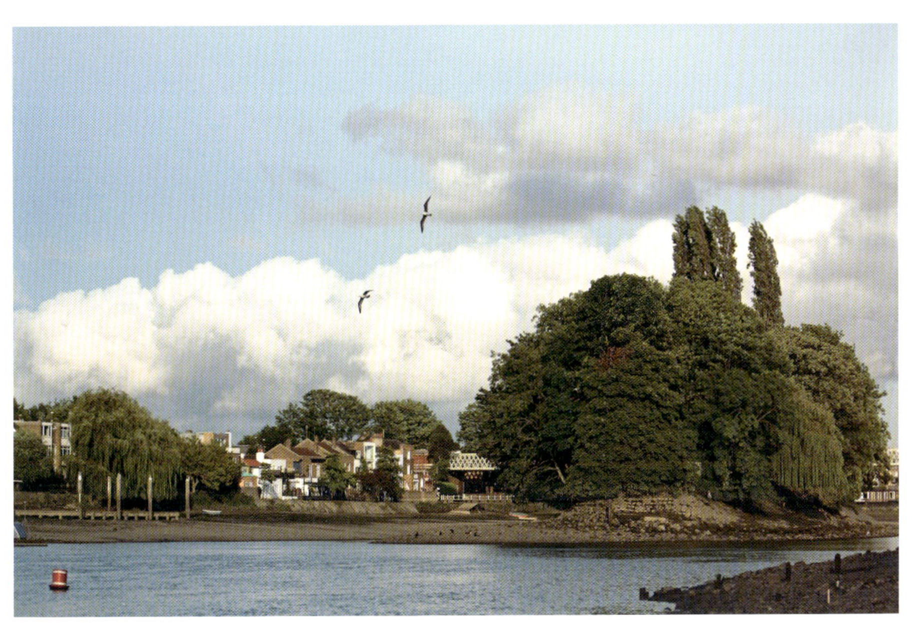

Bottom and Left: The view across to Kew from Brentford and including the controversial sculpture by Simon Packard, which was objected to by some riverside dwellers for blocking their view.

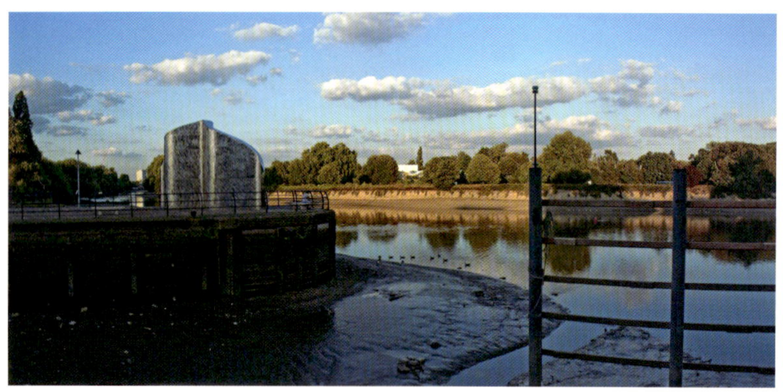

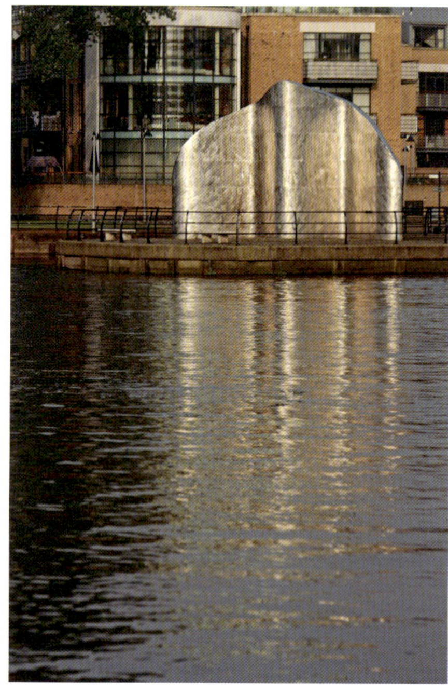

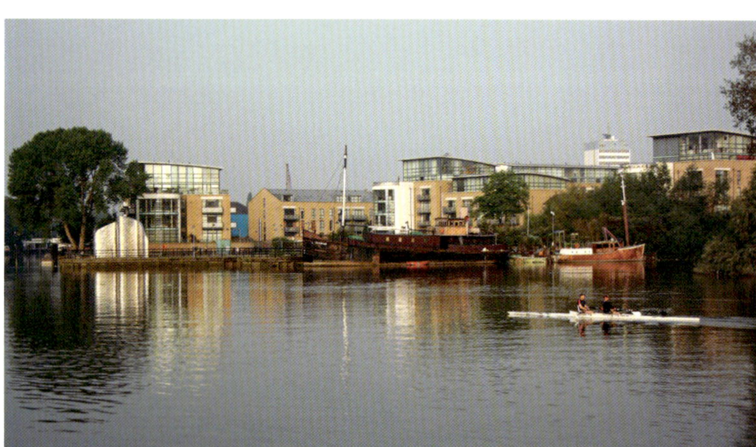

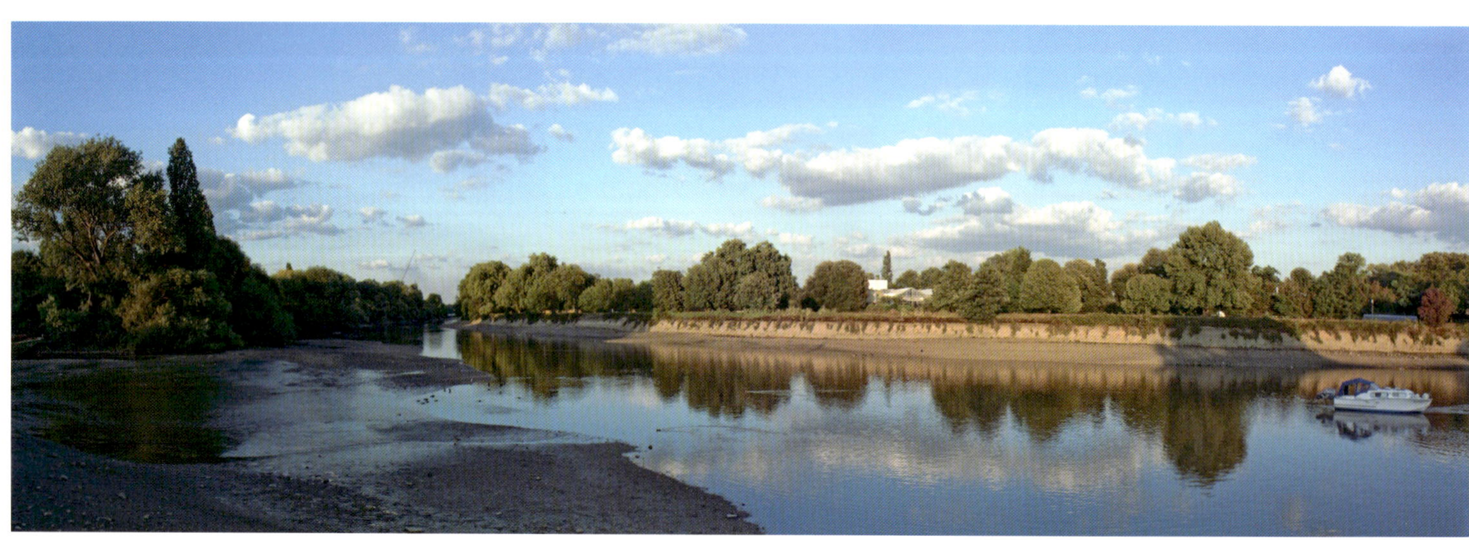

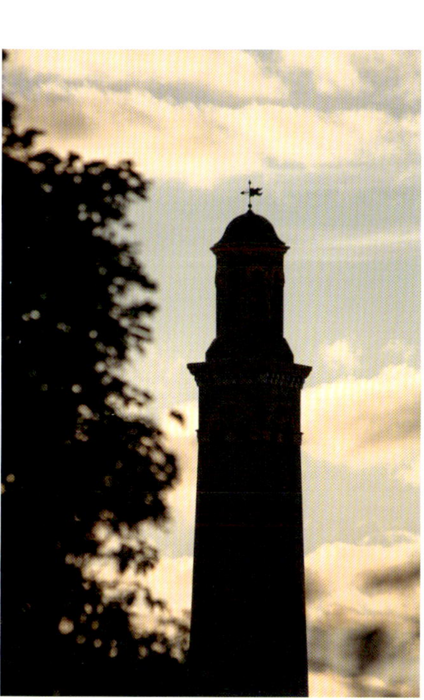

The Steam Museum and tower in Brentford as seen from Kew.

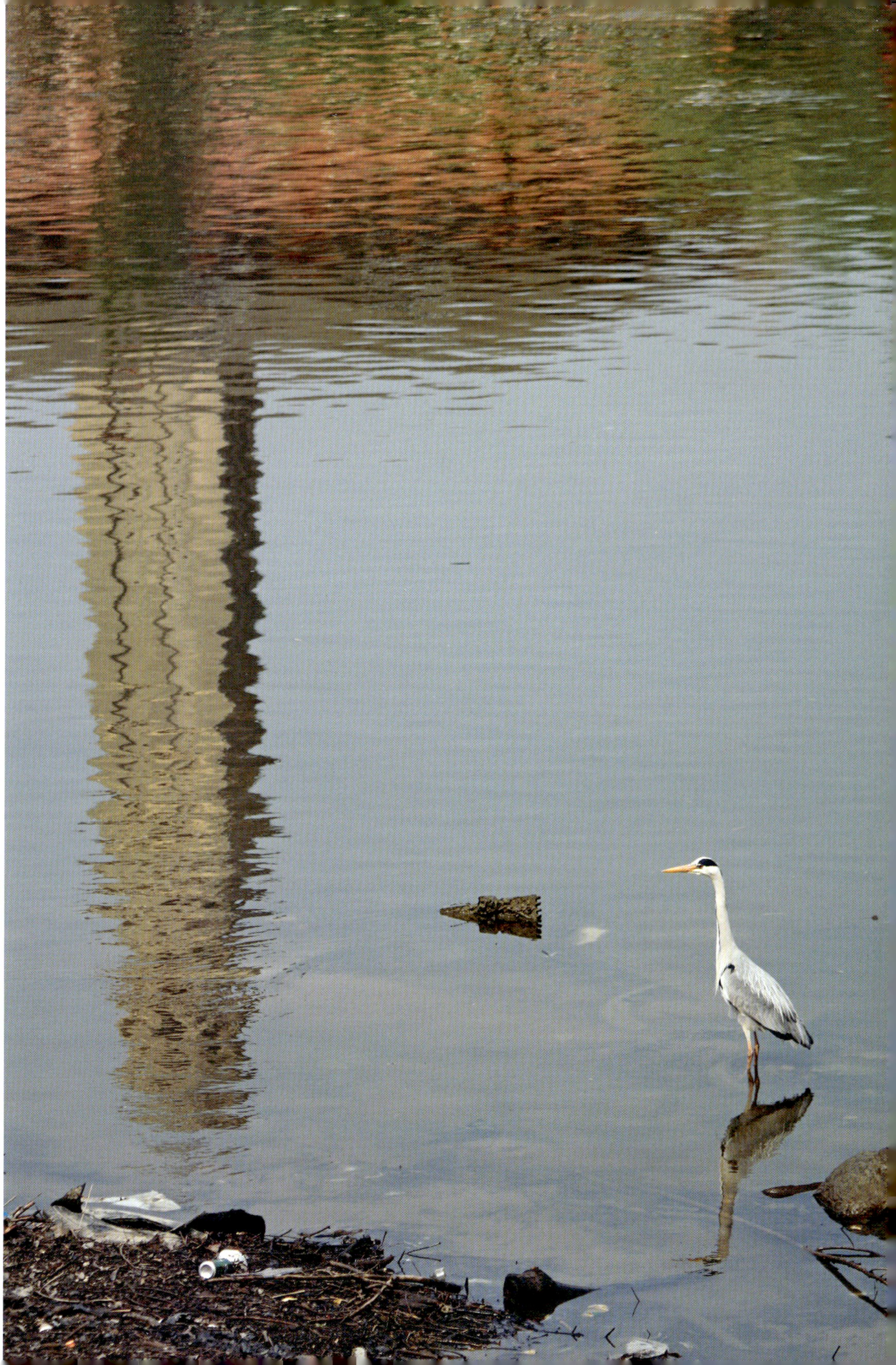

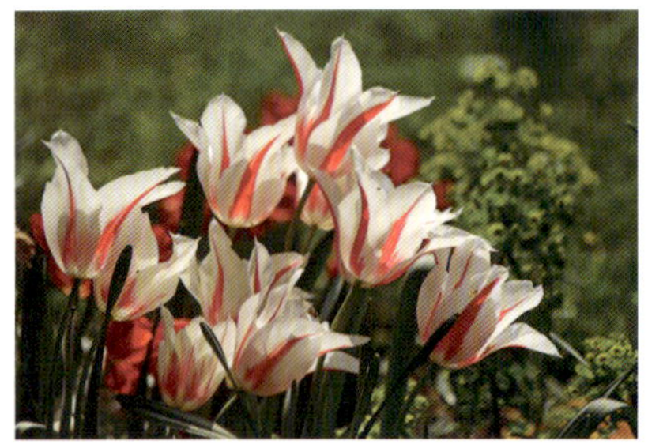

Pictures left and below: The towpath and the keyhole sculpture at Kew Pier: it is generally agreed that 'Cayho', the earliest known spelling for Kew, indicated 'a landing place on a promontory', as indeed it was in the 14th century. However, 'Cayho' could also be translated as 'a key', the inspiration for this striking work of art.

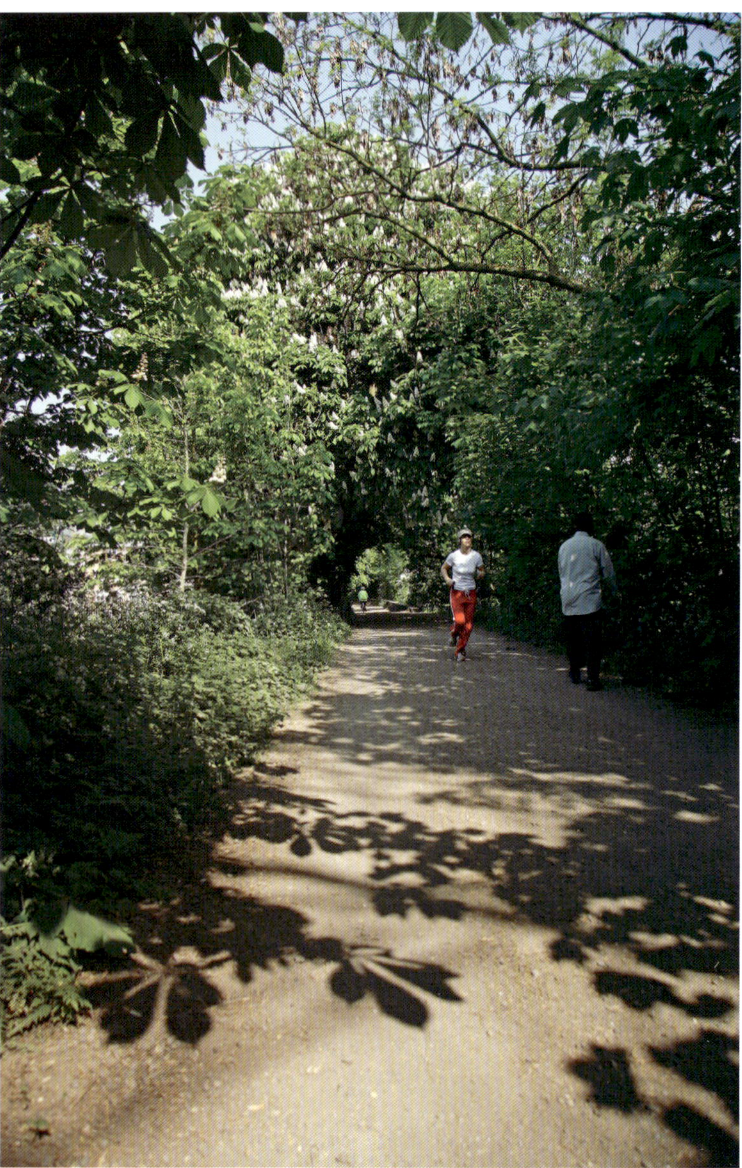

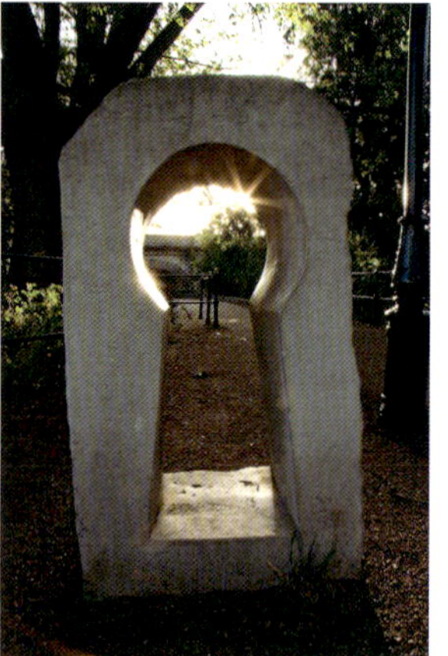

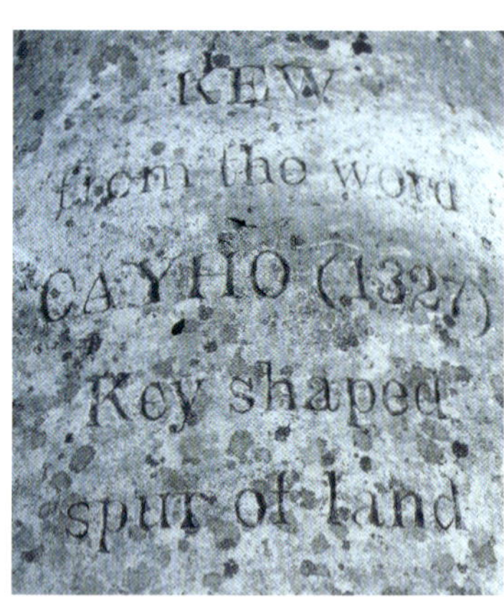

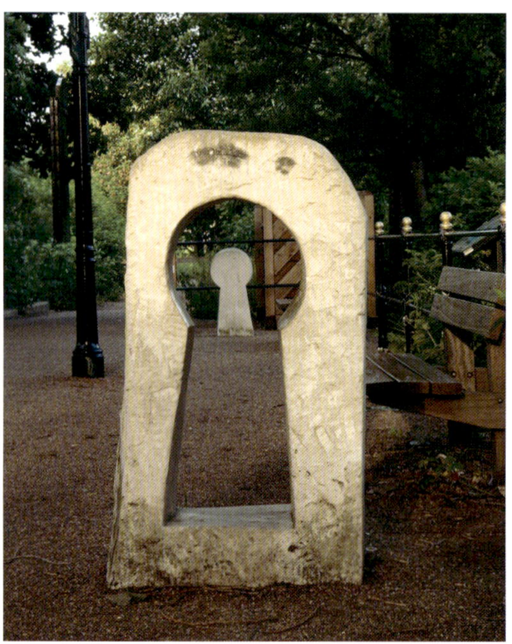

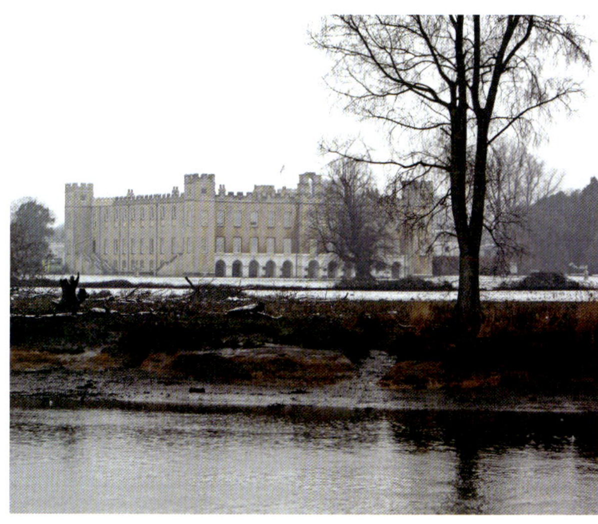

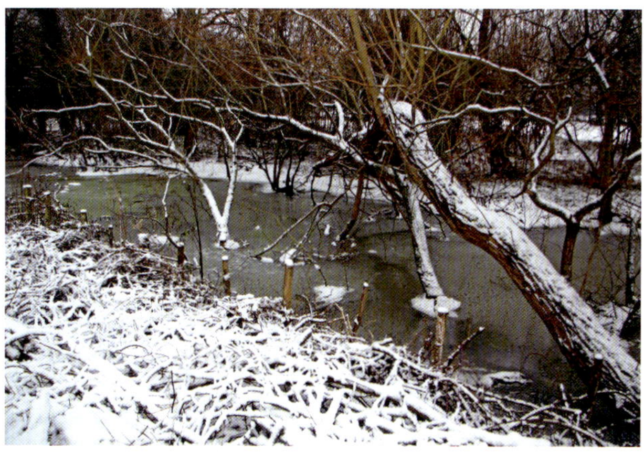

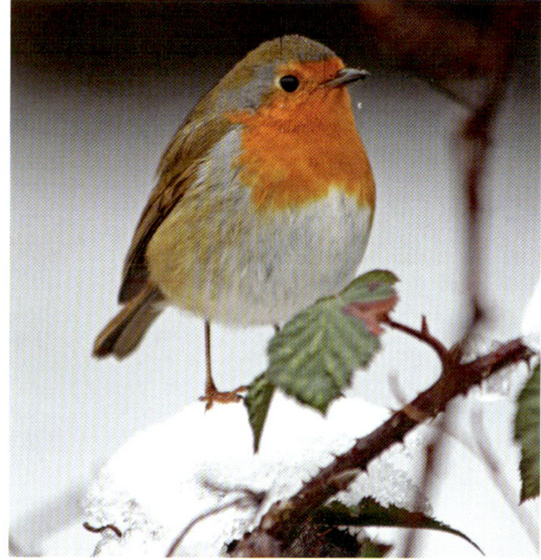

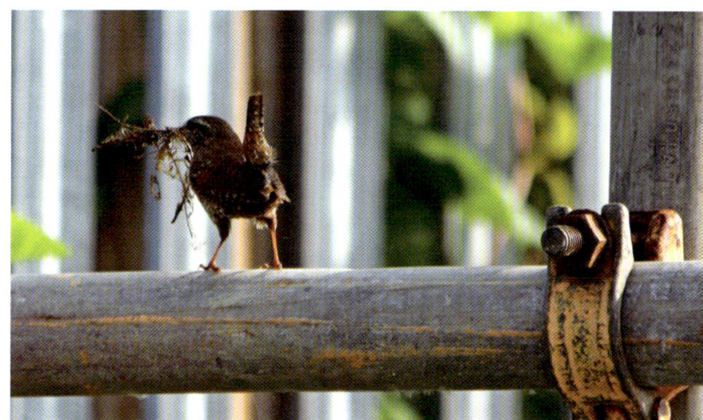

Above and top:
The towpath in winter and the view across the river to Syon House.
Right: A wren has taken up residence in an upturned rowing boat at one of the clubs stationed alongside the river.

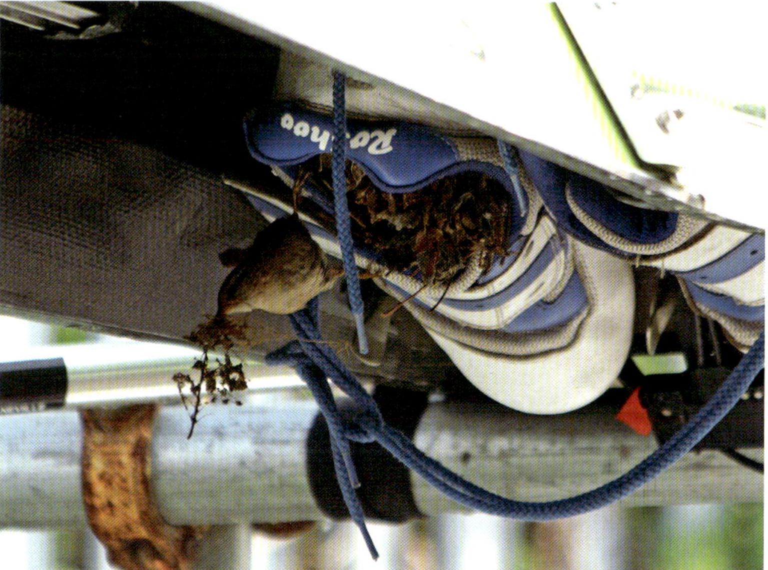

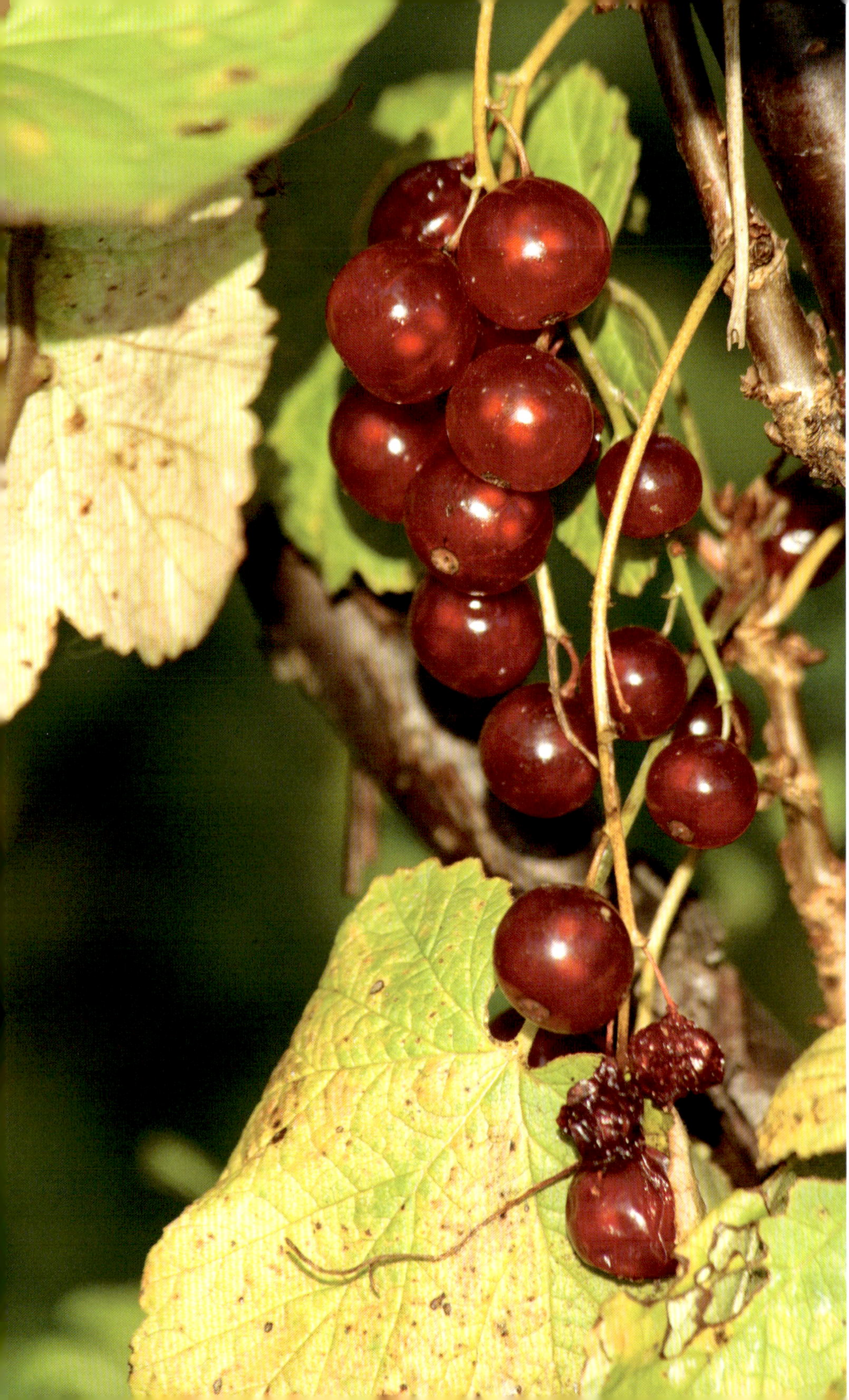

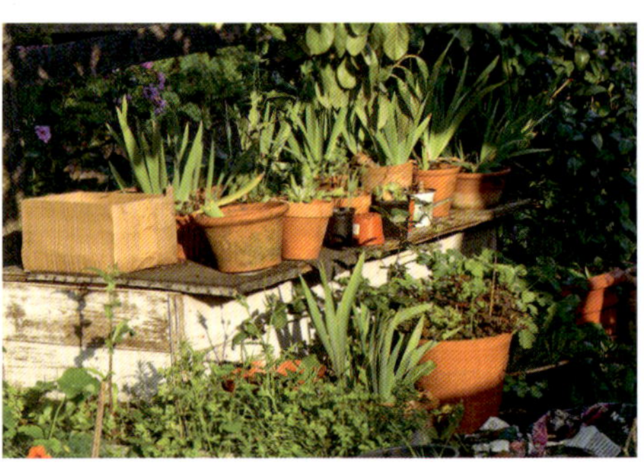

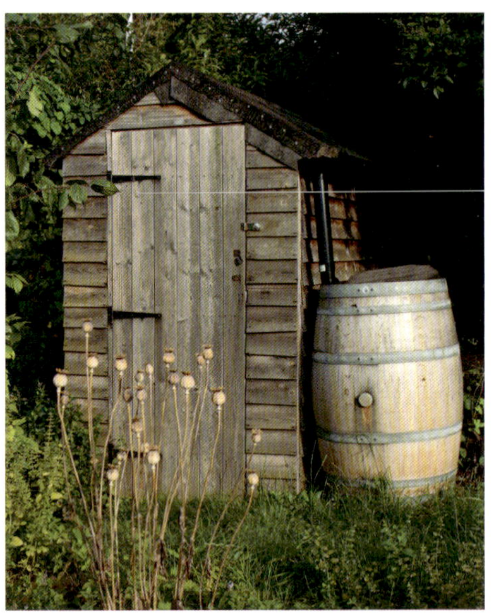

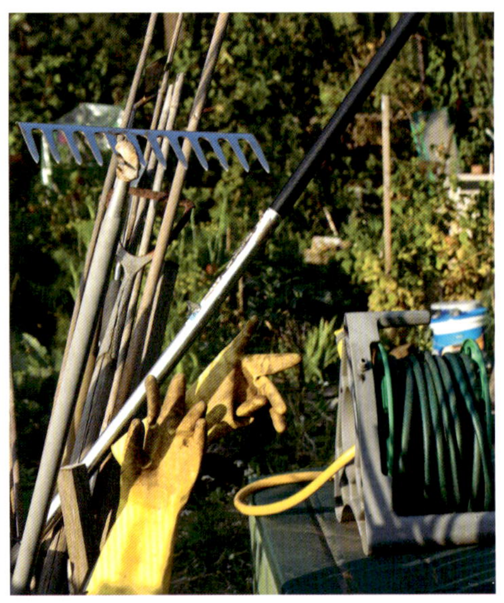

Short Lots:
A strange name it may be, but it forms the spiritual home of the Kew Horticultural Society and can be found down by the river. A huge plot teaming with life.

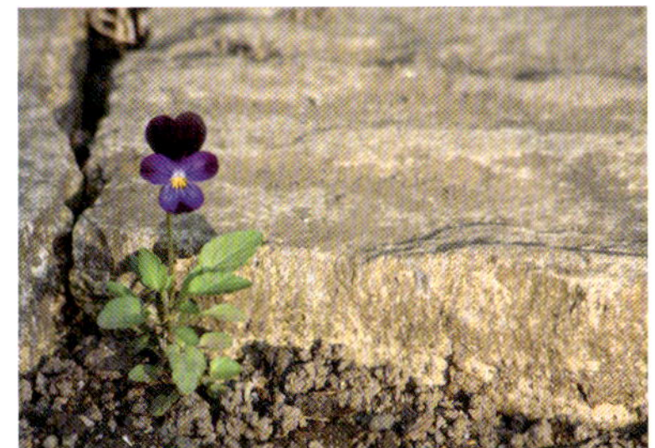

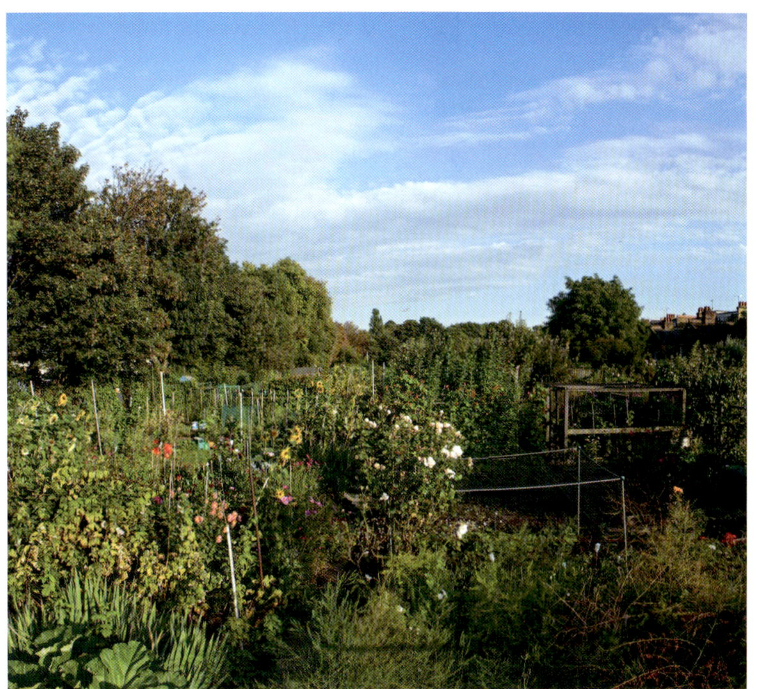

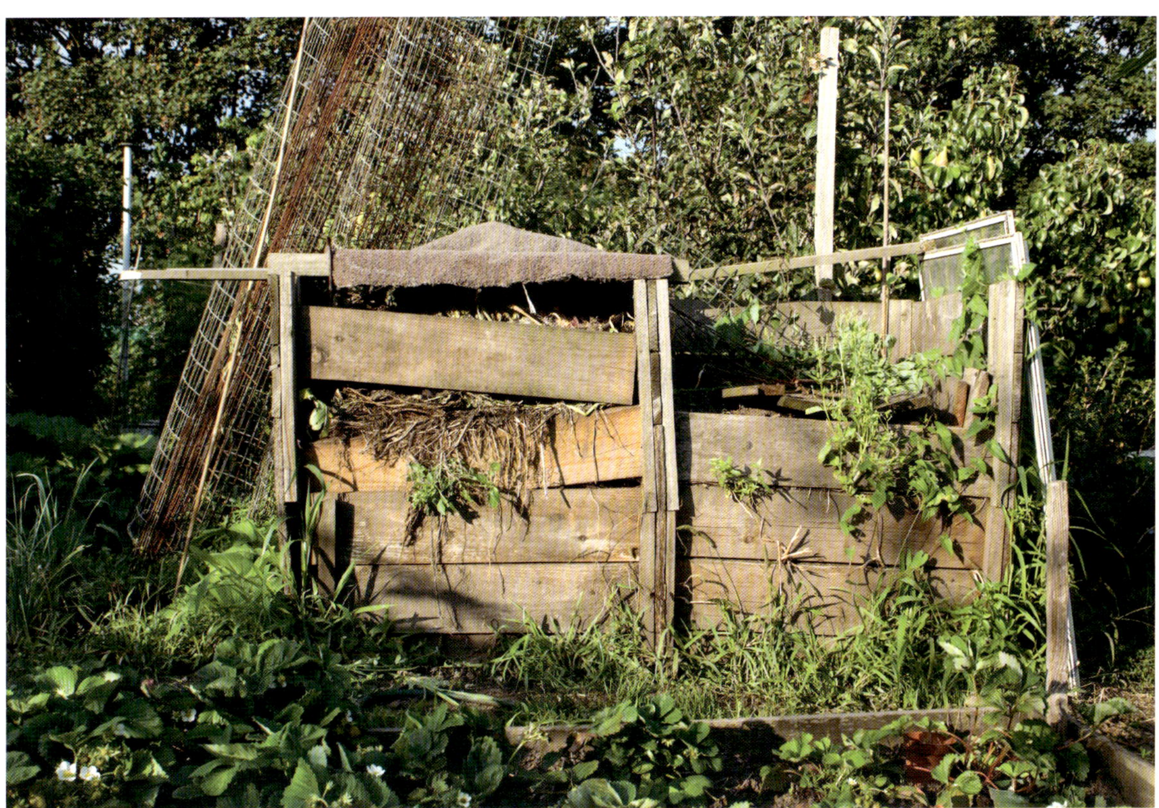

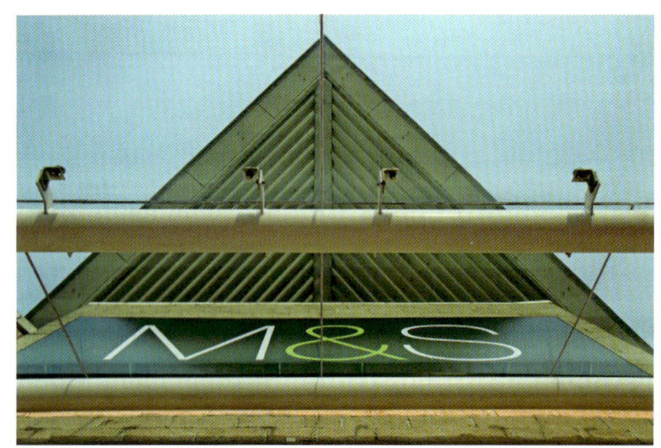

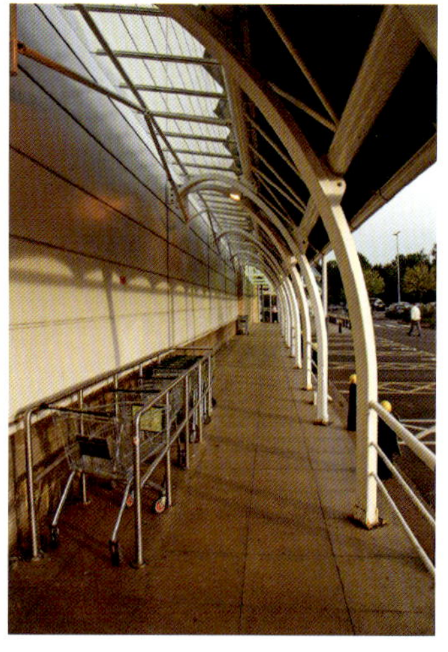

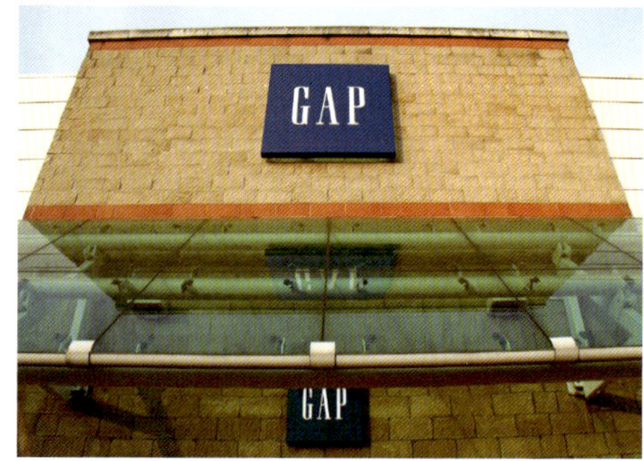

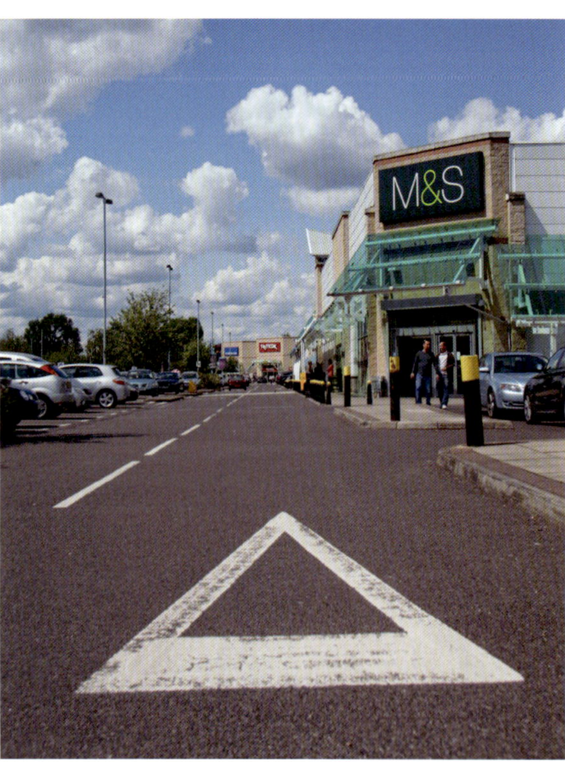

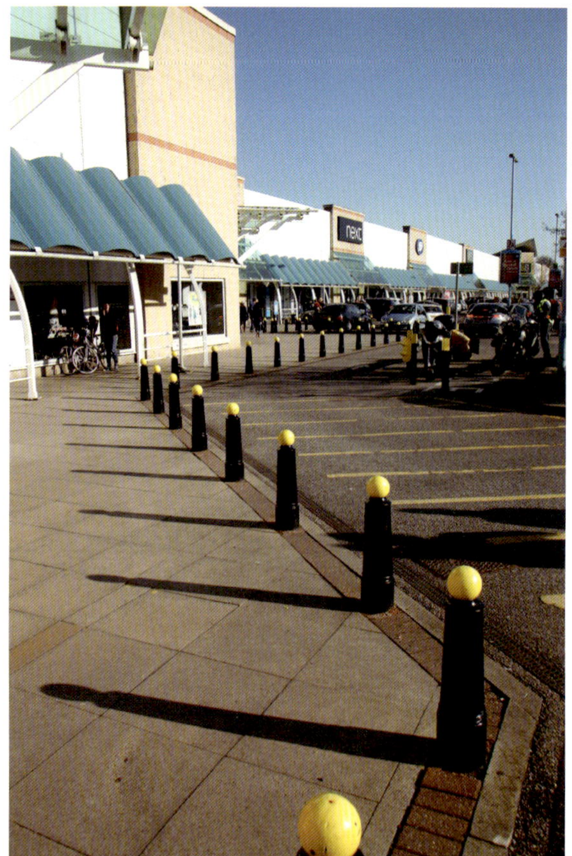

Kew Retail Park: off Mortlake Road

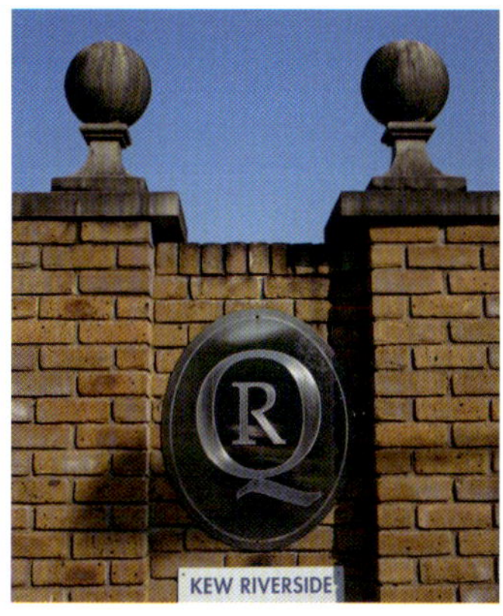

Kew Riverside Park:
Formerly water meadows, this area that stretches alongside the river next to The National Archives has now been fully developed.

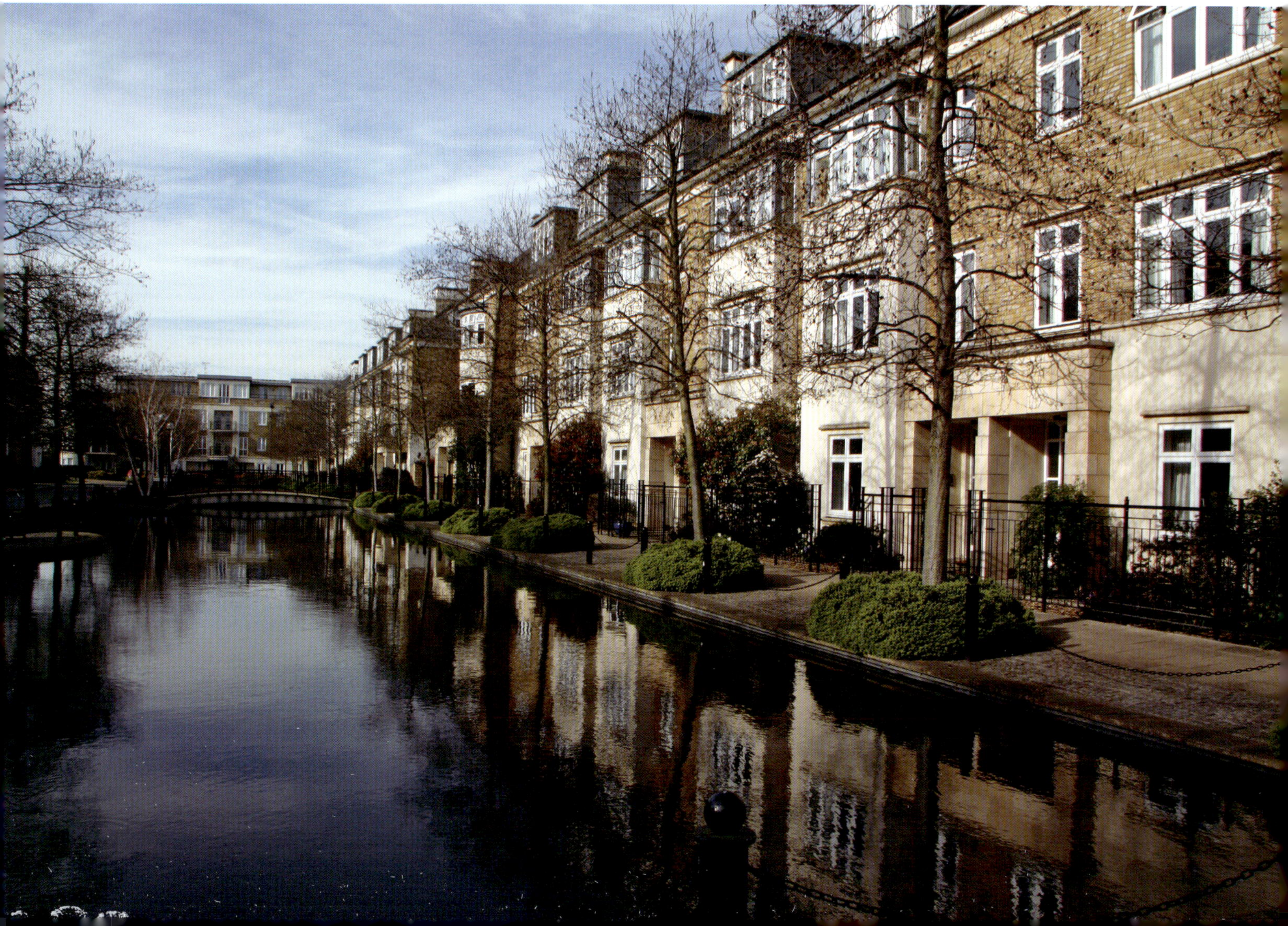

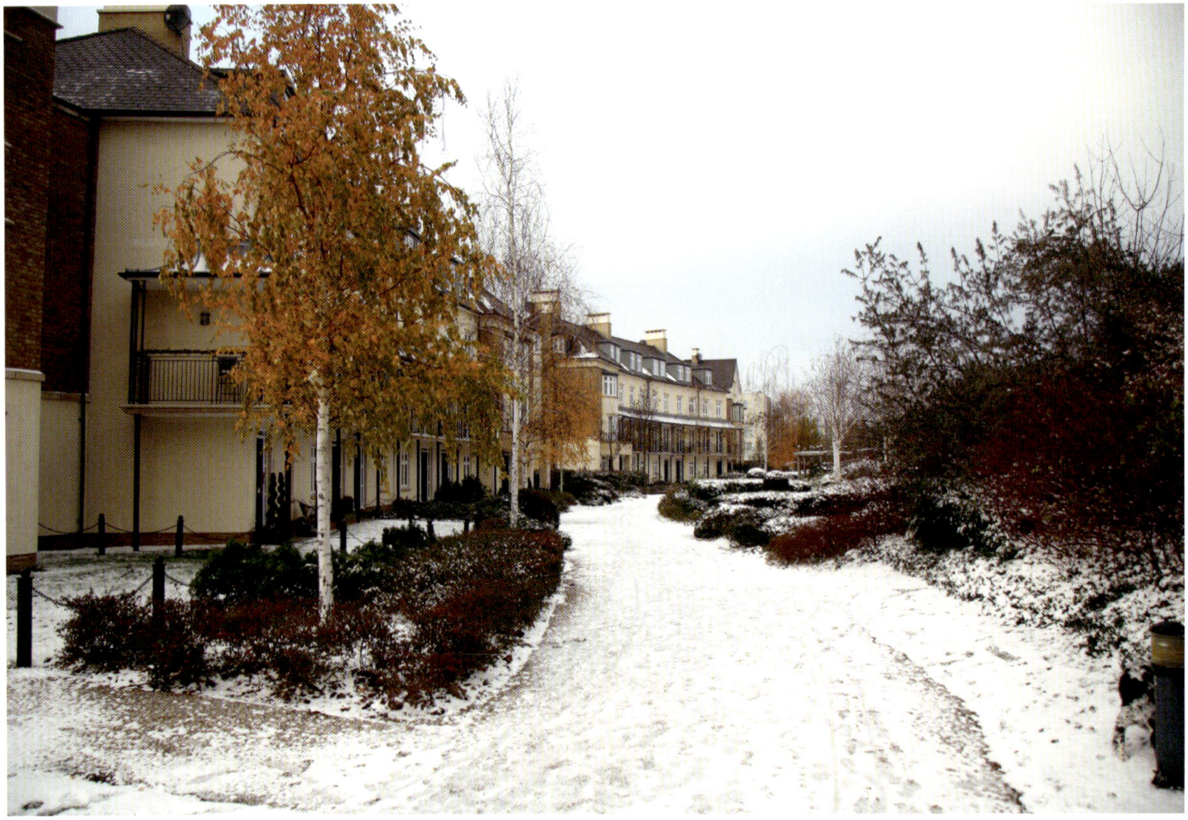

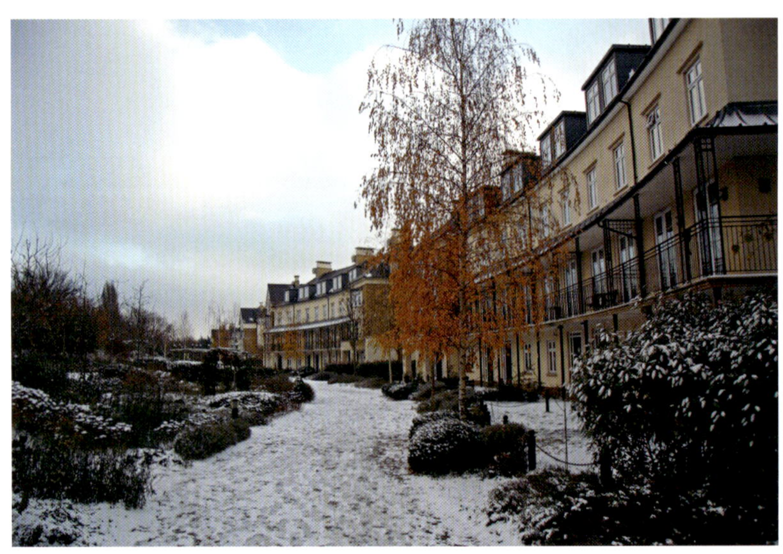

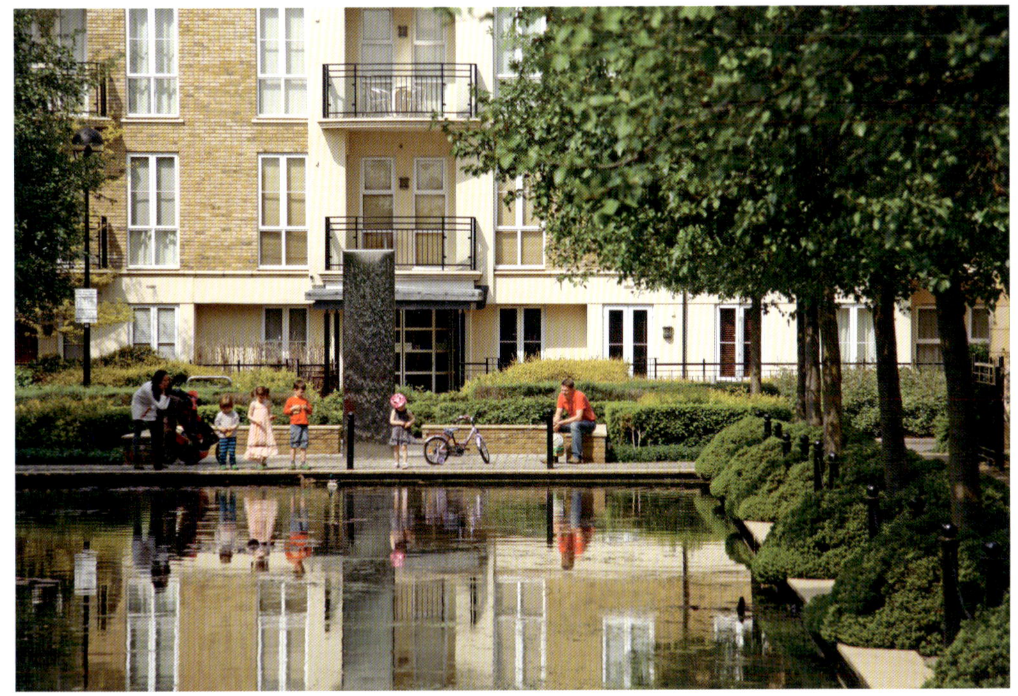

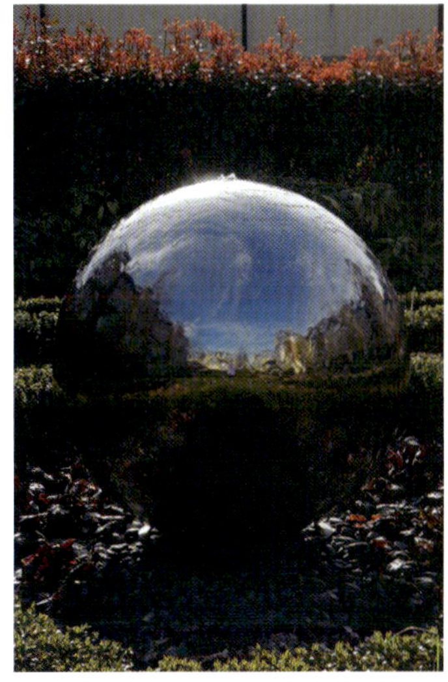

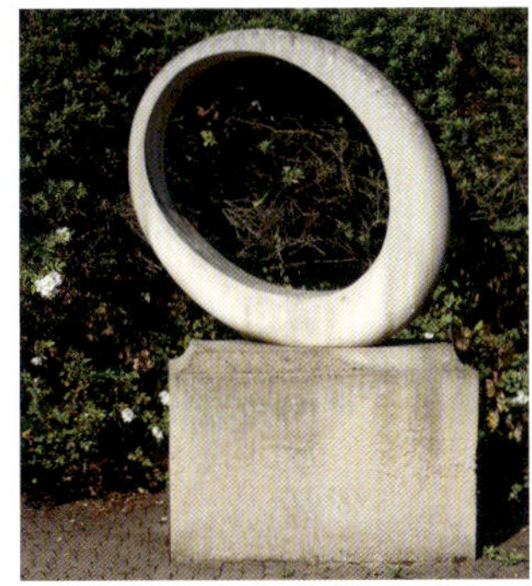

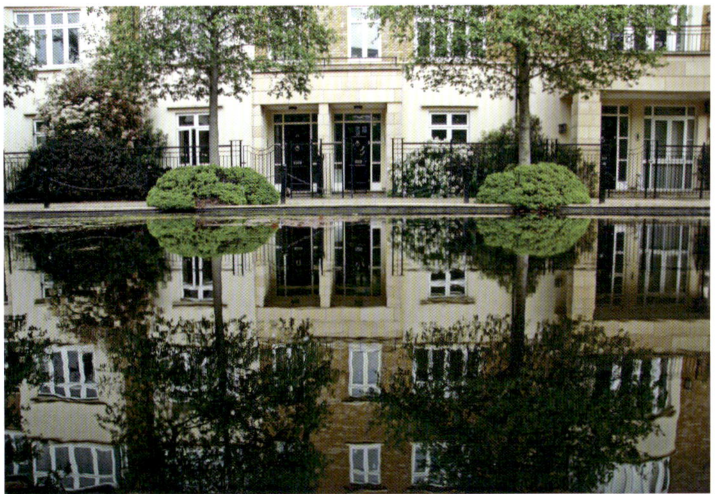

This page and opposite:
Kew Riverside Park. The sculpture above right can be found beside the gates as you enter via Townmead Road.

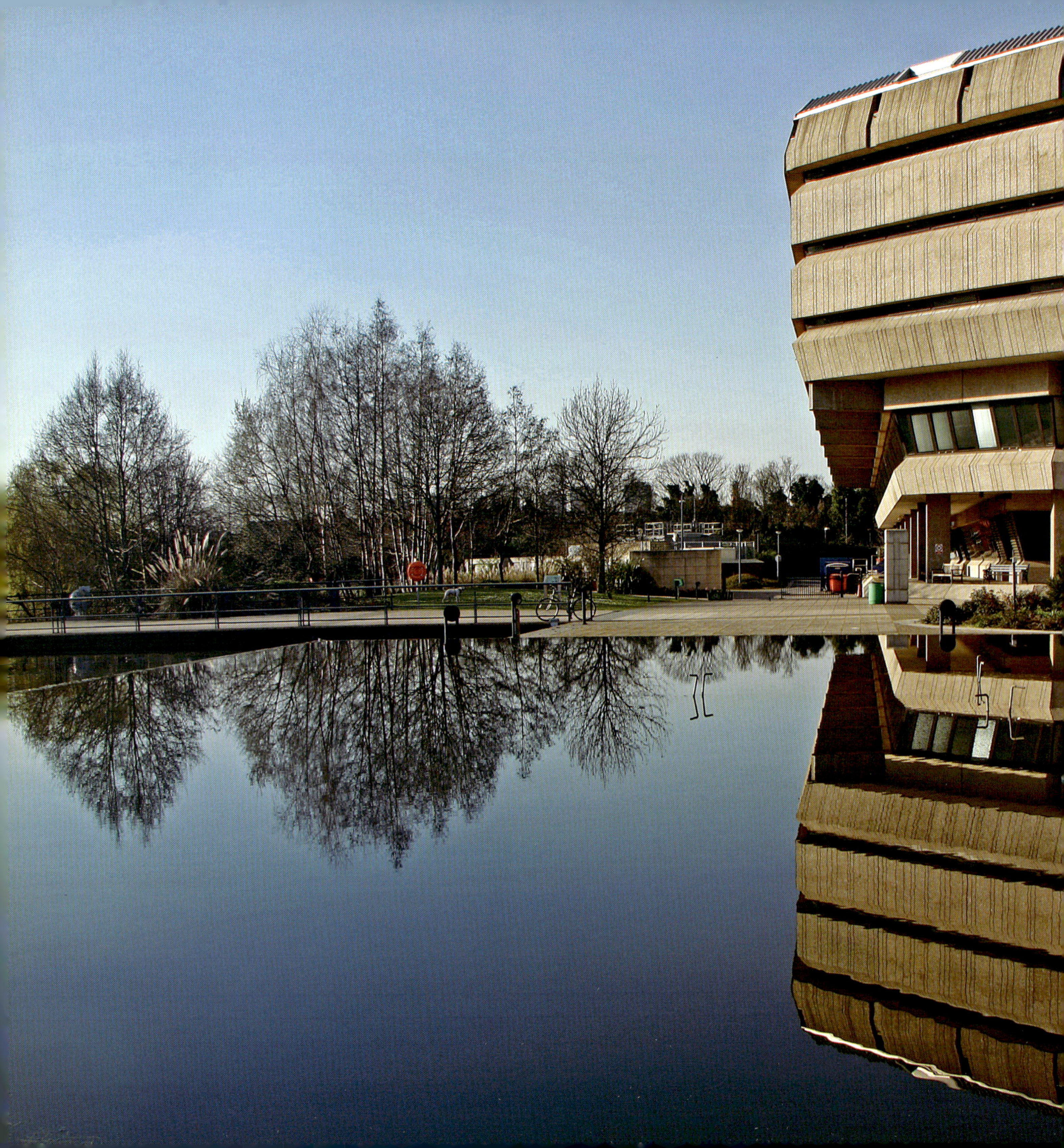

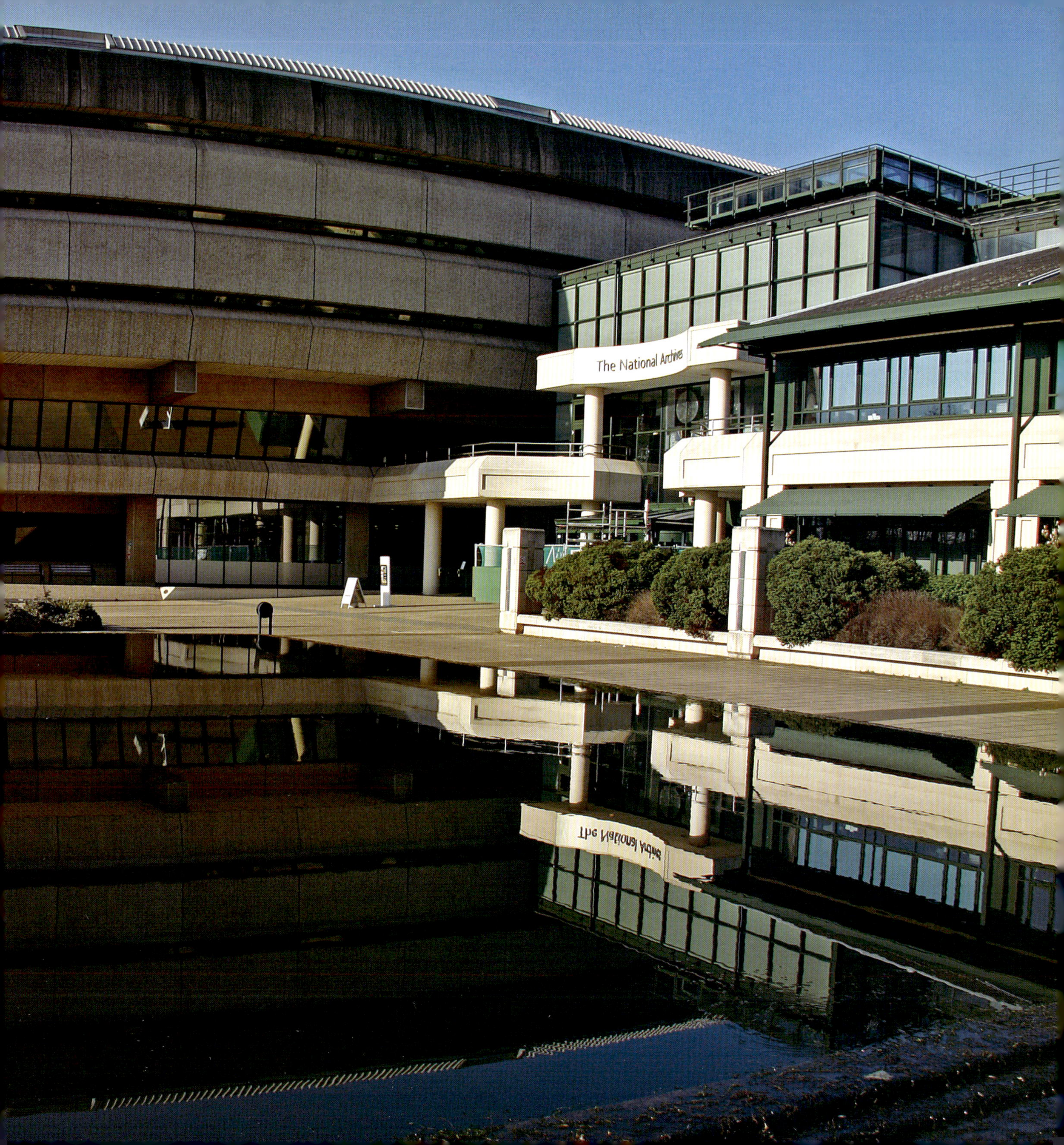
The National Archives

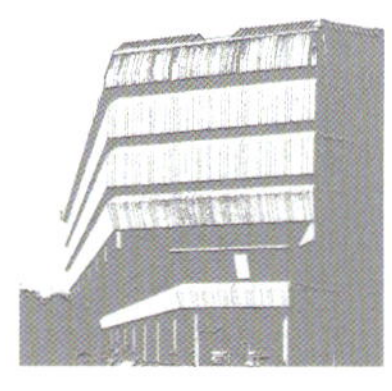

THE NATIONAL ARCHIVES

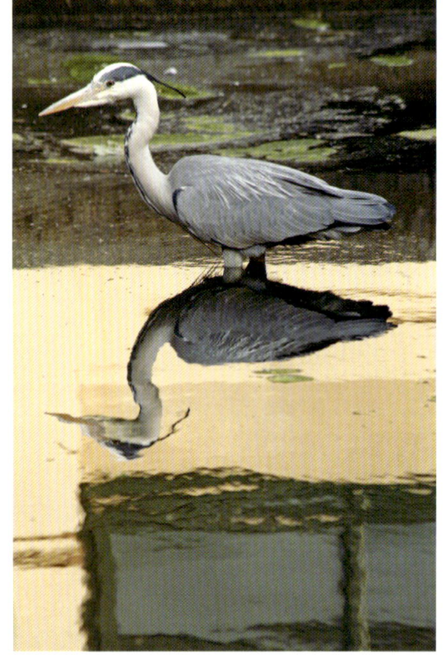

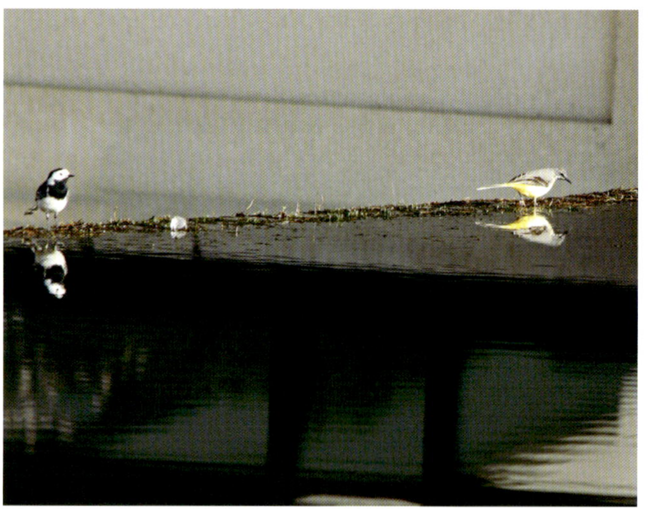

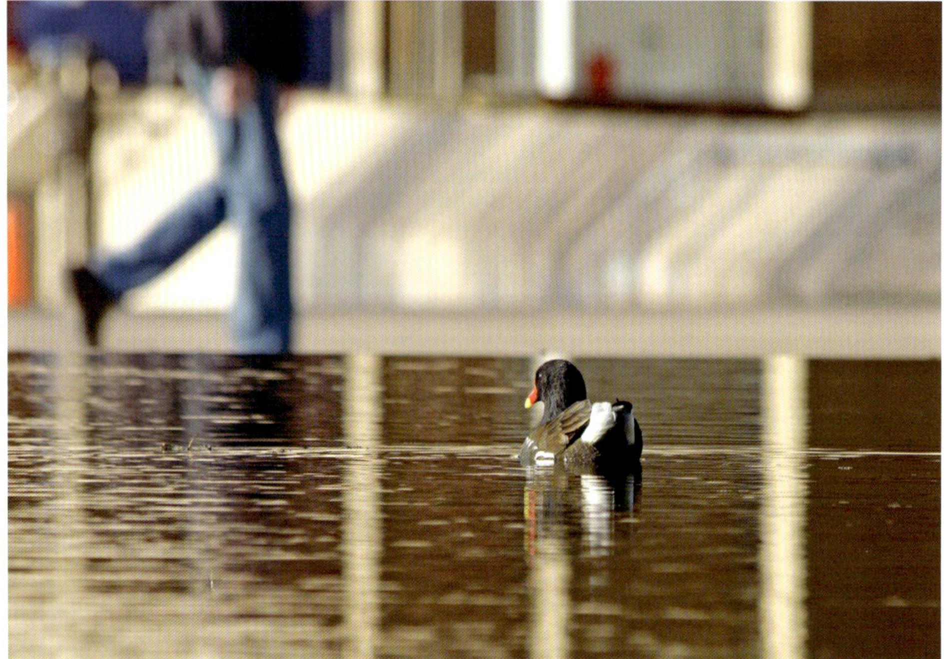

An imposing building, built during the 1970's and then called The Public Record Office, The National Archives is the destination both in person and increasingly online for all those seeking information about our past. It has in its grounds a lake, which is open to the public during daylight hours and amongst the wildfowl that you will see is their resident Grey Heron, pictured top left, Wagtails top right and Moorhens, bottom left.

Previous Page:
The National Archives as seen reflected in the lake.

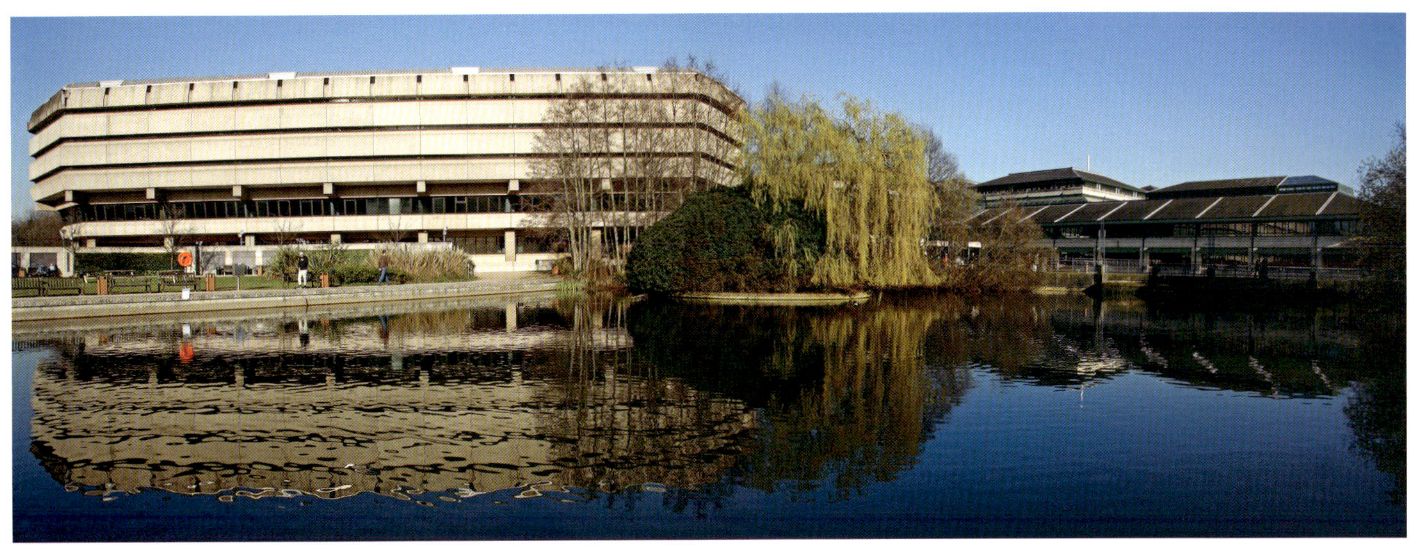

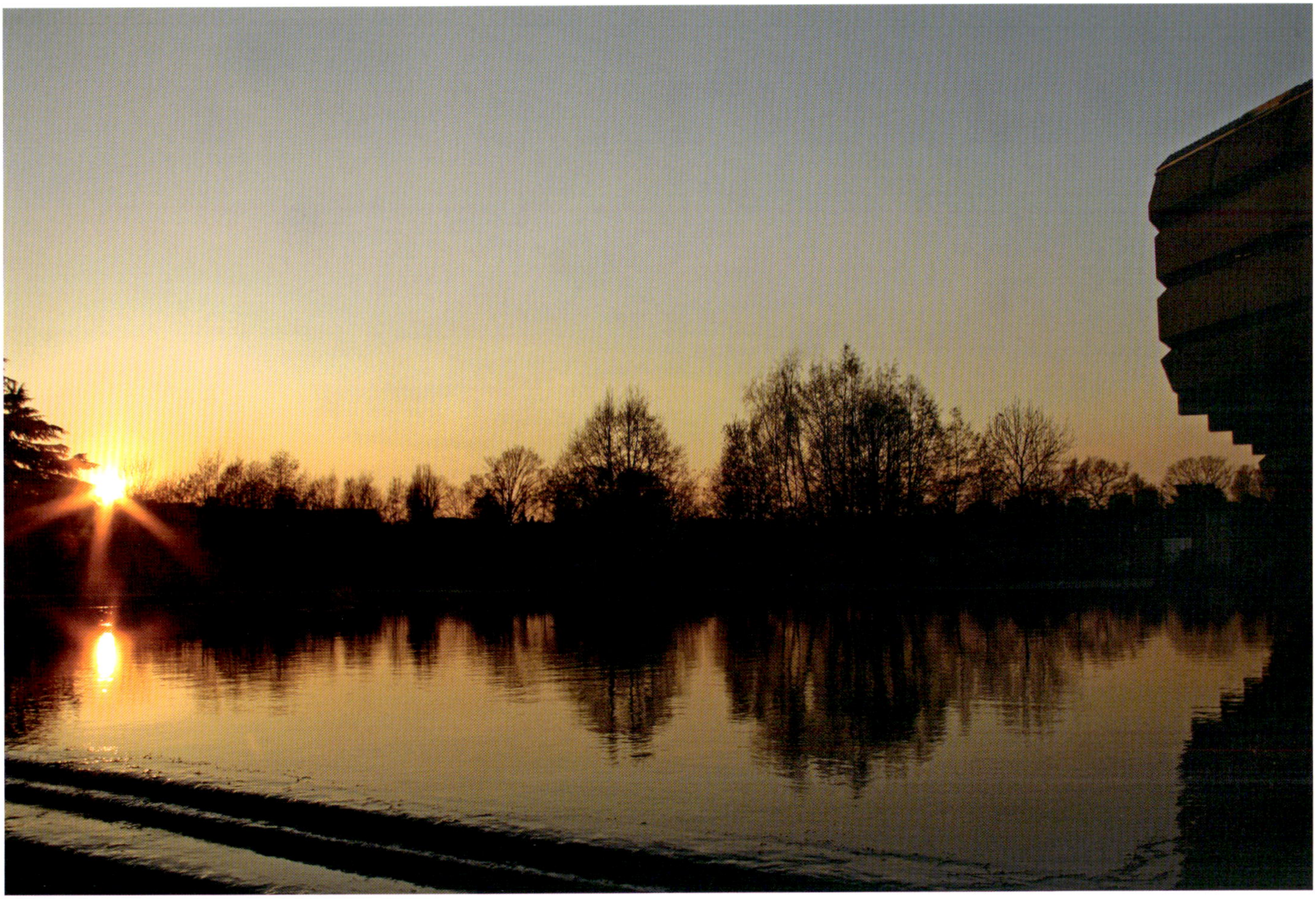

THE BRIDGE AND PIER

There has been a bridge here since 1759 and the current one is its third incarnation and was completed just over 100 years ago. The Bridge is actually named after the then King, Edward VII, and he performed the opening ceremony, as commemorated by the stone on the bridge, see below.

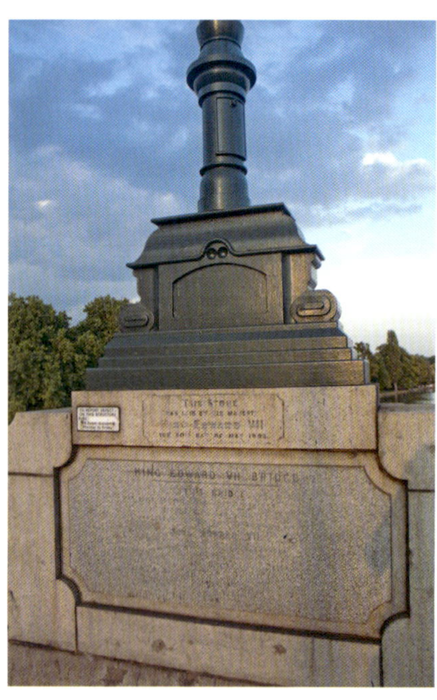

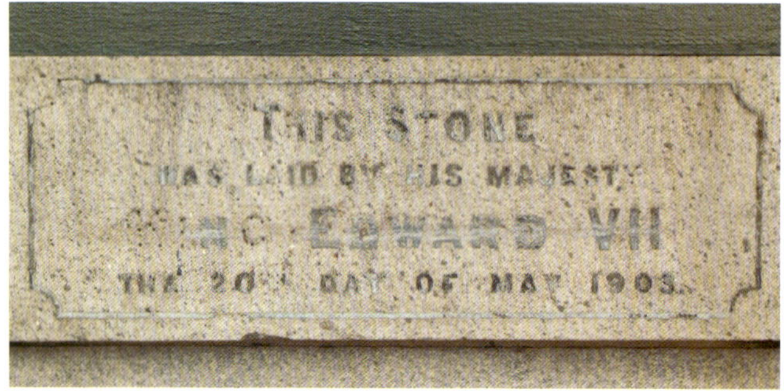

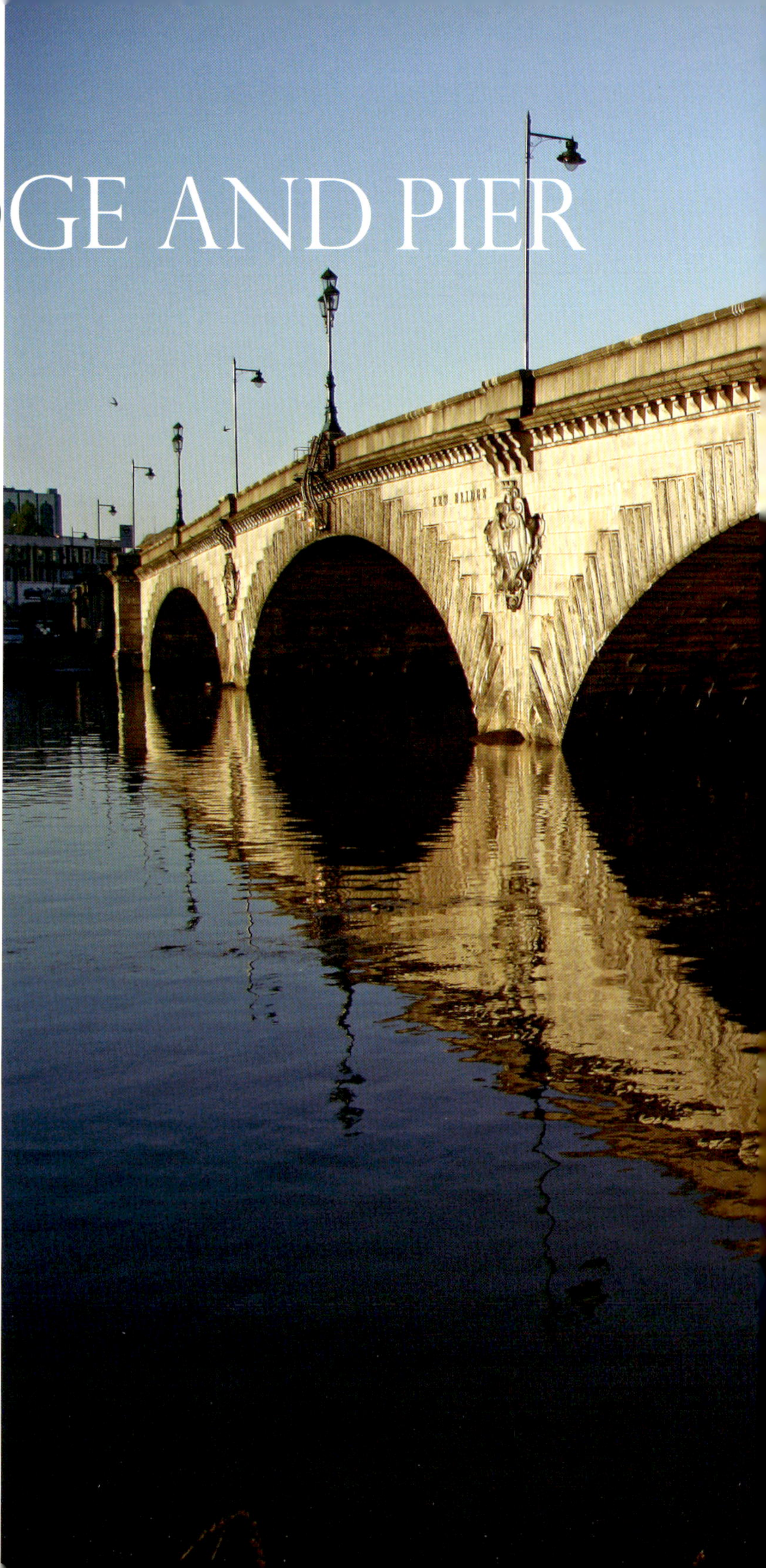

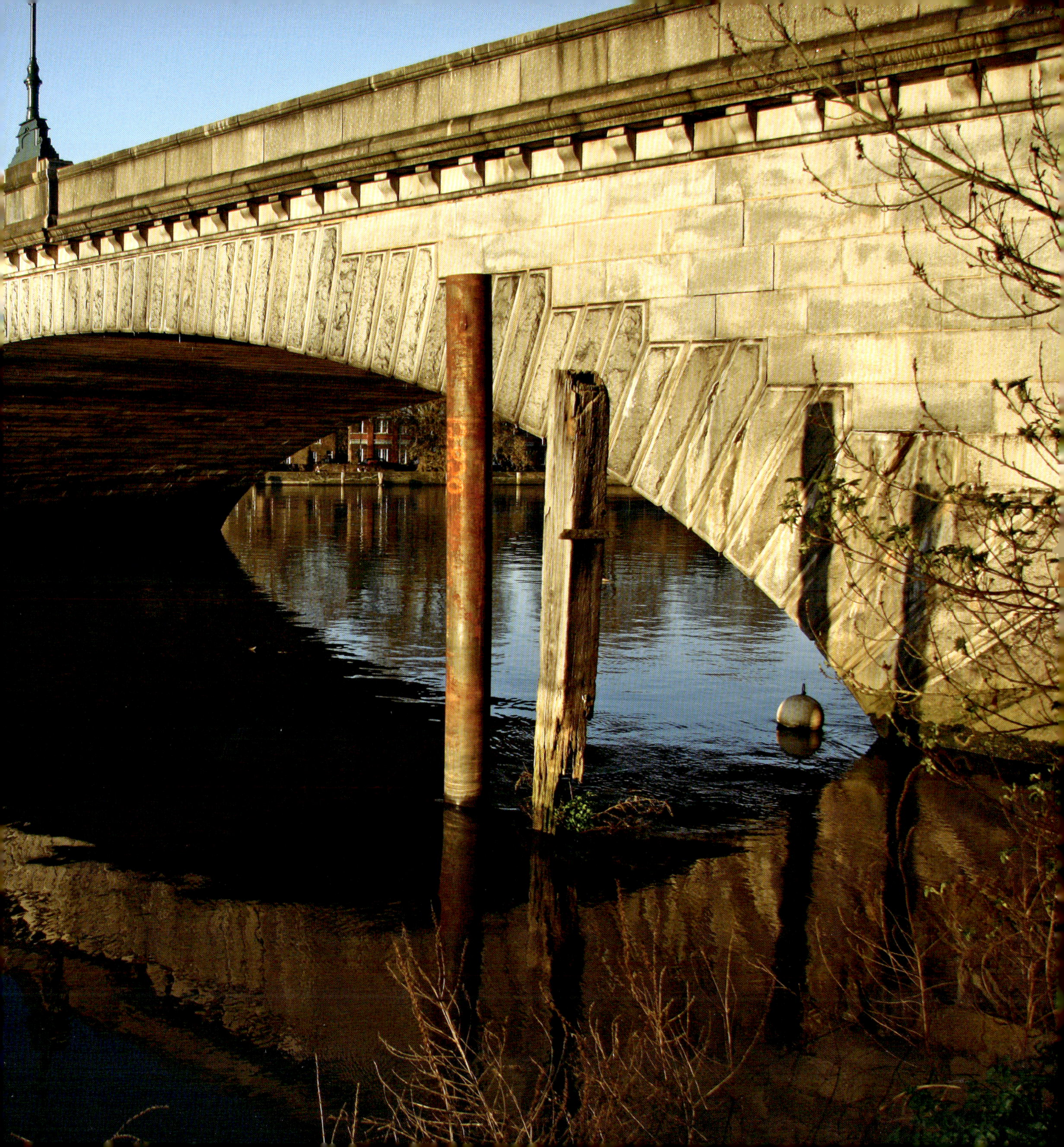

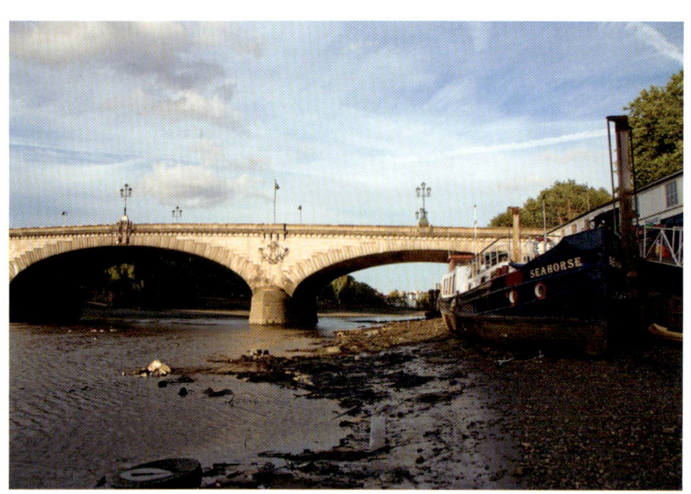

This and the next three pages: Kew Bridge from a variety of angles and in all weathers.

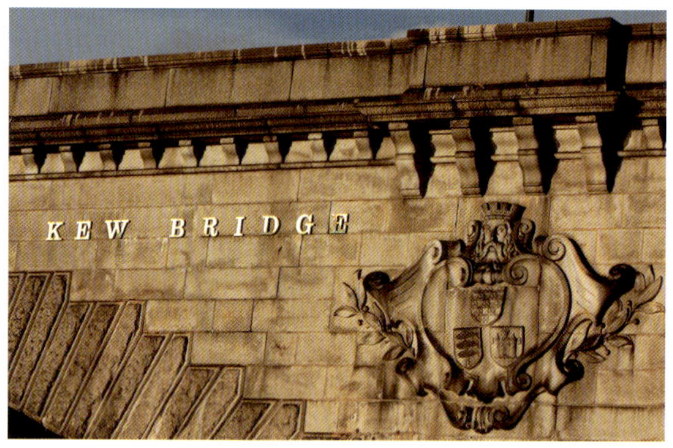

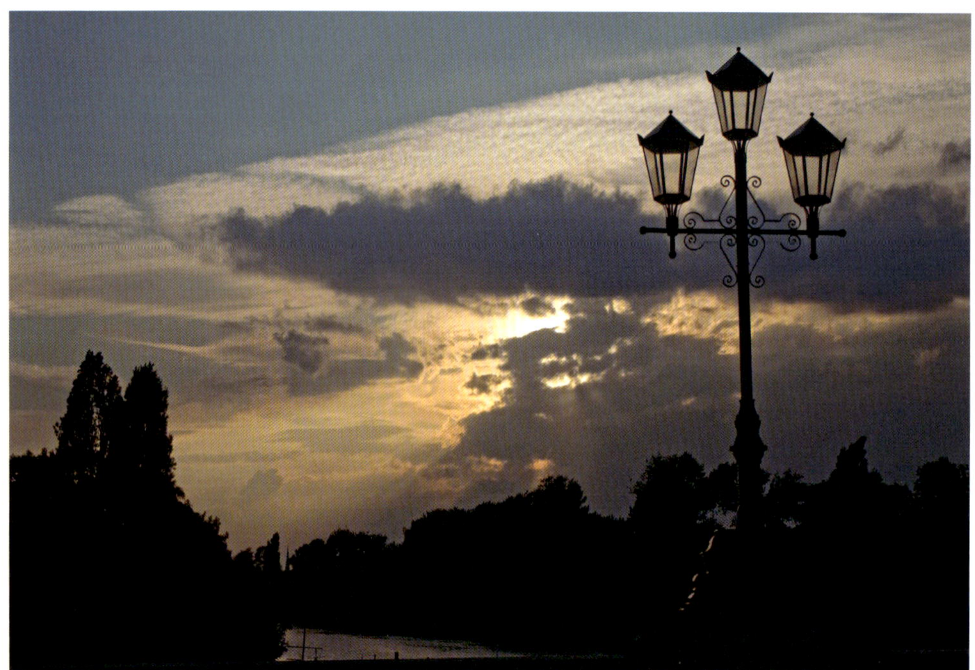

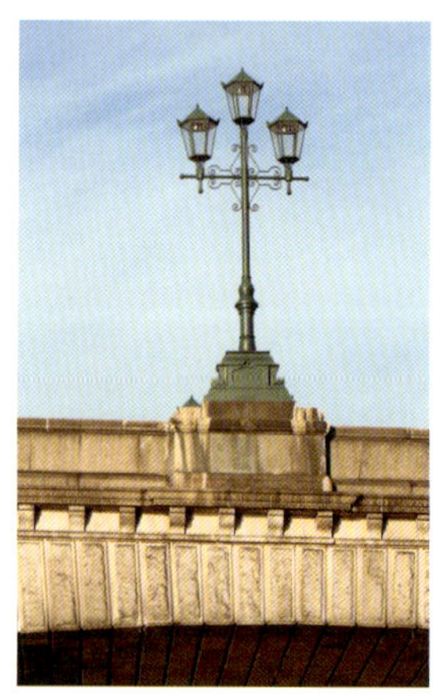

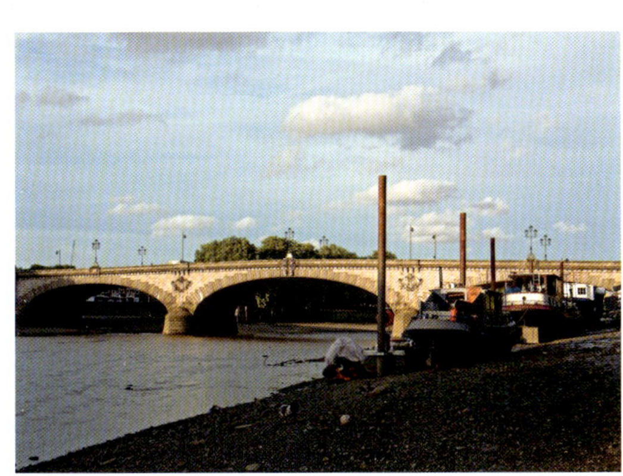
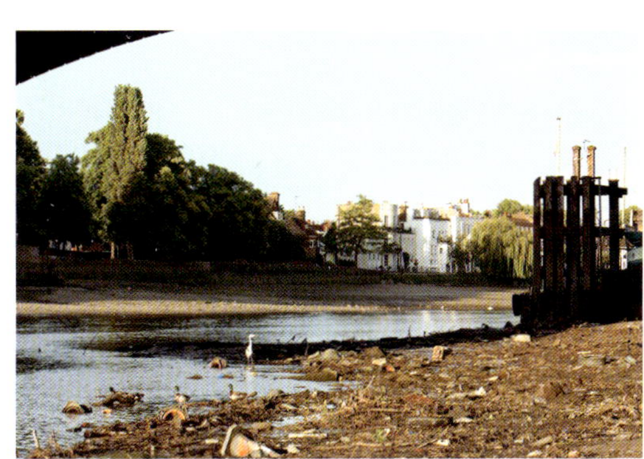
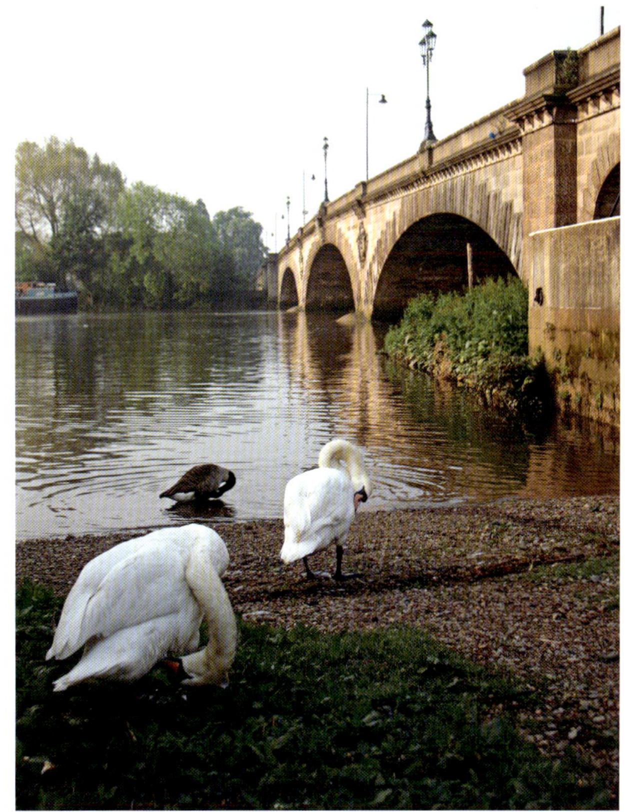
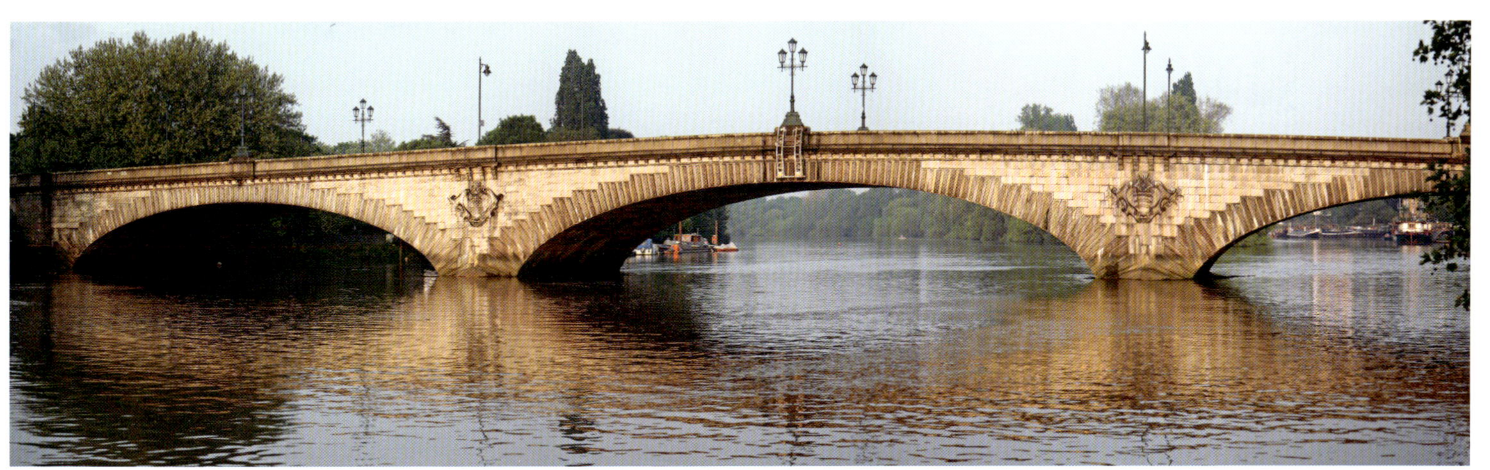

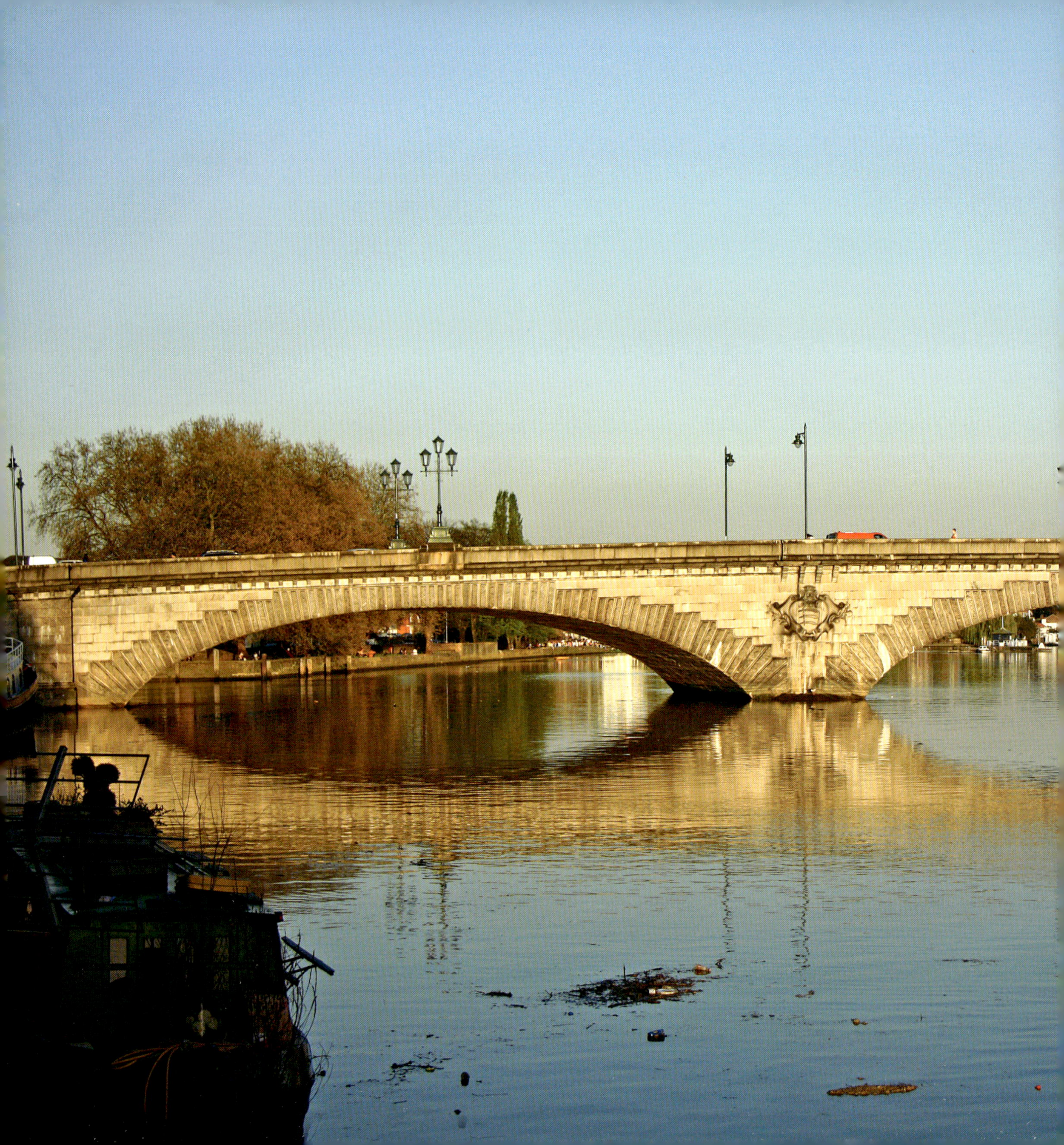

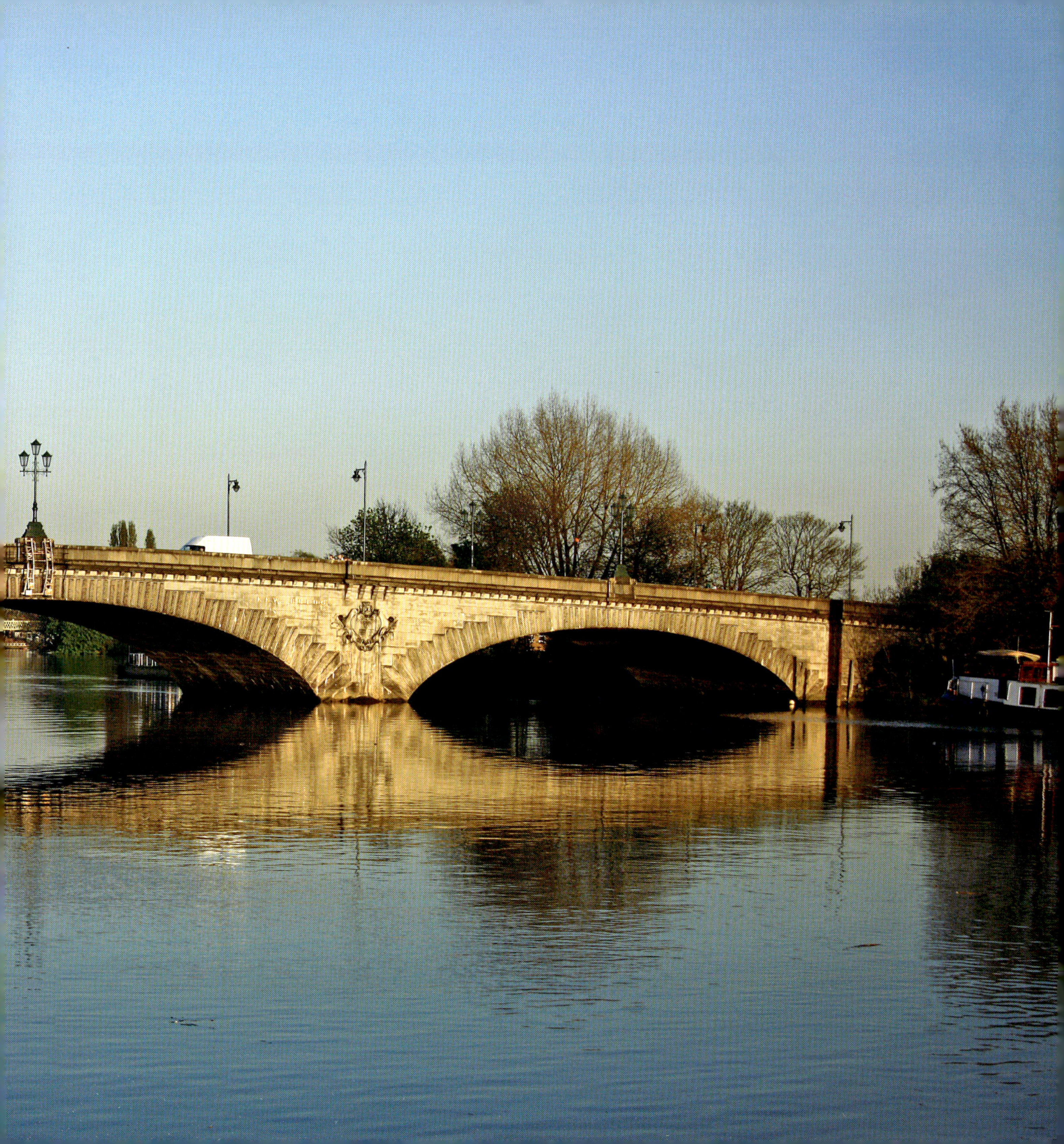

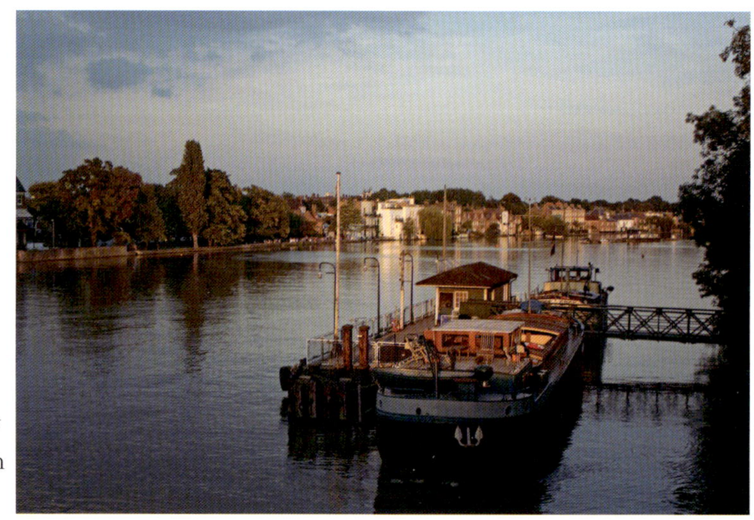

This page and opposite:
Kew Pier looking East from Kew Bridge with Strand-on the-Green in the distance.

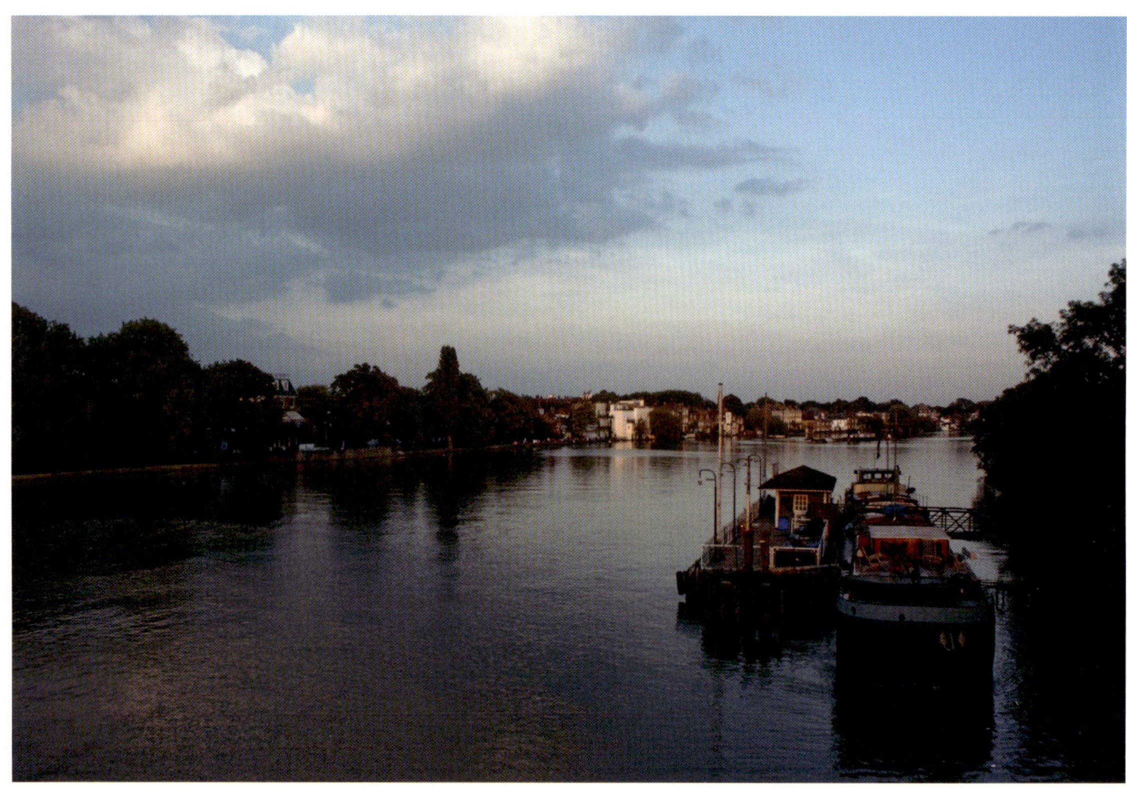

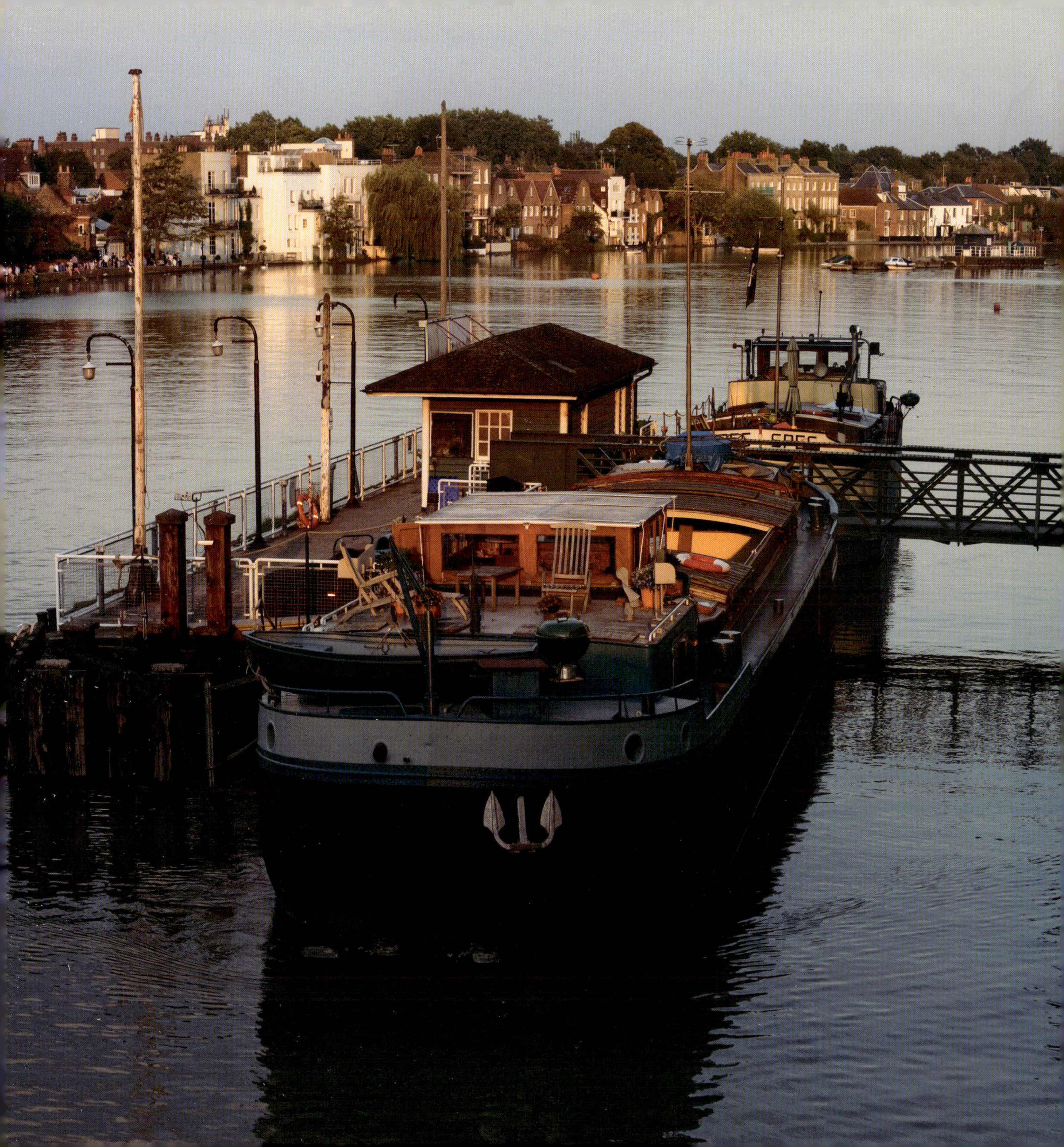

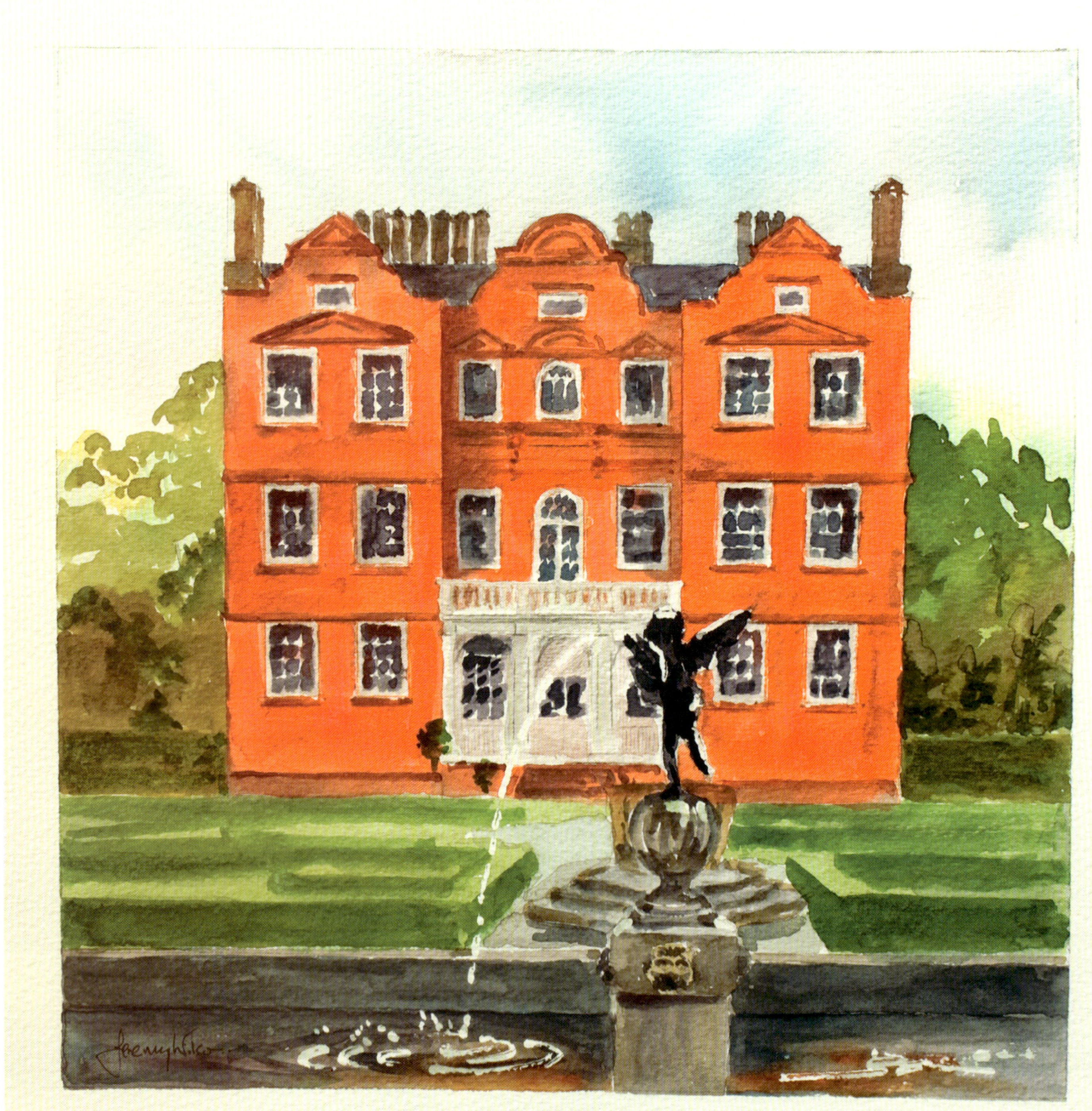

Kew Palace - this is an original watercolour by Jeremy Wilson produced exclusively for this book. A limited number of prints will be available after publication - please contact the publisher for more information.

KEW AT PLAY

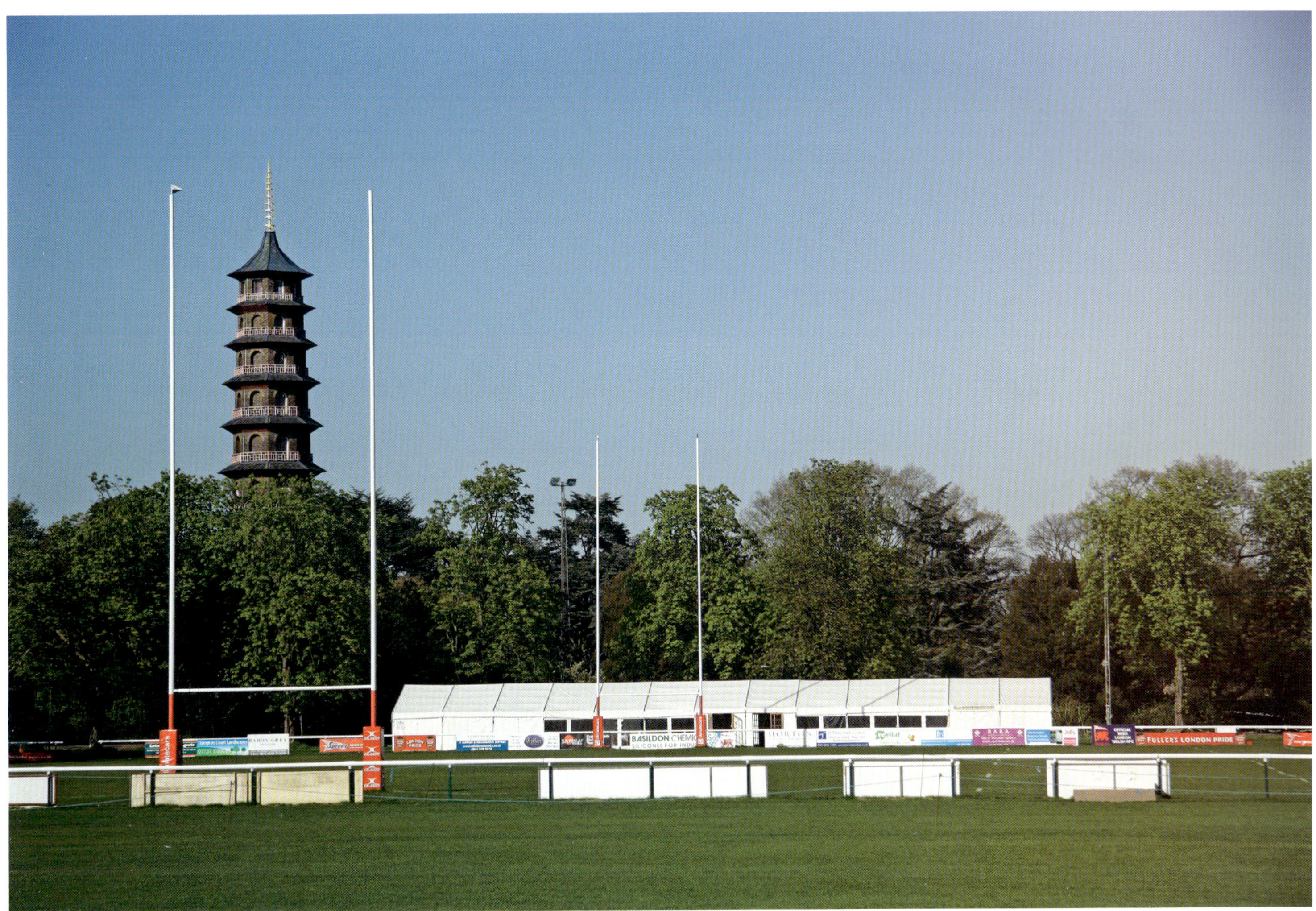

The London Welsh Rugby ground, Old Deer Park, off Kew Road with the Pagoda from Kew Gardens poking out from behind the trees.

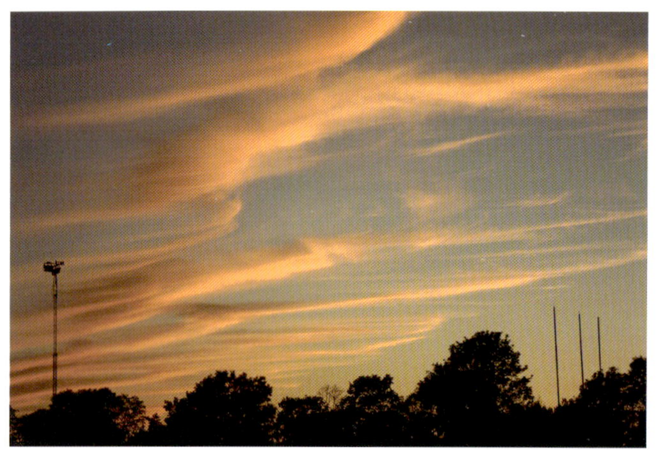

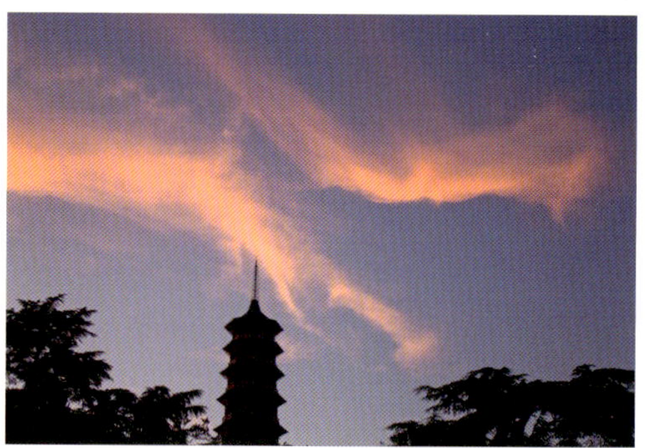

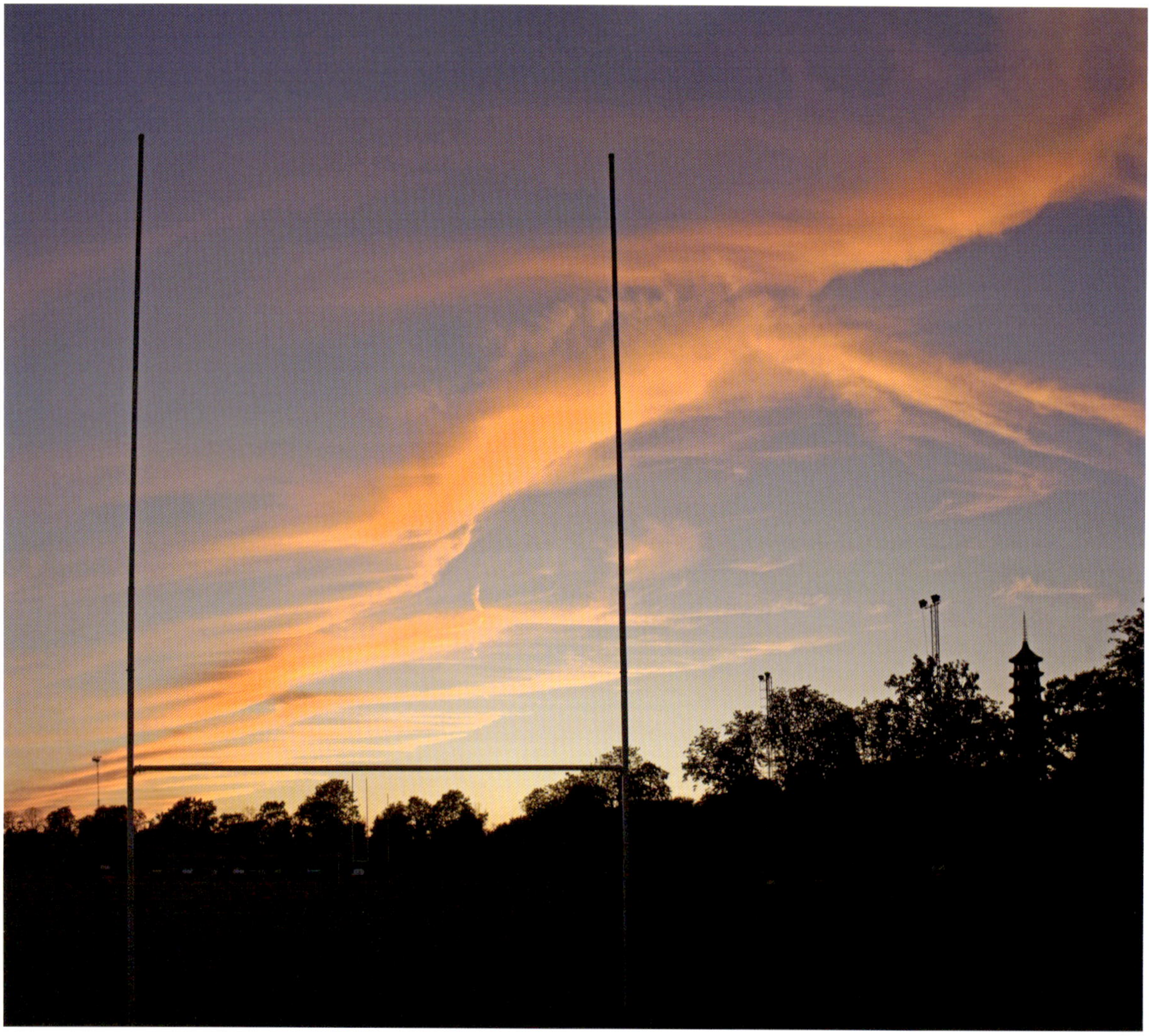

This page and opposite:
The London Welsh Rugby ground on Old Deer Park next to Kew Gardens.

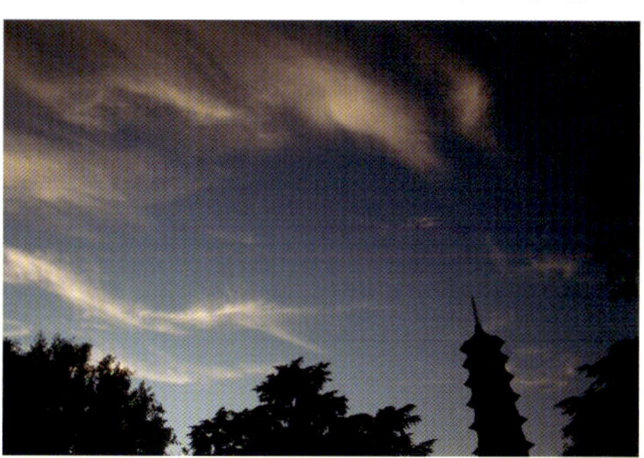

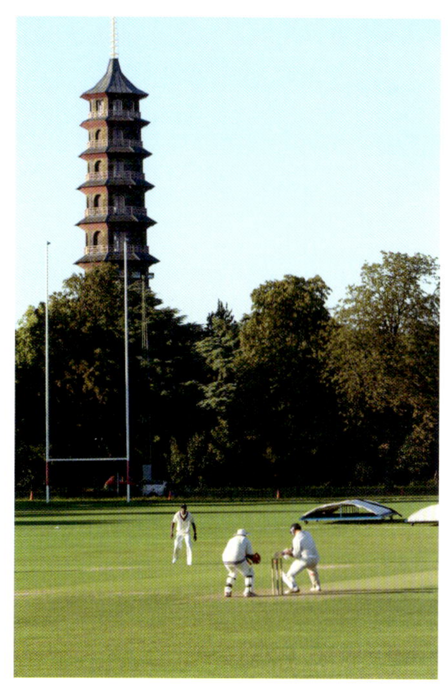

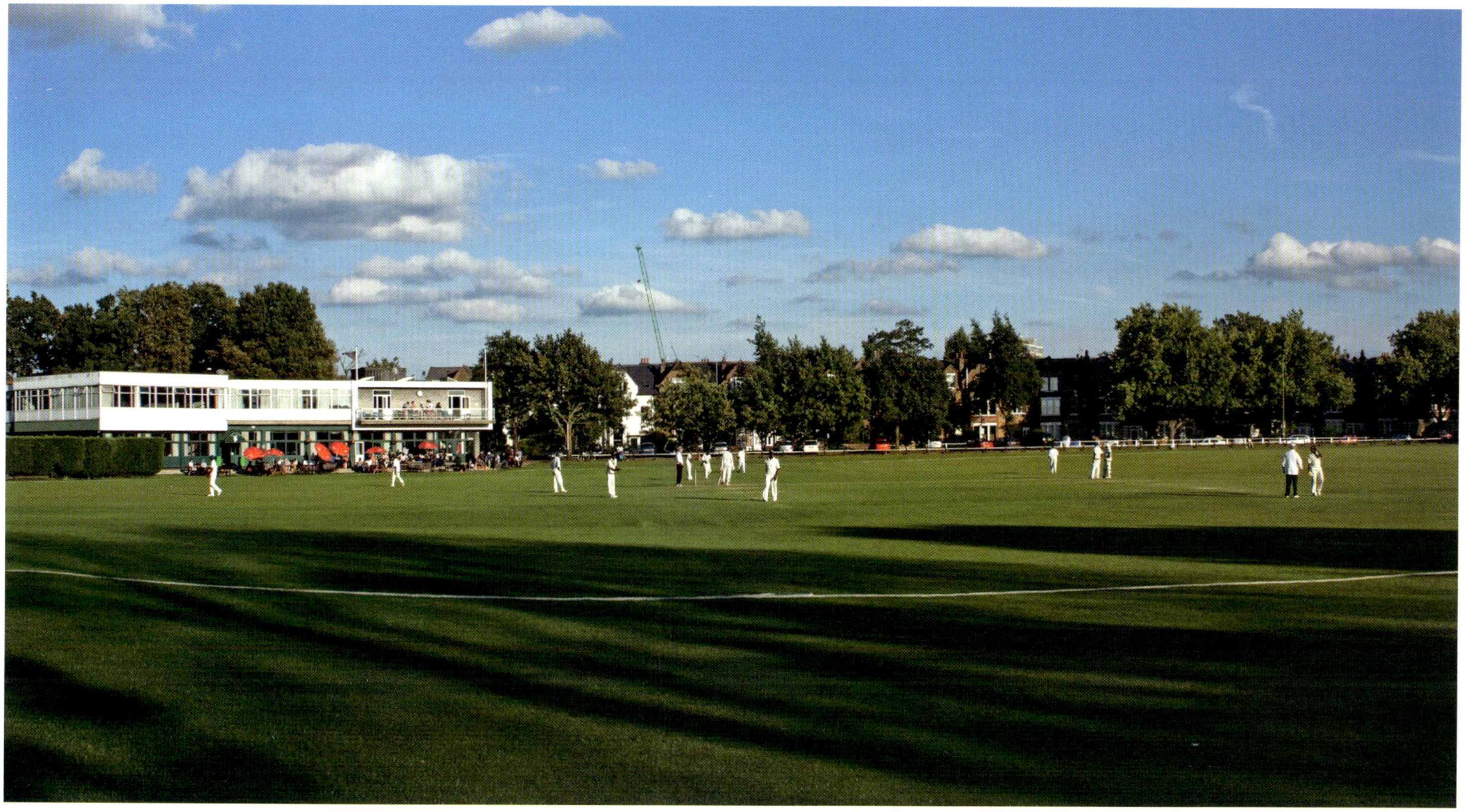

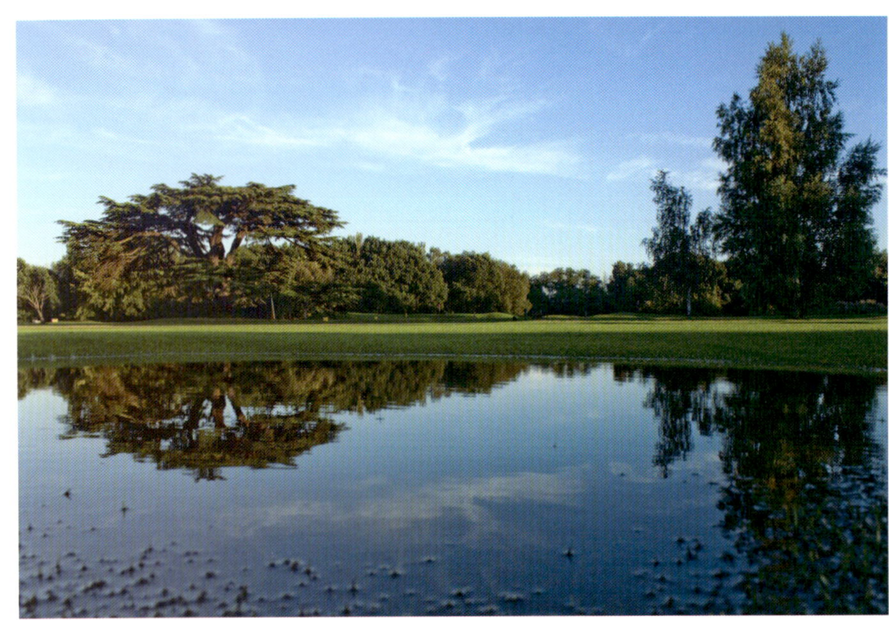

Royal Mid Surrey Golf Course: At the centre of the course can be found the Kew Observatory, which was built in 1769 for George III, who was a keen astronomer.

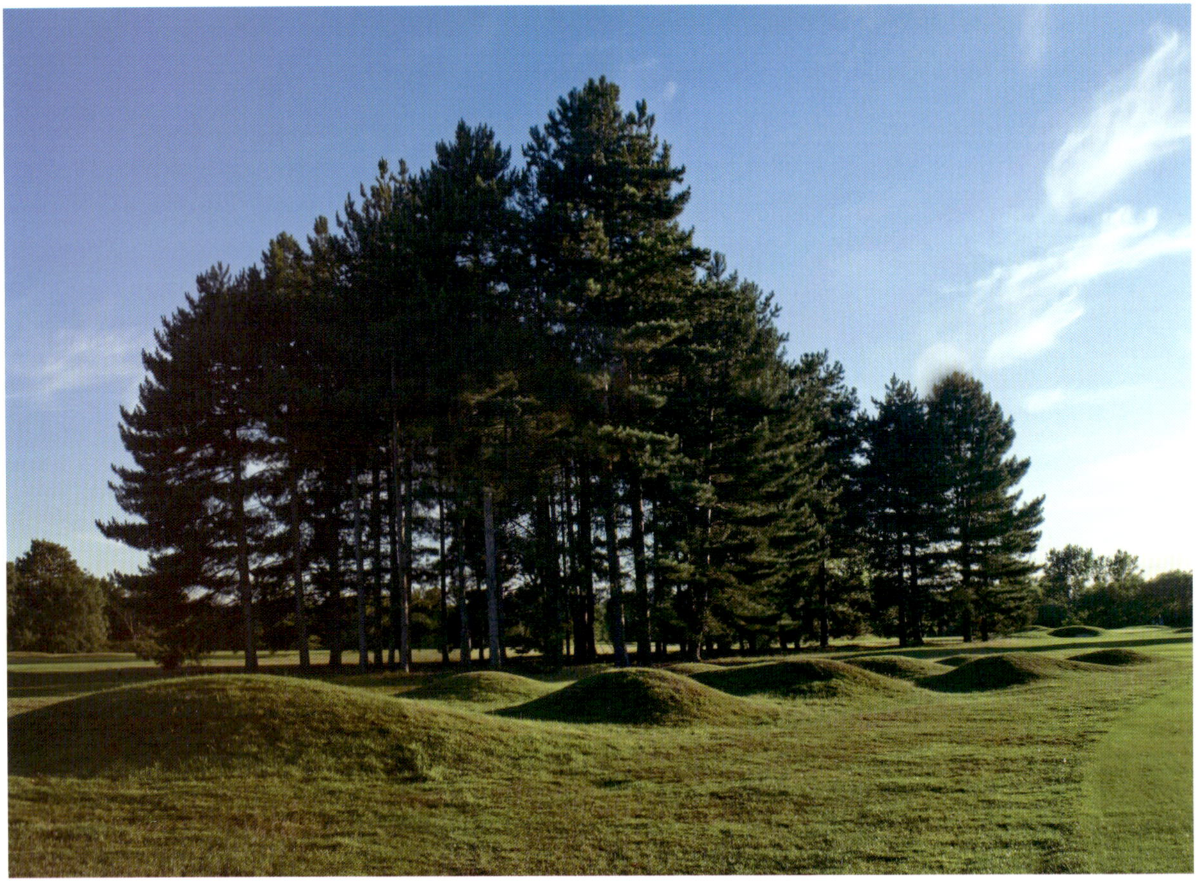

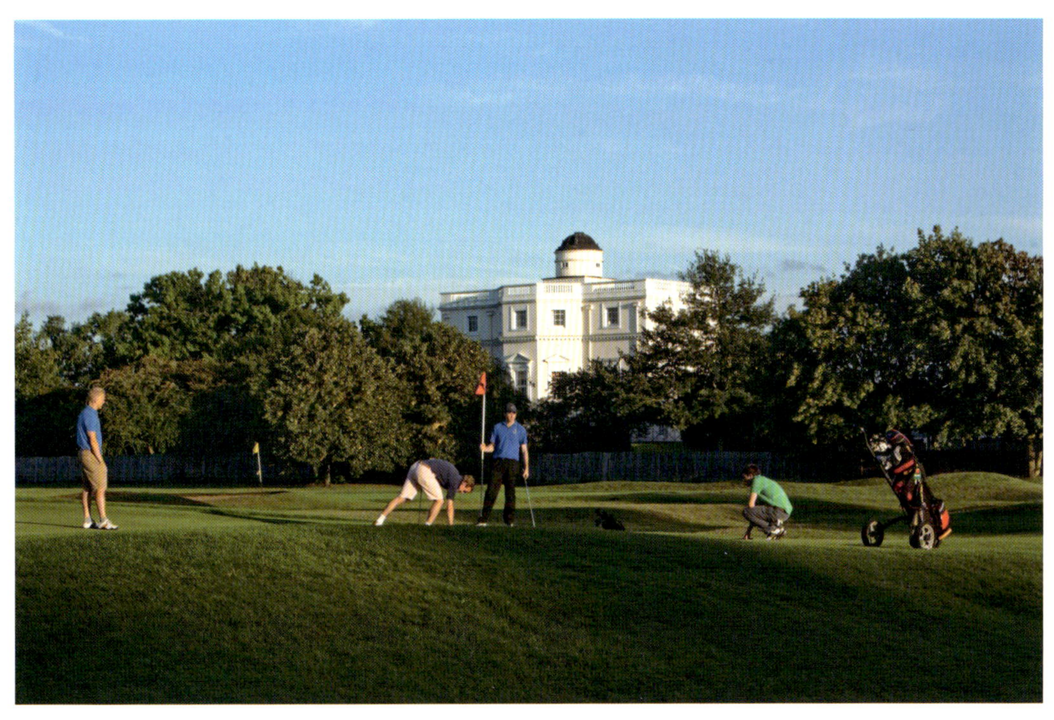

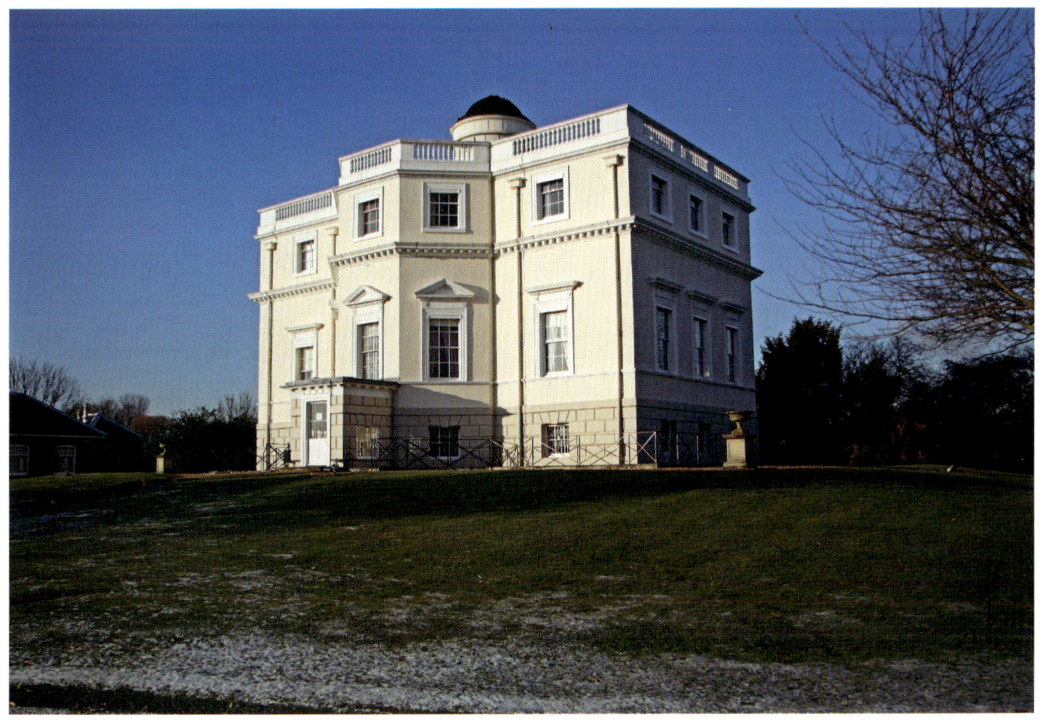

NORTH SHEEN BOWLS CLUB

The club was started in 1927. It came from what was the lawn garden at the back of the 'Beehive' public house (the publican was a Mr Jack Kisby) and the first President was Ald. J.H.Mears, of Chelsea Football Club. In 1940 a very large bomb virtually destroyed the green and for the next 10 years North Sheen played all their games away from home. The green and its buildings were rebuilt in 1949 and the ground was re-opened in 1950. The club is still going strong with a Ladies section introduced in 1990.

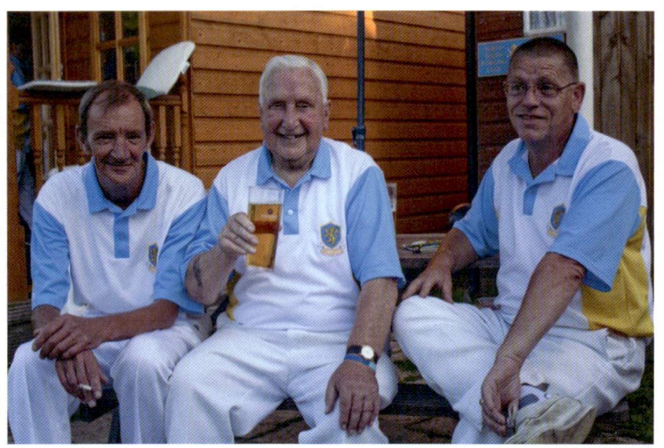

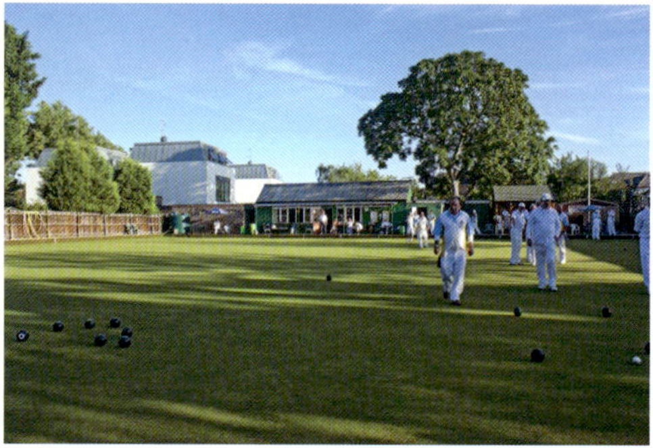

Pictured far left: in their fine club colours are from the left Gordon Dymock, John Wells (aged 91) their oldest member and Kevin Knight.

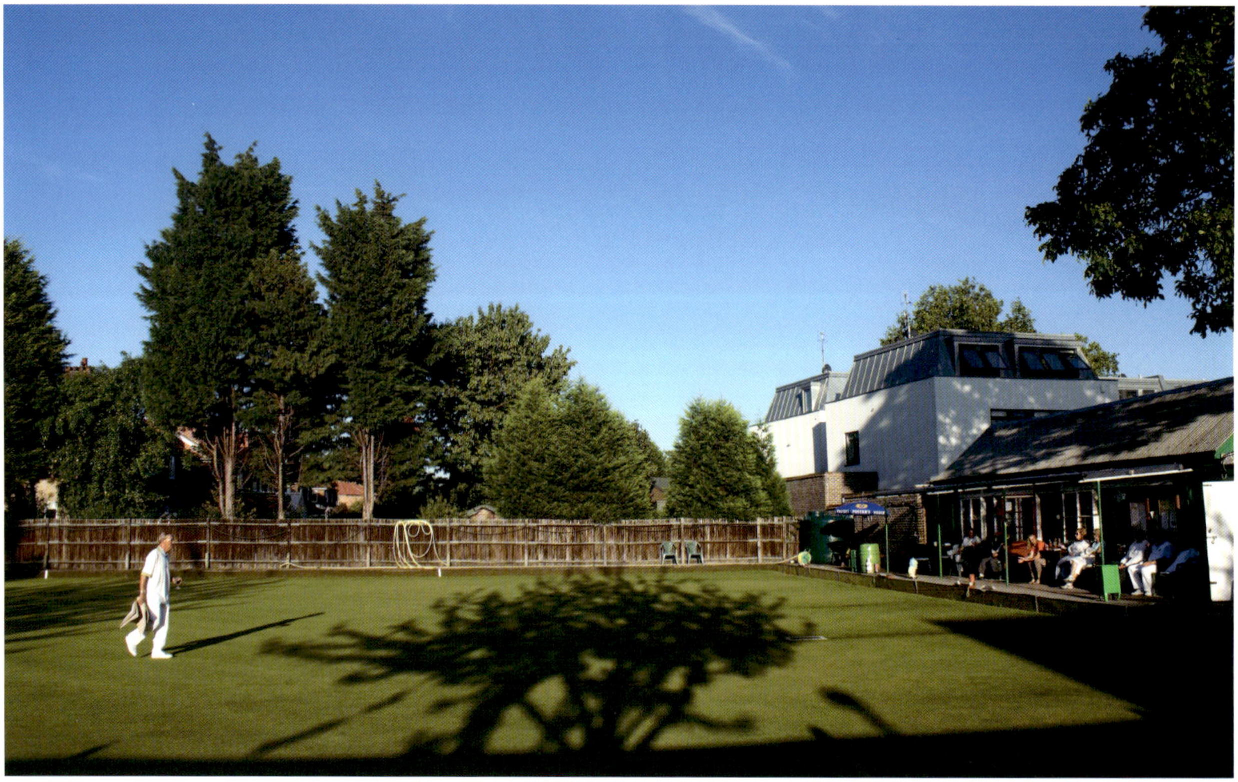

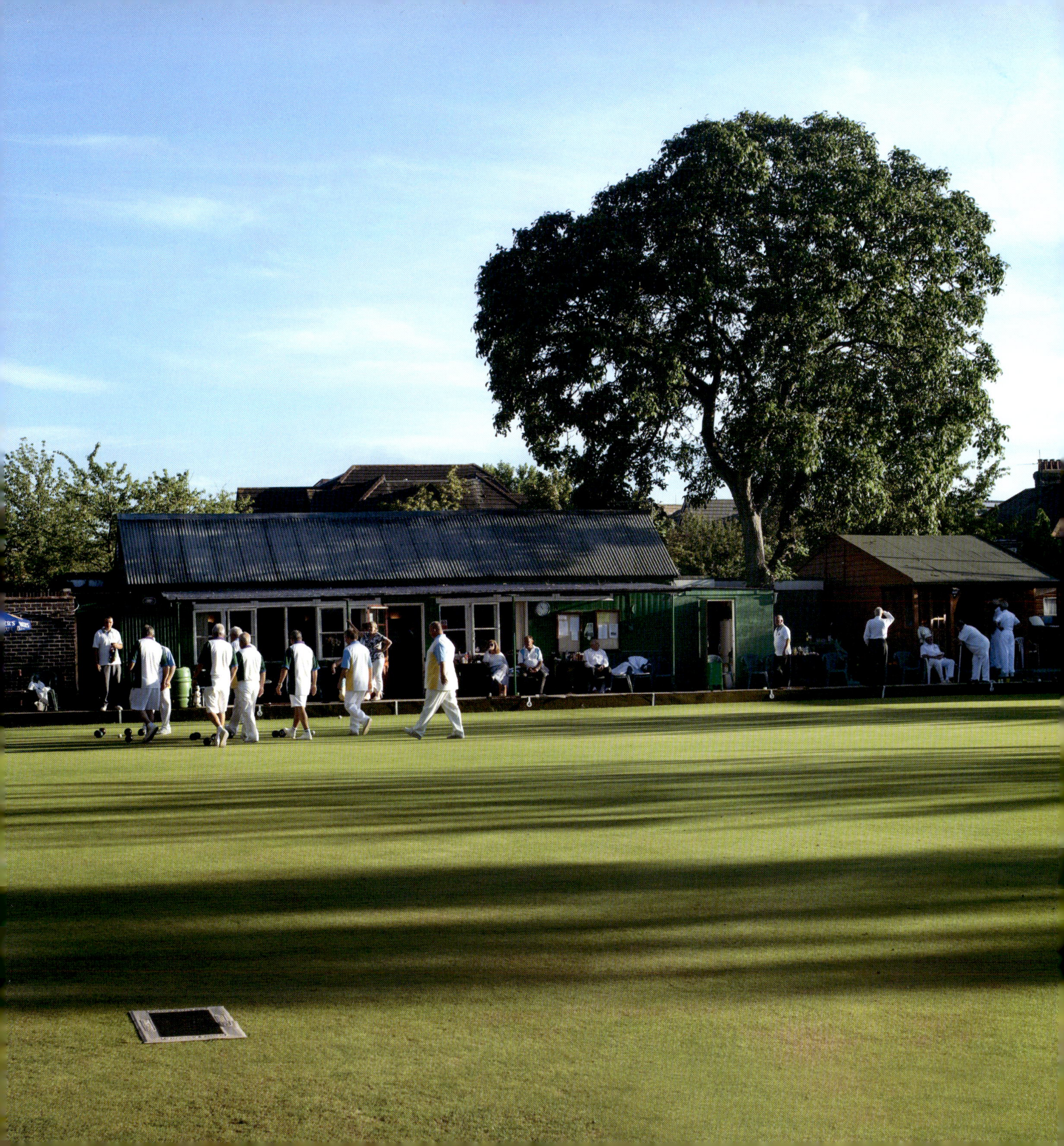

NORTH SHEEN RECREATION GROUND

Opened in 1909 and extended in 1923, this park was originally part of an orchard belonging to the Popham Estate.

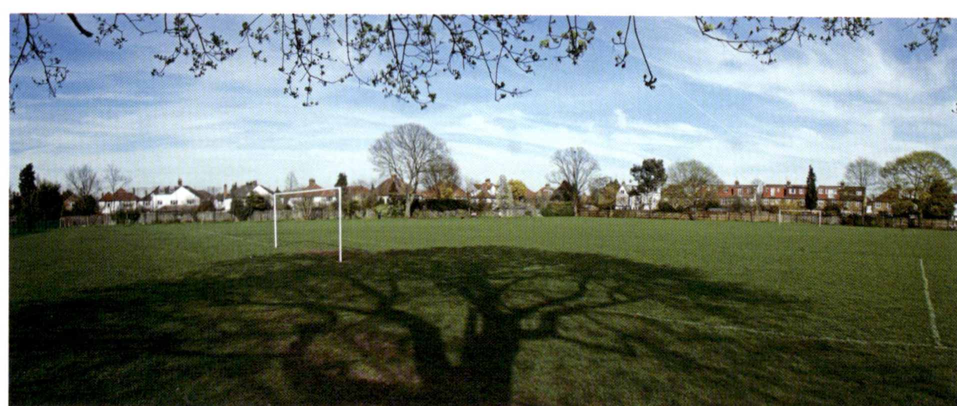

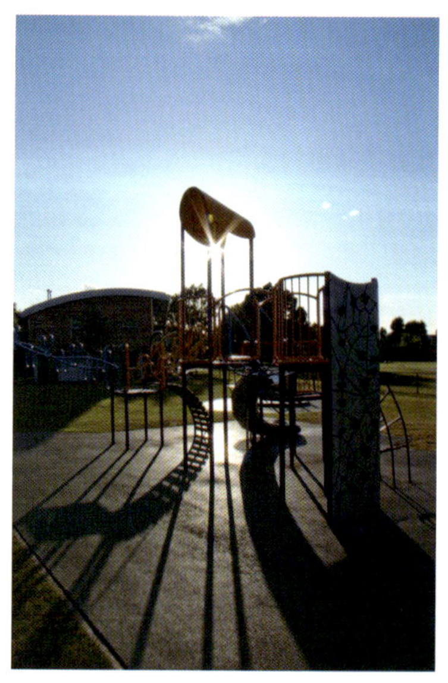

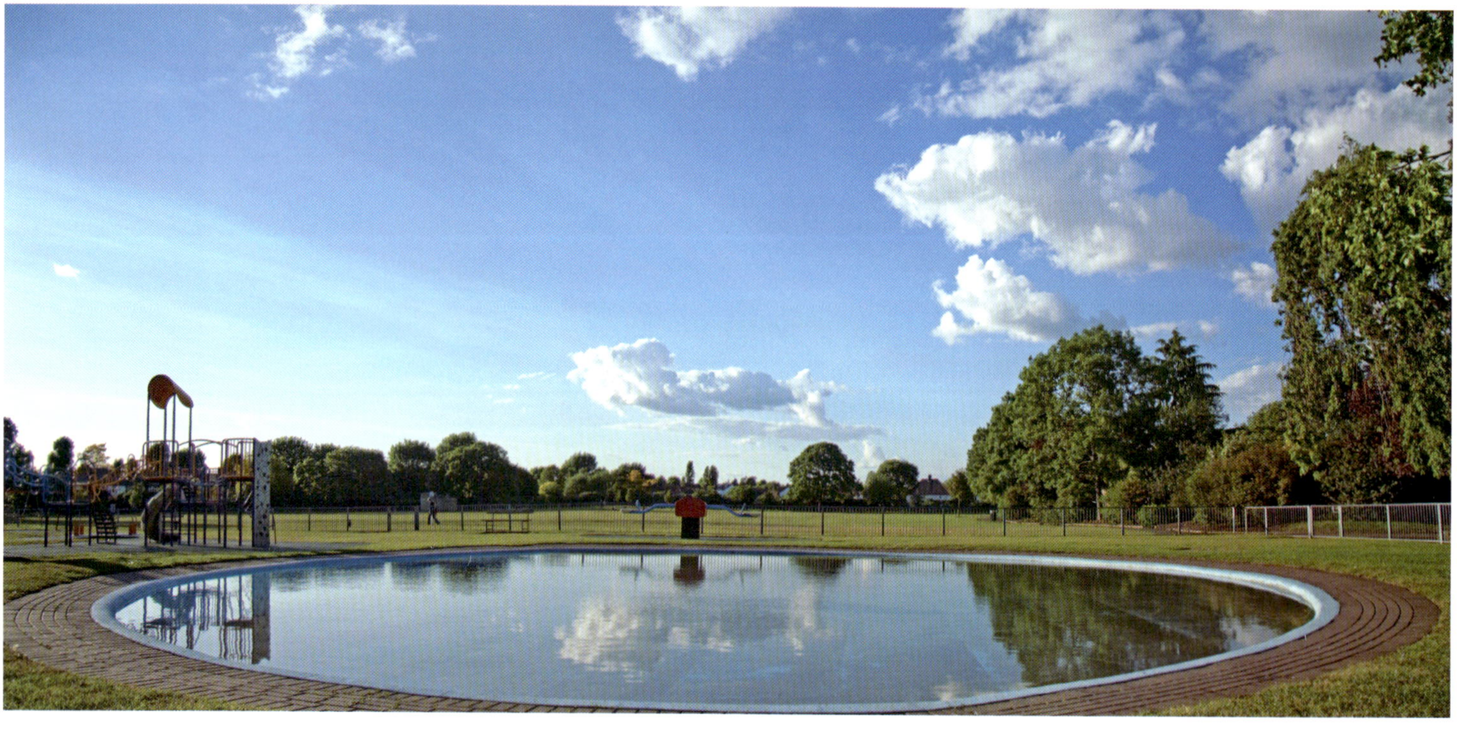

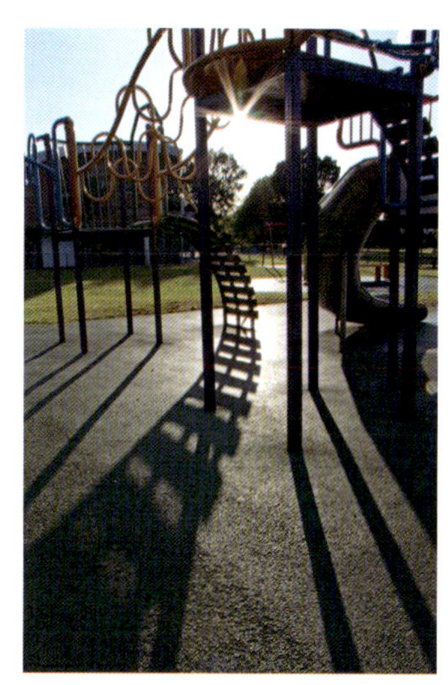

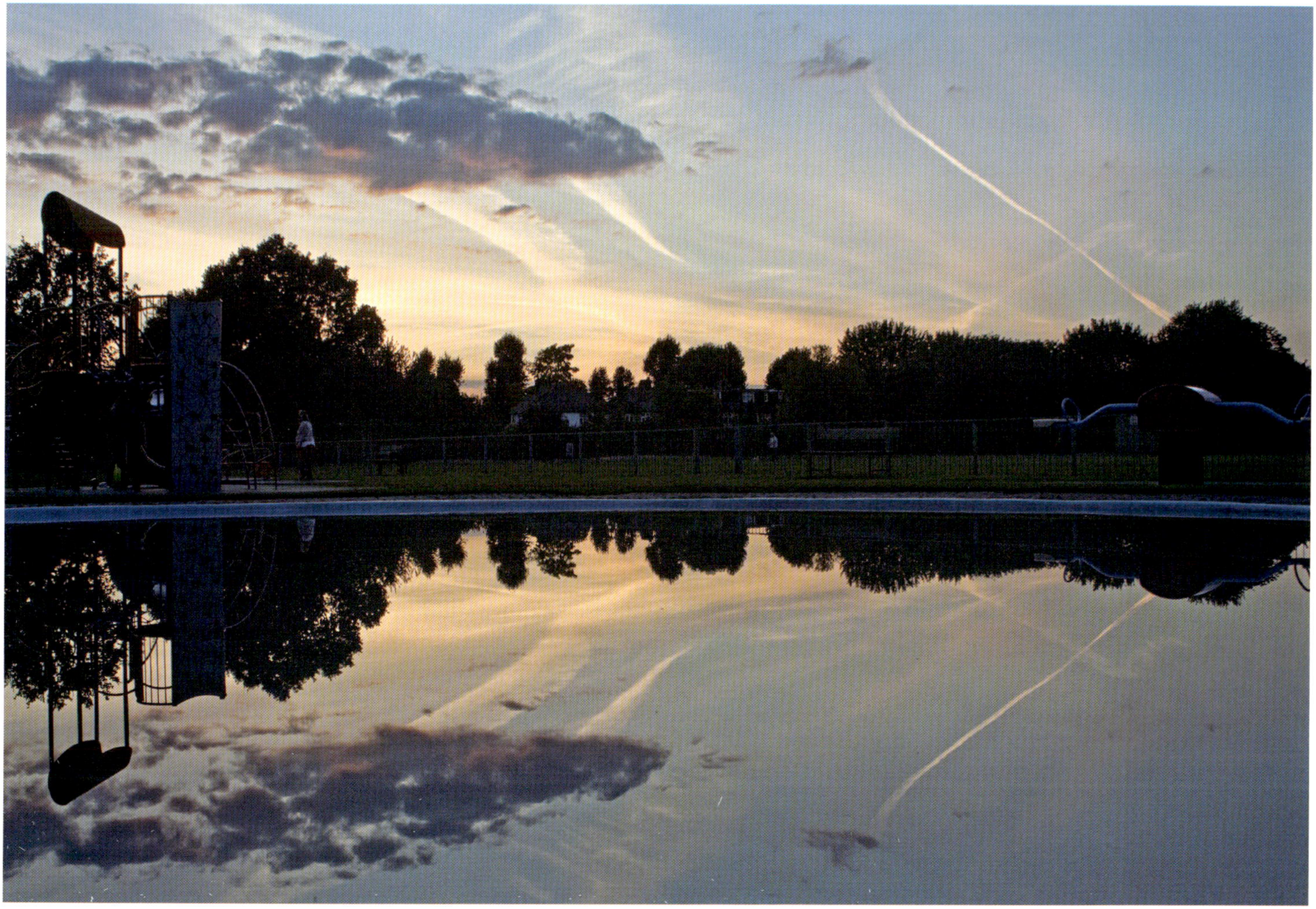

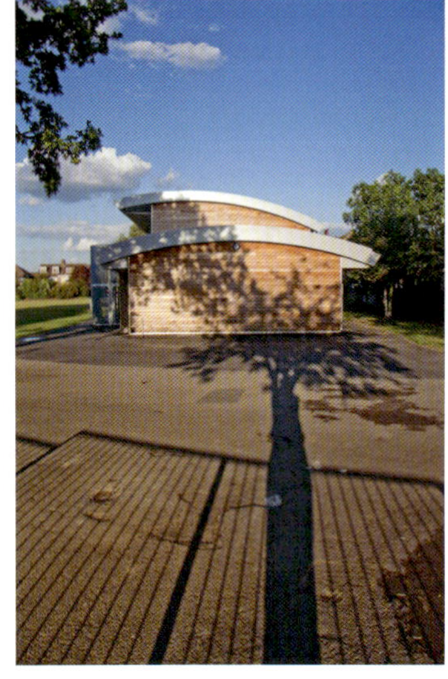

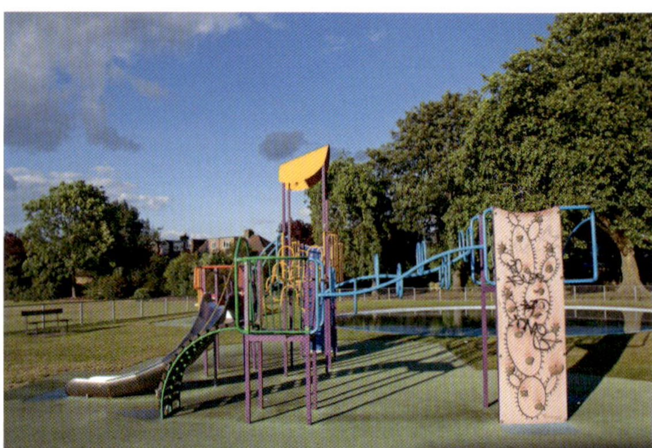

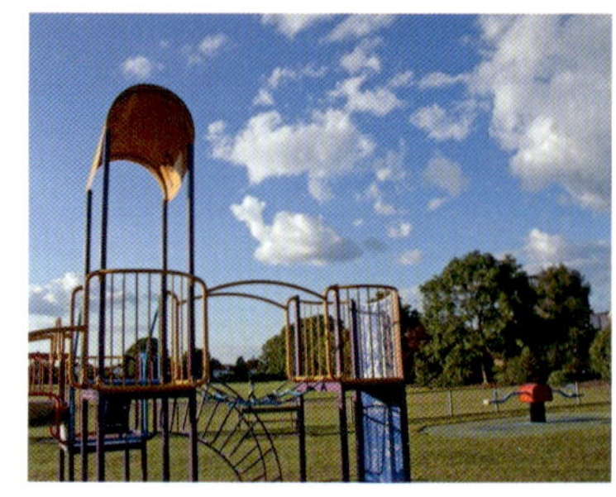

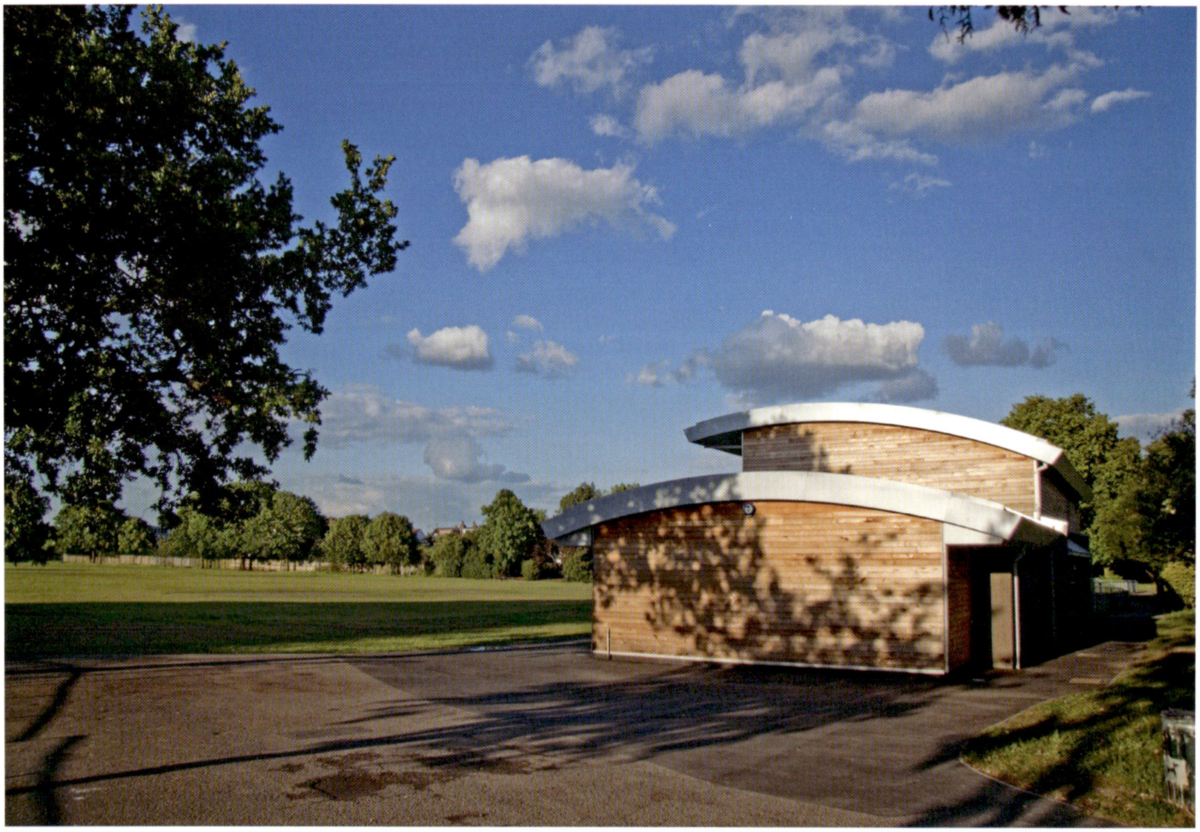

Left and top left: The pavilion in North Sheen Recreation Ground
Top middle & right: The playground

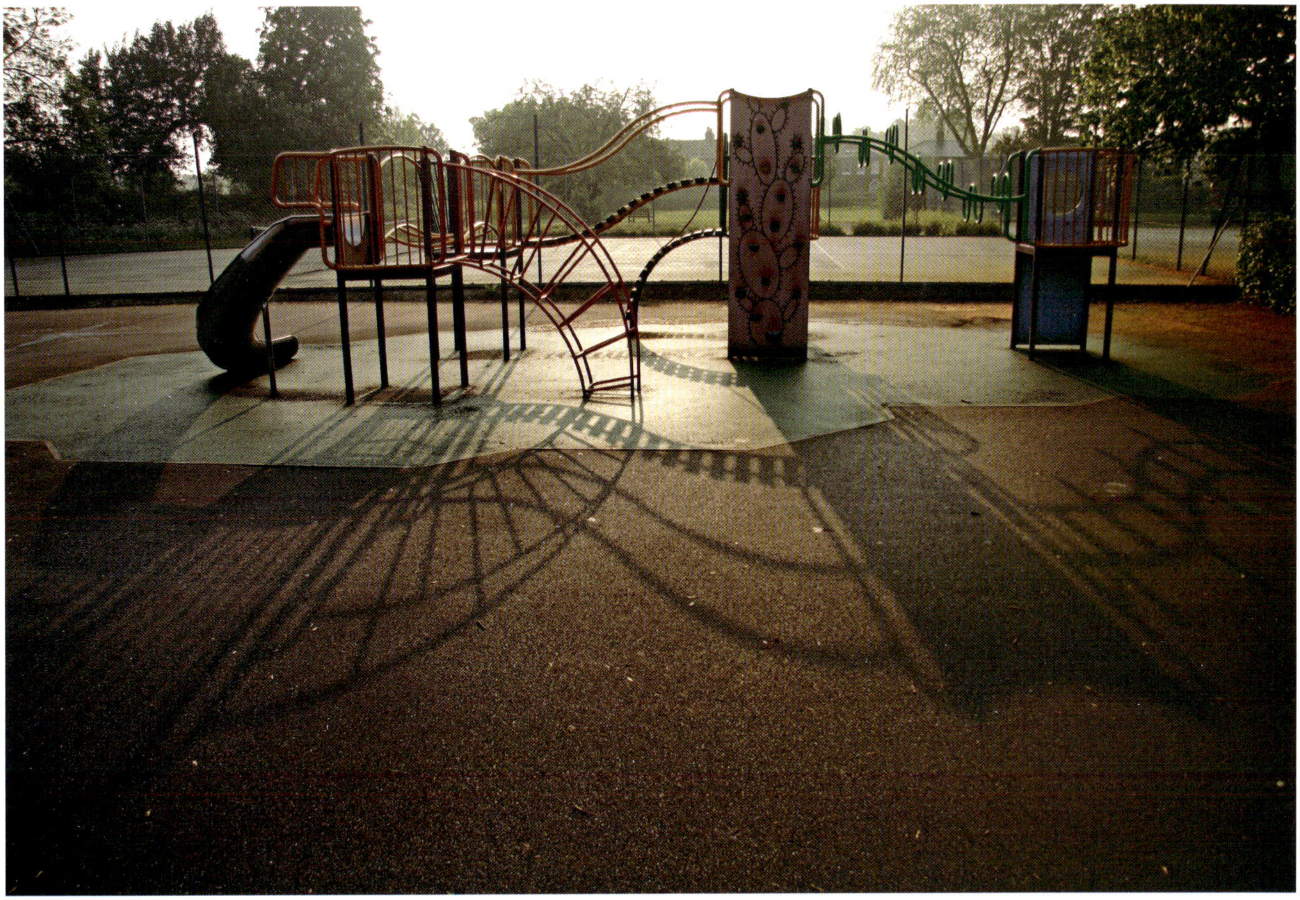

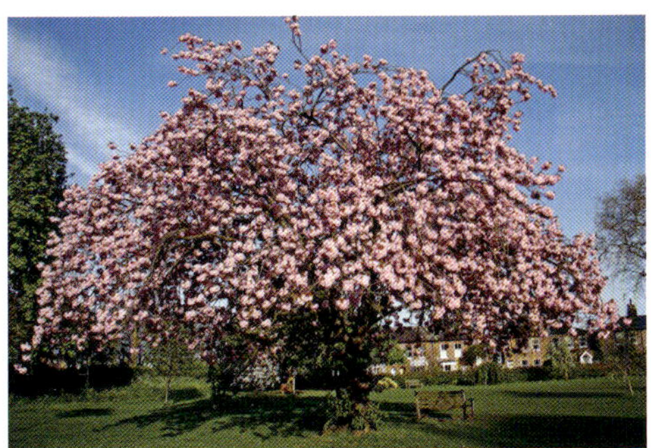

Westerley Ware:
Bordering the river by Kew Pier, this small park also contains tennis courts and a playground.

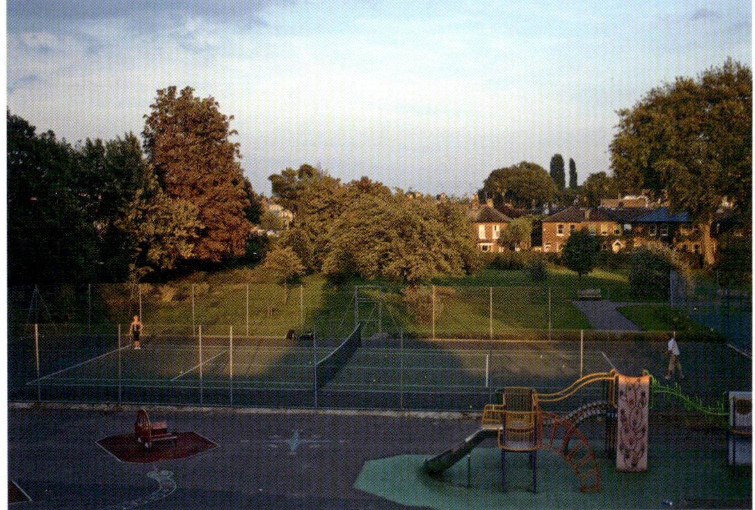

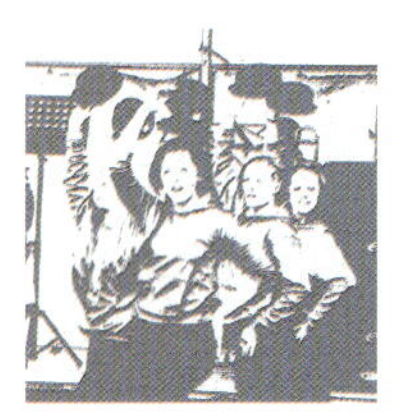 SHOWS ON THE GREEN

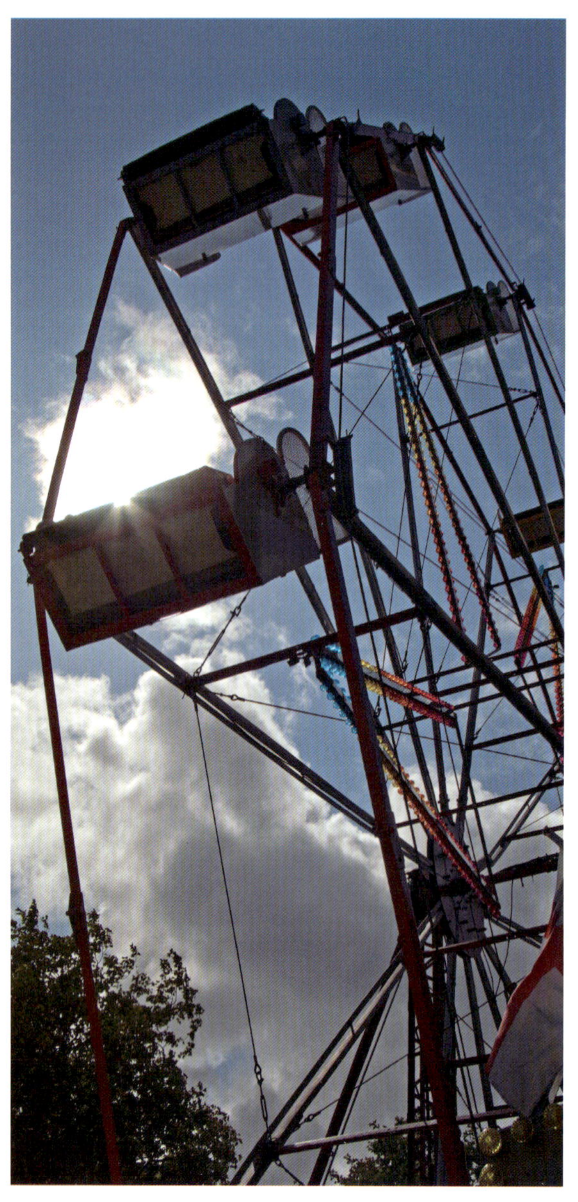

The Kew Midsummer Fete 2011 was a huge success despite the weather trying to dampen down the festivities. Lots of money was raised for local good causes and much fun enjoyed by the masses of people who came along.

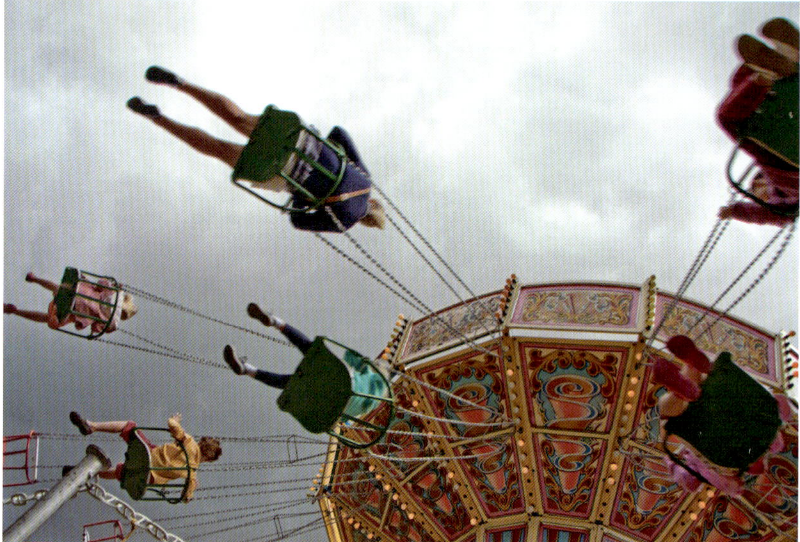

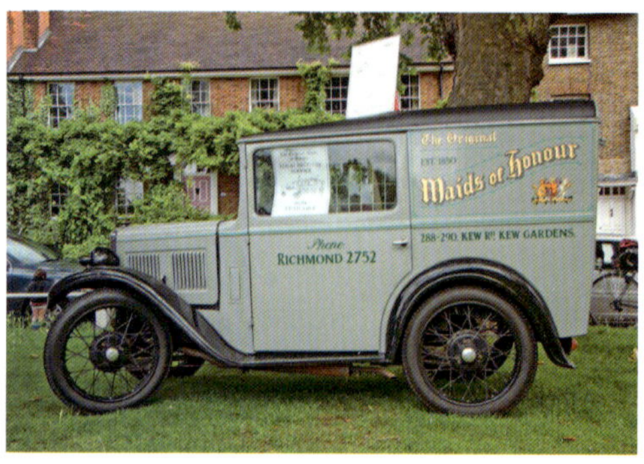

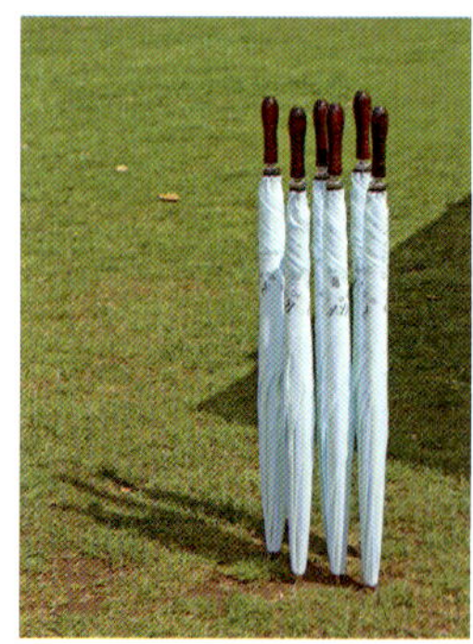

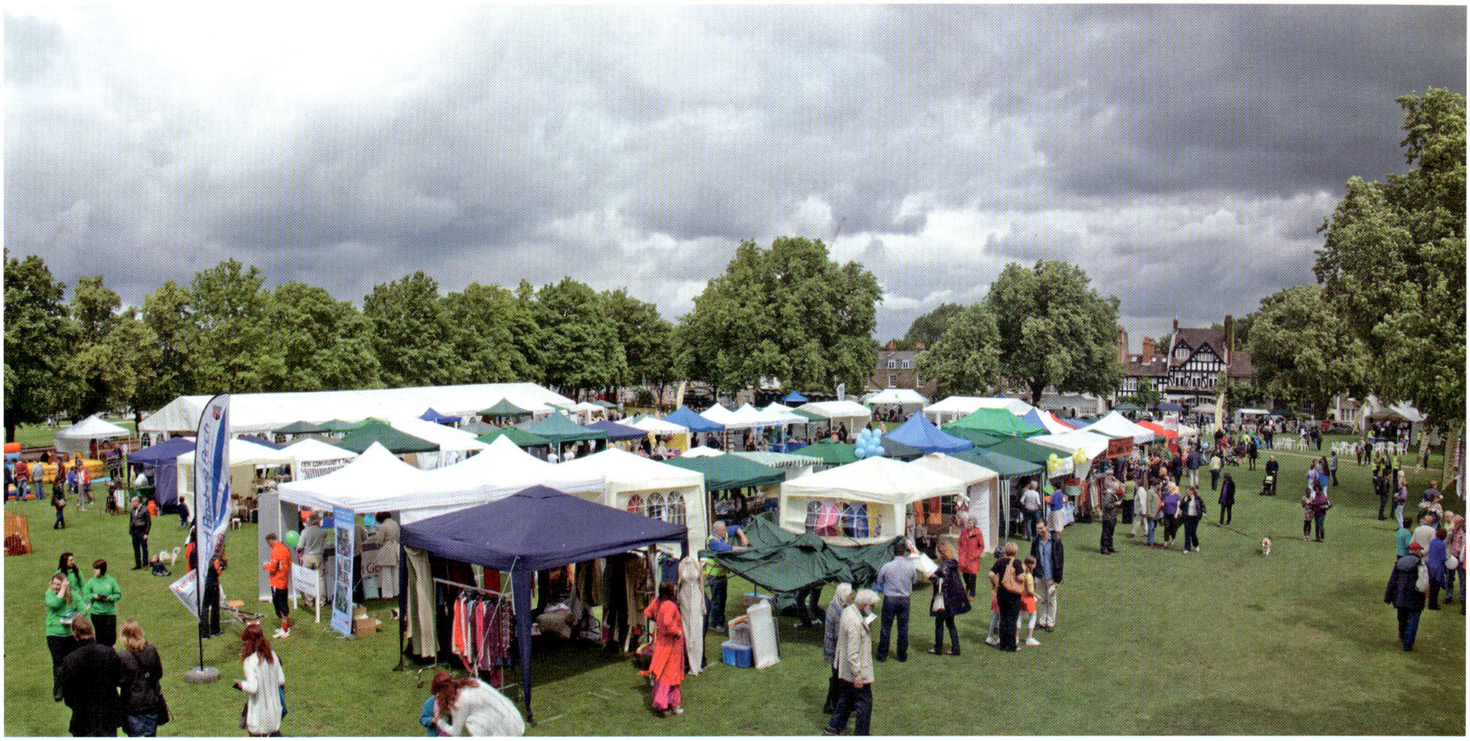

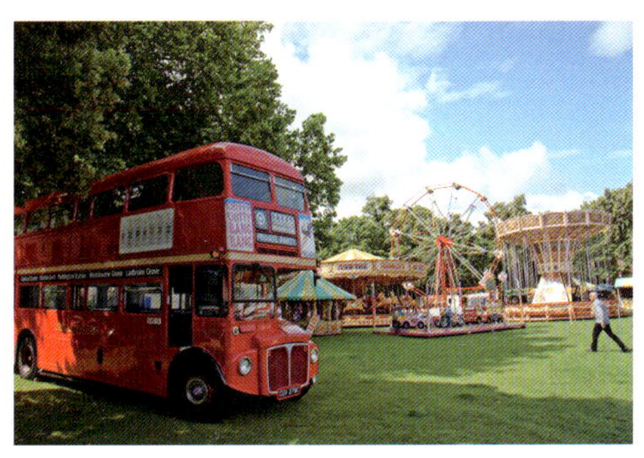

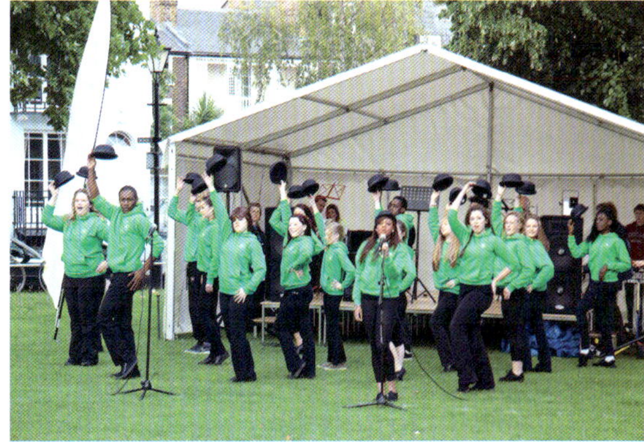

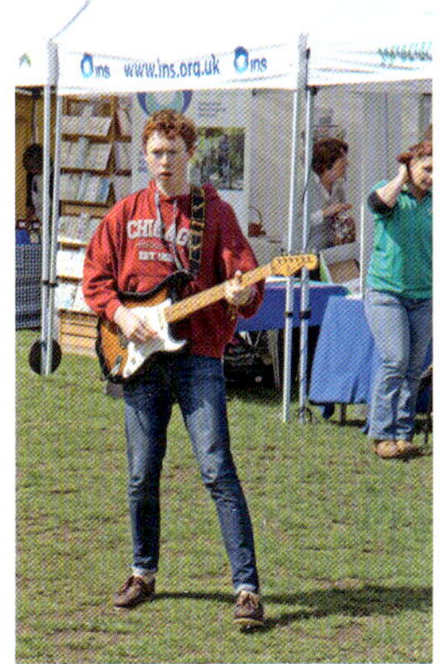
www.ins.org.uk
CHICAGO

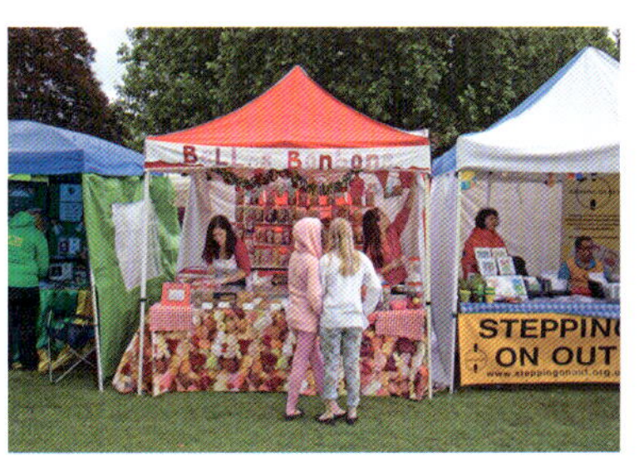
ON OUT

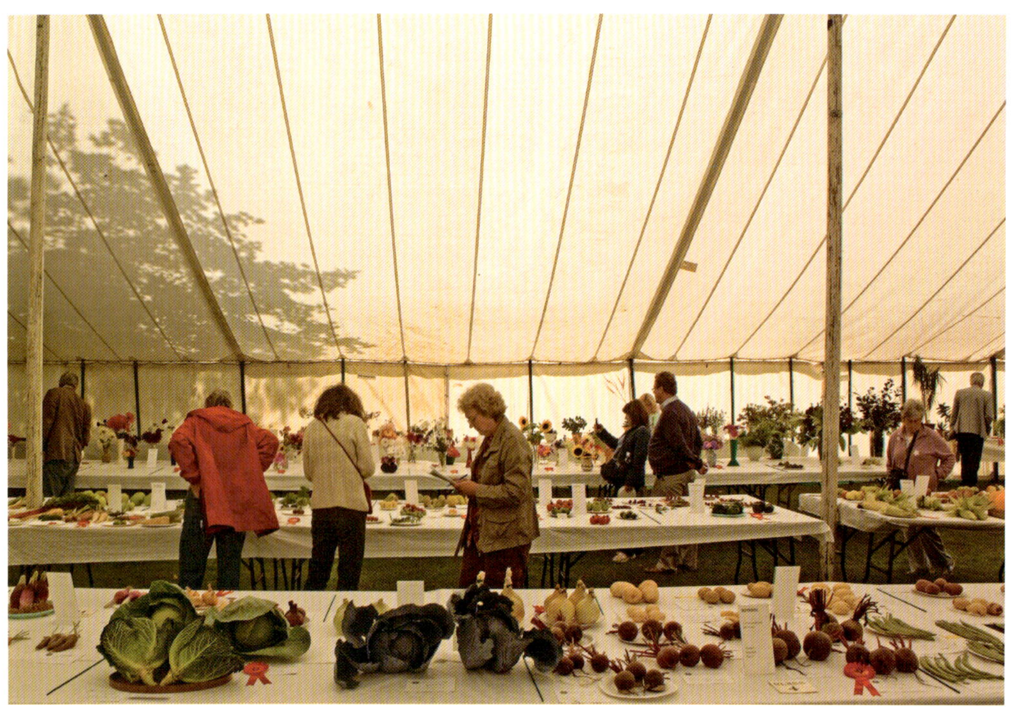

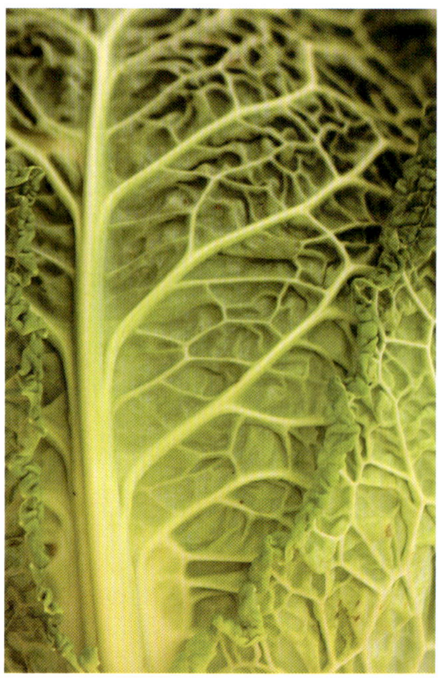

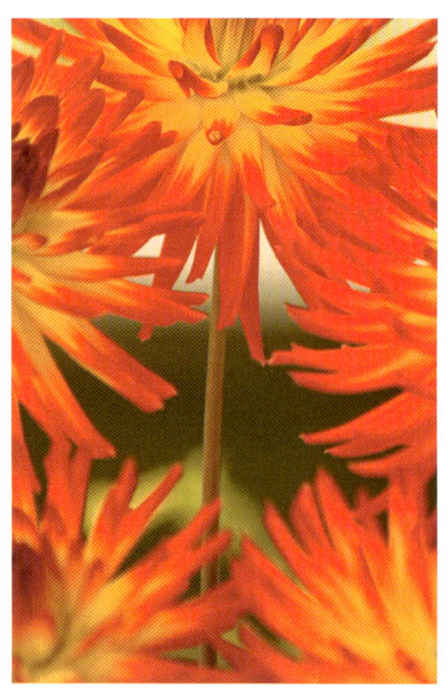

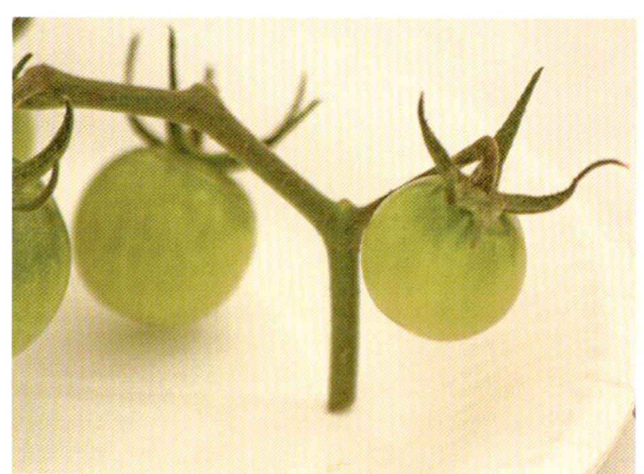

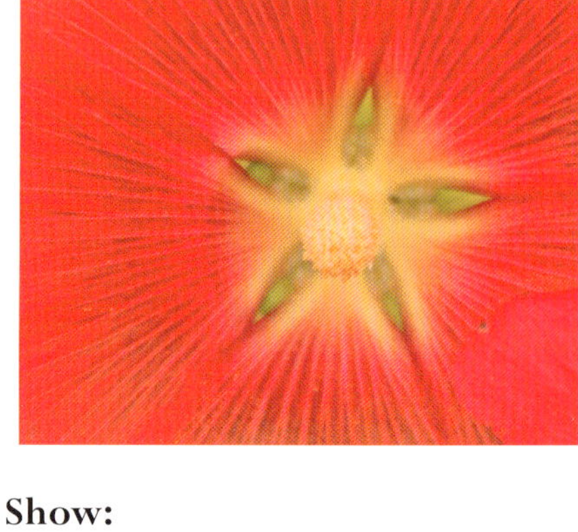

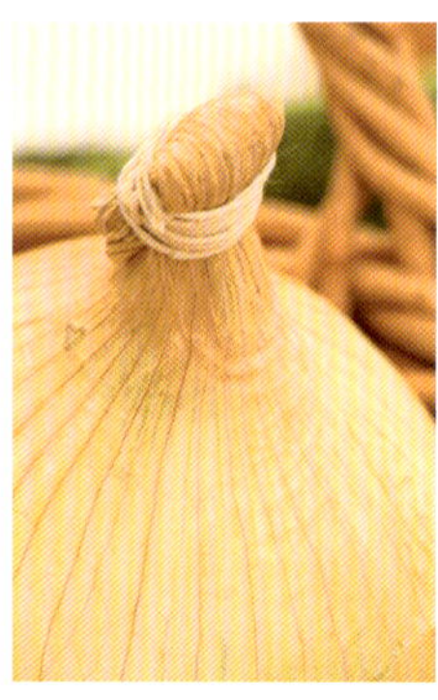

Kew Horticultural Show:
This is the pride and joy of Kew's Horticultural Society, an extremely lively organisation that formed in 1938. For the keen amateur as much as the seasoned gardener, many members can be seen tending their plots down by the river at Short Lots (see page 82).

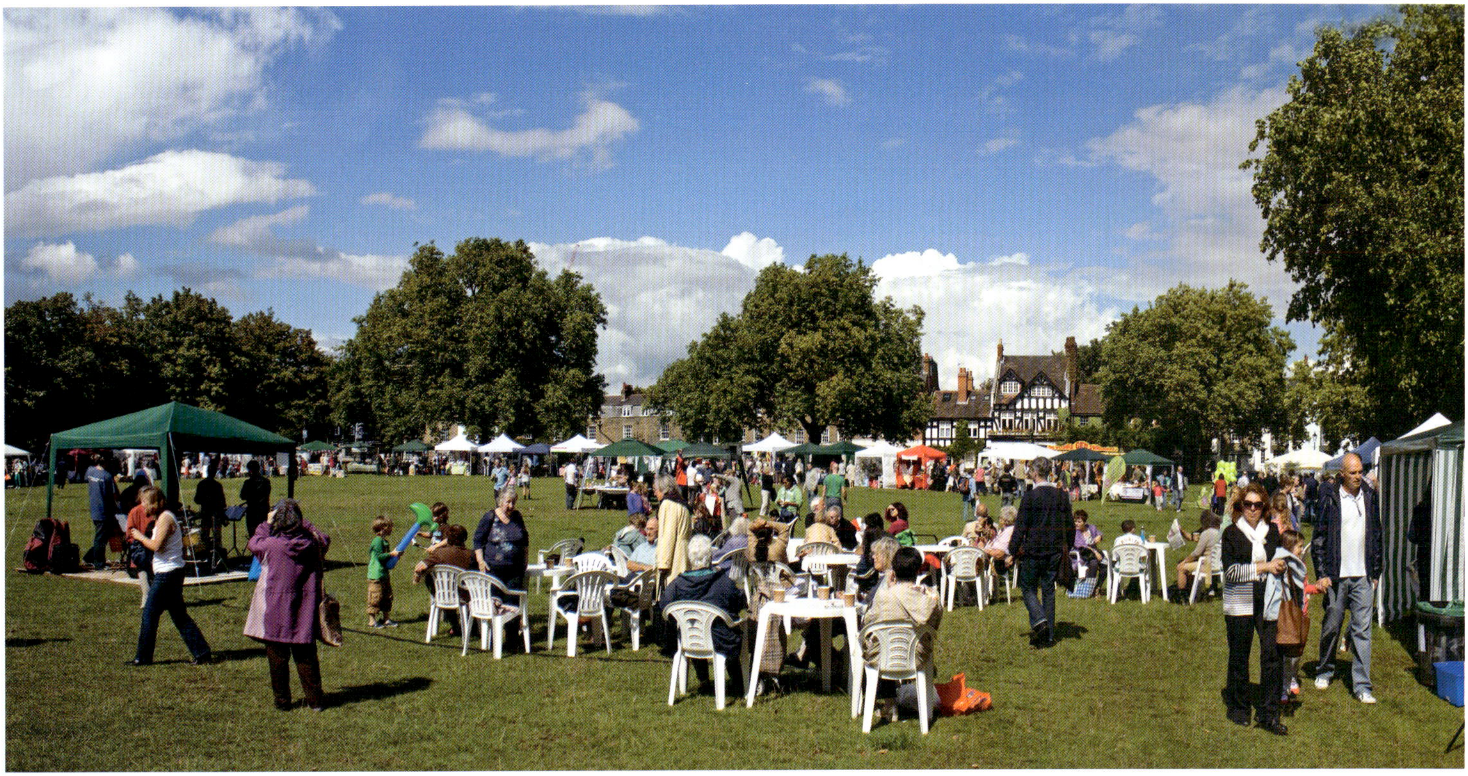

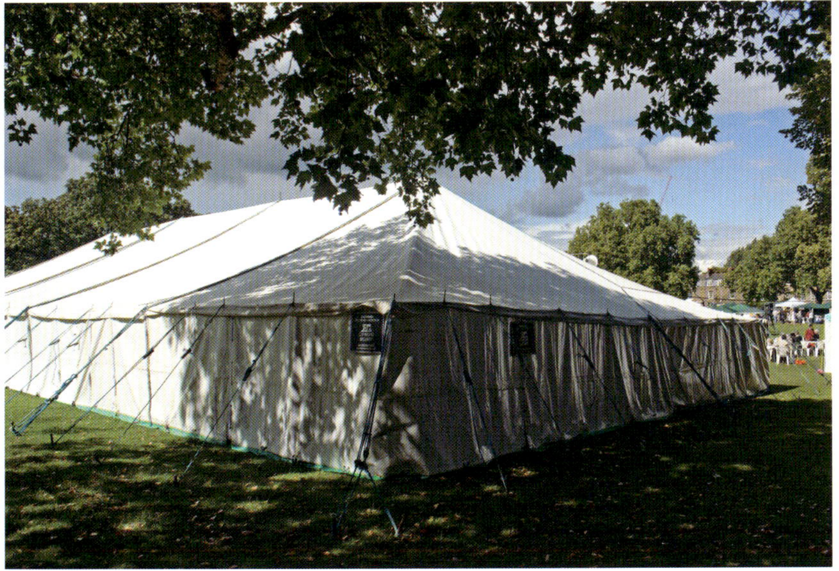

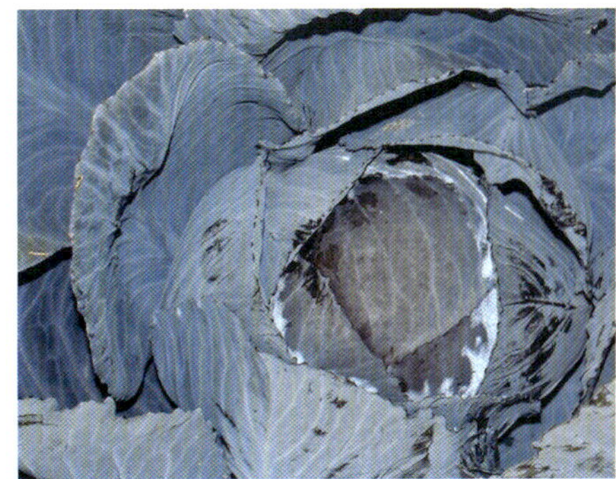

The show, traditionally held on the Saturday of August Bank Holiday, is when The Green comes alive with stalls selling food, plants, books and bric-a-brac. Forming a great circle in front of the marquee, the action really gets going as members present their fruit, flowers and vegetables for the judges to award their annual prizes. Keenly contested, there are no less than 20 cups and medals to be won.

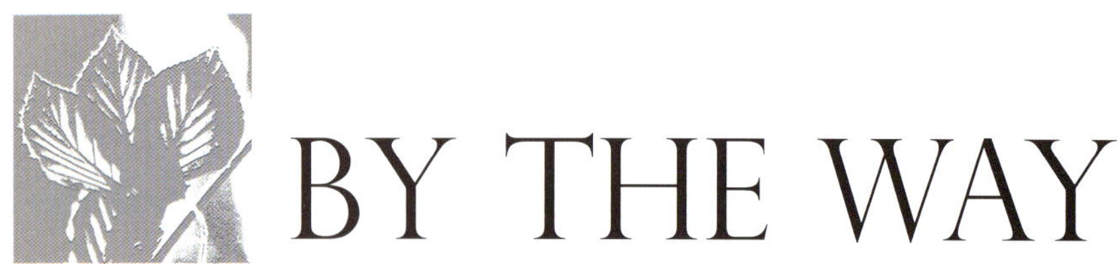

BY THE WAY

KEW'S LITTLE TREASURES AND HIDDEN PLACES

Pensford Field:

Like much of Kew and the surrounding area, the Field was once used as market gardens. Hidden away behind rows of houses, Pensford is run by an Environmental Trust that was formed to care for this little oasis in the middle of residential Kew. A not for profit organisation, the charitable trust relies on donations, fund raising and the work of volunteers to manage the Field, which can be found off Pensford Avenue.

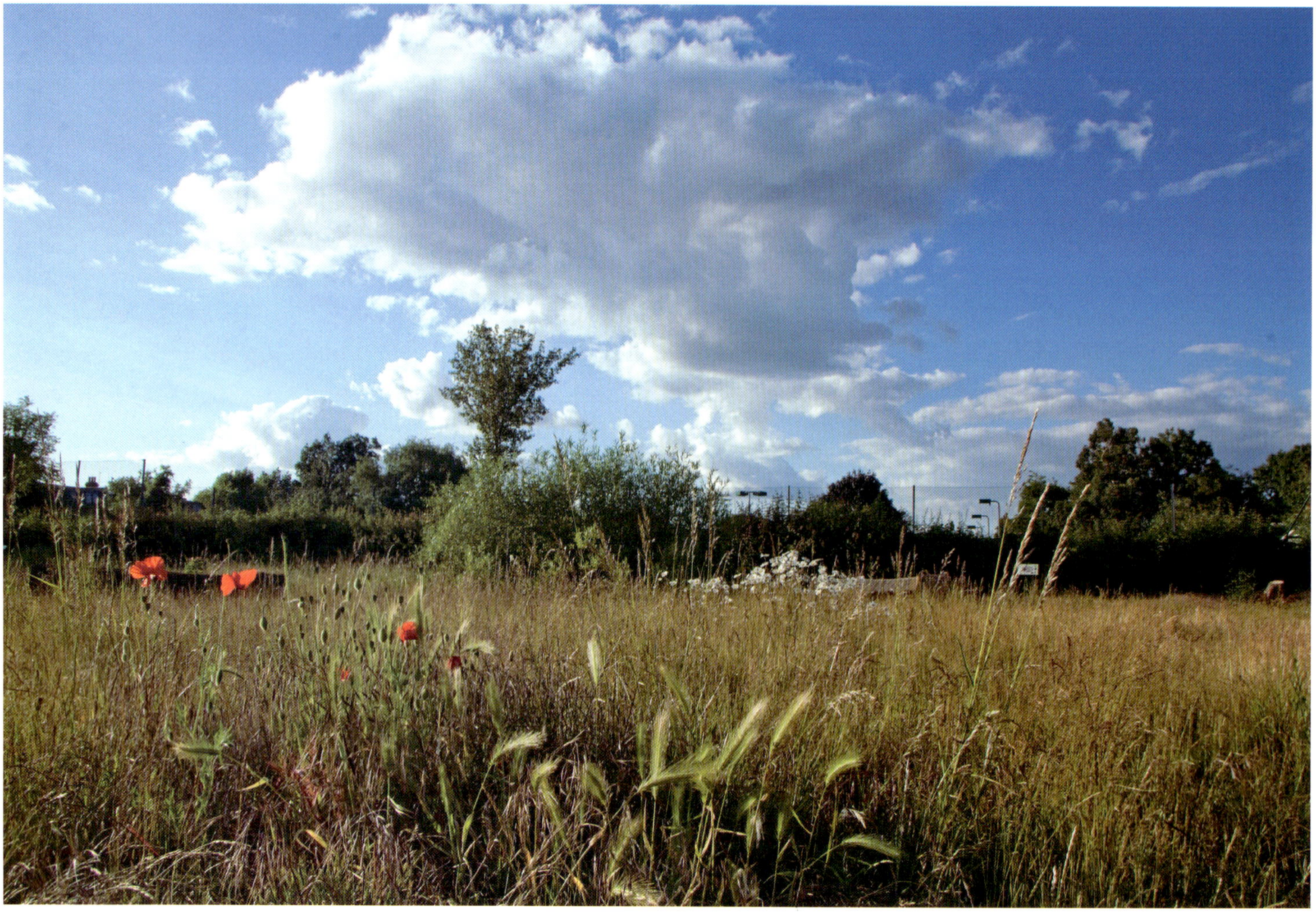

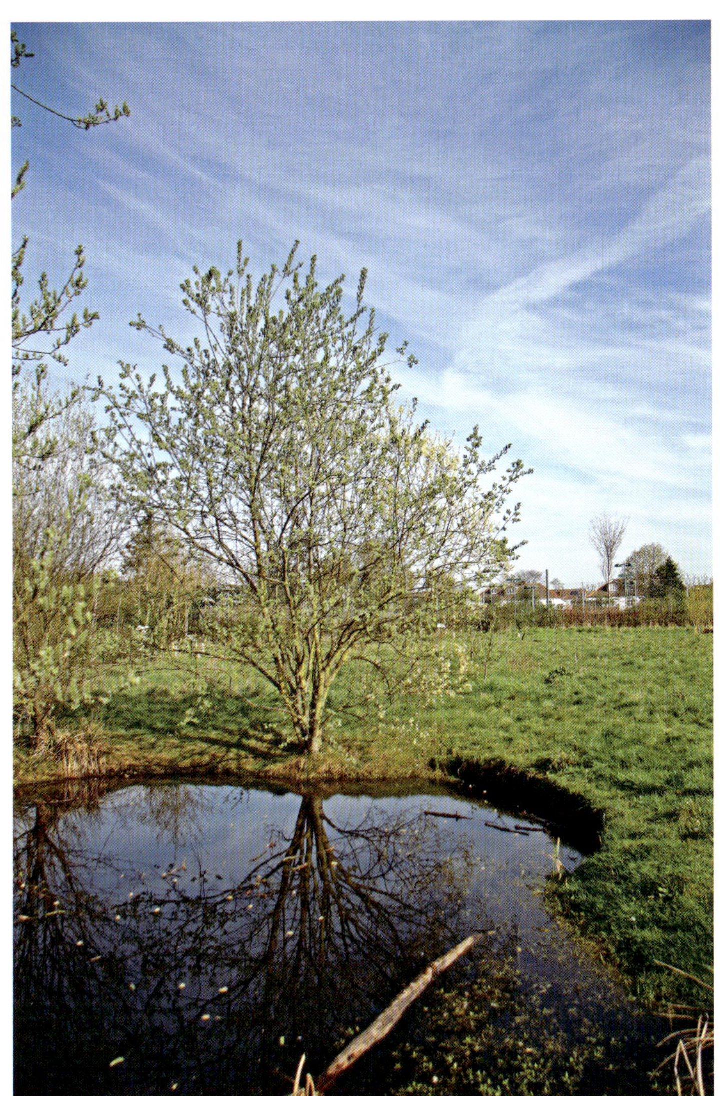

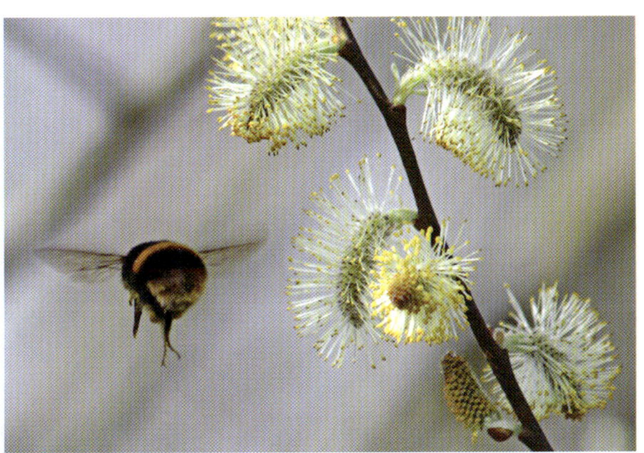

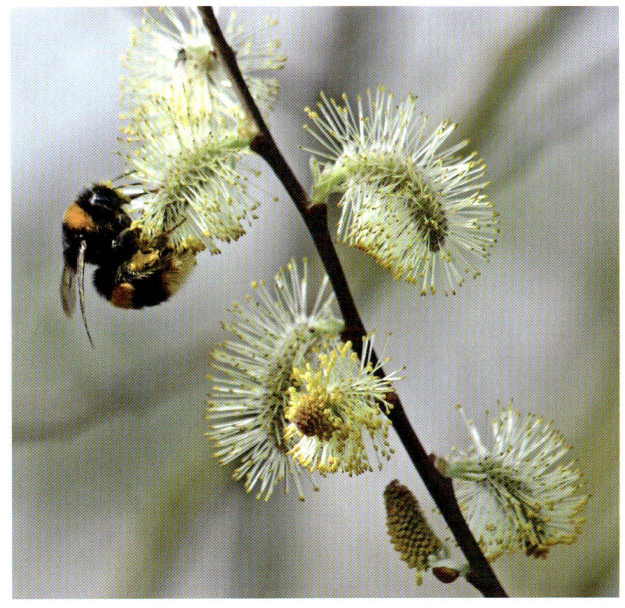

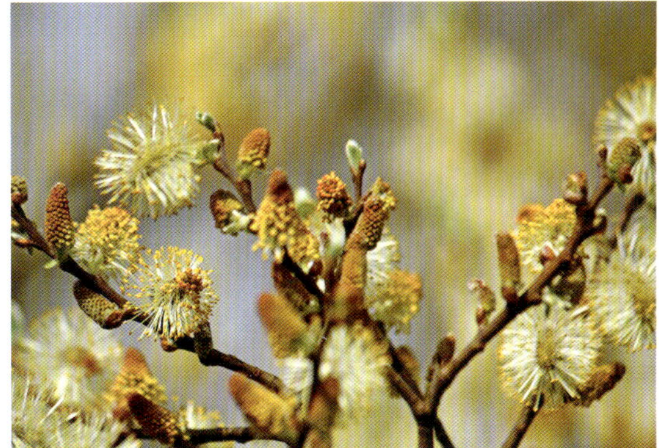

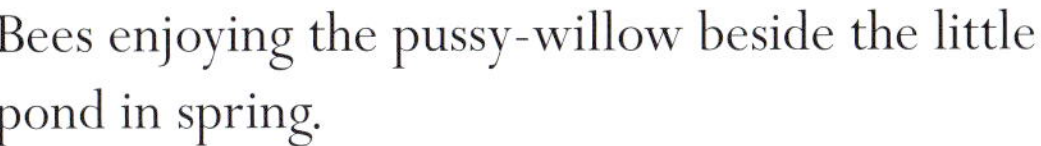

Bees enjoying the pussy-willow beside the little pond in spring.

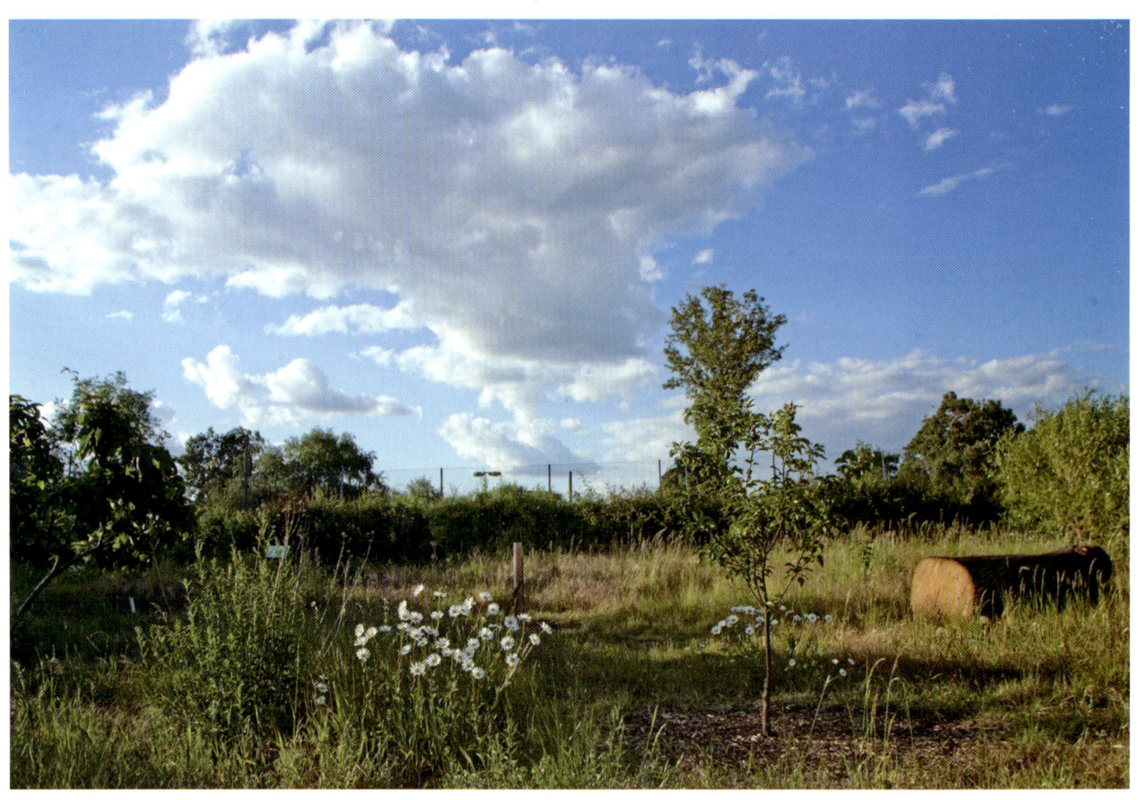

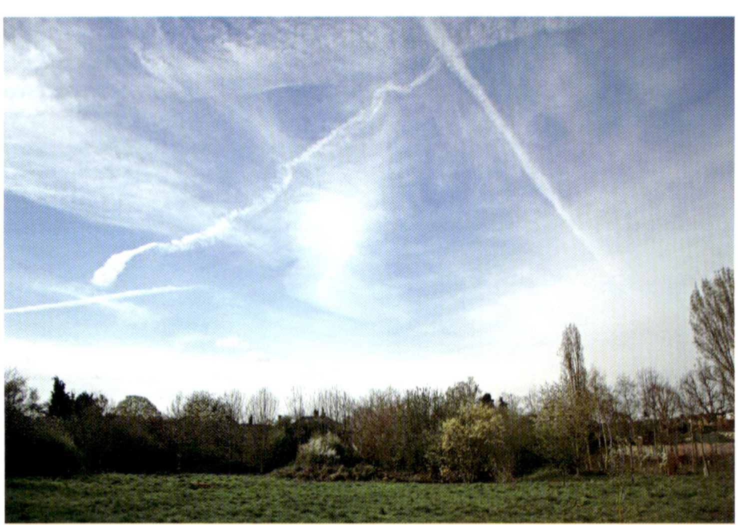

Right: Off to one side of the Field can be found some beehives.

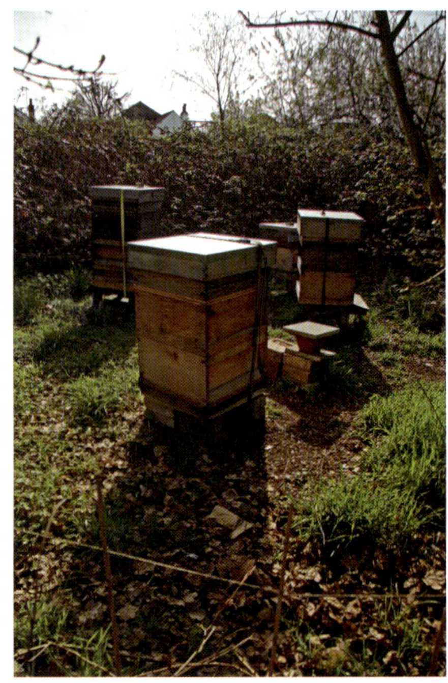

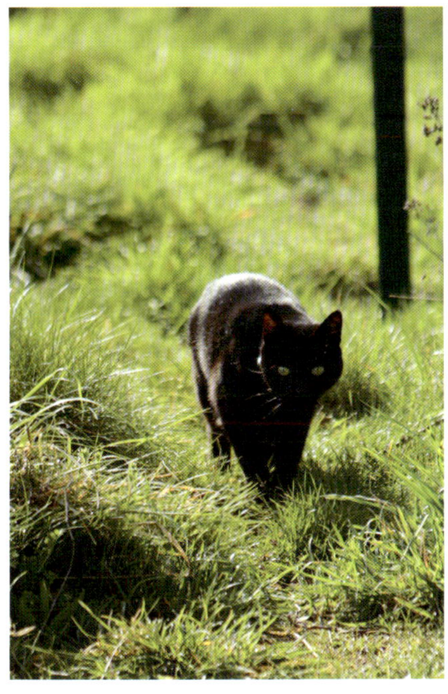

The Field is a quiet and peaceful place where cats can run and guitars be strum.

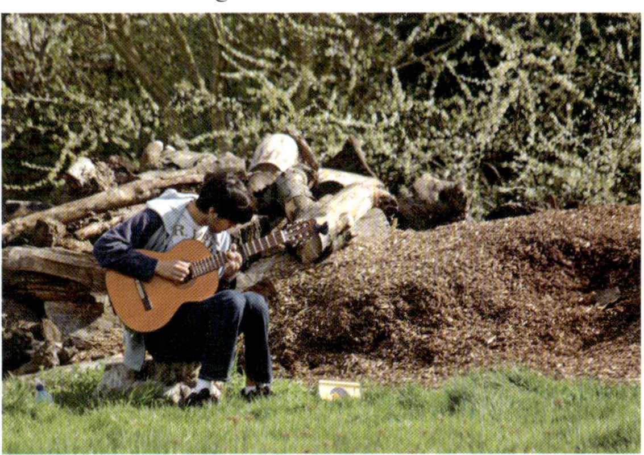

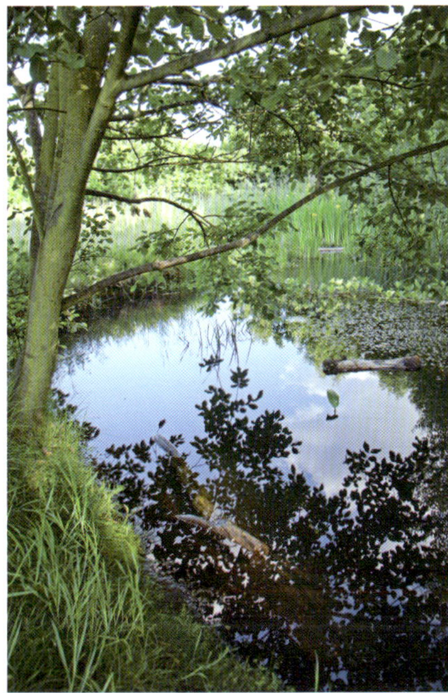

The little pond in early spring attracts many frogs and toads, who require water to lay their spawn.

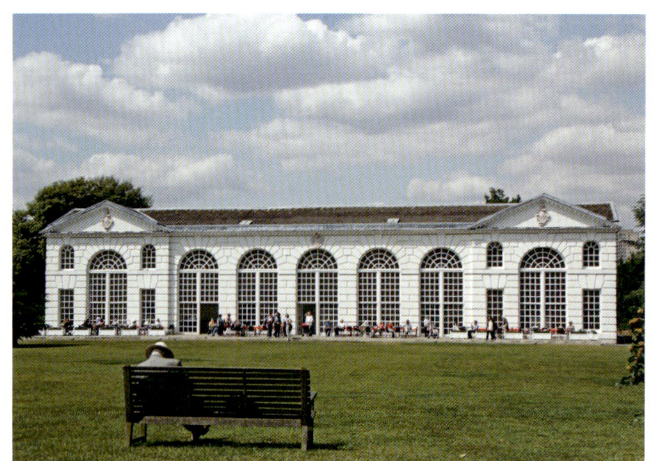

Kew Gardens:
Left: Orangery
Bottom left: By the lake
Bottom right: Walled Garden
Below: Kew Palace

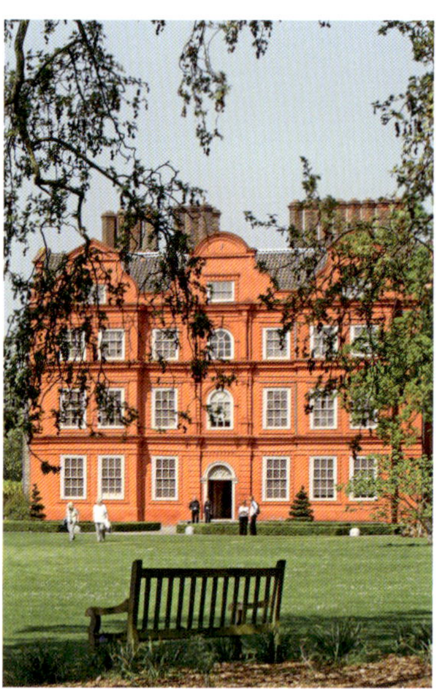

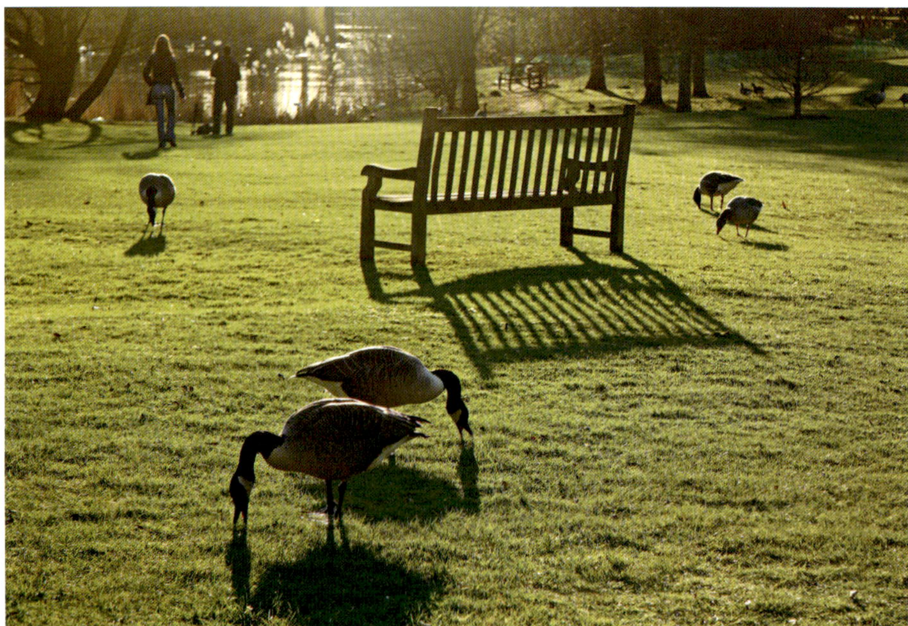

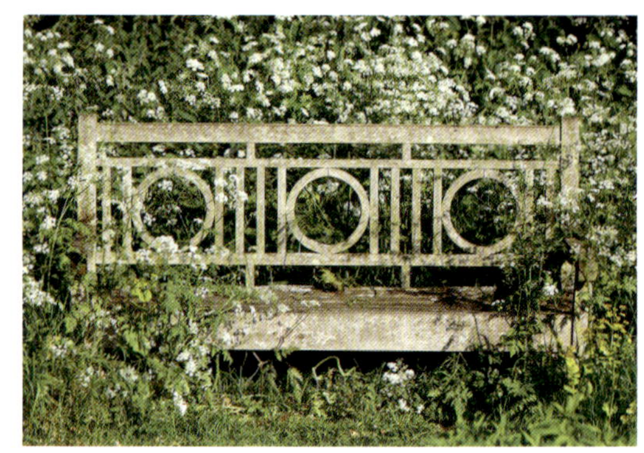

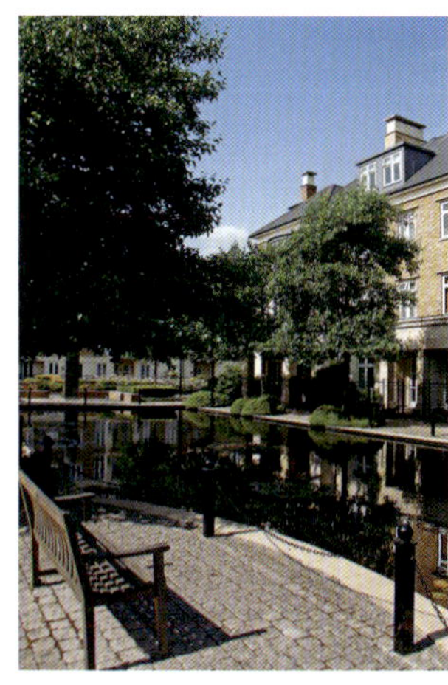

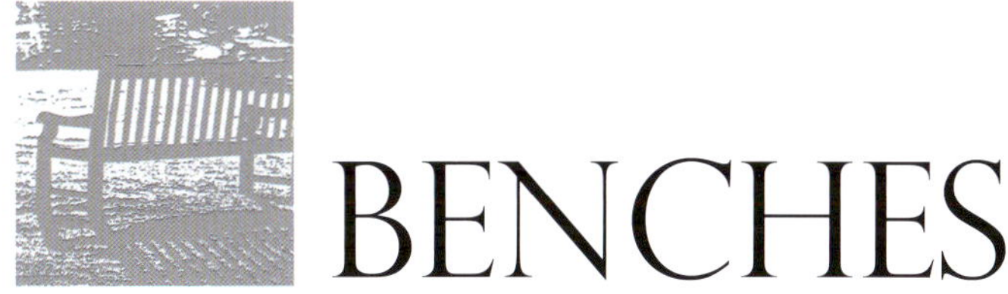

BENCHES

Do *you* have a favourite?

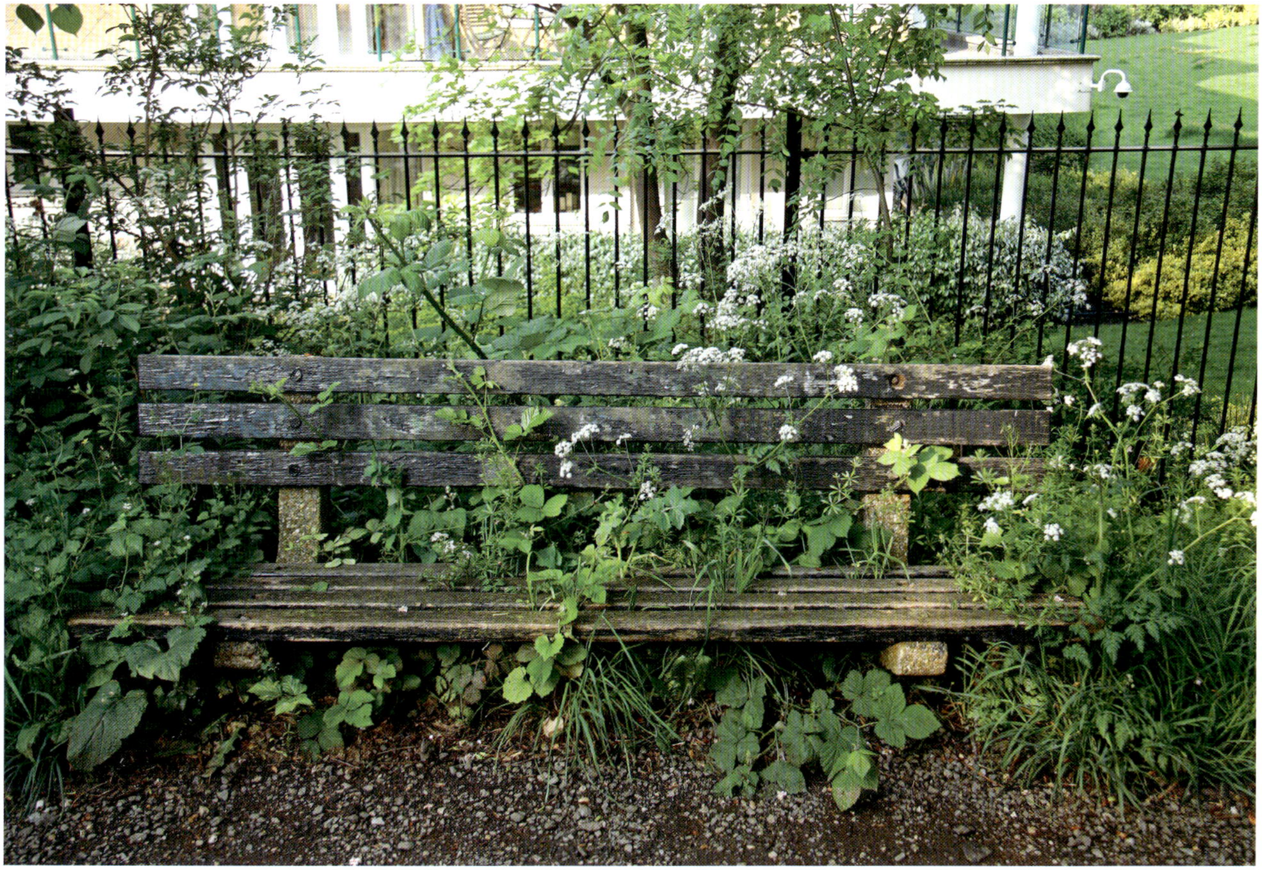

Top: Kew Riverside Park **Above:** River towpath

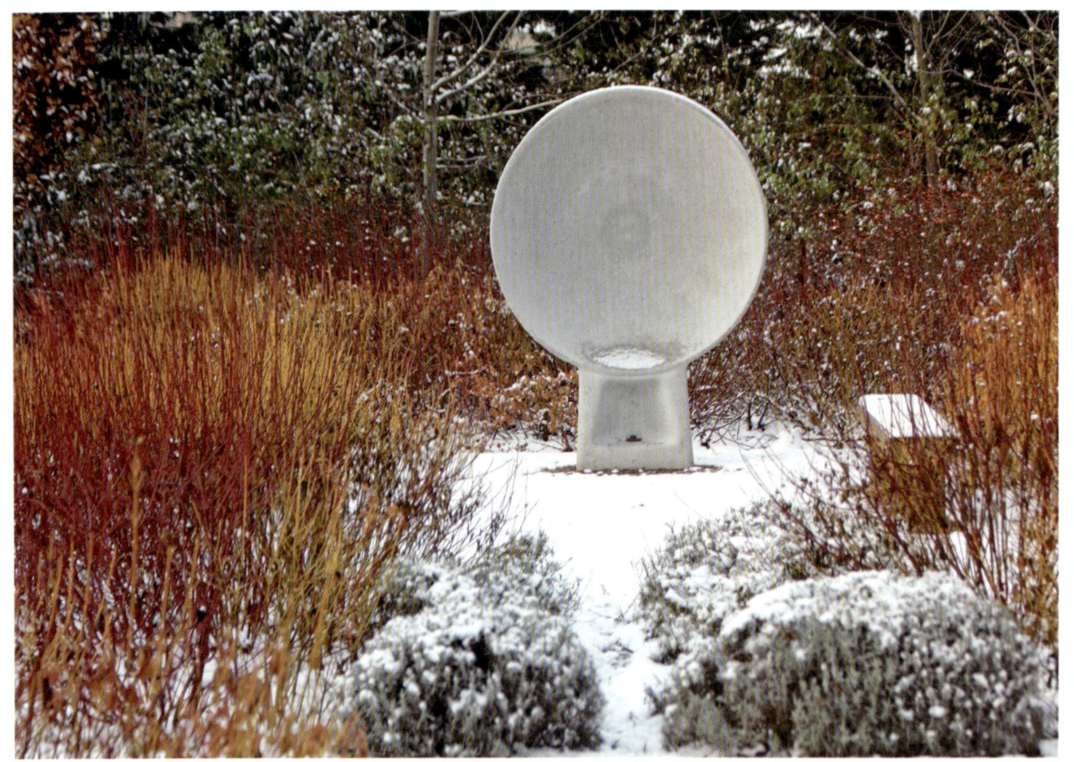

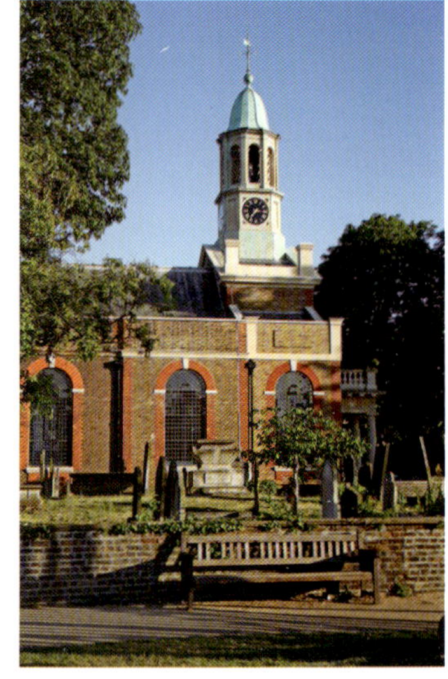

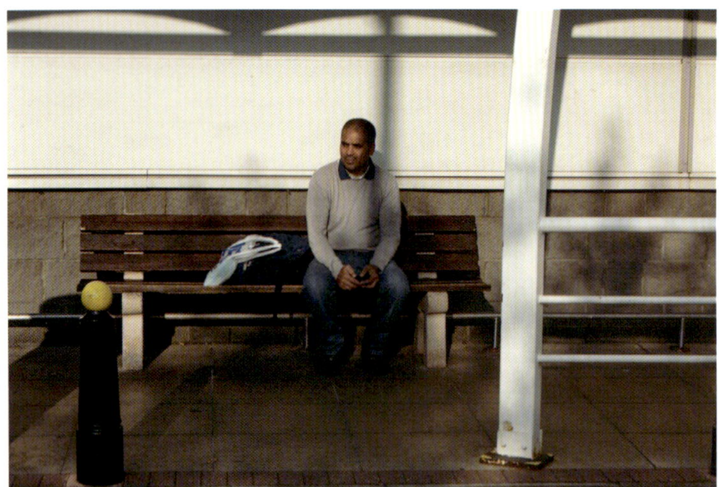

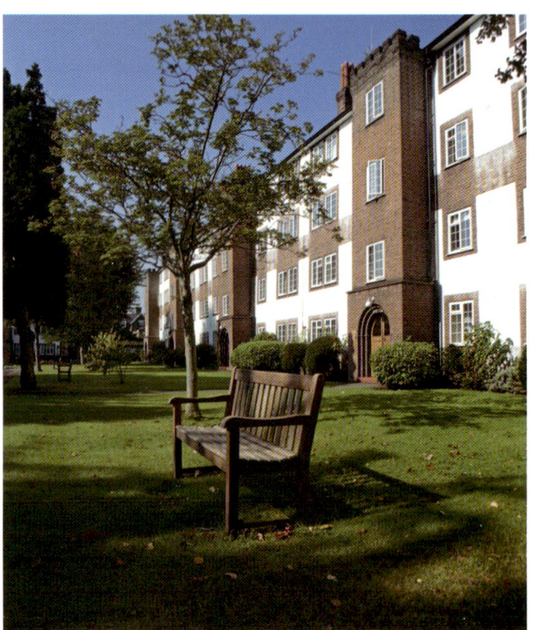

Top: Kew Riverside Park
Above: Kew Retail Park
Top Right: St Anne's, Kew Green
Right: Gloucester Court, off Kew Road

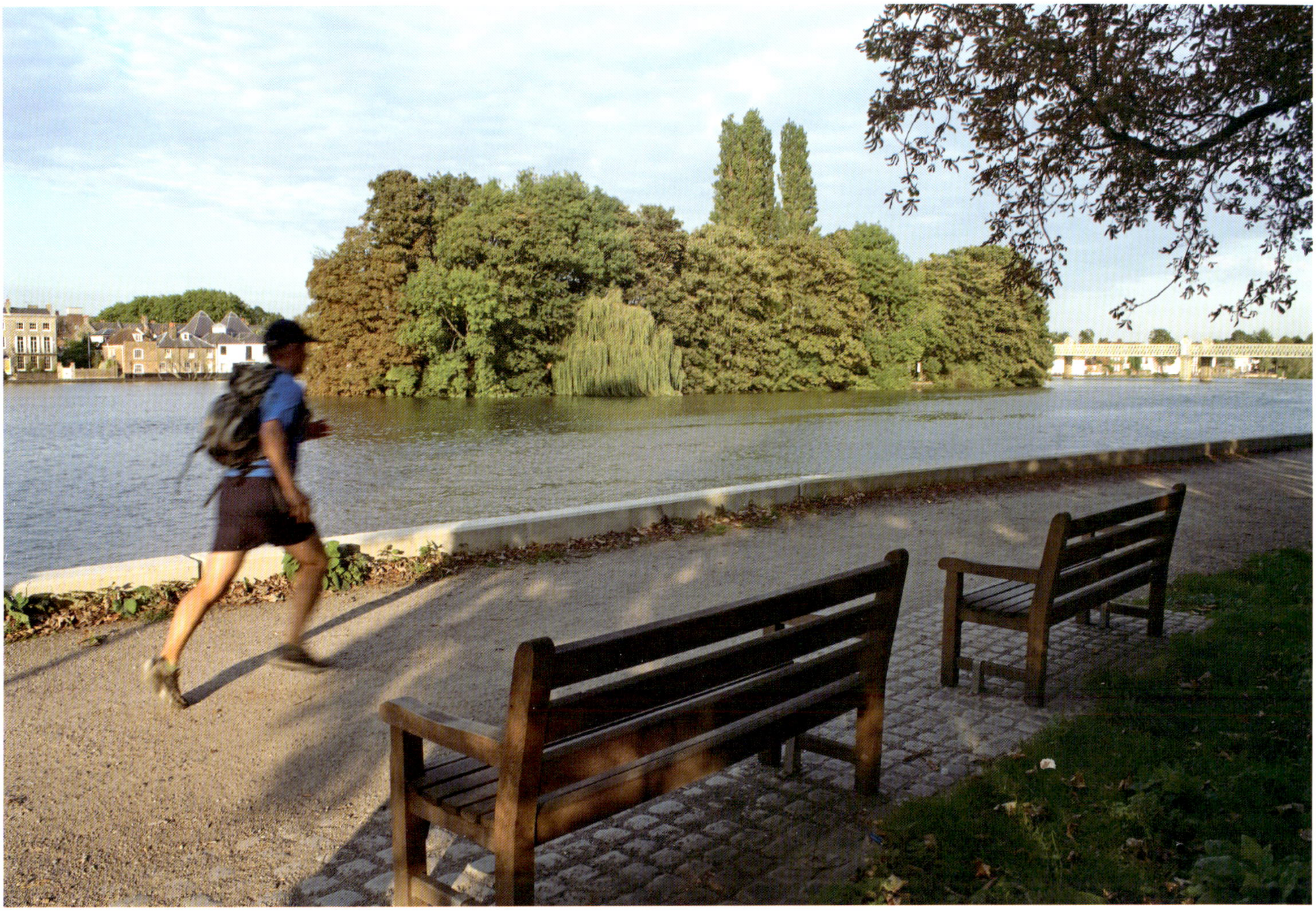

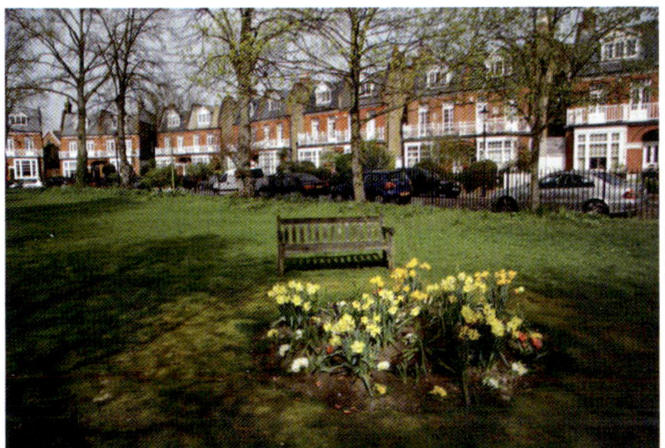

Top: The recently renovated part of the embankment overlooking Oliver's Island.
Above: Lawn Crescent **Right:** Barn Church

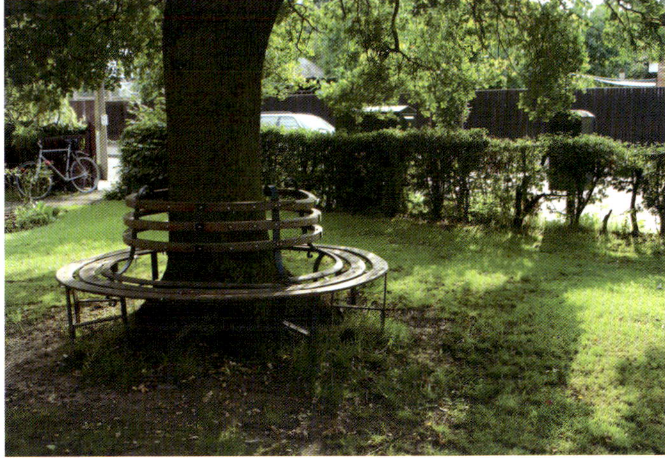

NORTH SHEEN CEMETERY

The cemetery was opened in 1909. They have just recently been letting some of the grass grow, as has been tried in one or two other local cemeteries. Leaving the grass longer on some sections allows plant species to flower and provides a better habitat for local wildlife. This policy is in keeping with the grade II listing as a Site of Importance to Nature Conservation.

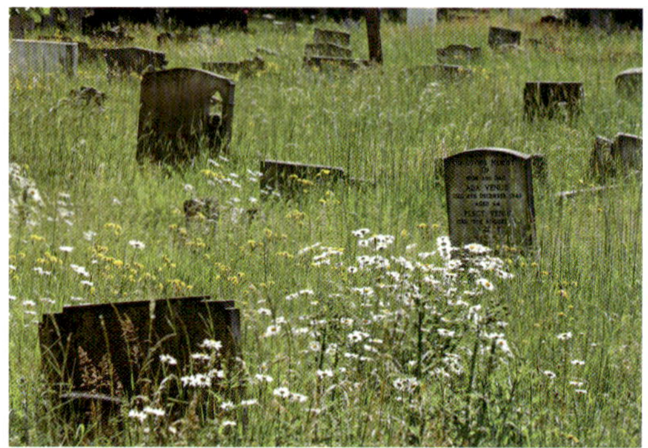

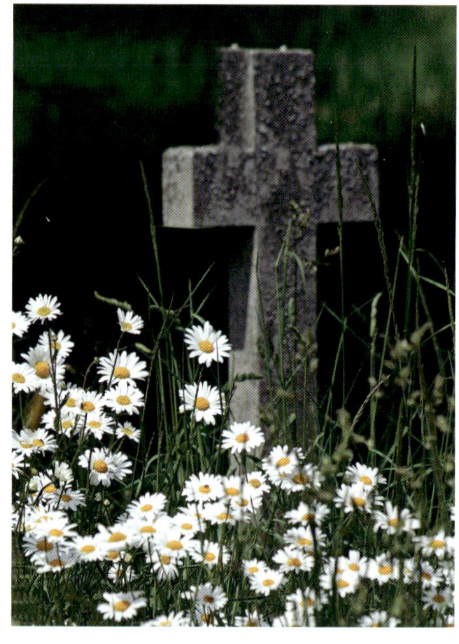

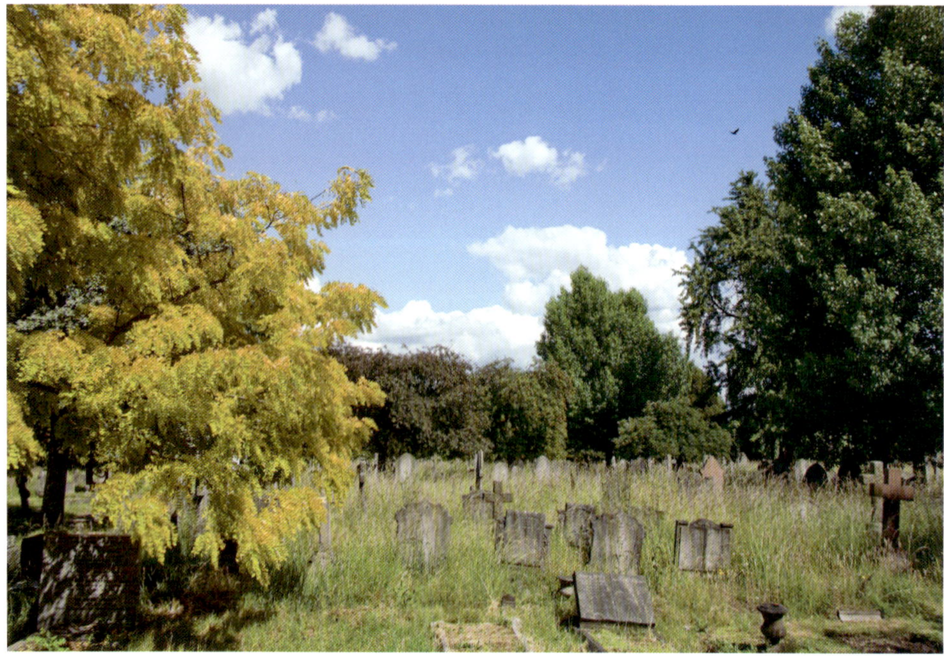

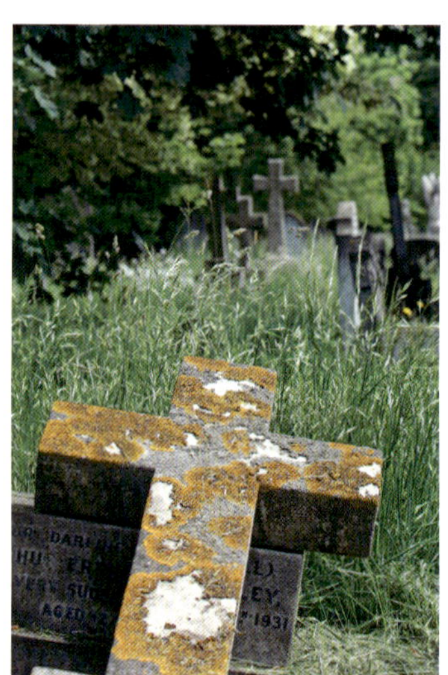

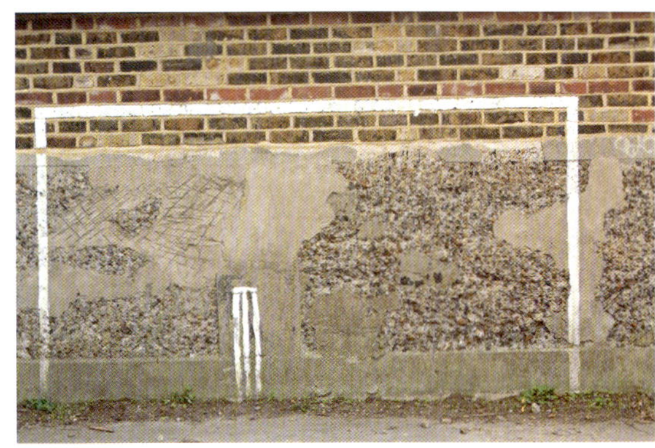

When just a wall will do.

The row of garages off Forest Road, beside the railway line.

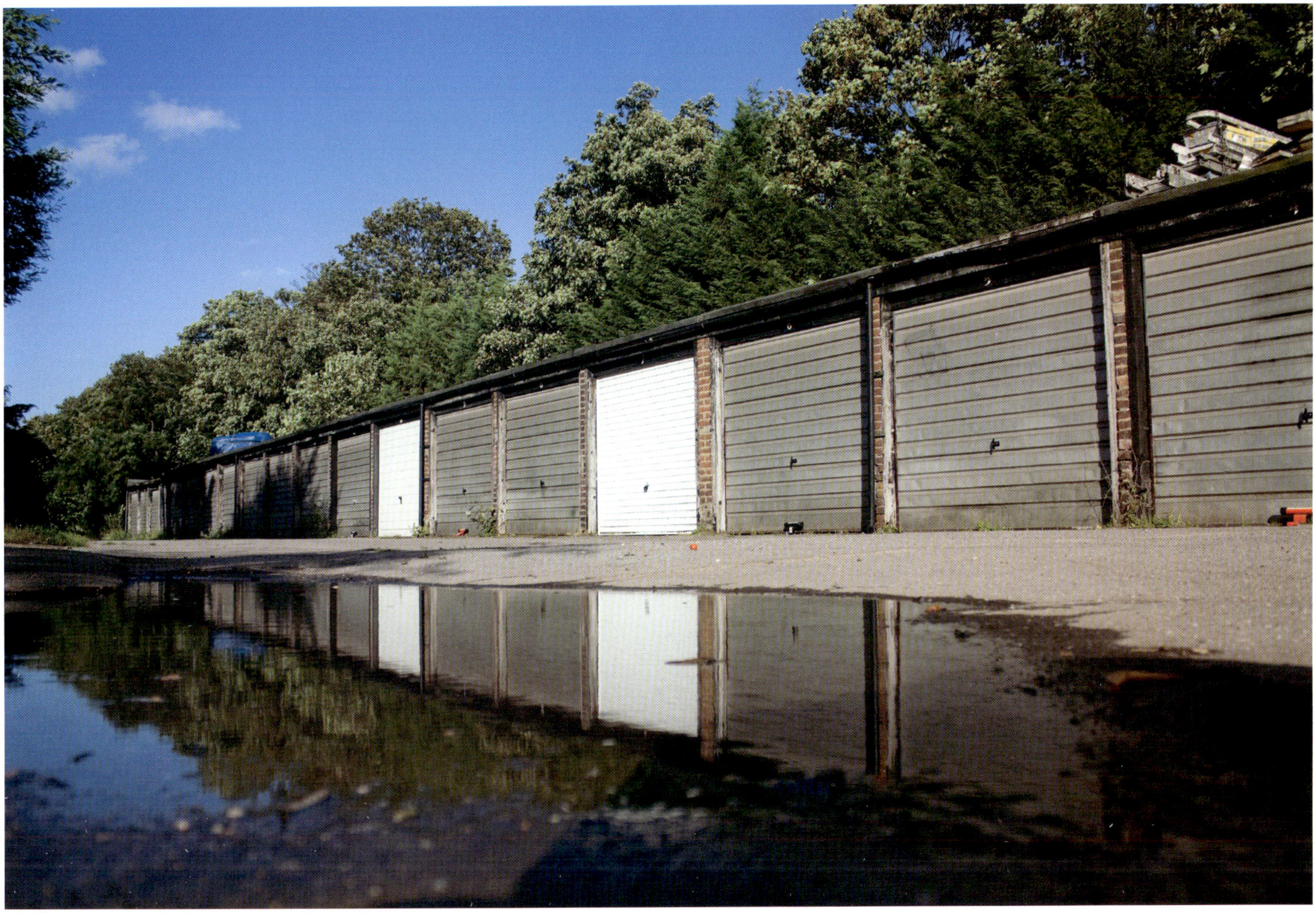

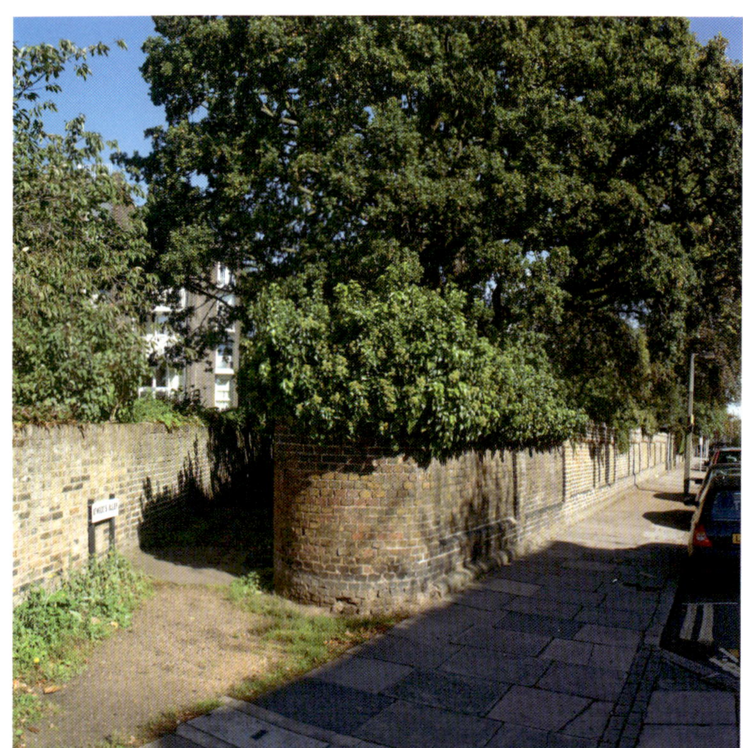

Left: Atwood's Alley, named after the market gardener of the same name, who had land near here. It runs behind the houses in Leyborne Park.

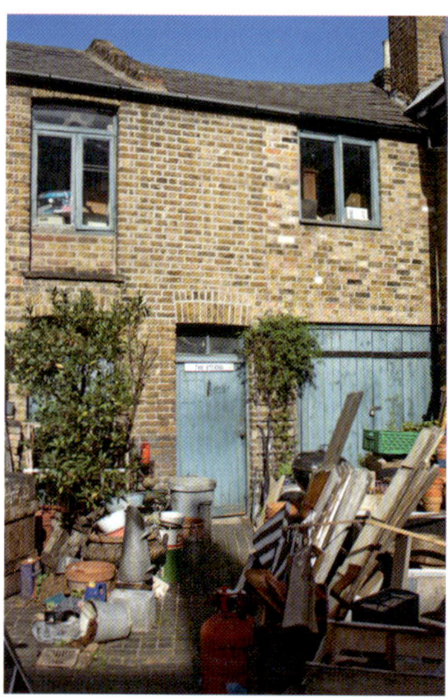

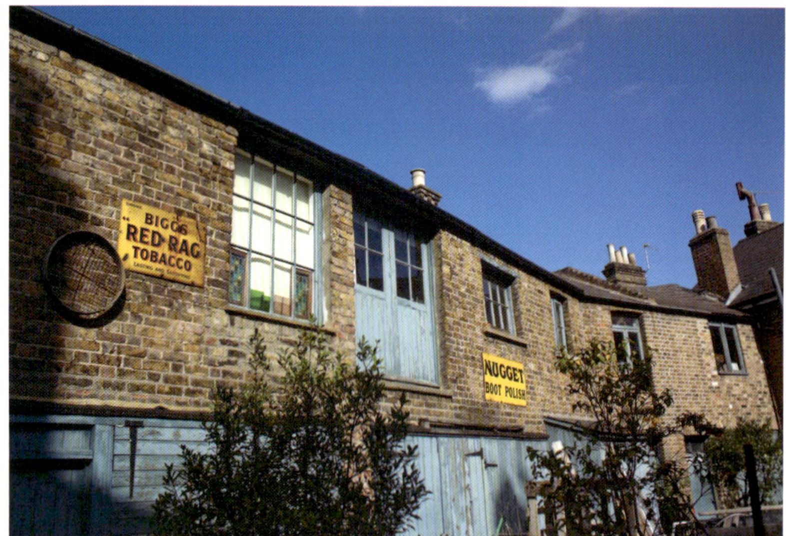

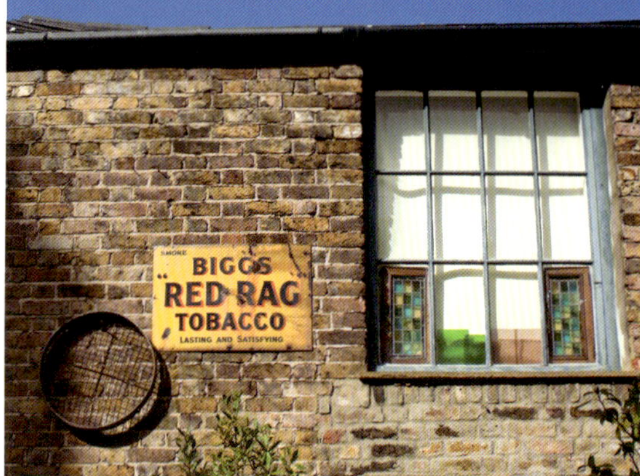

Left, top right and above: The are some old buildings that retain a lot of character to be found off Cambridge Road.

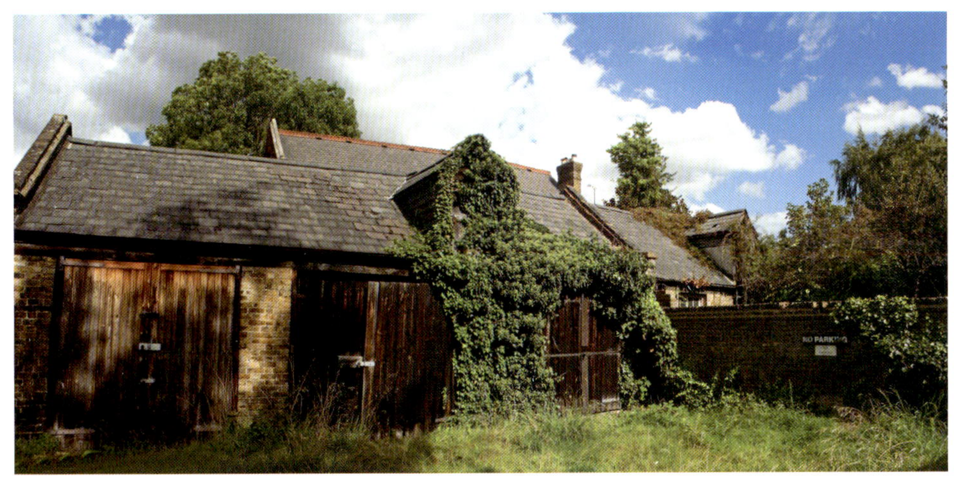

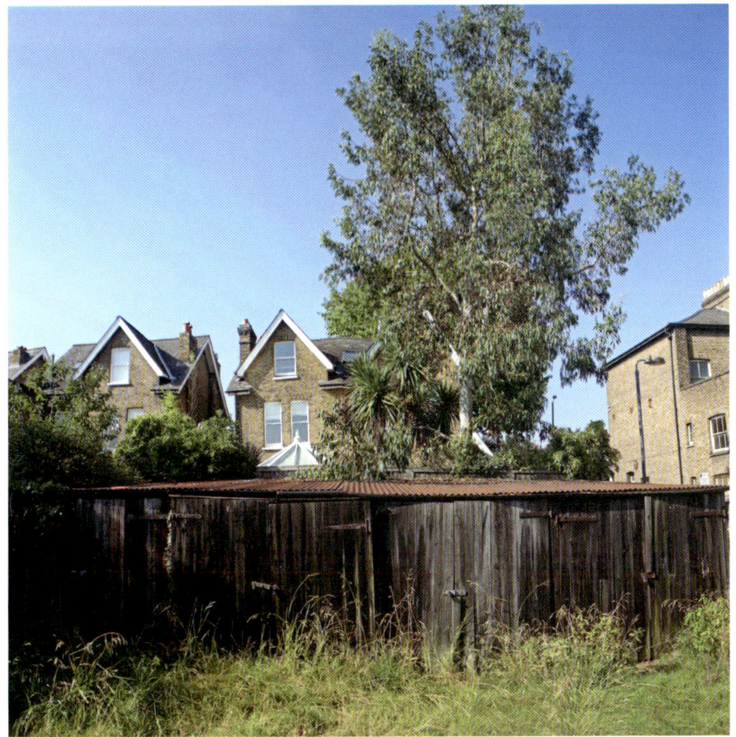

Top and above: The old garages off Cambridge Road and next to the old chapel that can be seen in the pictures on the right.

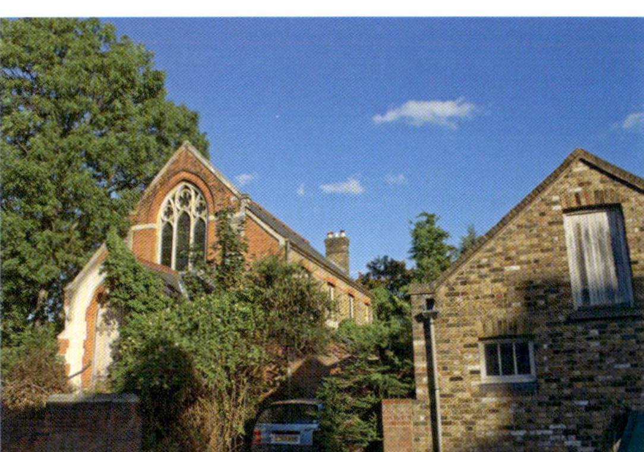

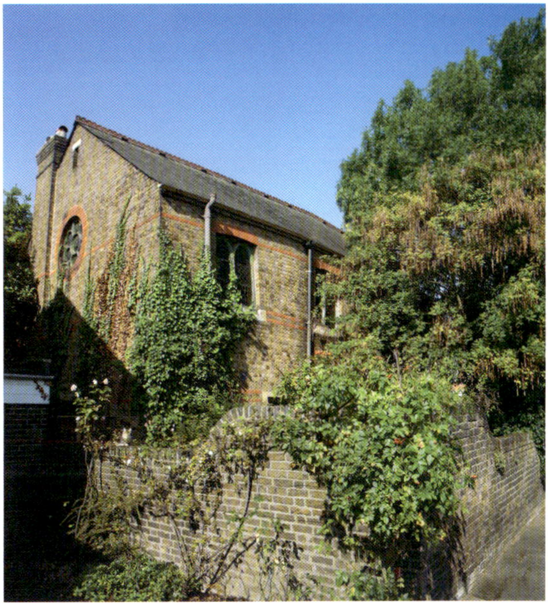

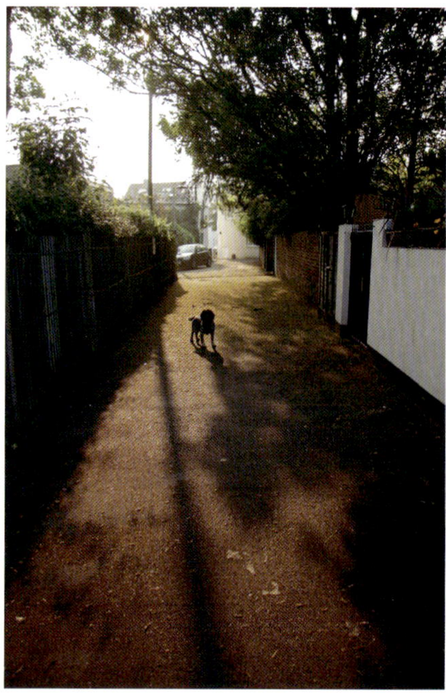

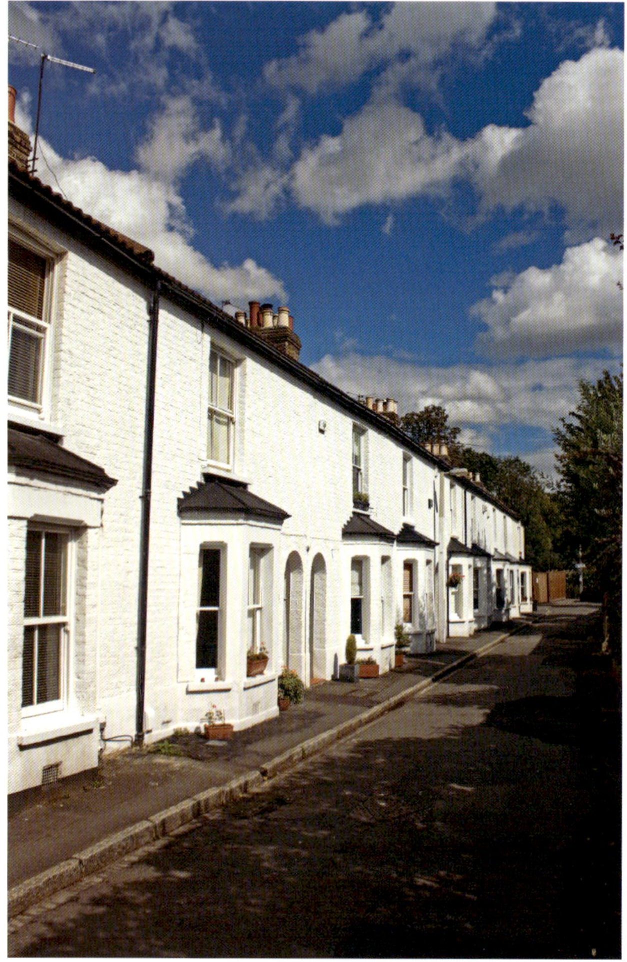

Right: Watcombe Cottages, which date from 1887, were built on land by the river that in times past was used for willow harvesting. But as the demand for willow waned the land was sold to developers.

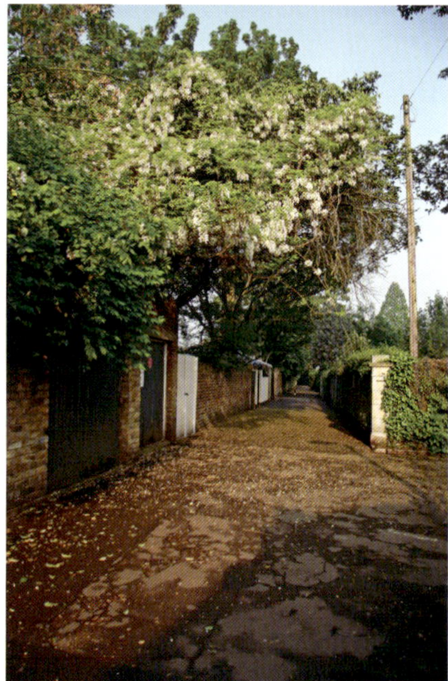

Top and above: Greyhound lane, which runs behind The Greyhound pub.

ROYAL BOTANIC GARDENS

The Royal Botanical Gardens' official foundation date is 1759. Kew has long been associated with Royalty, who in turn attracted rich noblemen to settle here also. It is mainly through this connection that we are able to enjoy today the wonderful open space that is Kew Gardens. Prince George, later George III, was living in the White House, which stood opposite what we now know as Kew Palace (see next page), and it was from here that Augusta, Prince George's mother, and Lord Bute set about creating a feature garden. Comprising little more than 9 acres, the Gardens over the next 80 years lacked both proper direction, enough money to prosper and almost closed. It was only on the appointment of Sir William Hooker in 1840 as its first director did change really take place. The Gardens expanded massively and this together with the vision of the new director, saw the building of such iconic structures as the Palm House (see below). All of which made the Gardens a huge draw for the public, and would ensure that the Gardens would never again be in danger of closure.

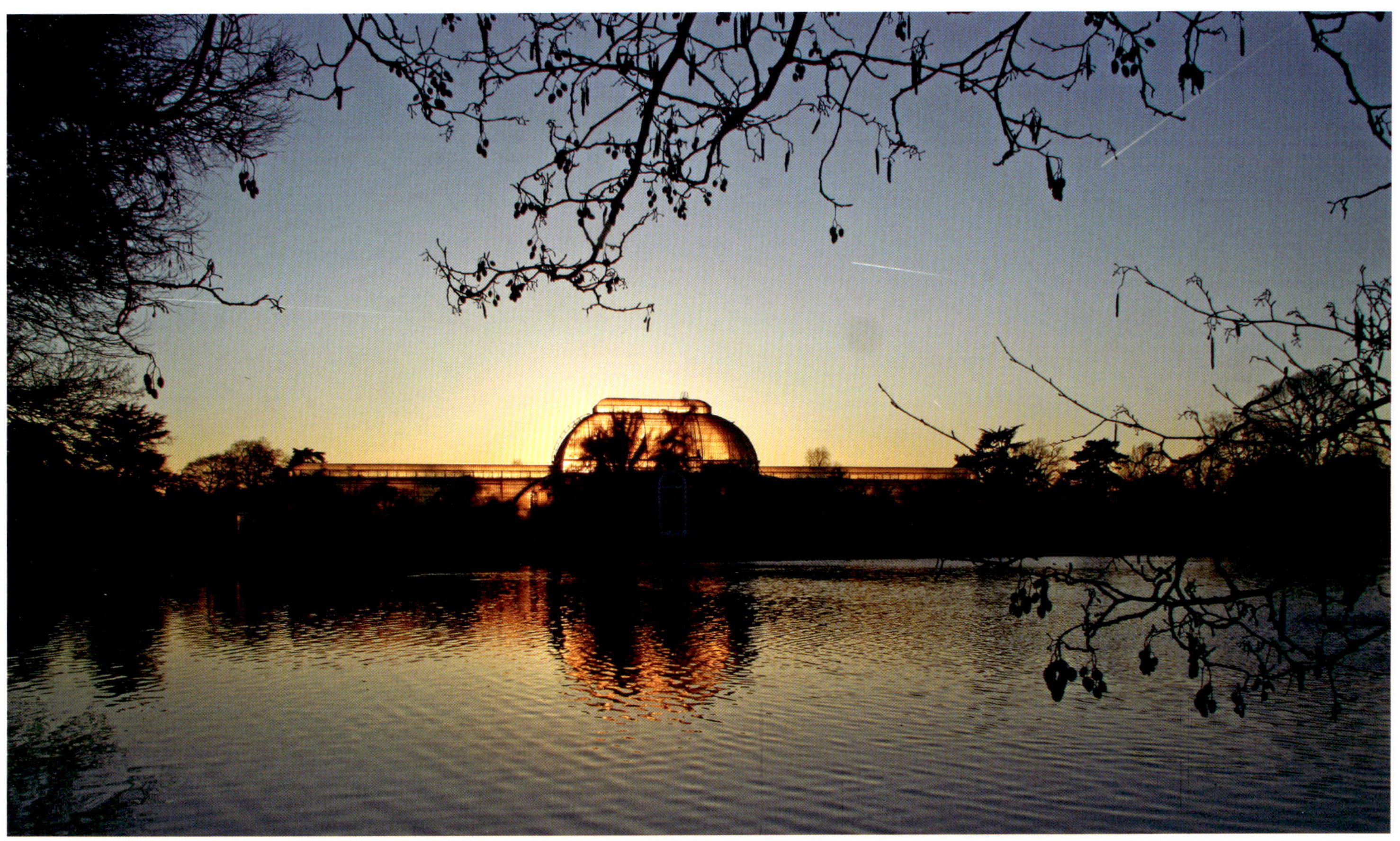

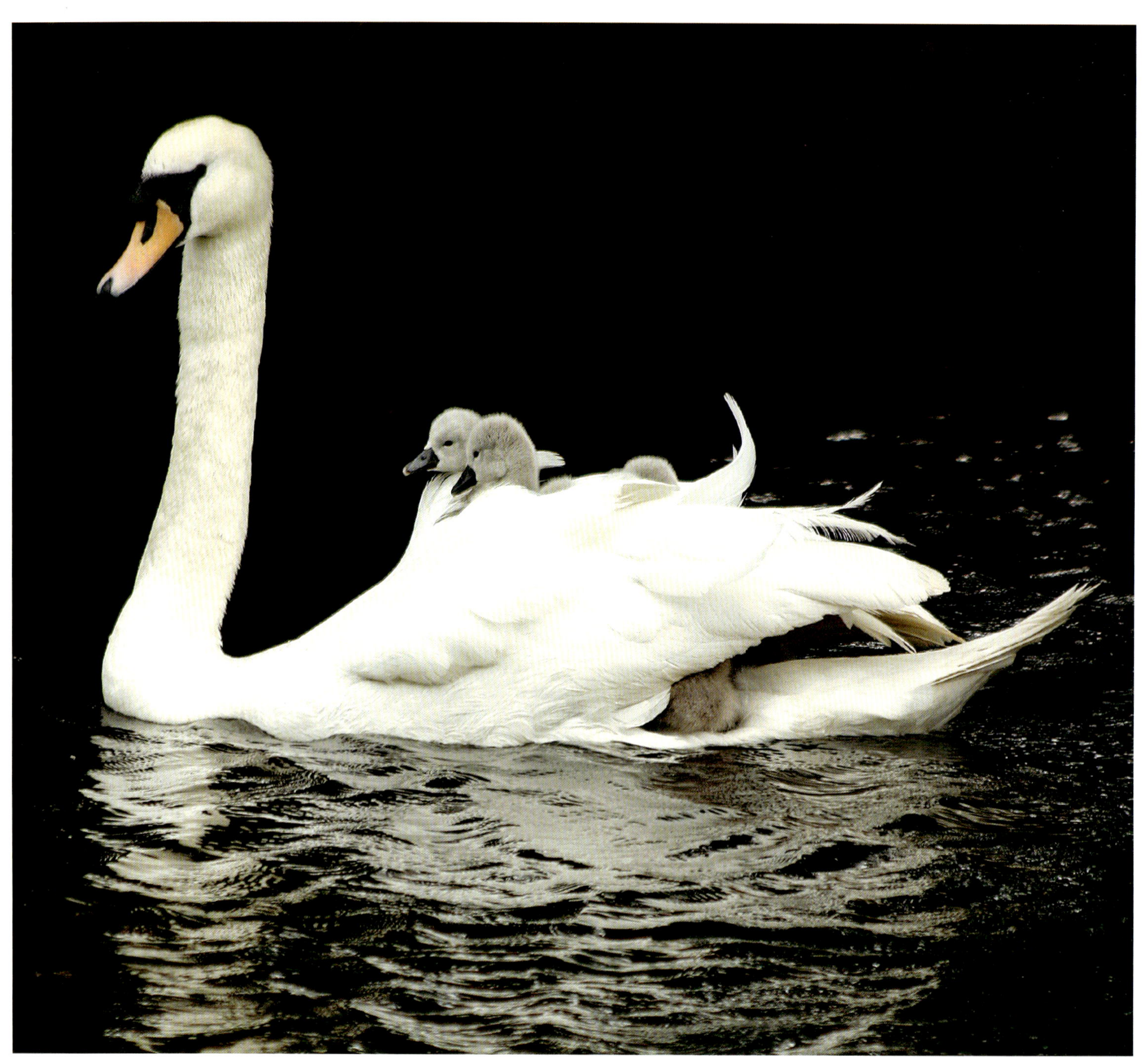

Two images that show off the best of Kew Gardens and the rich diversity of things on show. **Above:** Mute Swan carrying her cygnets on the lake. **Opposite page:** Kew Palace

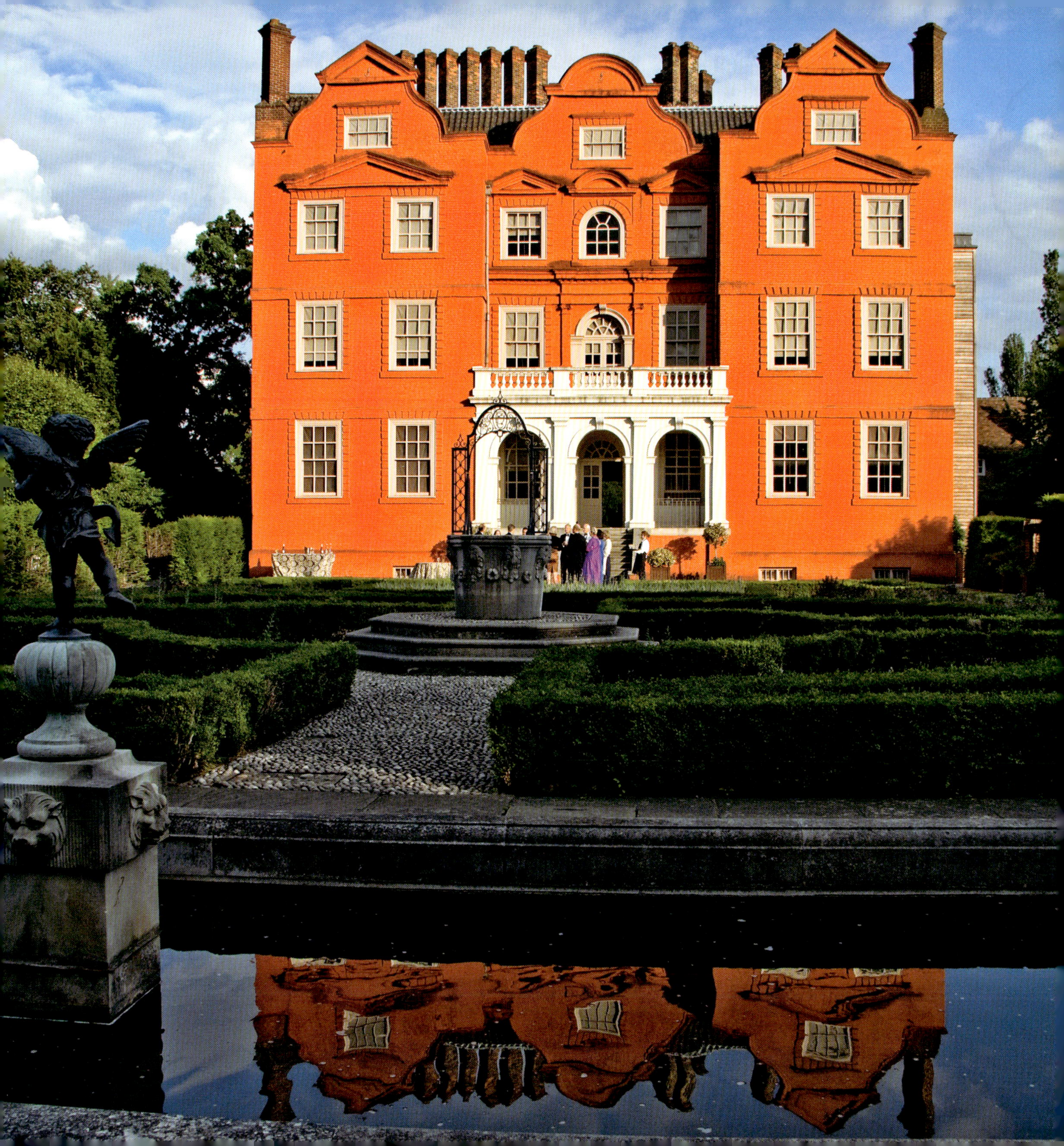

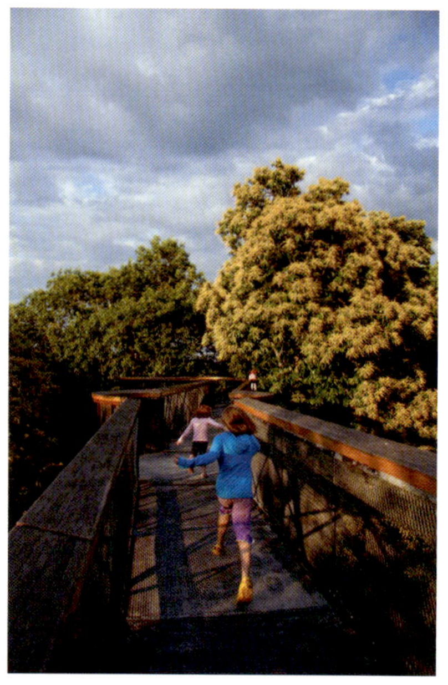

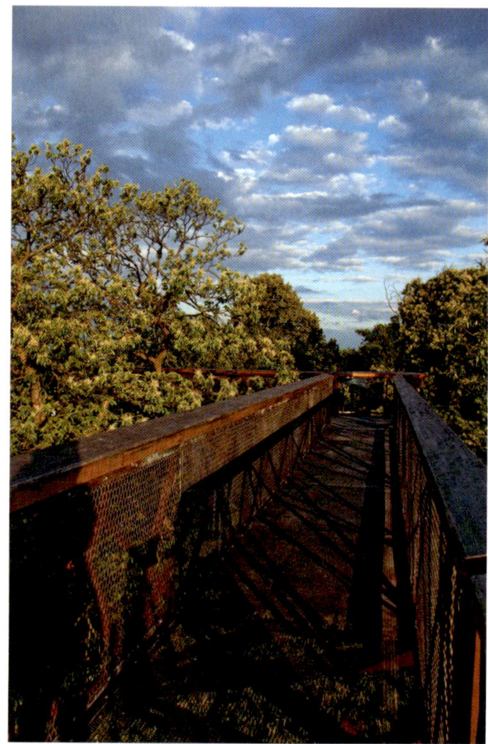

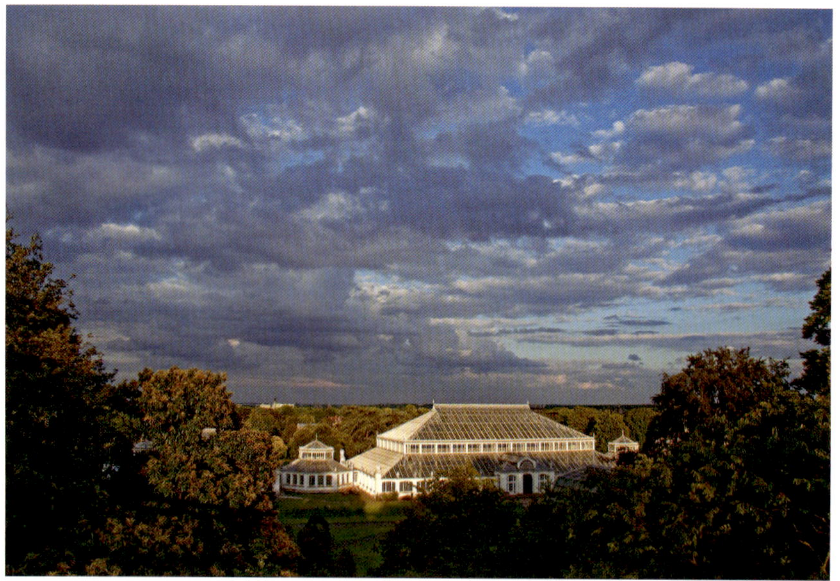

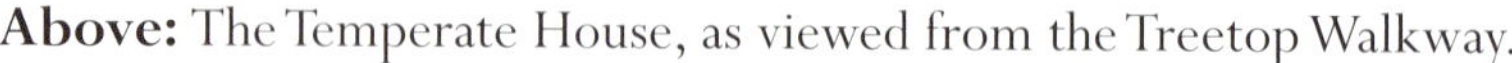

Above: The Temperate House, as viewed from the Treetop Walkway.

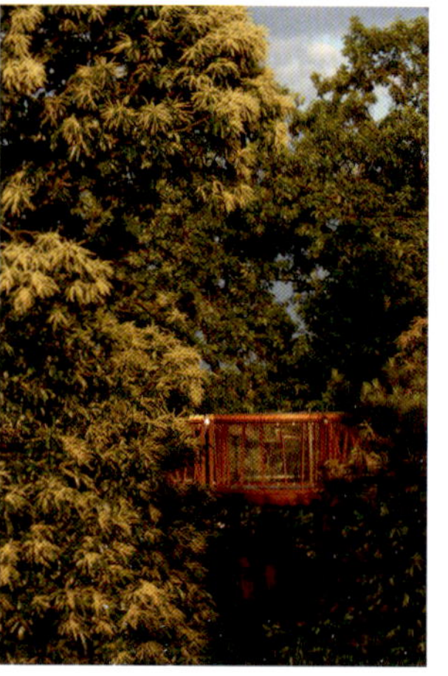

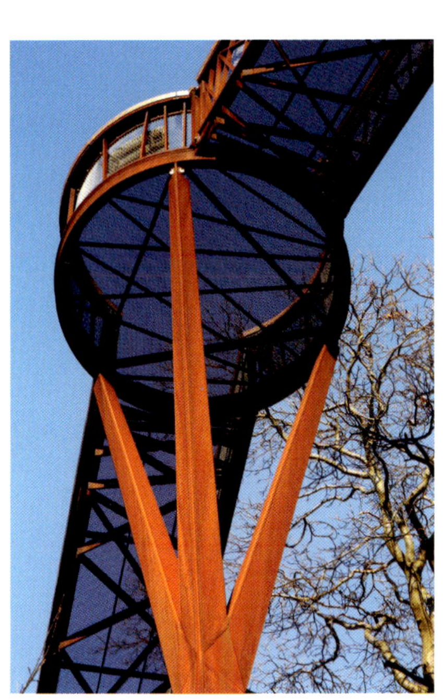

This page and the three pictures opposite:
Xstrata Treetop Walkway

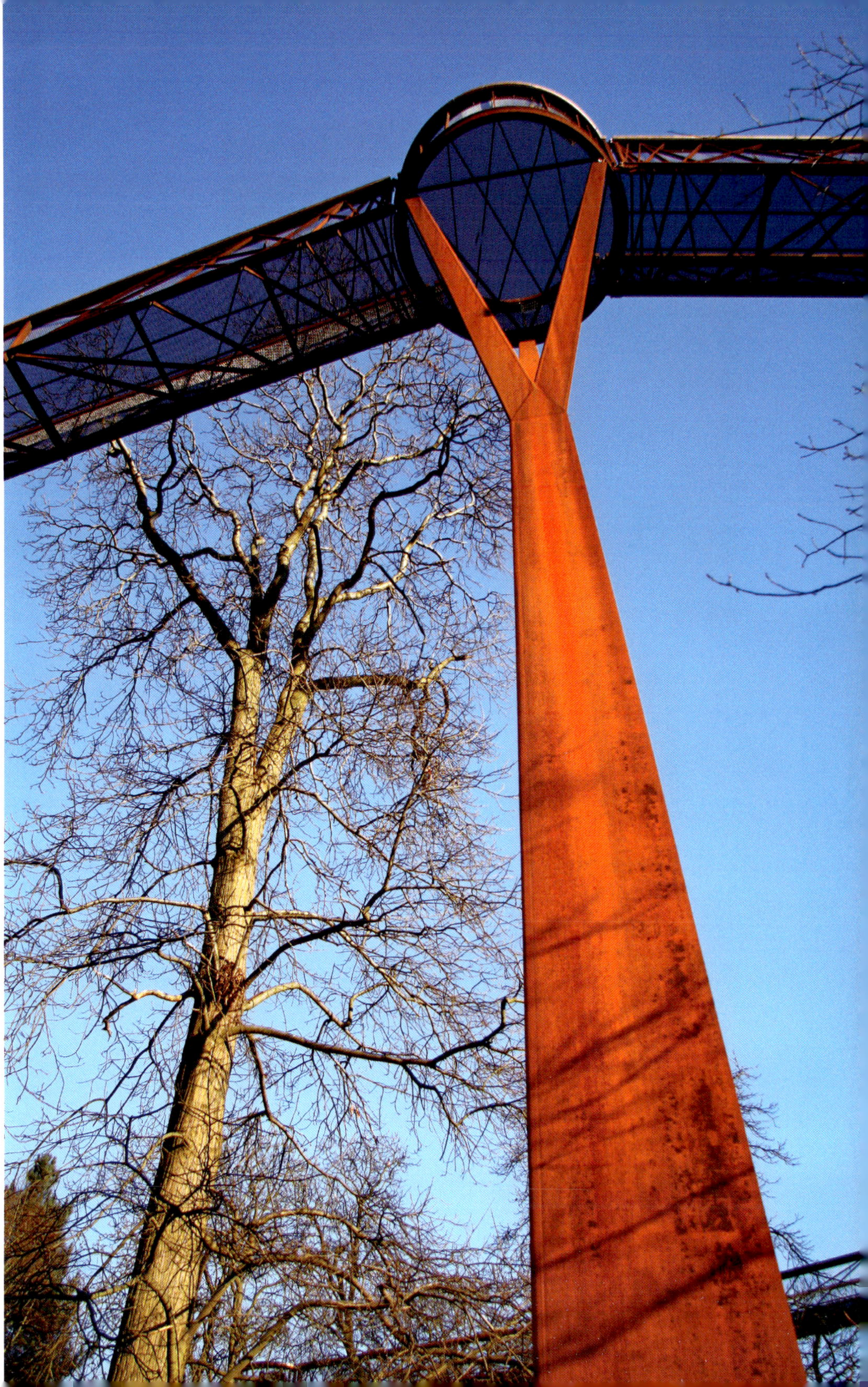

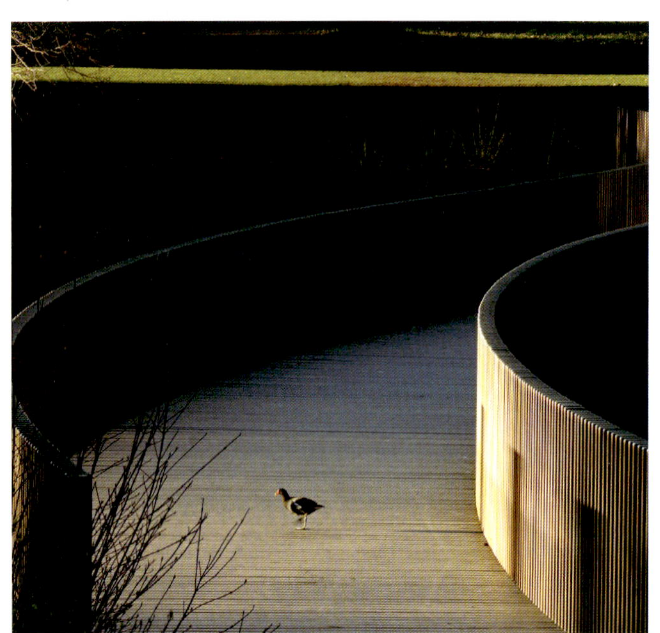

This page and opposite:
The Sackler Crossing, which crosses the lake, opened in 2006. The bridge is named after Theresa Sackler, one of the philanthropists whose money made the project possible.

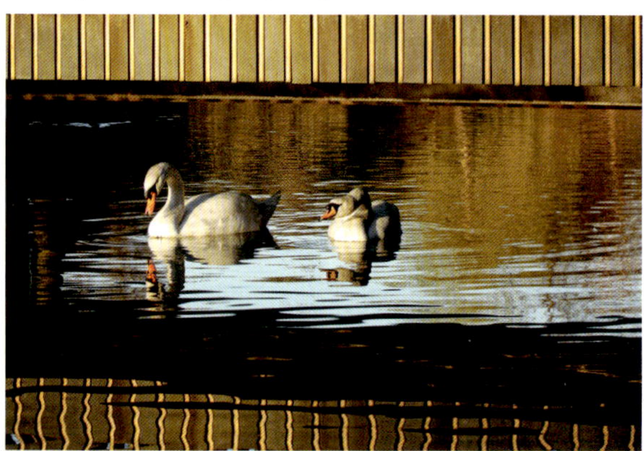

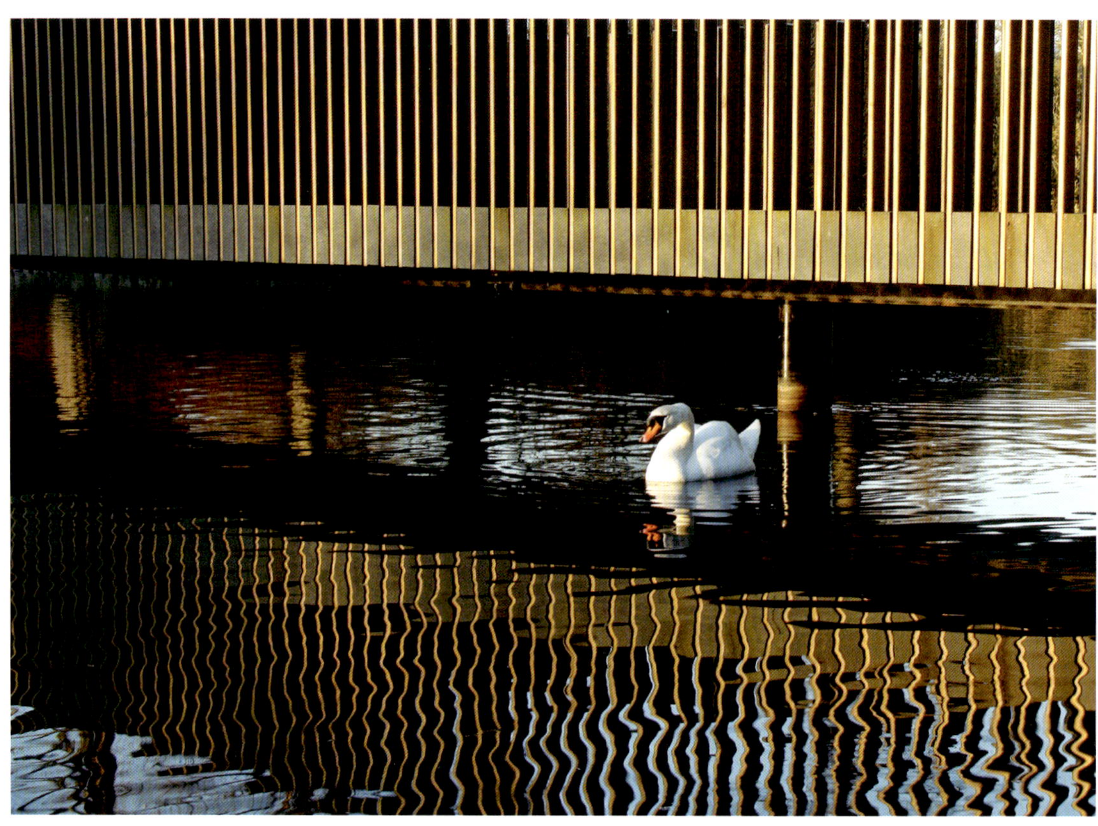

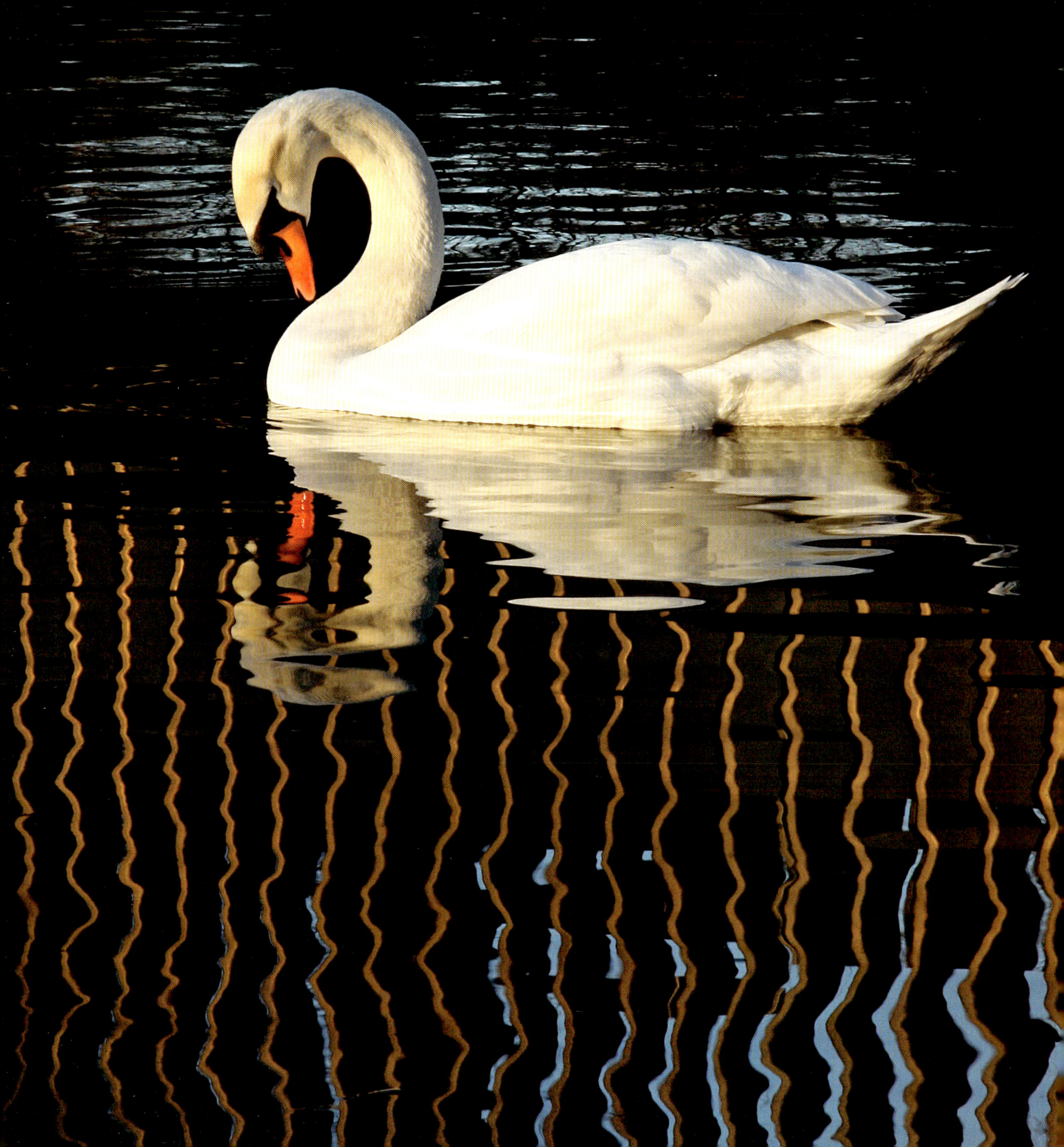

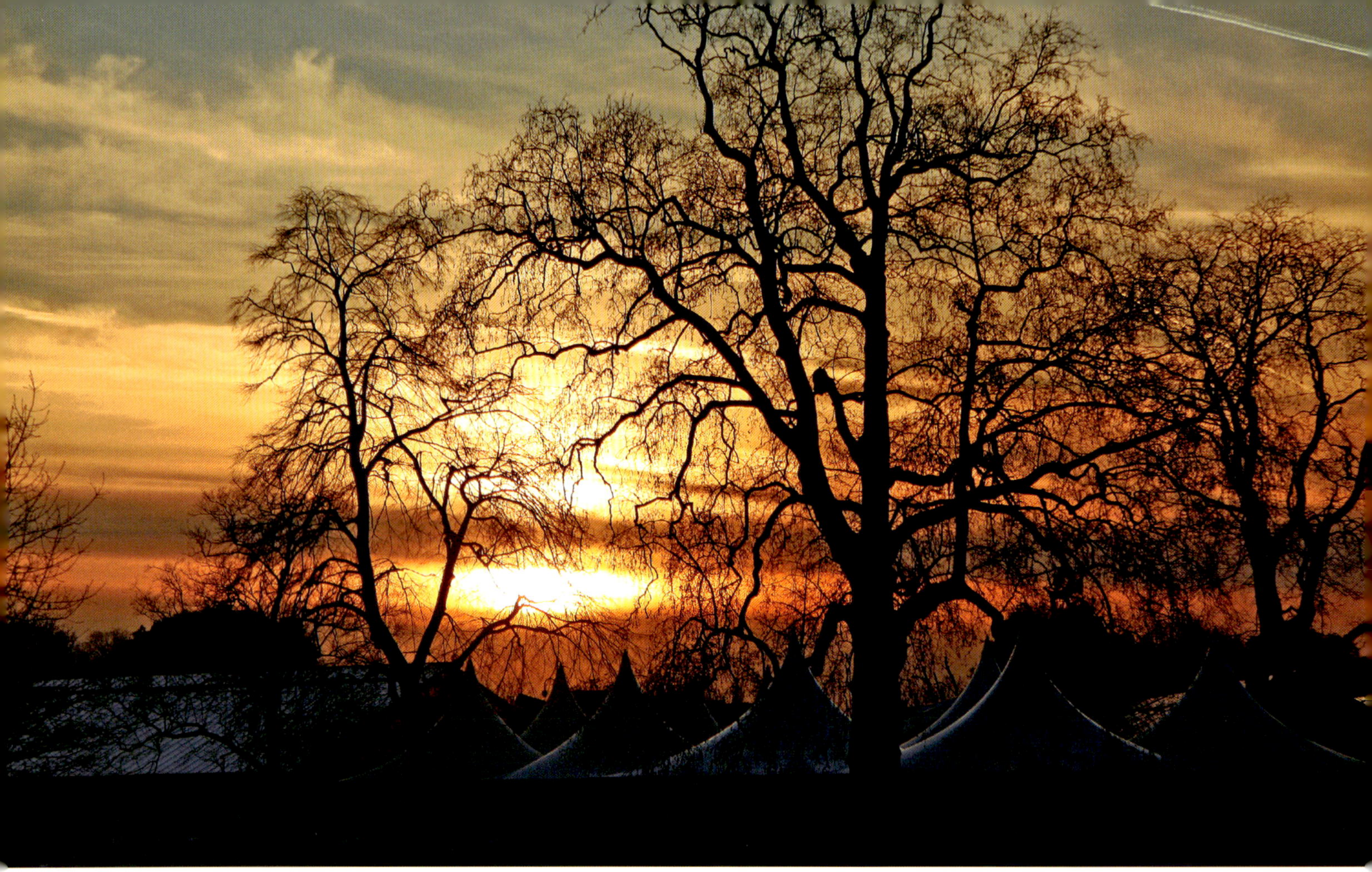

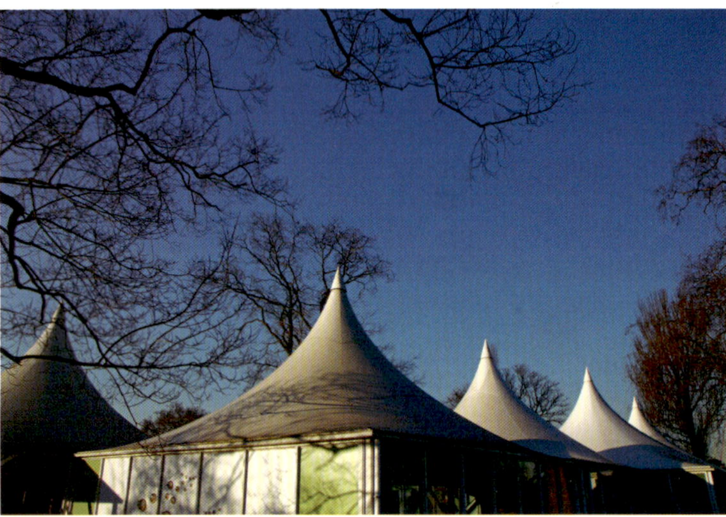

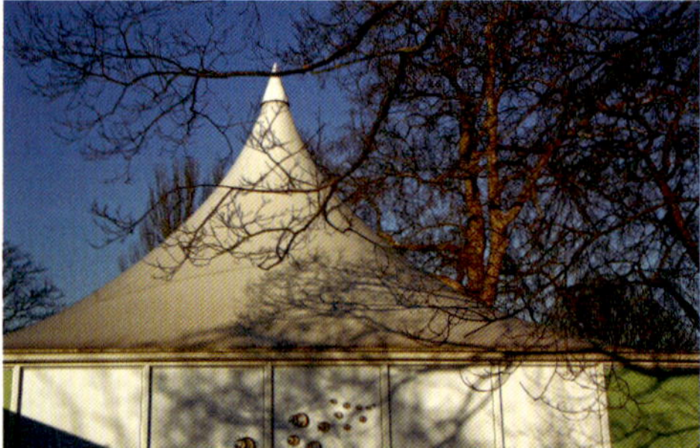

This page: White Peaks Café and Shop

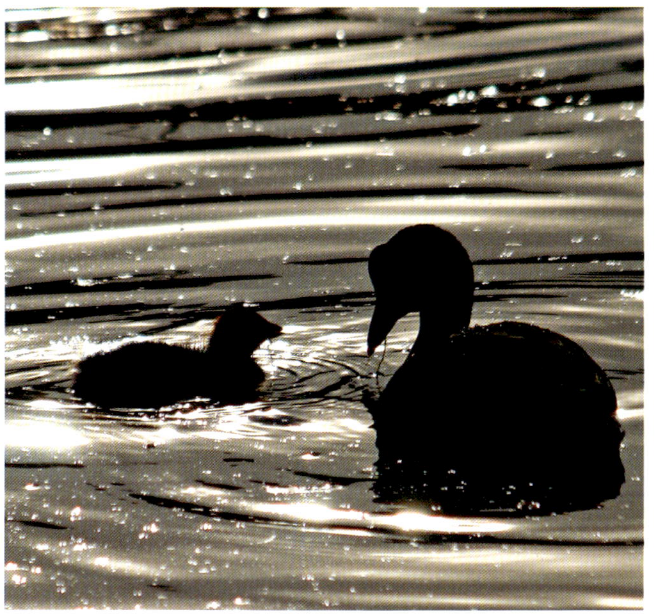

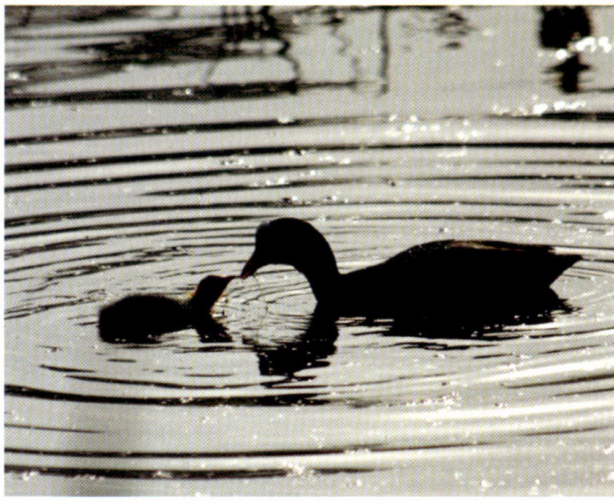

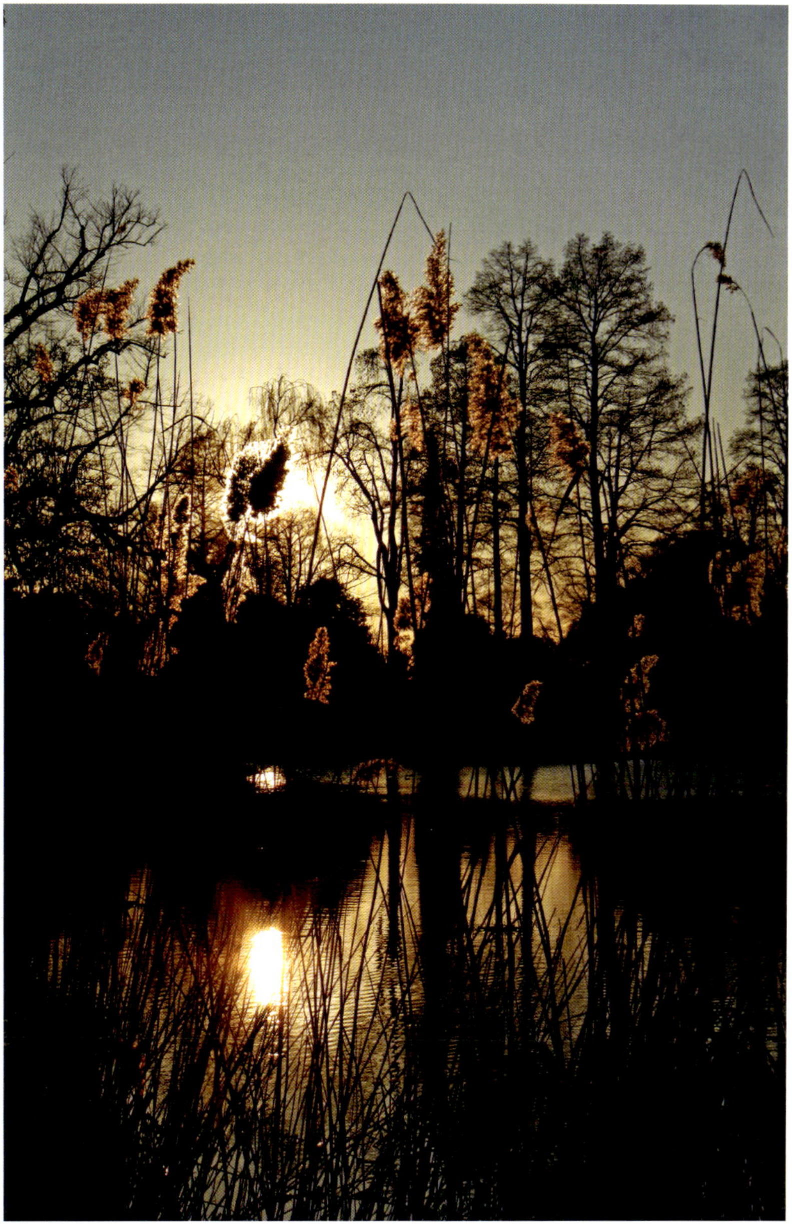

This page: The lake at dusk and a coot feeding its young.

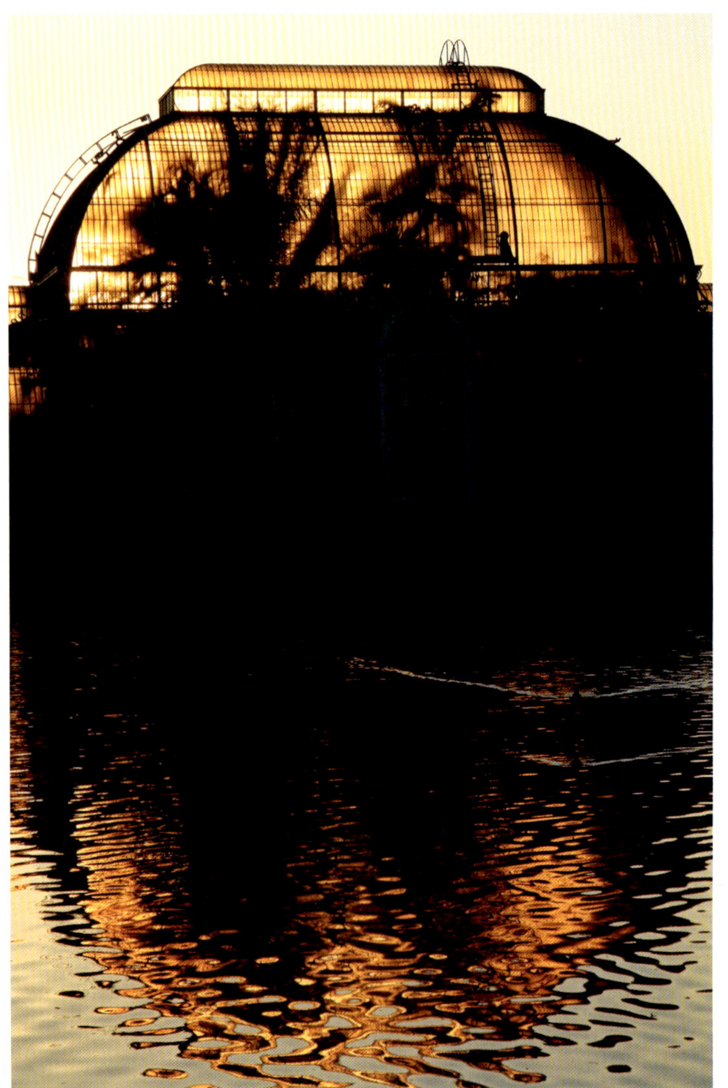

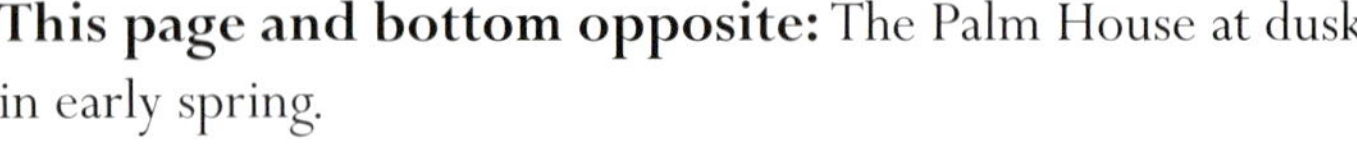

This page and bottom opposite: The Palm House at dusk in early spring.
Top opposite: One of the many museums; this one houses the Plants and People exhibit.

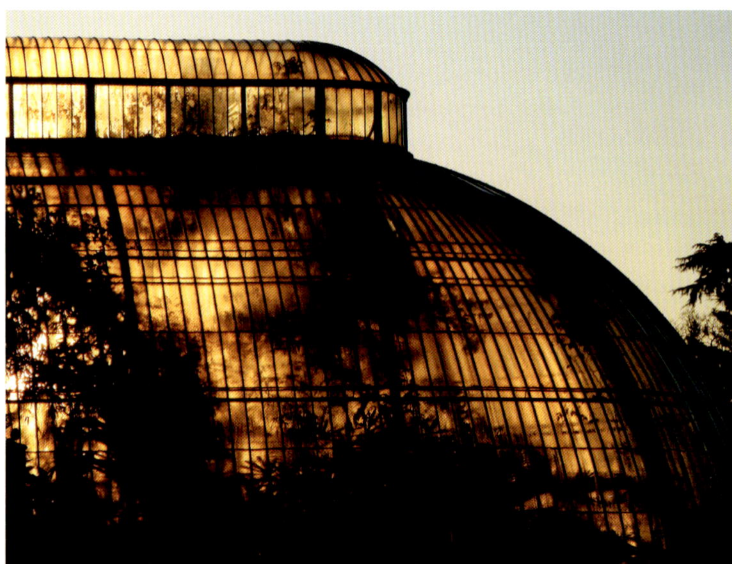

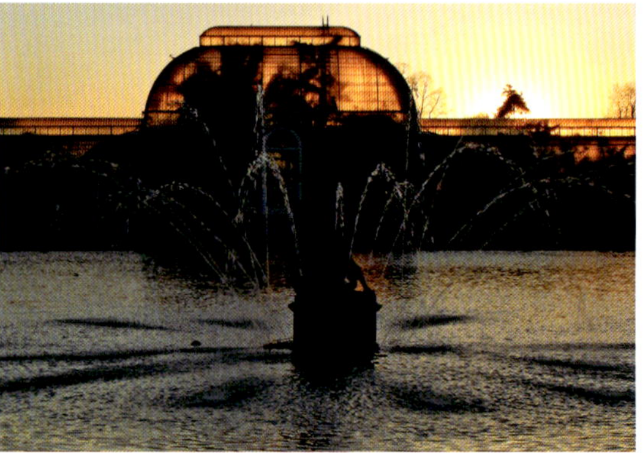

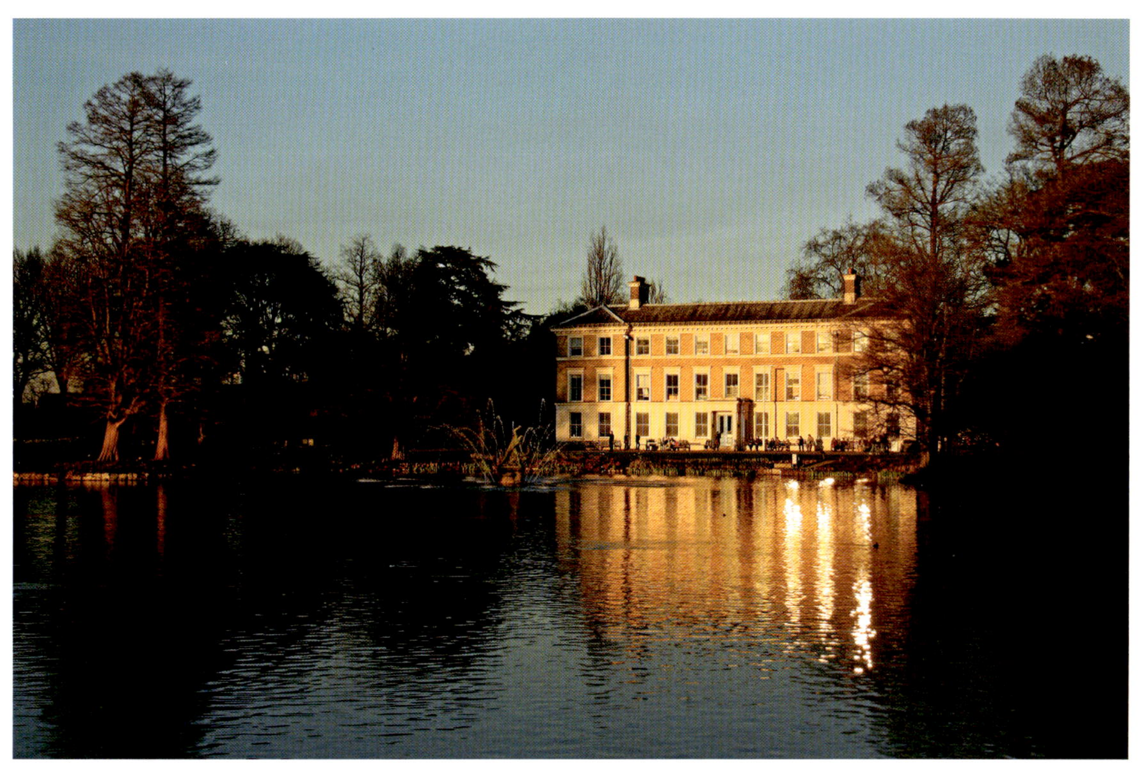

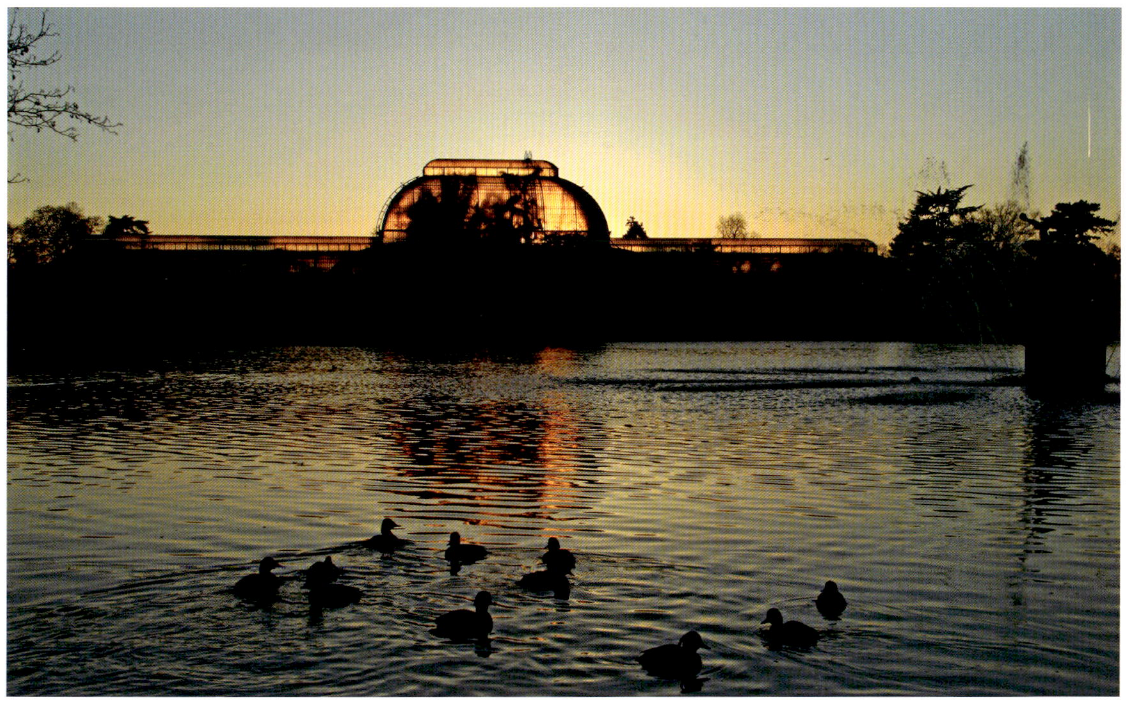

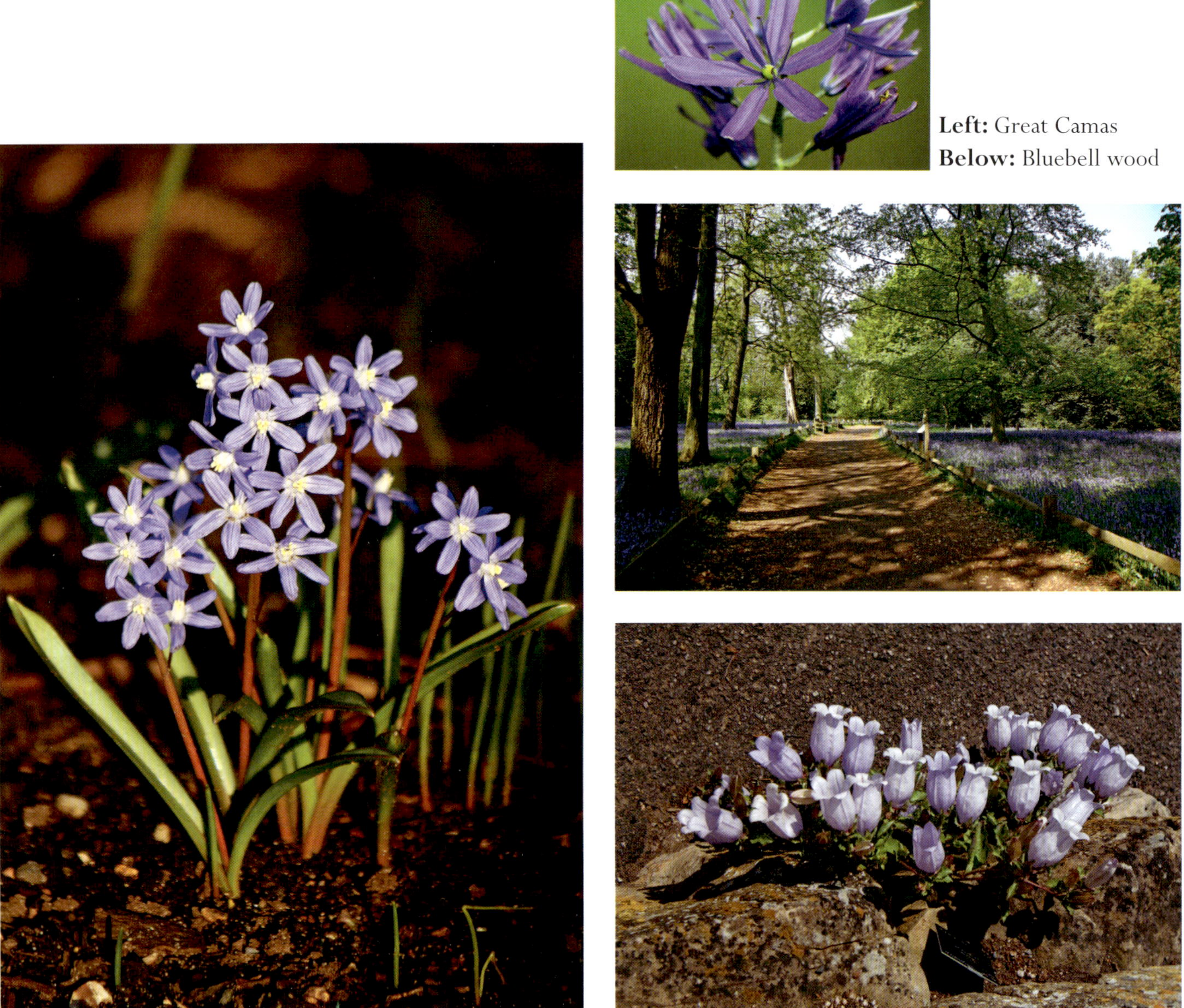

Left: Great Camas
Below: Bluebell wood

Above left: Glory of the snow - so called because they often appear when there is still snow on the ground.
Above right: Alpine Campanula

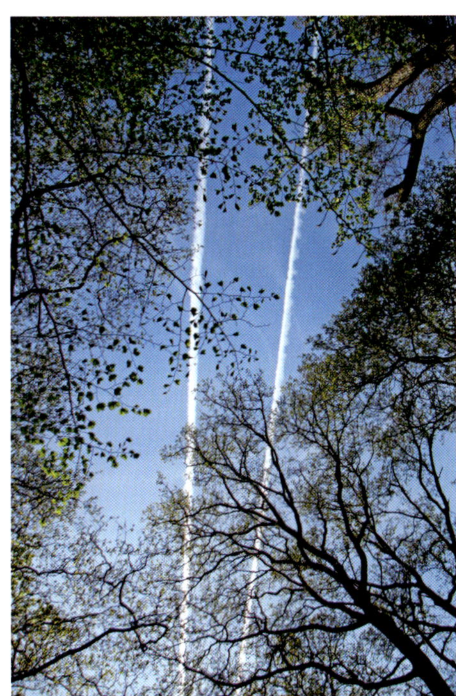

Above: Aeroplane vapour trails through the trees.
Right: The famous Pagoda, which dates from 1762.

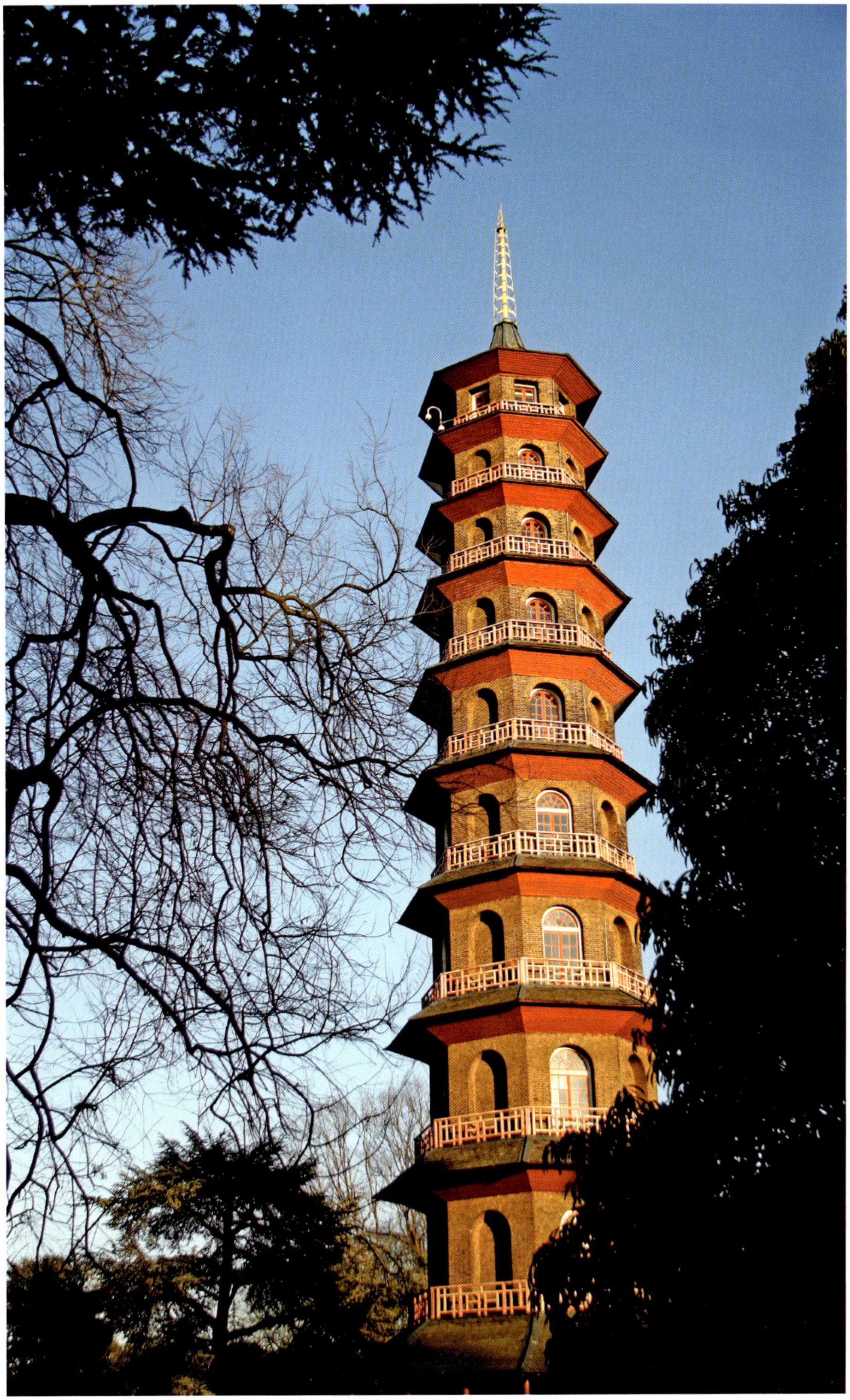

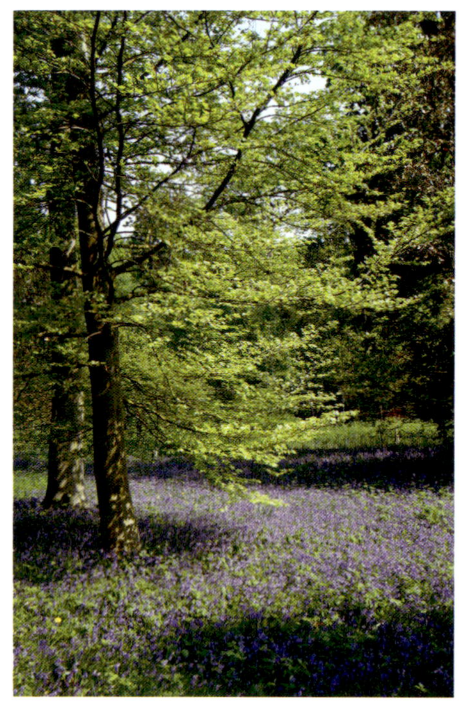

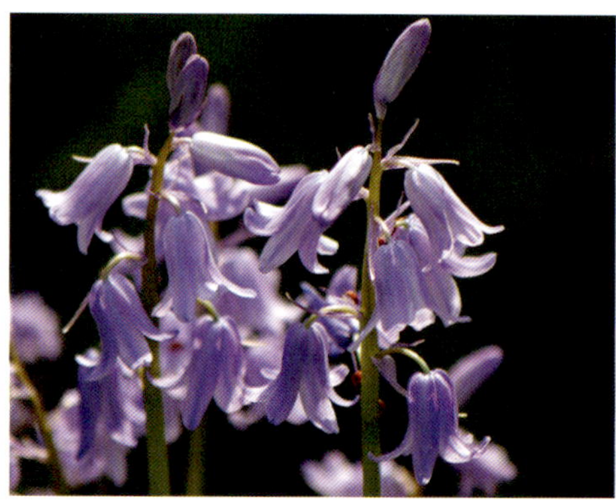

This page and opposite:
The Bluebell Wood

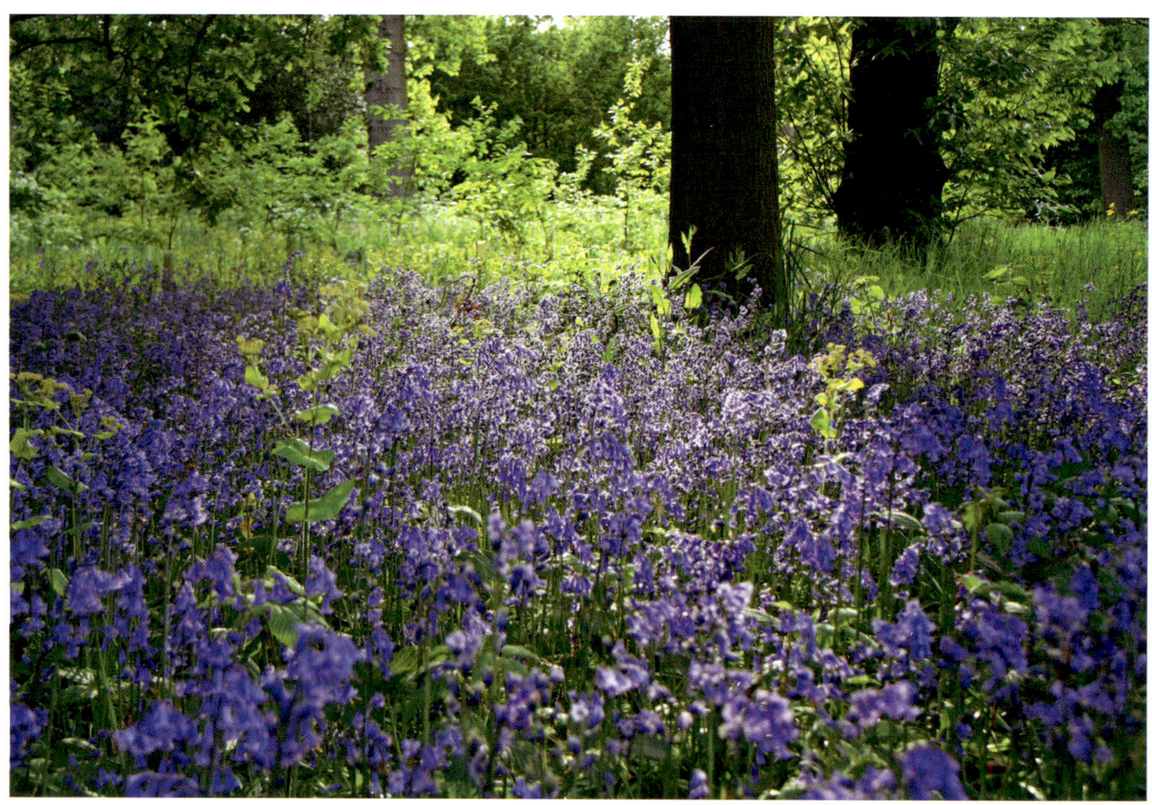

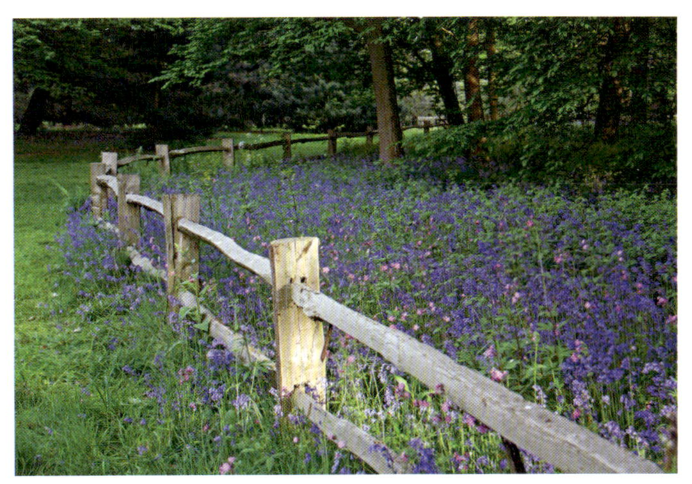

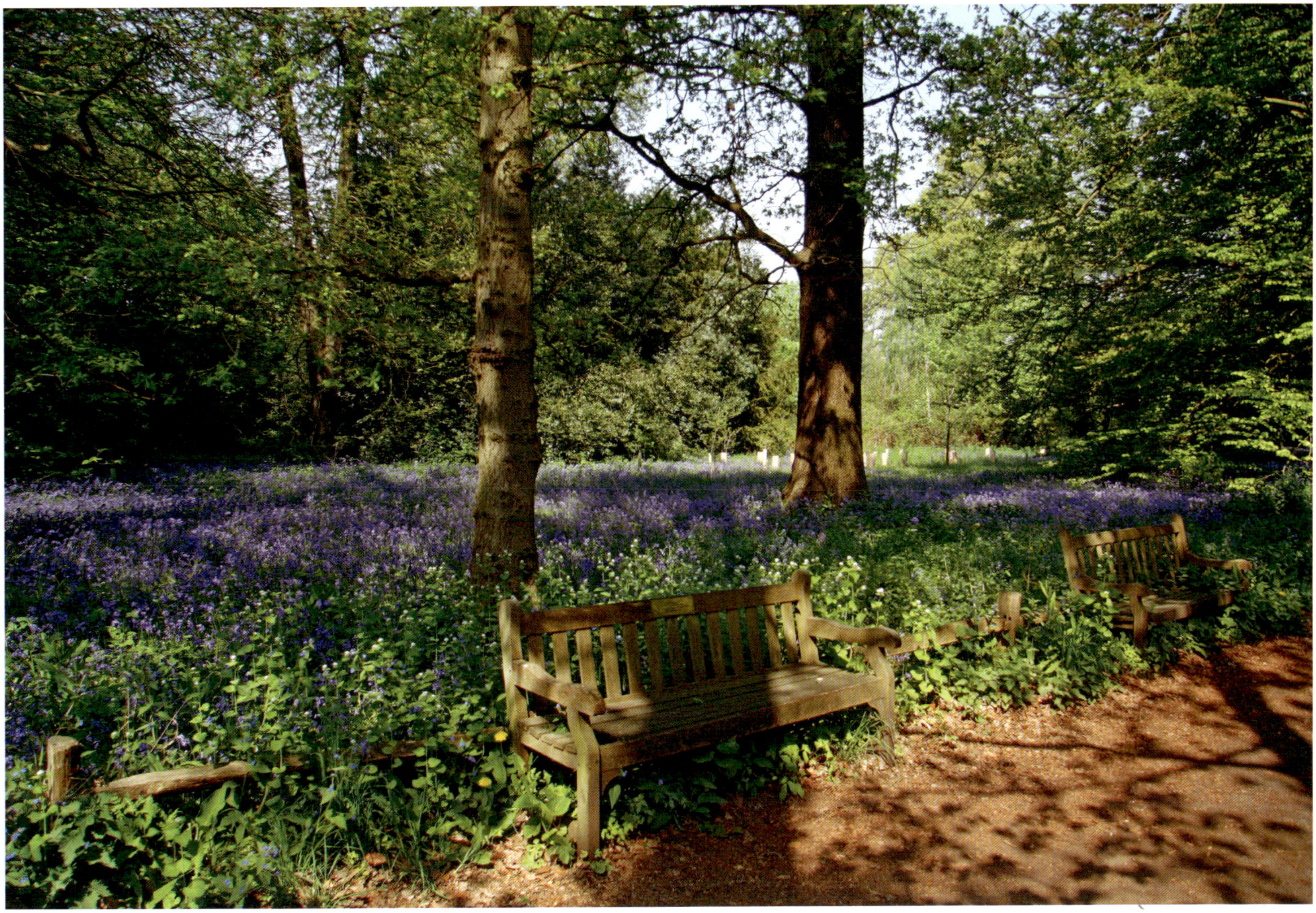

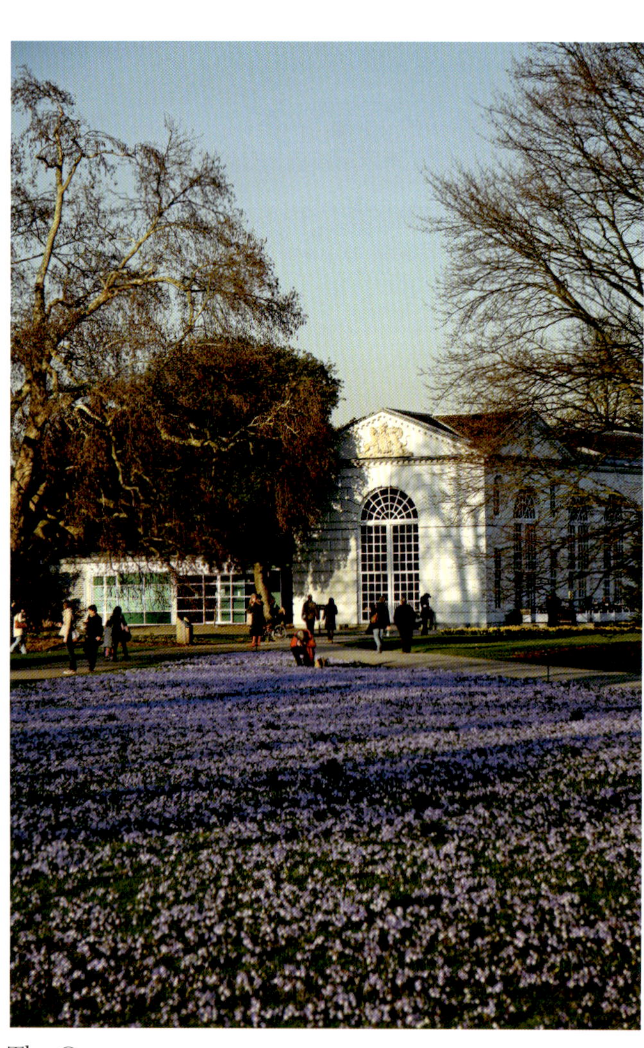

The Orangery

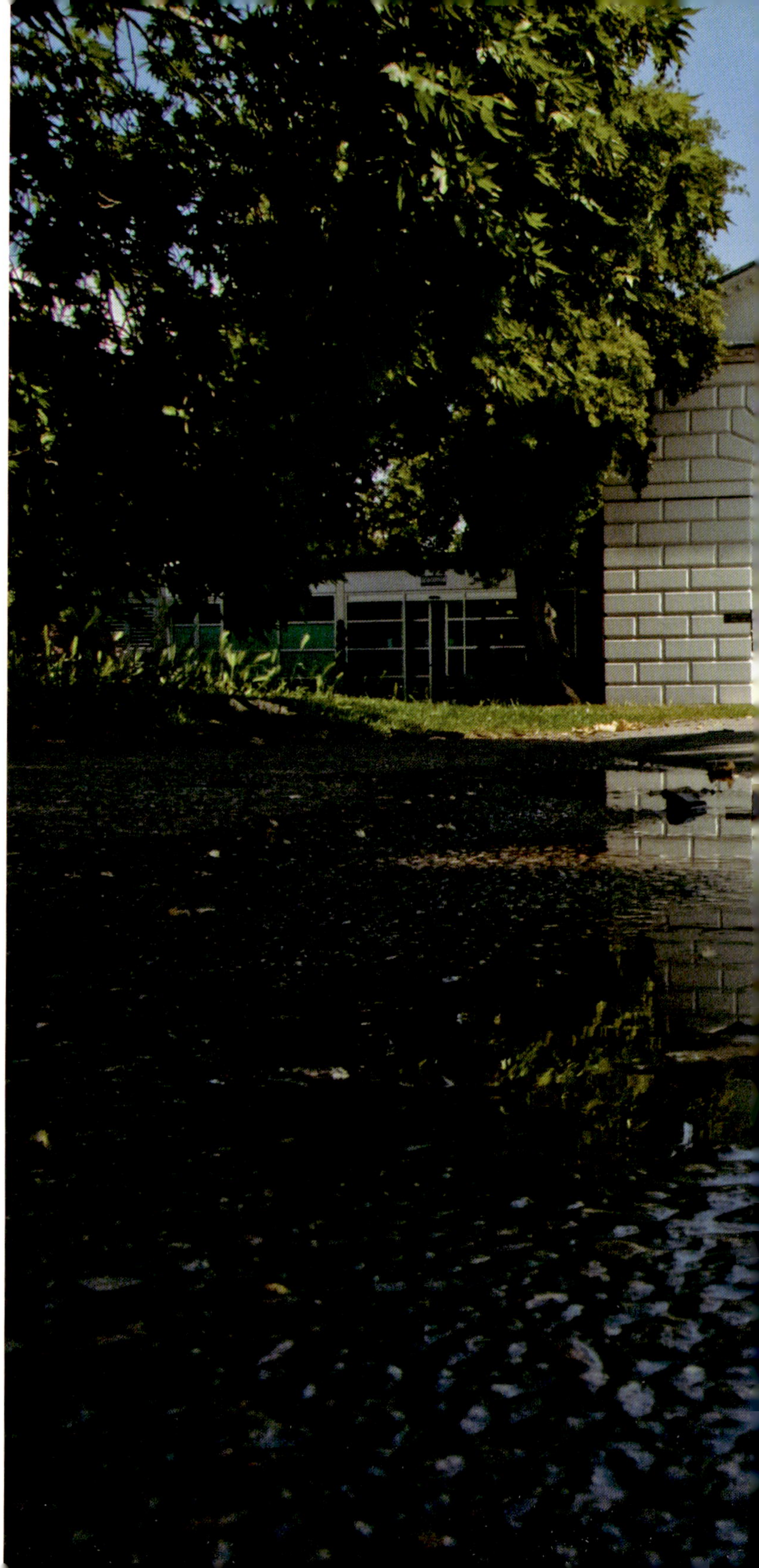

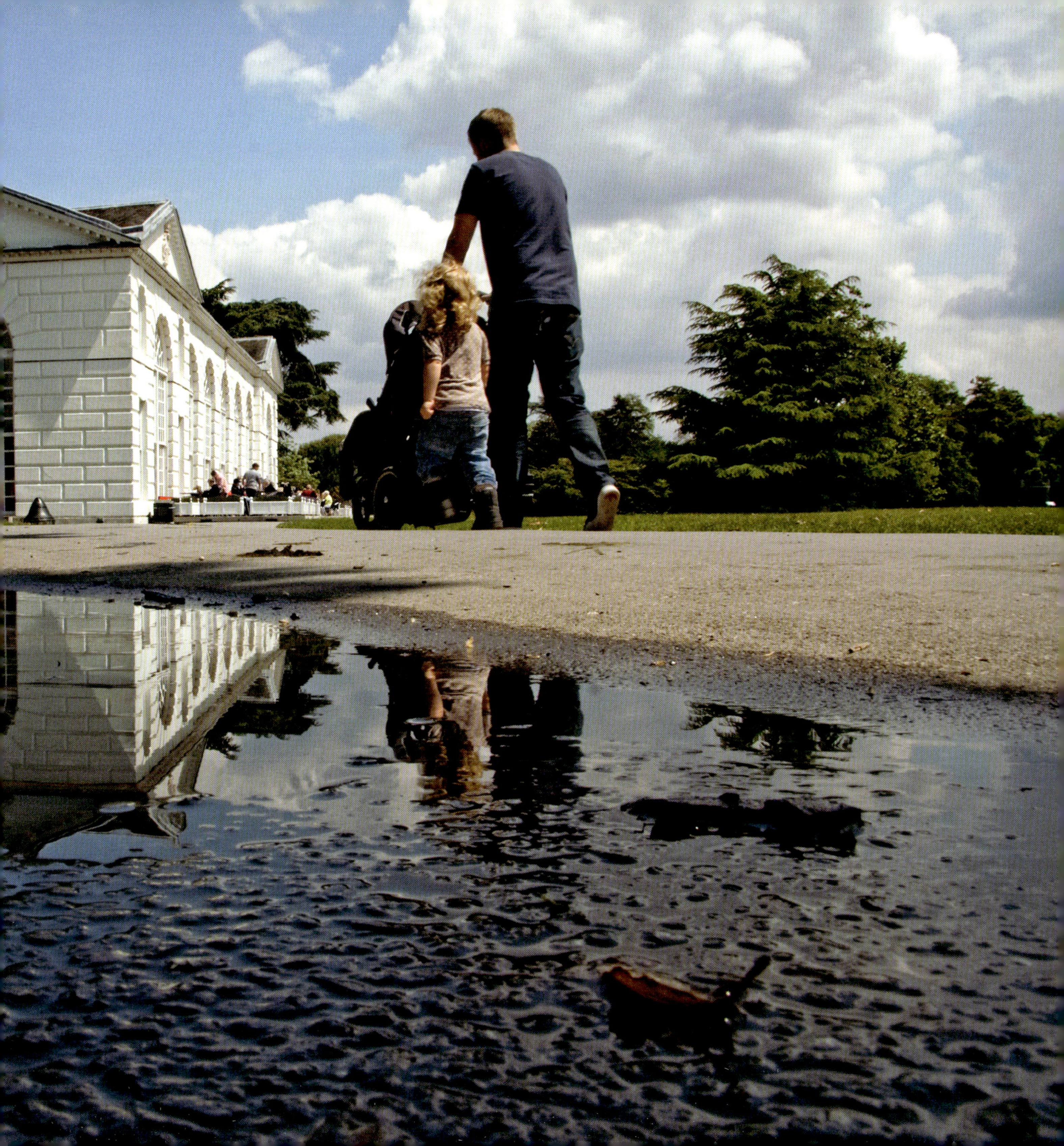

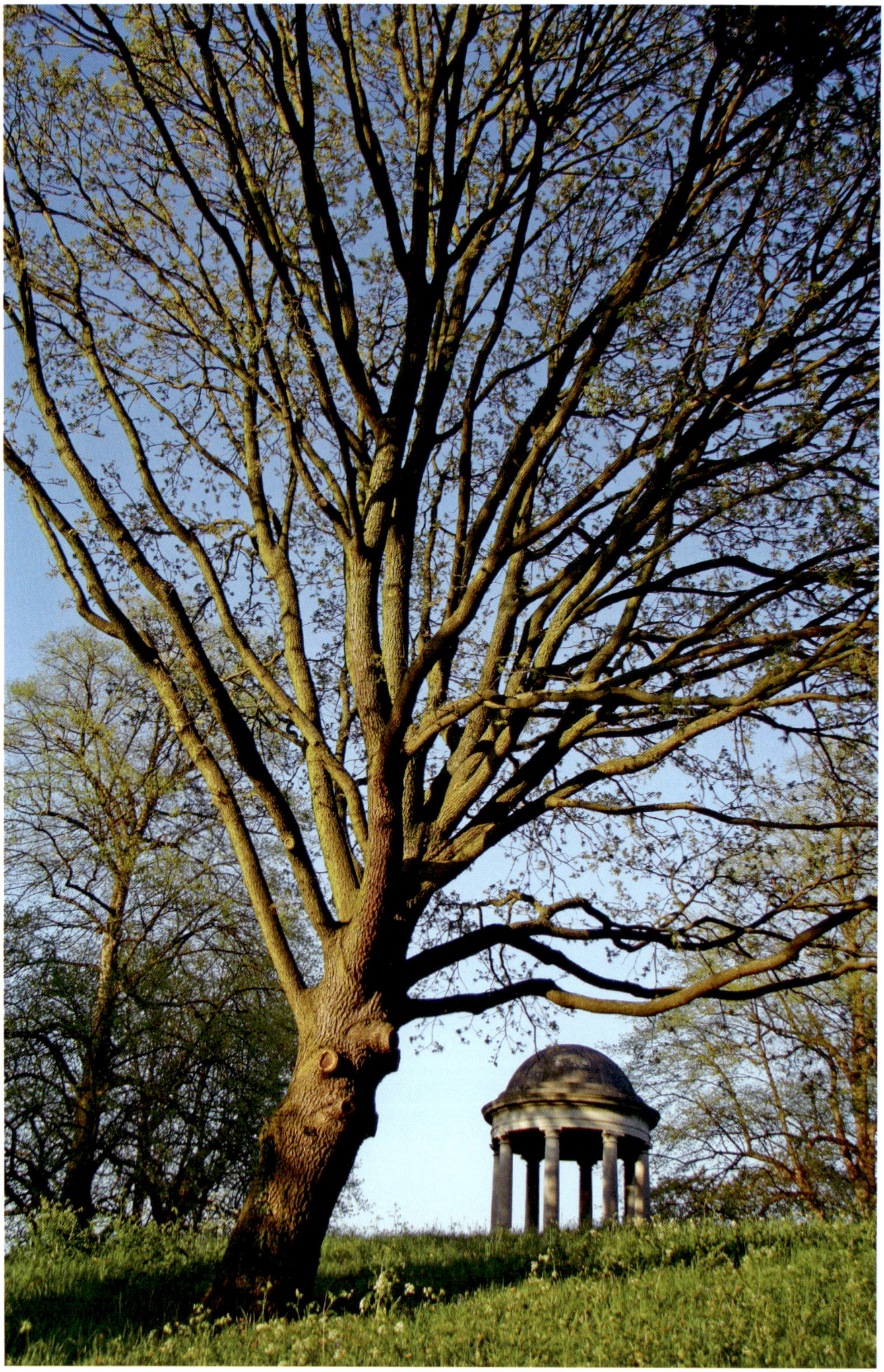

This page:
The Temple of Aeolus, which overlooks the Palm House Pond.

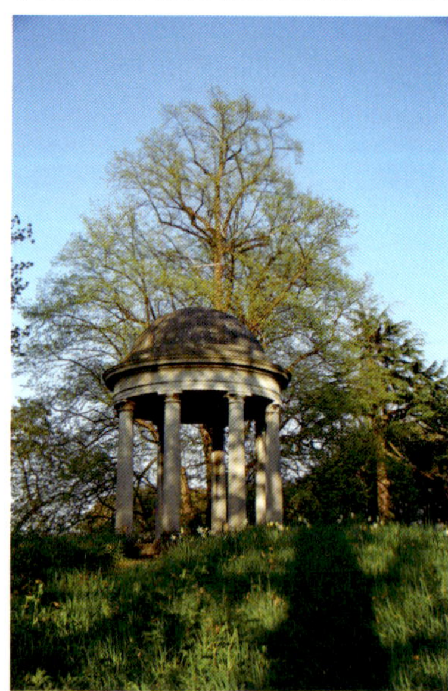

This page: The Walled Garden

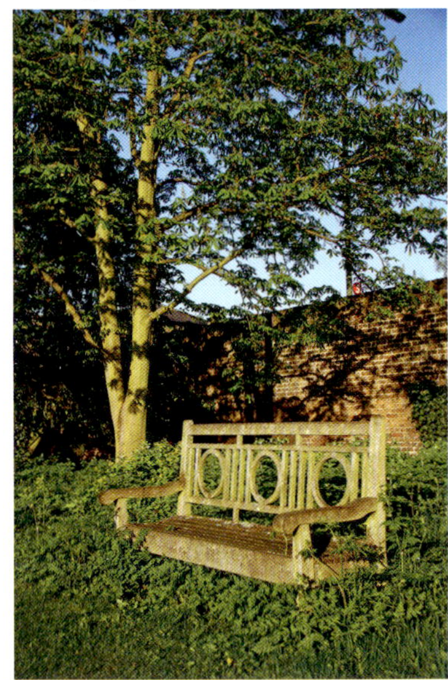

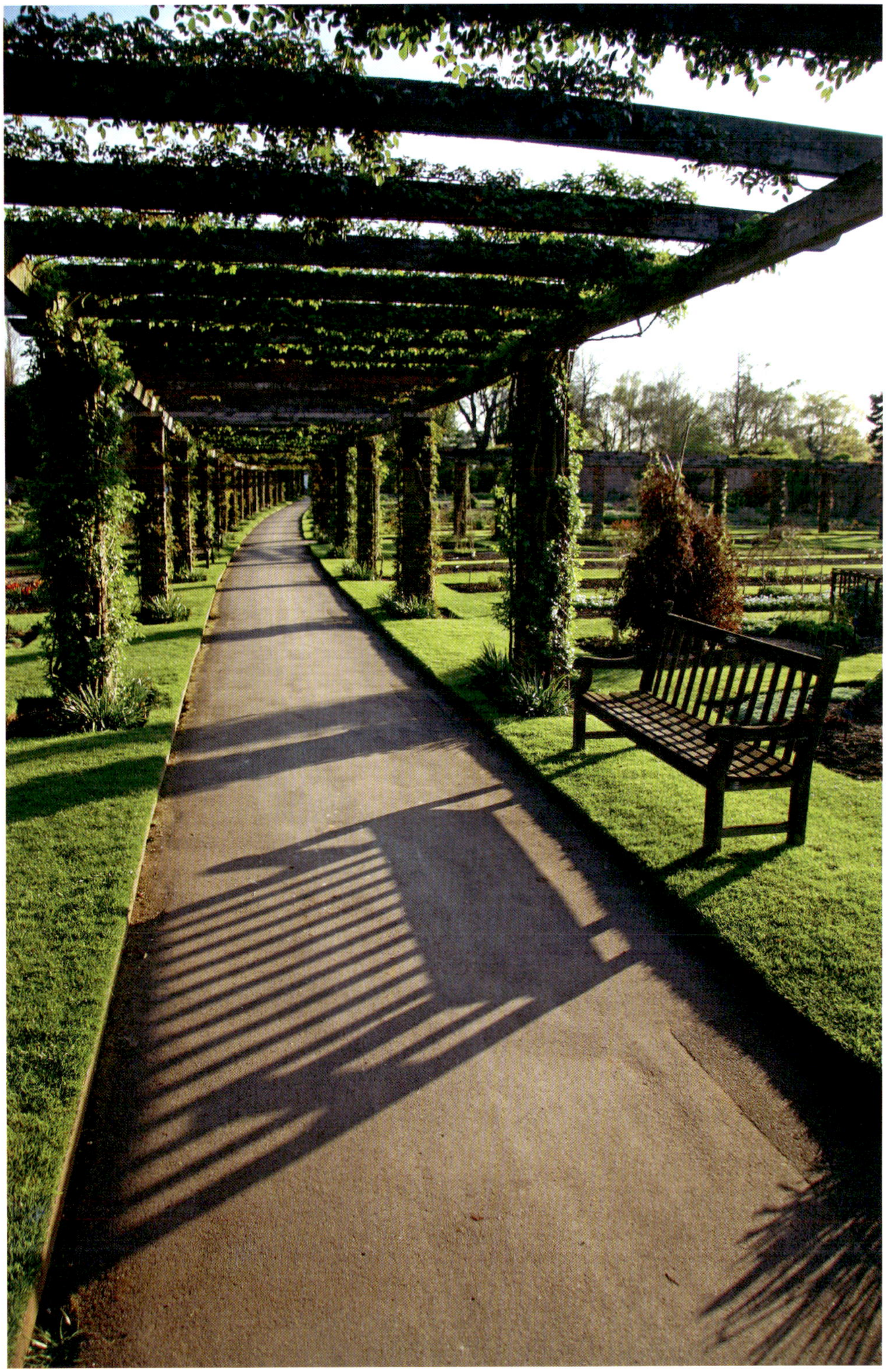

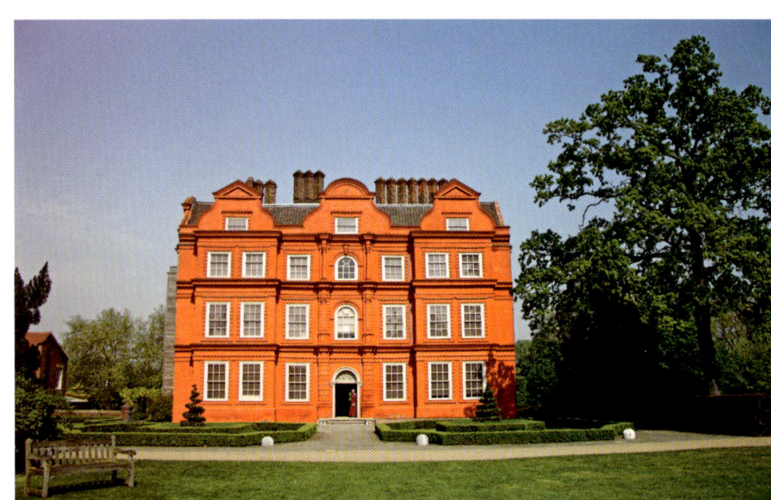

This page and opposite:
Kew Palace

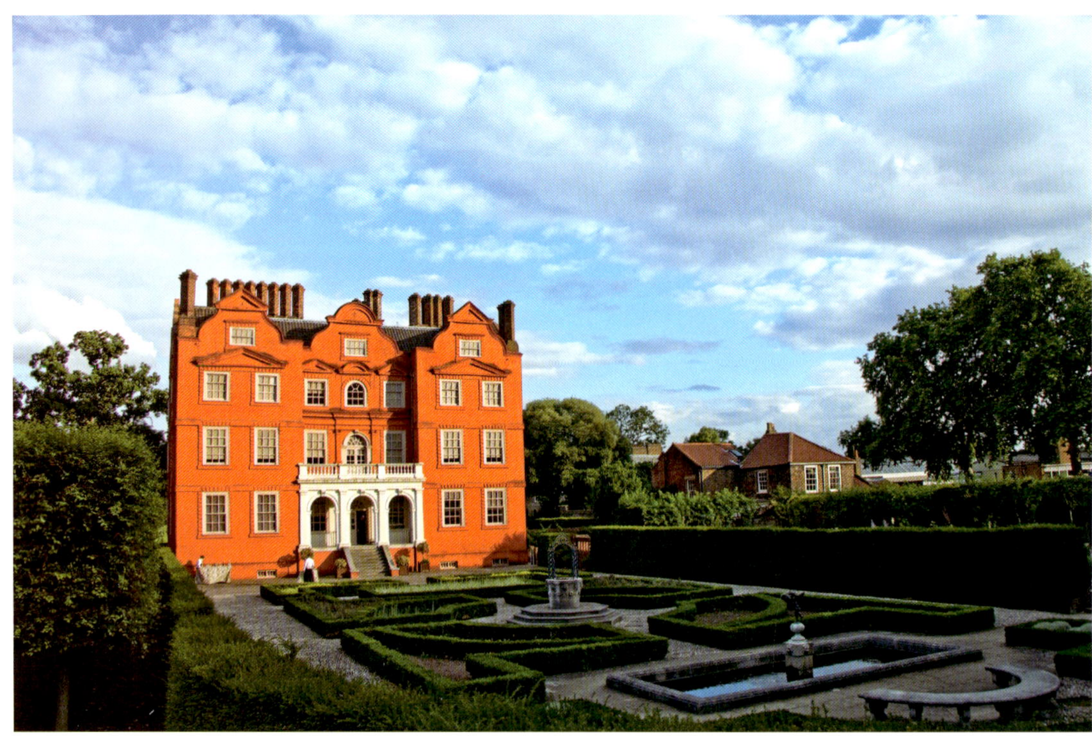

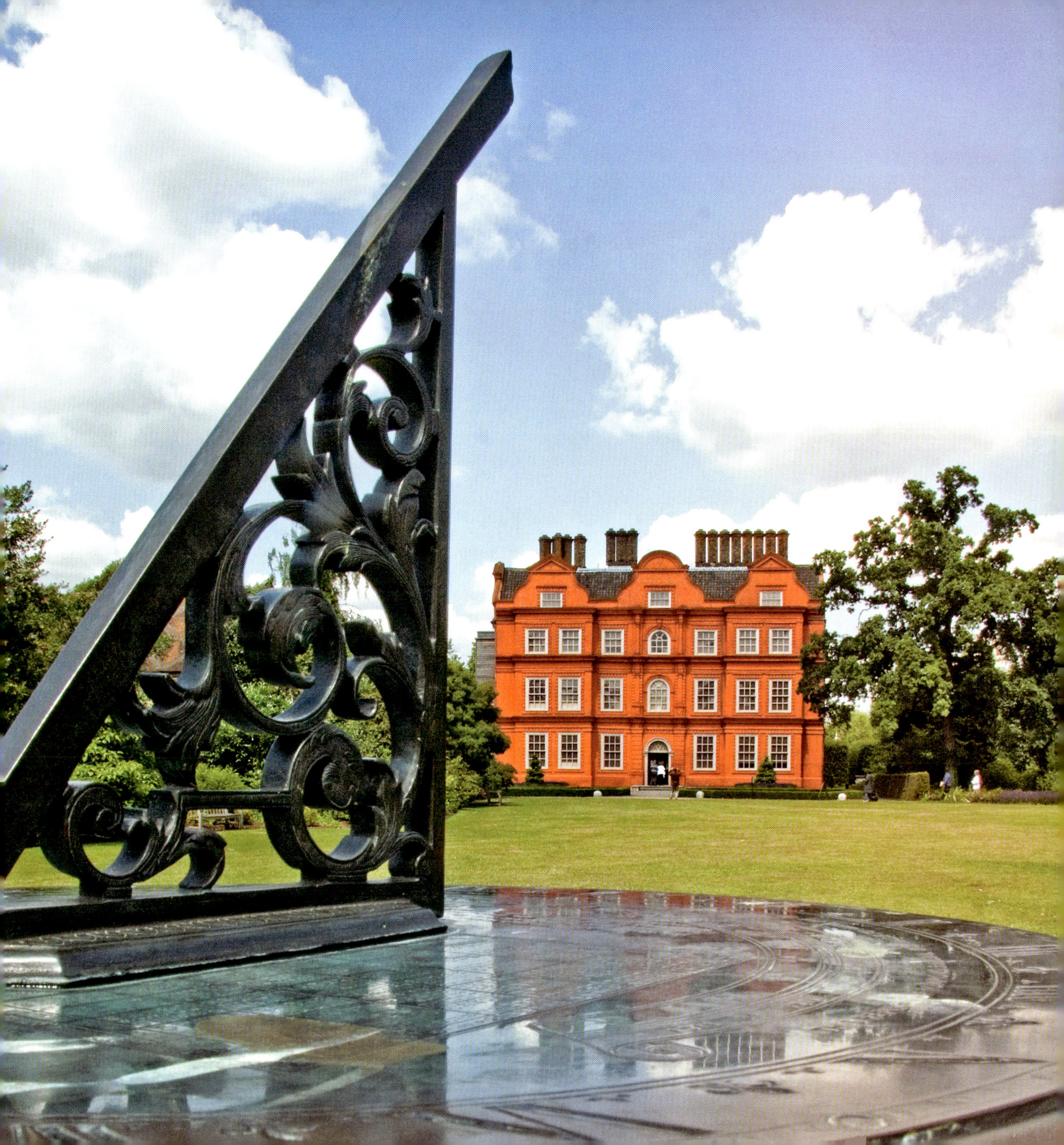

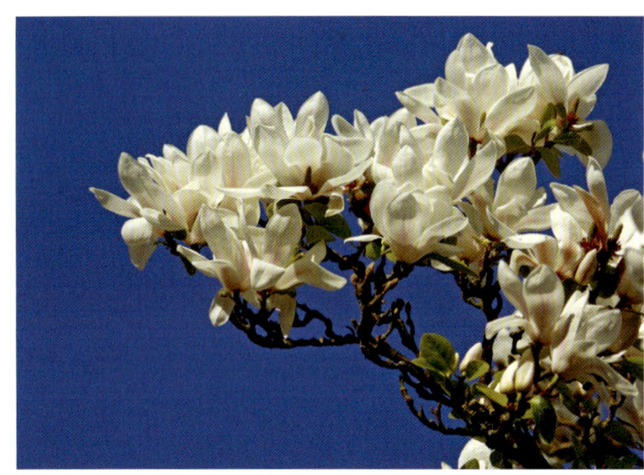

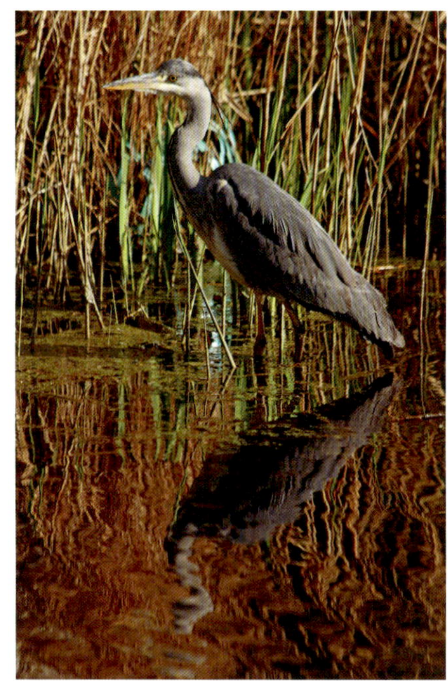

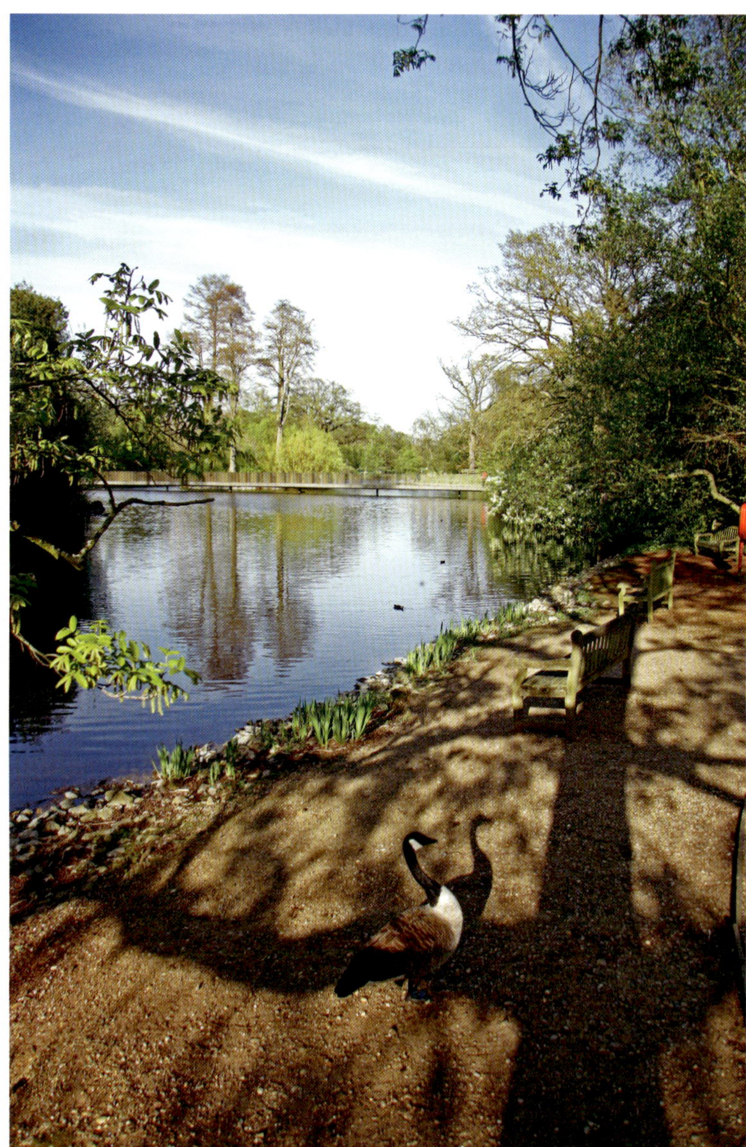

Top: Magnolia
Above: A Grey Heron on the lake.
Right: A Canada Goose beside the lake.

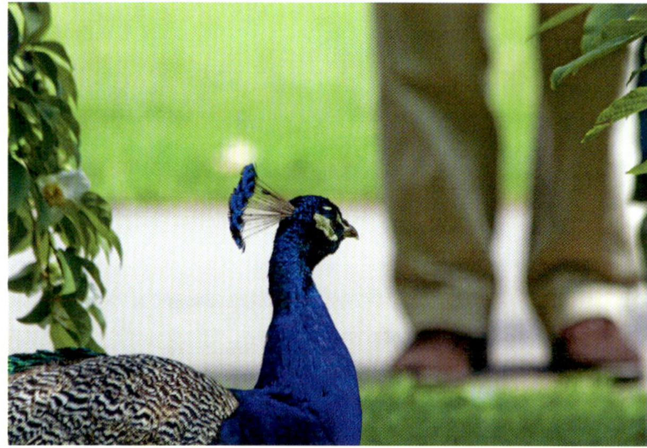

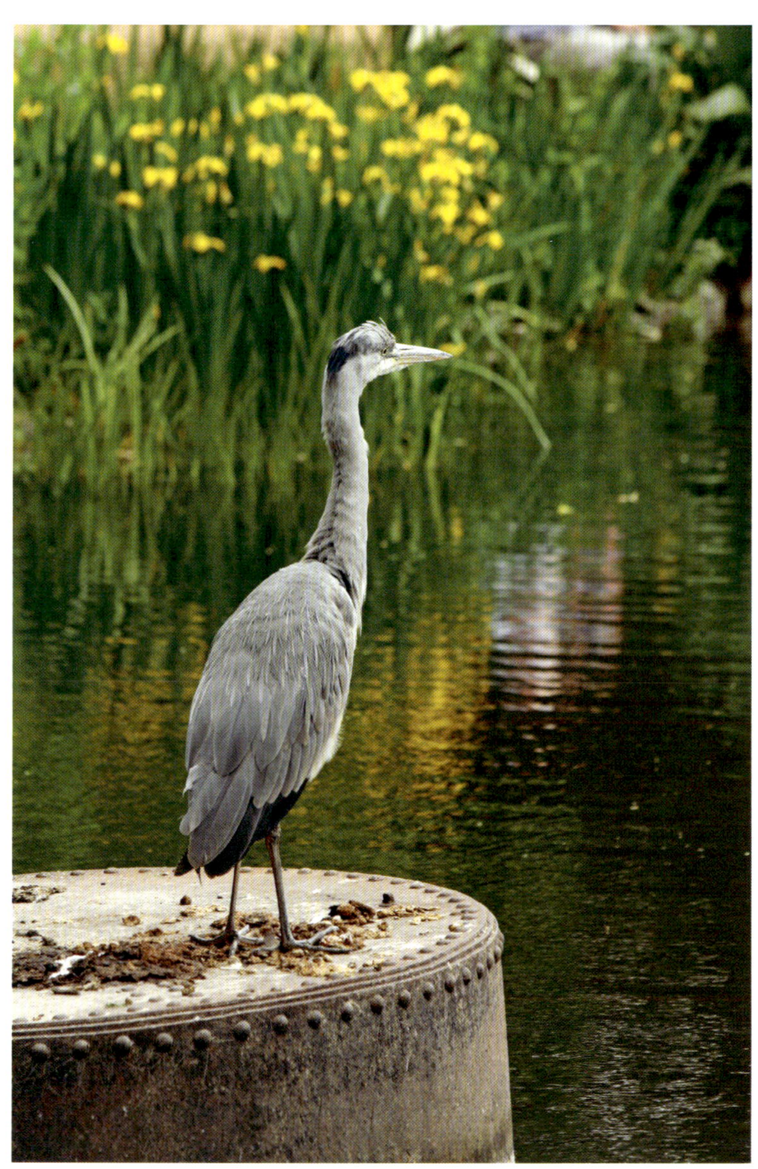

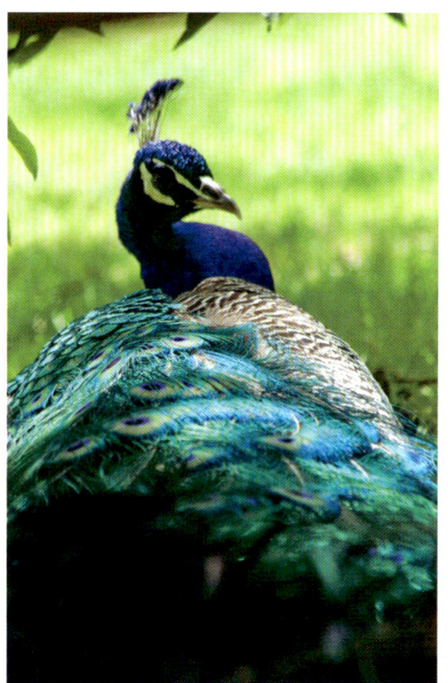

Left: A Grey Heron
Top and above: A Peacock

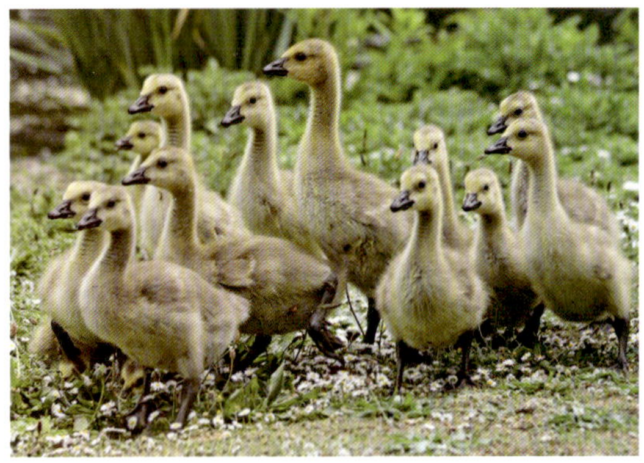

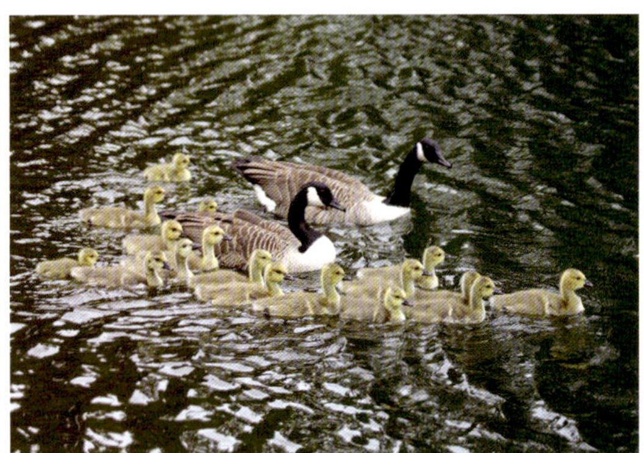

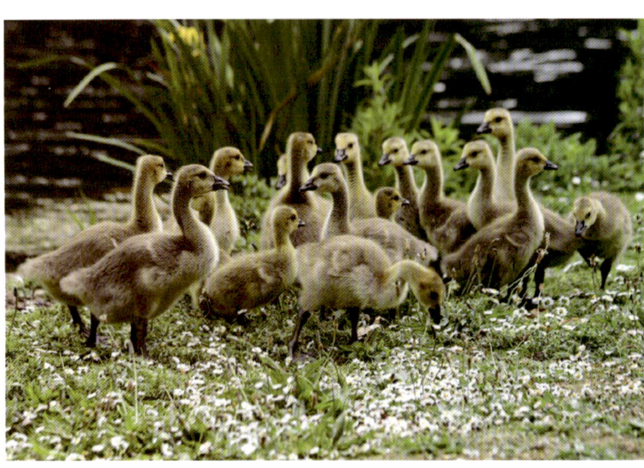

This page and opposite:
An unusally large Canada Goose family, seventeen in all.

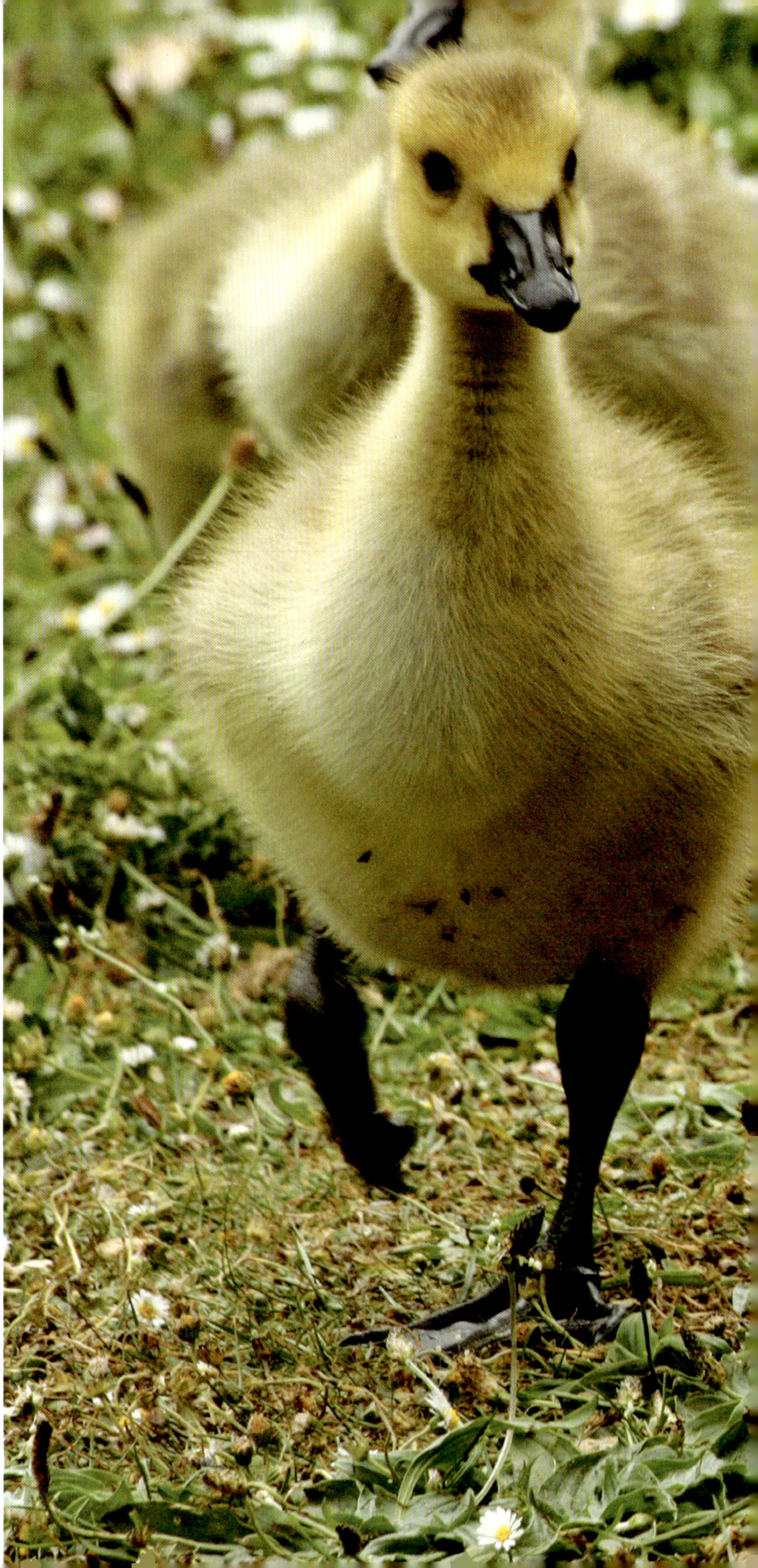

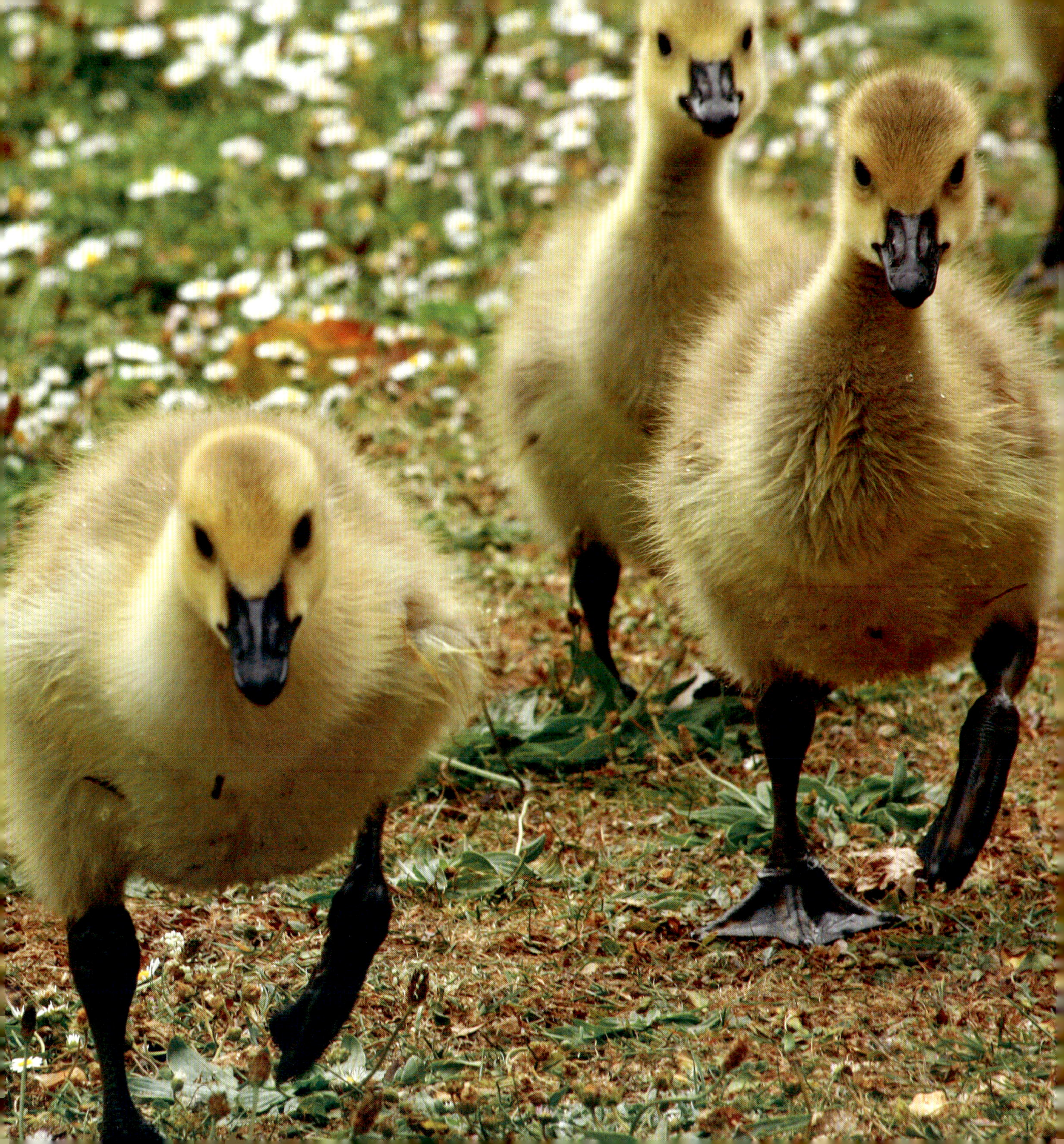

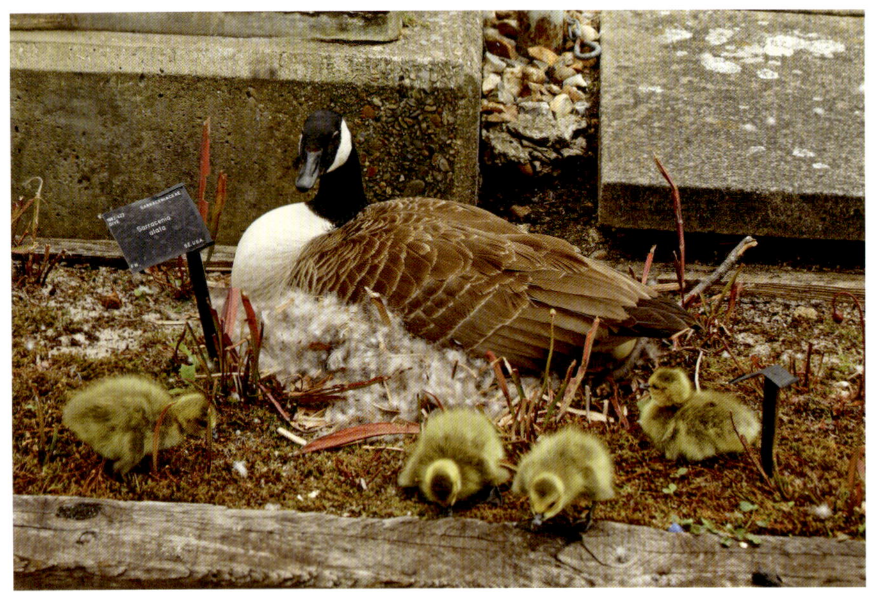

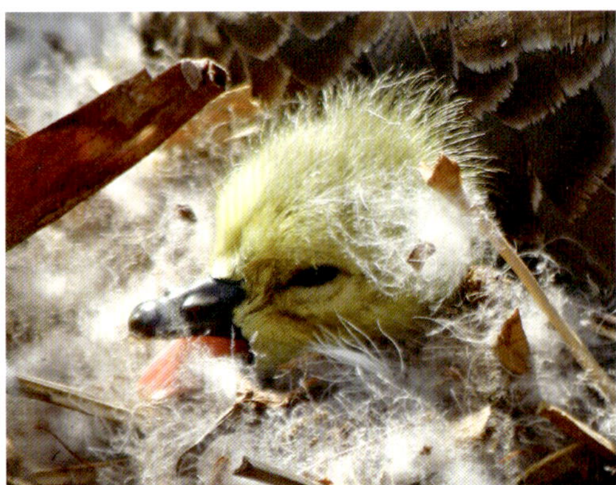

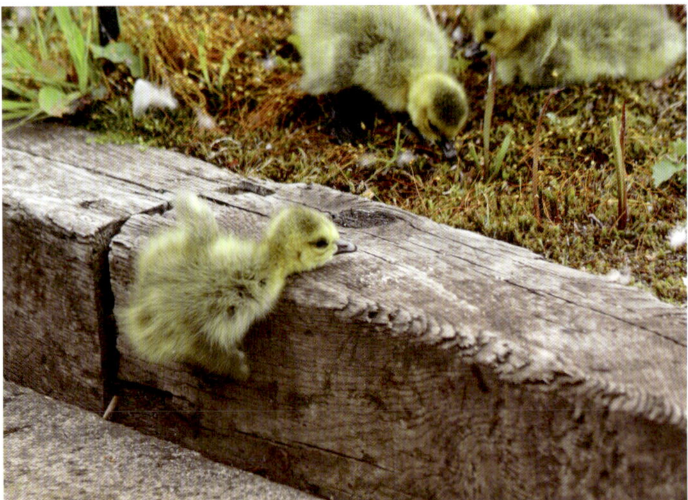

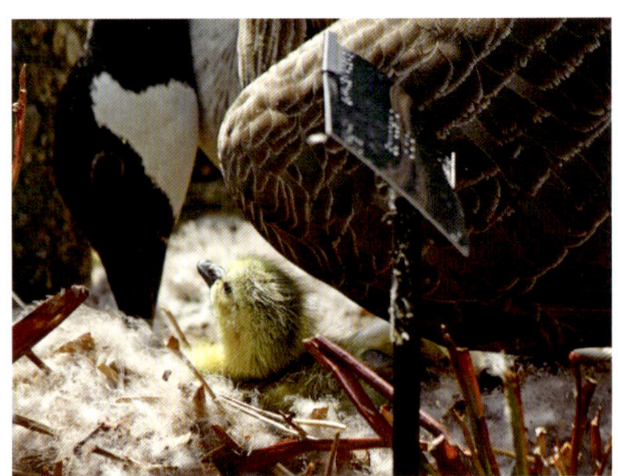

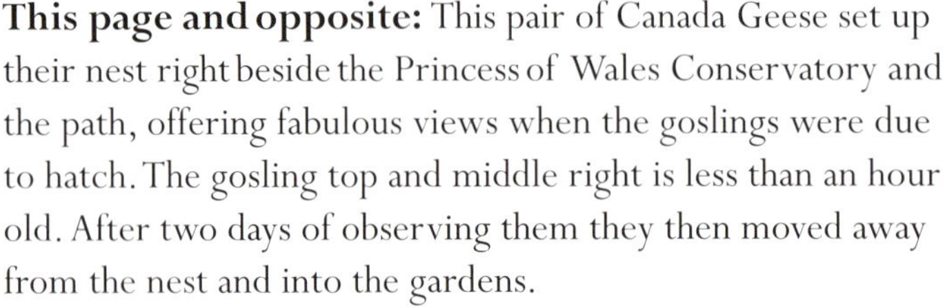

This page and opposite: This pair of Canada Geese set up their nest right beside the Princess of Wales Conservatory and the path, offering fabulous views when the goslings were due to hatch. The gosling top and middle right is less than an hour old. After two days of observing them they then moved away from the nest and into the gardens.

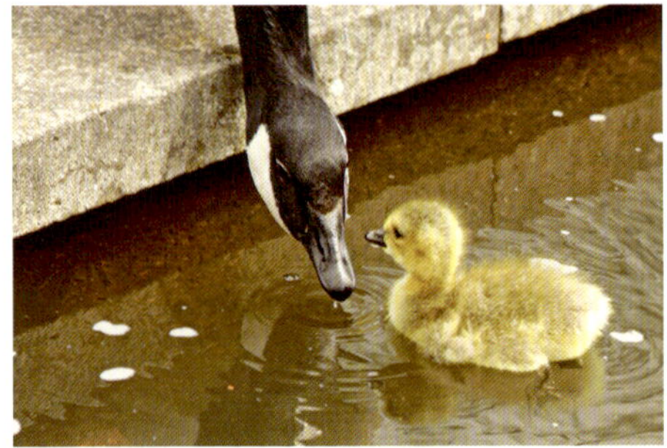

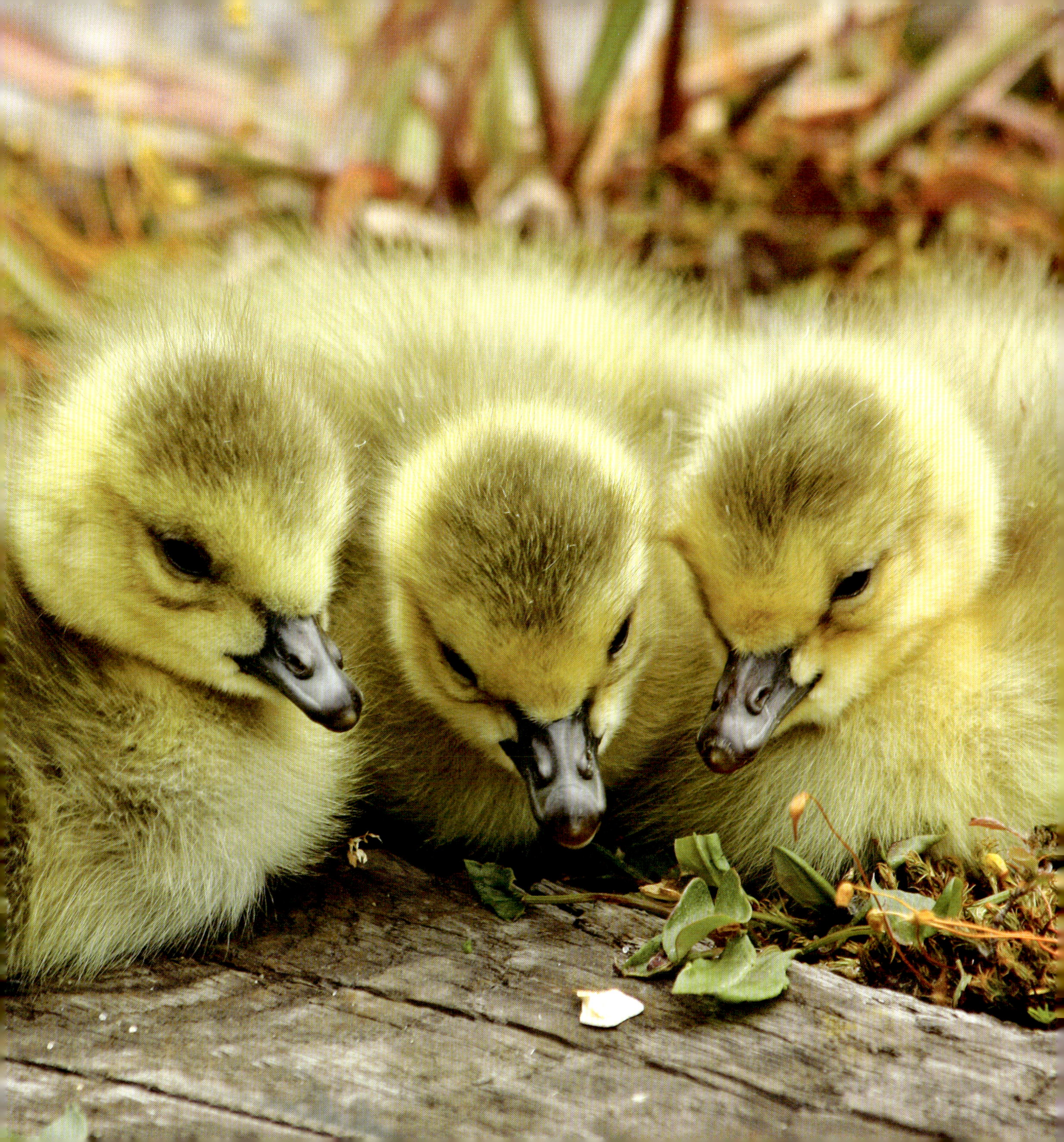

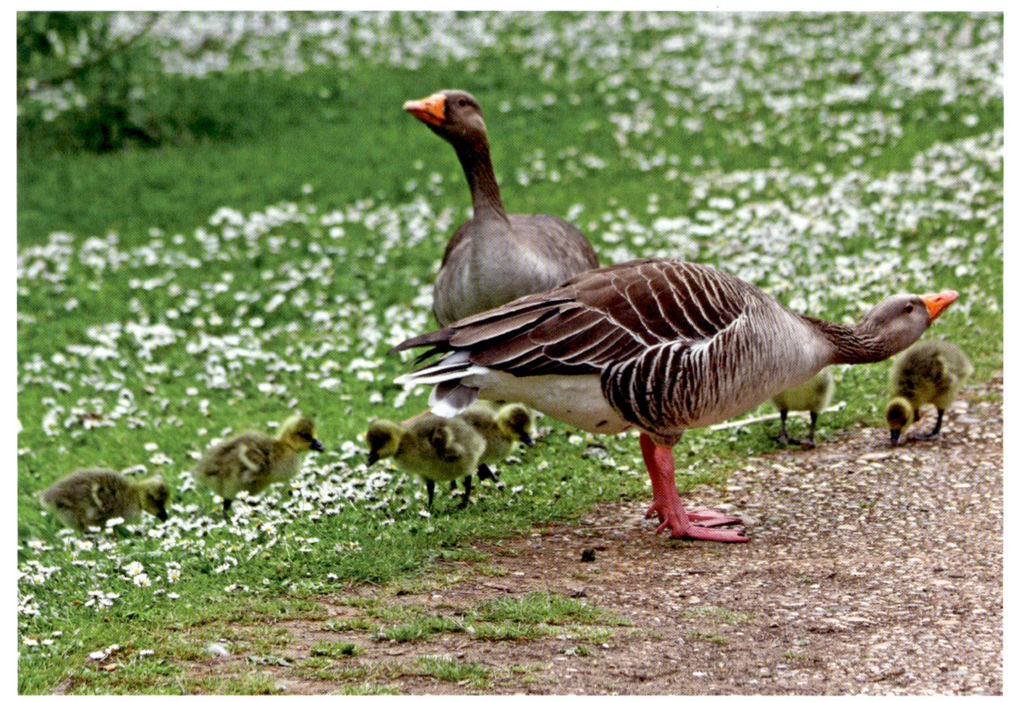

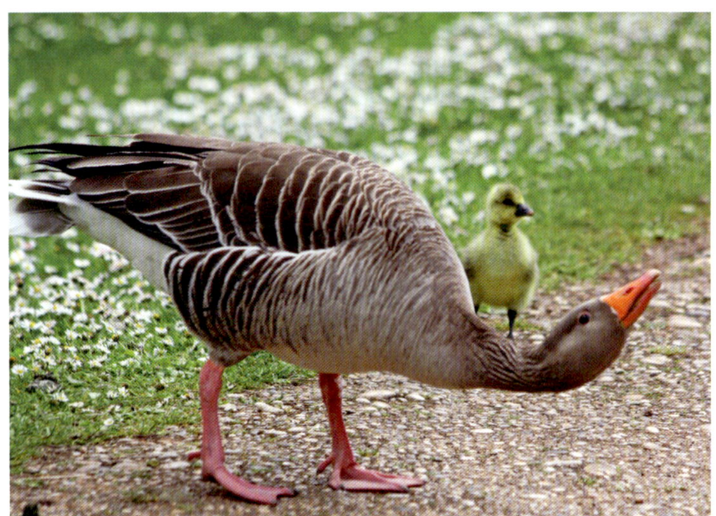

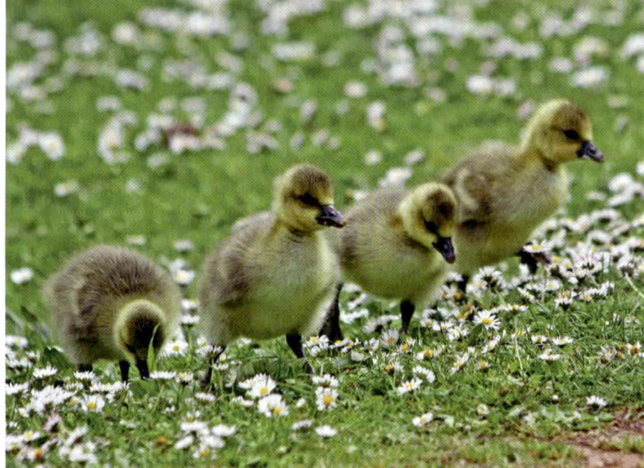

This page: Greylag Geese and their goslings, displaying some extravagant neck movements.

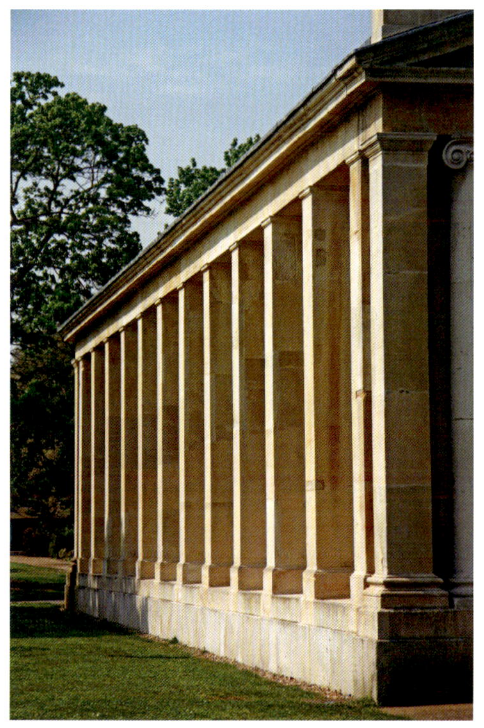

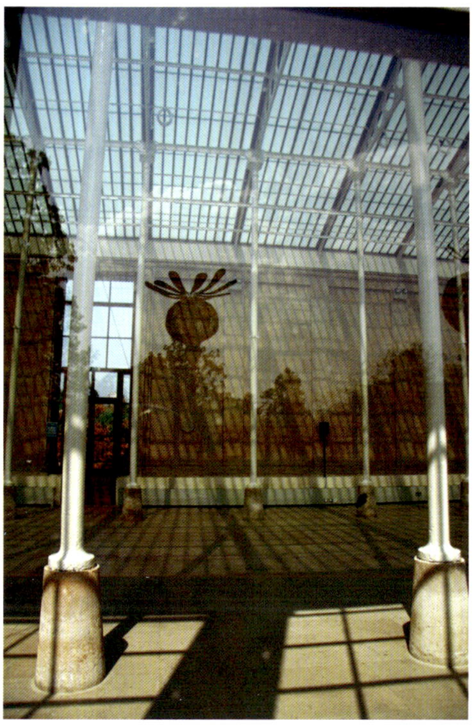

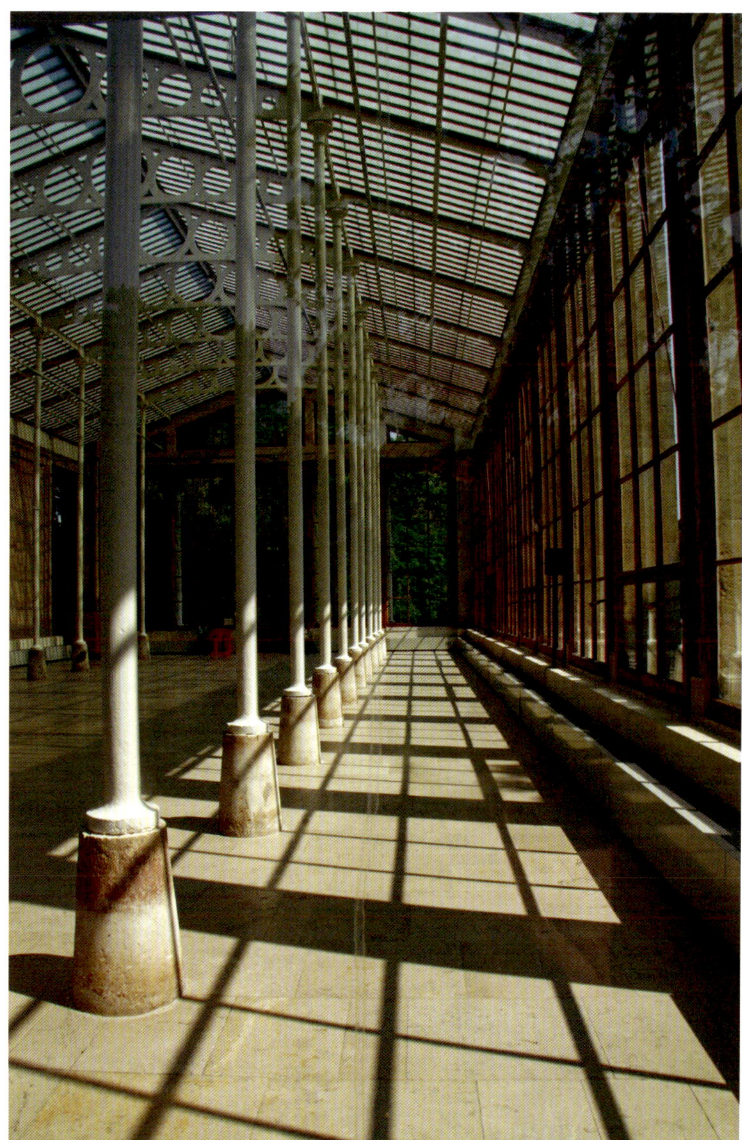

This page: The Nash Conservatory is just inside the main gate. It originally came from Buckingham Palace and was given to Kew Gardens by William IV.

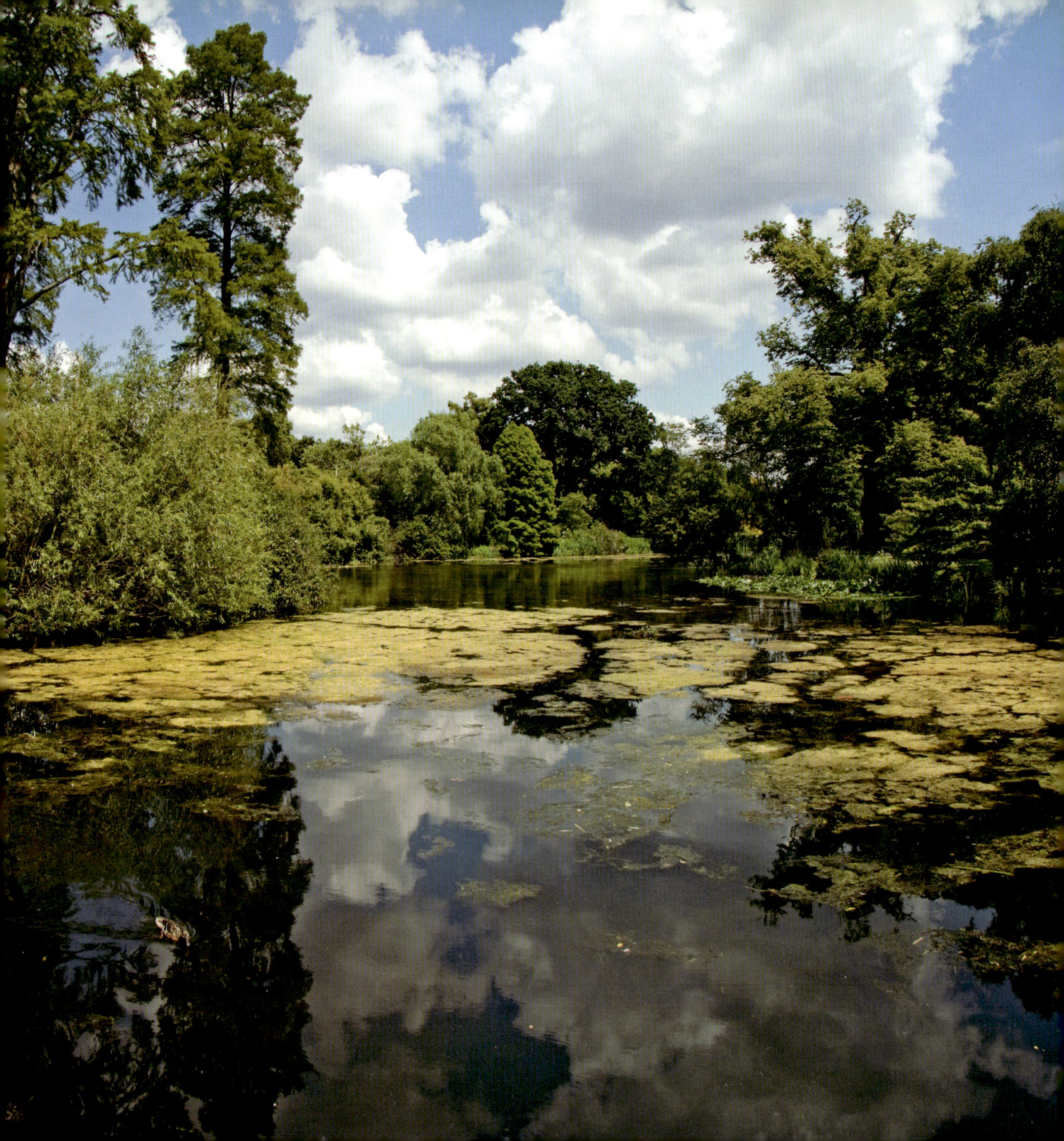

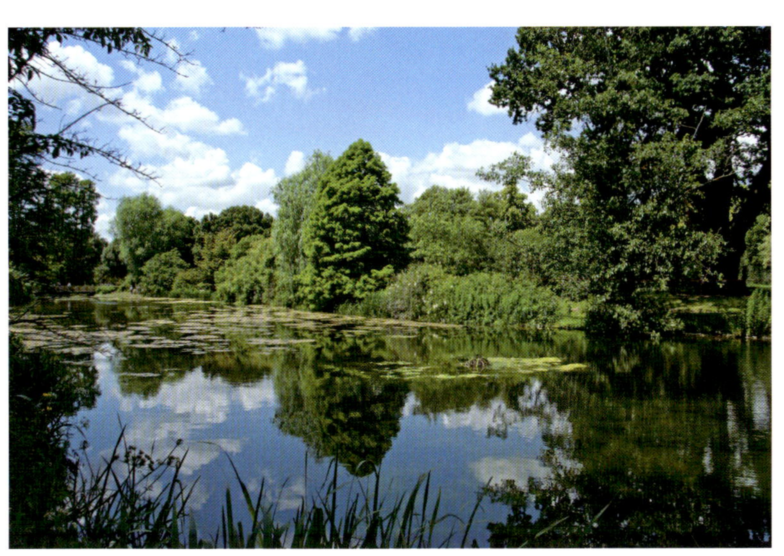

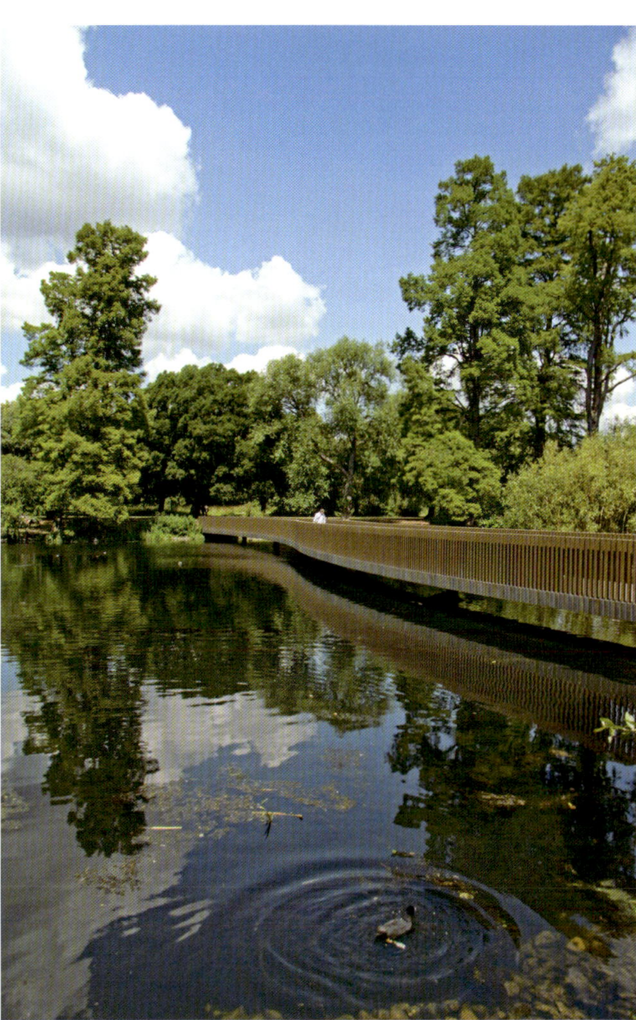

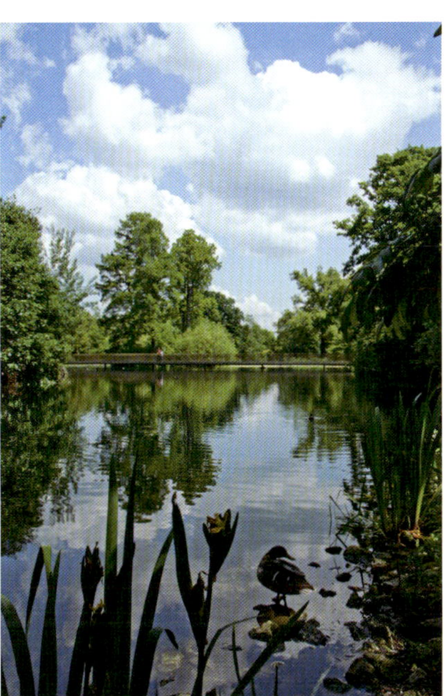

This page and opposite:
The lake in summer

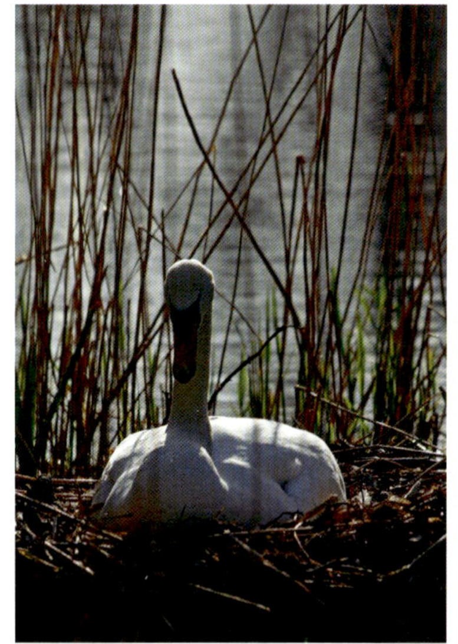

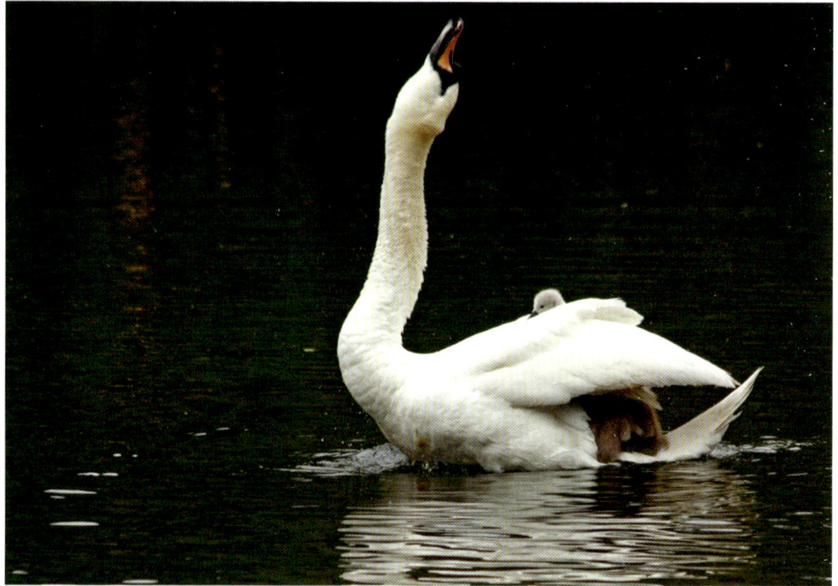

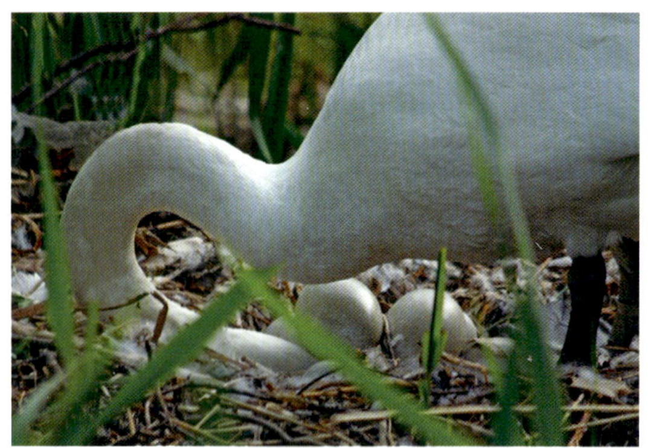

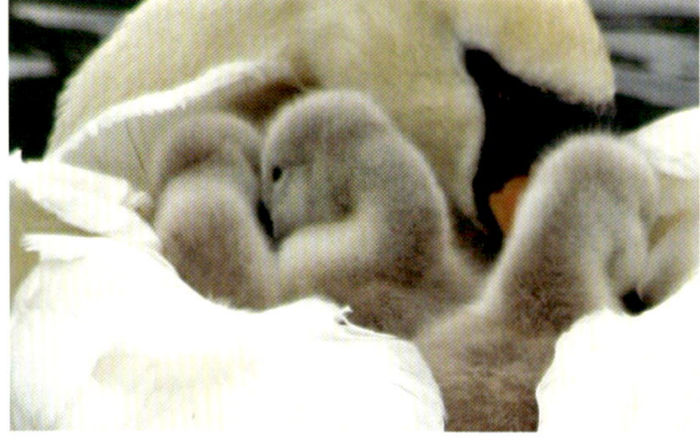

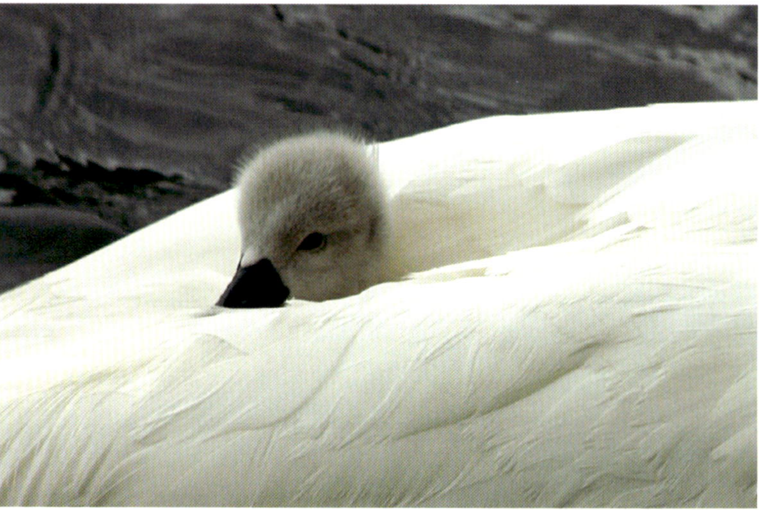

This page and opposite: The pair of Mute Swans on the lake successfully bred in 2011 and although common to see the pen carry them on her back, all six were a surprise.

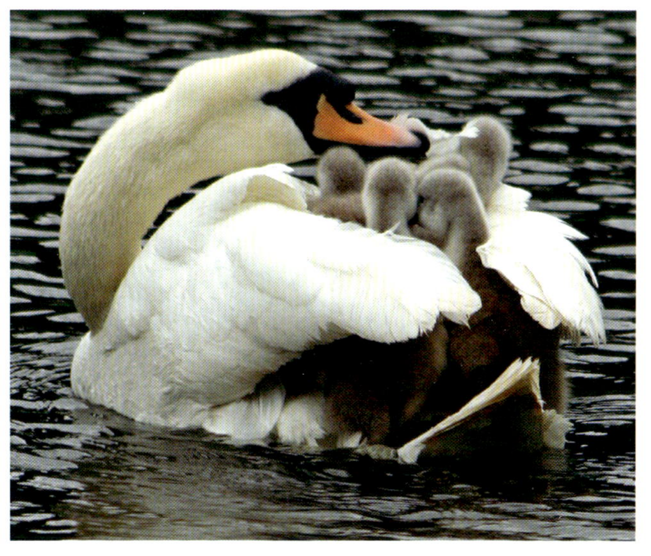

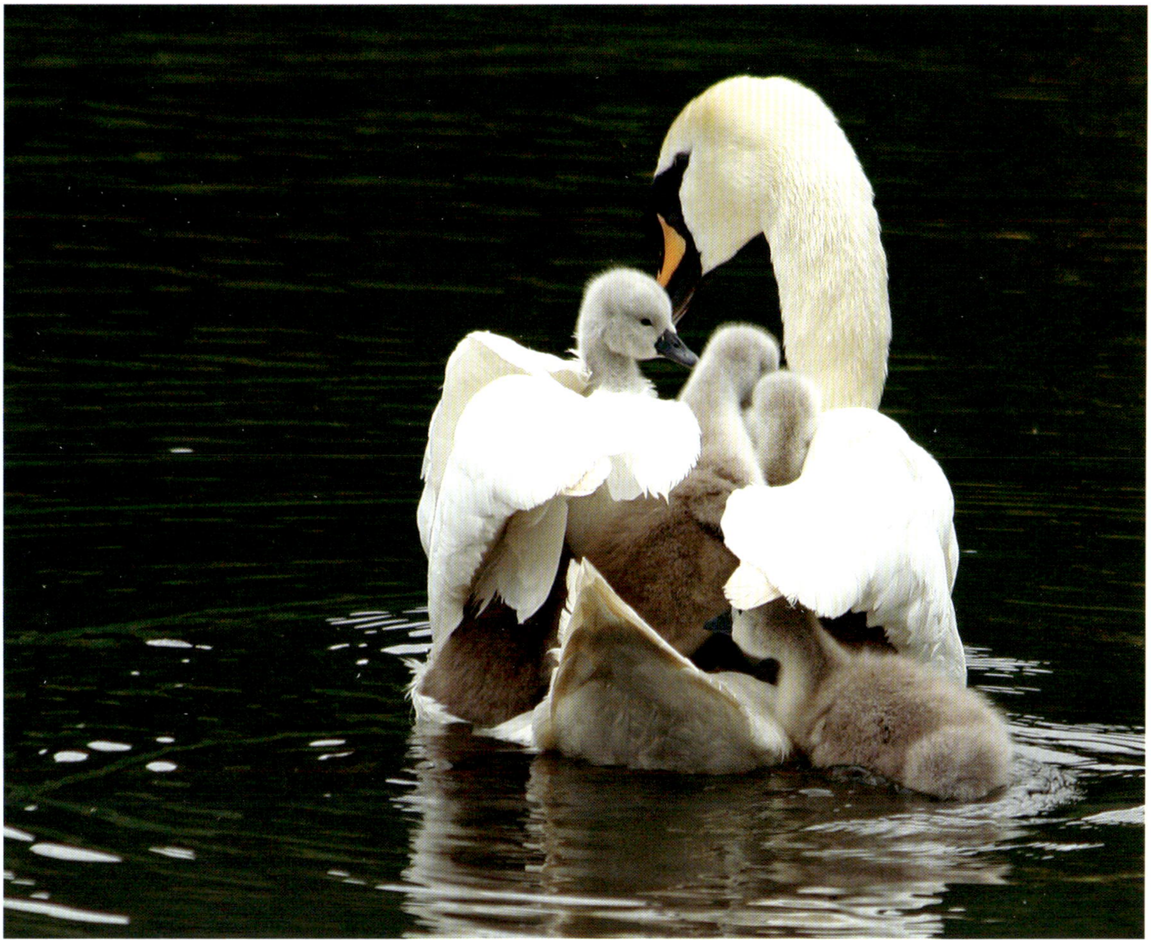

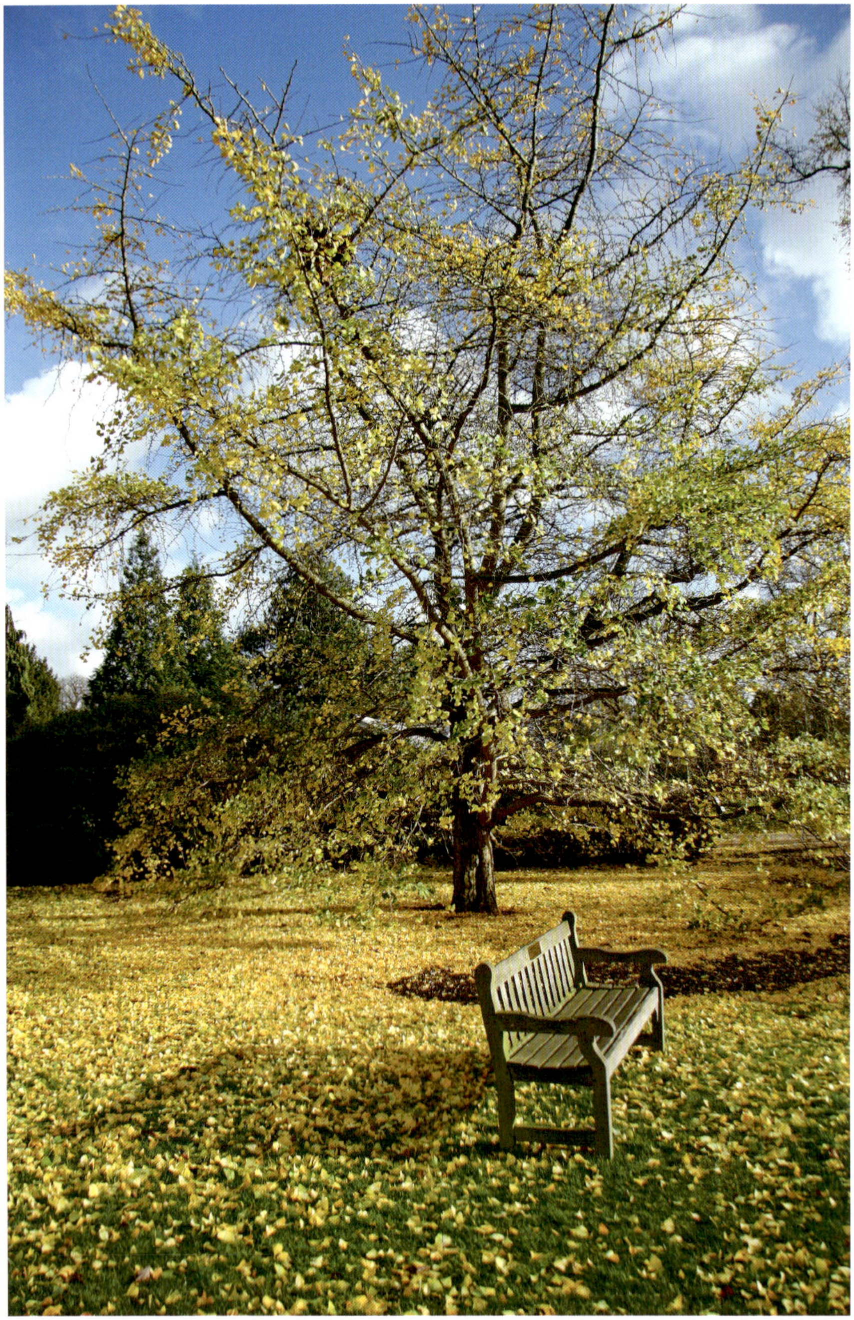

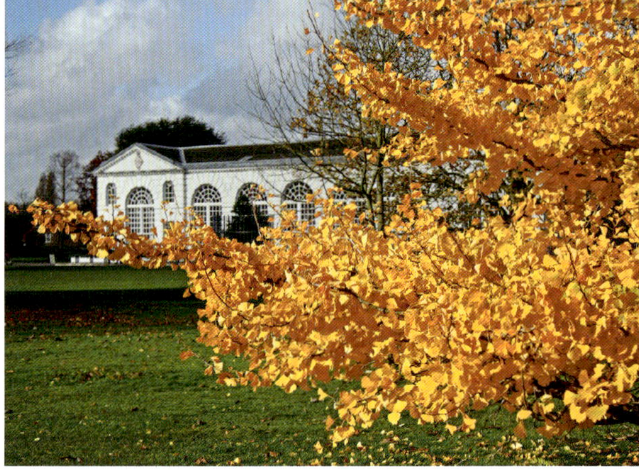

Above: The Orangery

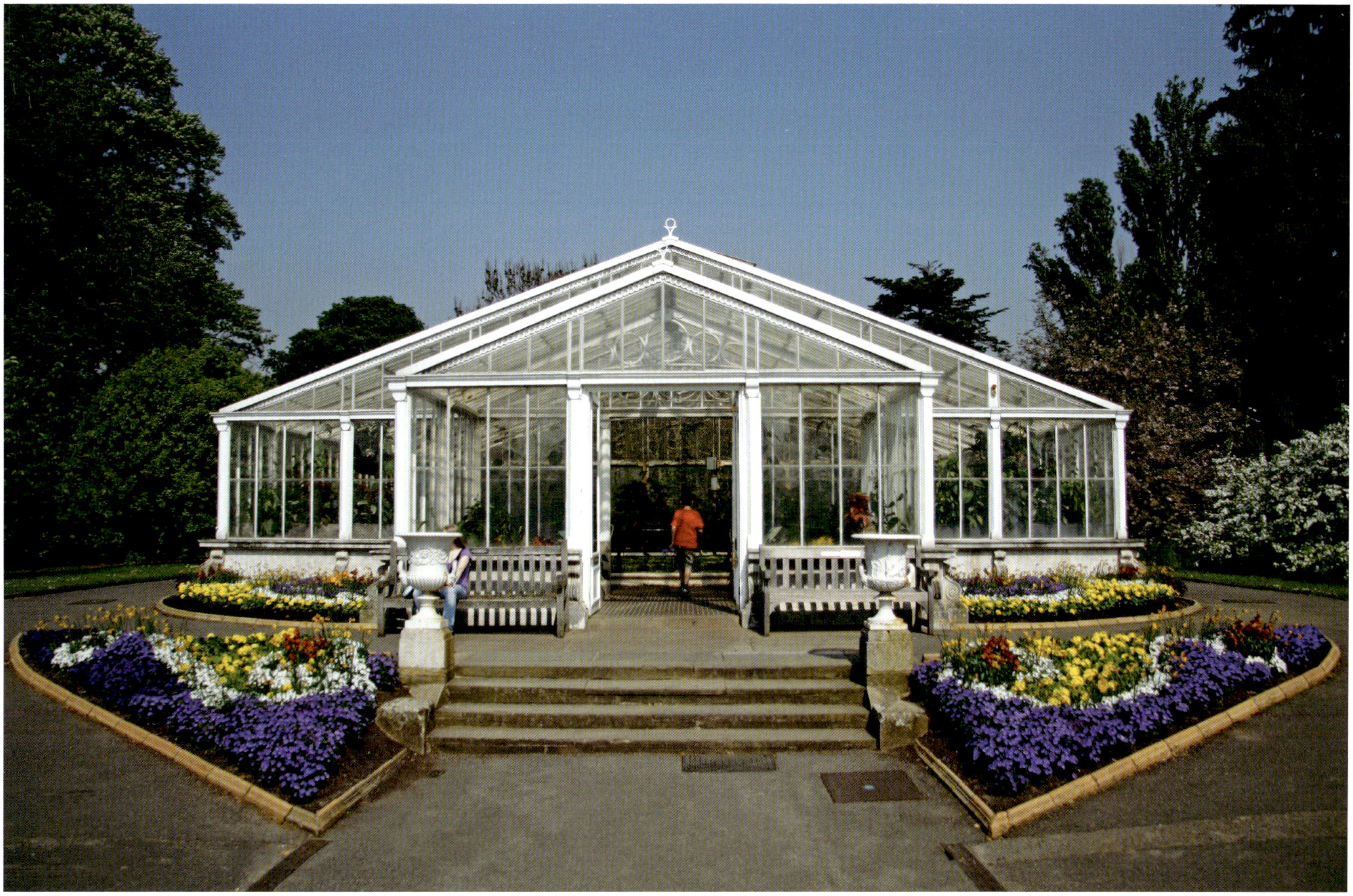

This page: The Water-lily House
Opposite: Autumn colours
The next page: The Palm House

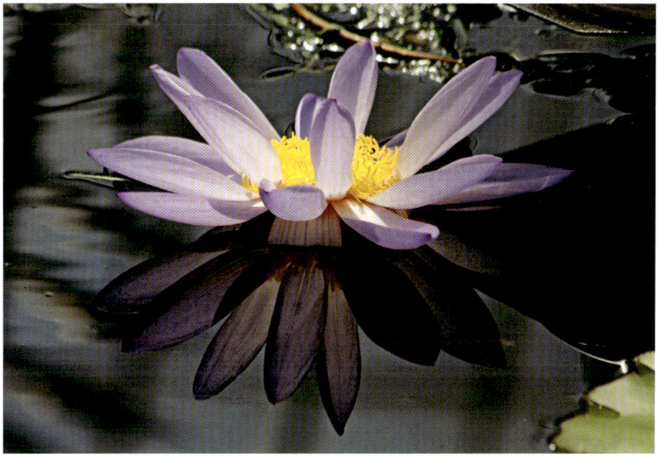

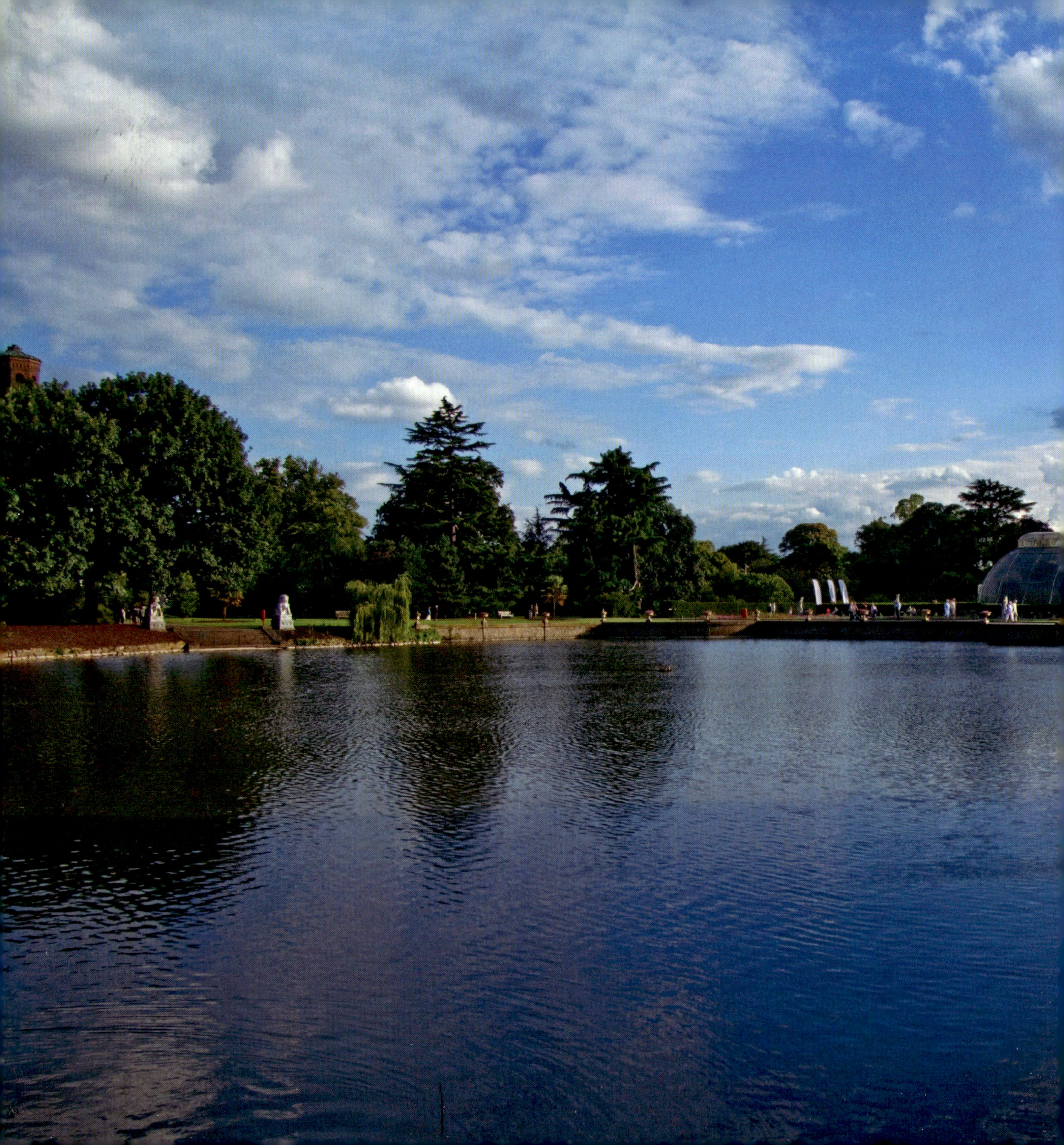

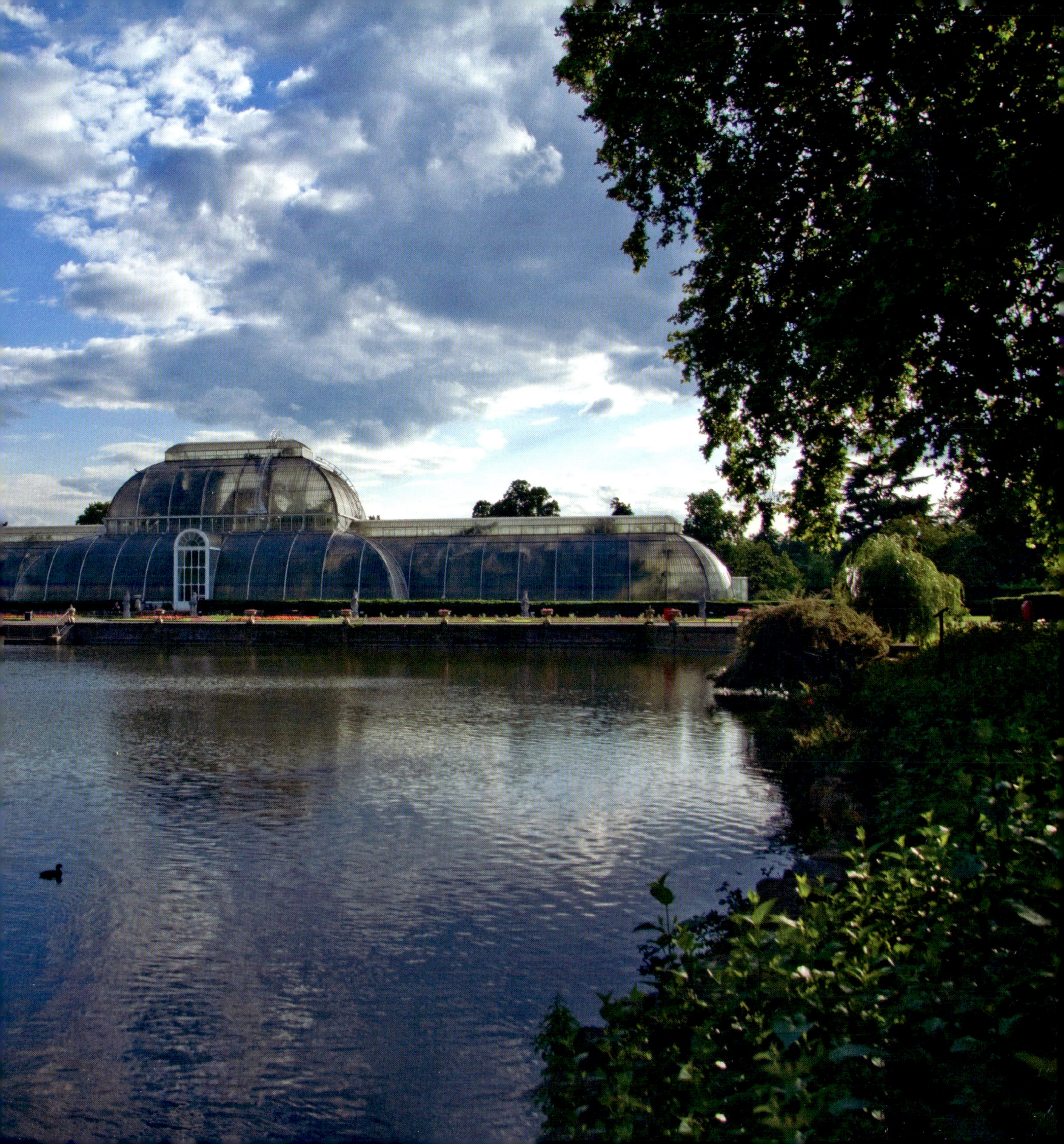

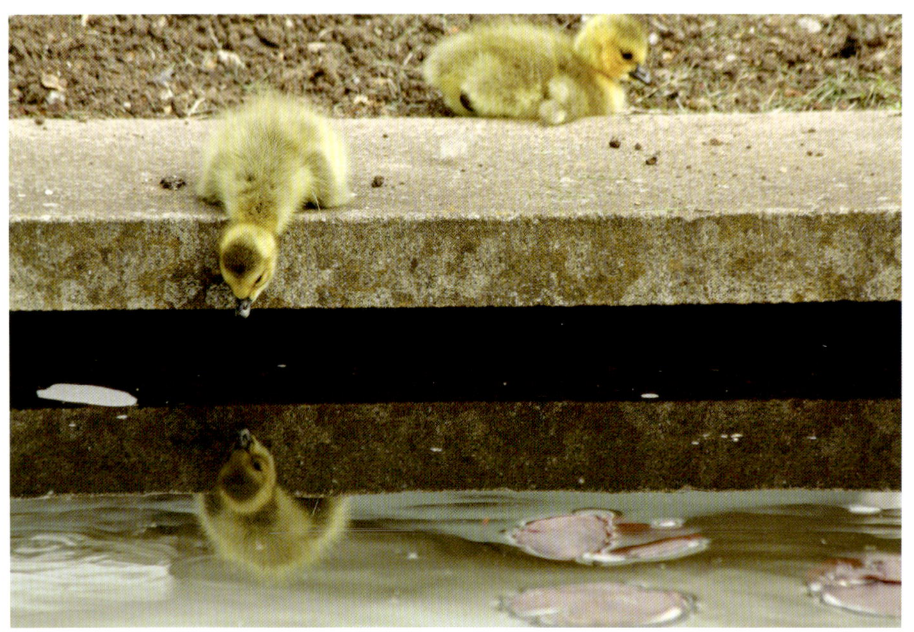

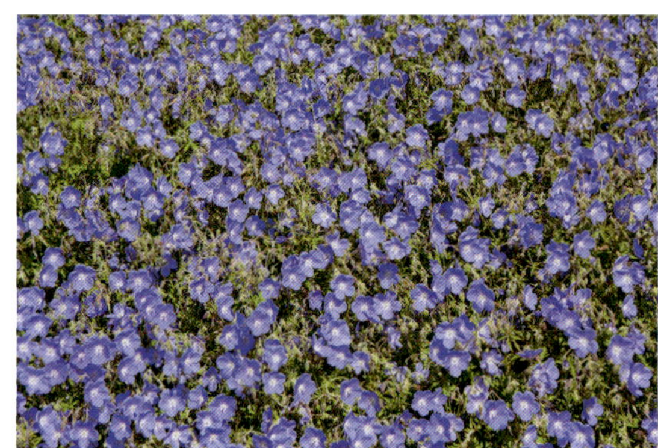

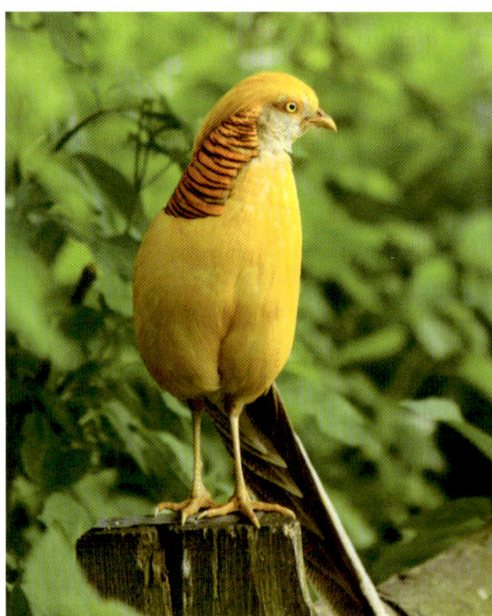

Top left: Canada goslings
Above: Golden Pheasant

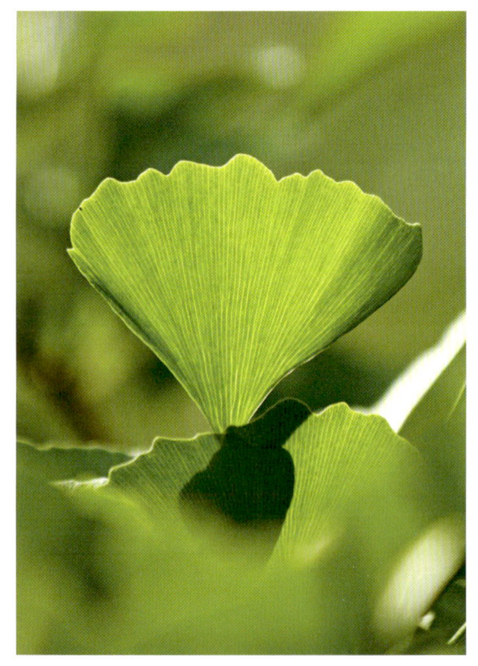

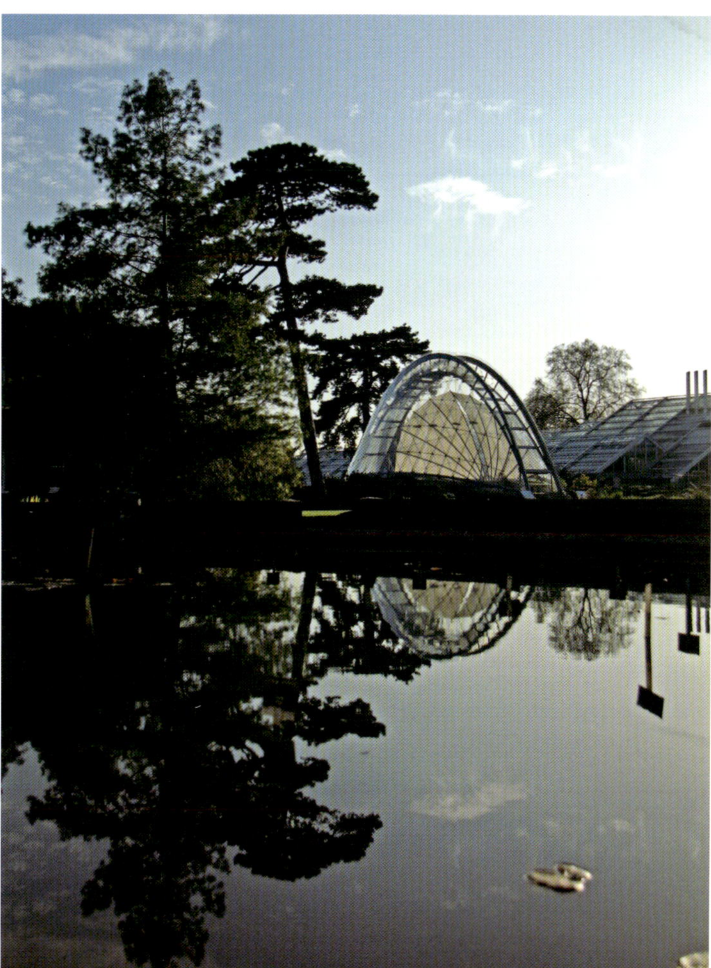

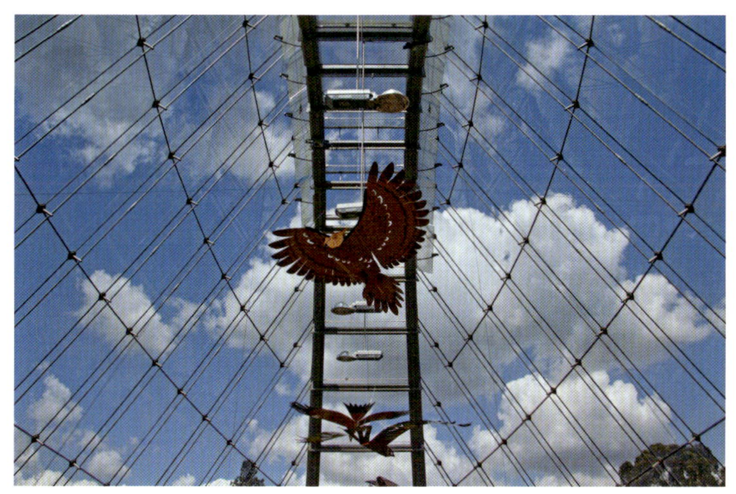

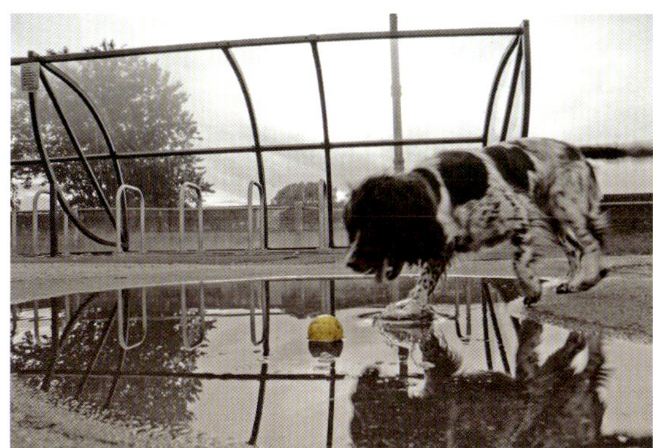

Top left and right: The Davies Alpine House
Above: The Brentford Gate bike racks and one excited dog.
Right: The Brentford Gate

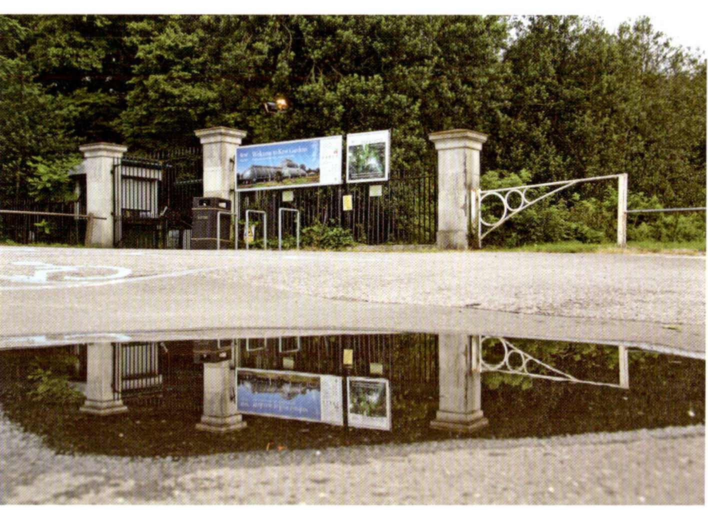

With thanks...

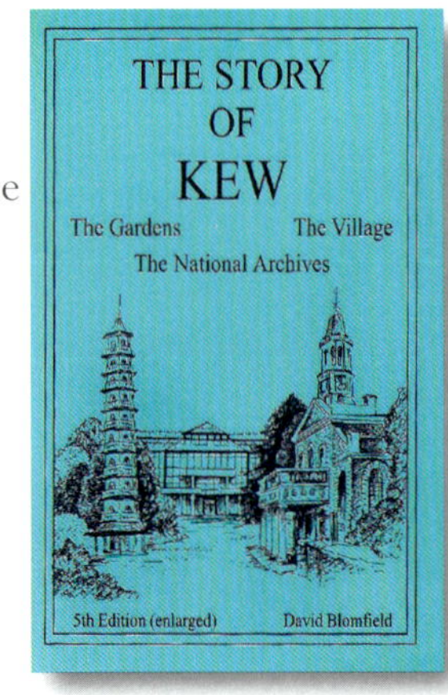

This book has taken the best part of a year to produce and I am indebted to numerous people for their help in making it happen - Mark Brighton, Isla Dawes and all the staff at Kew Bookshop, David and Caroline Blomfield (the cover of one of David's books is on the right), Jeremy Wilson, James Naughtie, Diana Hutchings, David Collison, Richard Nye, my wife Diana, Justin for the loan of his lens, Gina Fullerlove and Rebecca Evdoka of The Royal Botanic Gardens, Ian Dobie, Jem Peck, Norton York, Cathy Tilley, Michelle Warburton, Michael Dillon, Angela Catlin, Lisa Jones, Richmond Council and my Mum.

Over such a long period it is hard to remember quite who I have seen and what I have cast my lens over and my apologies if I have inadvertently forgotten to mention you.

Other books by Andrew Wilson from the WILD series

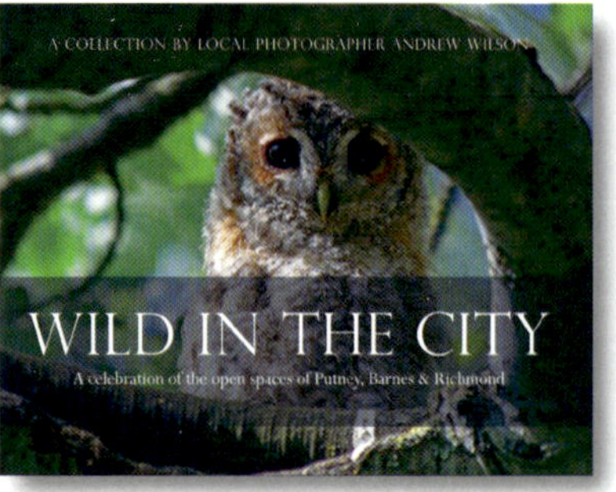

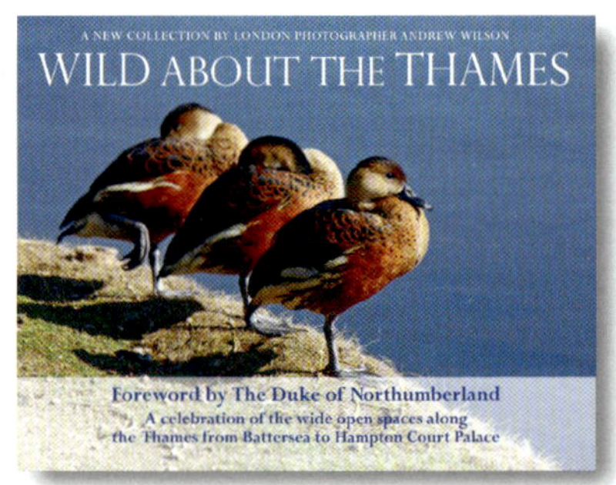

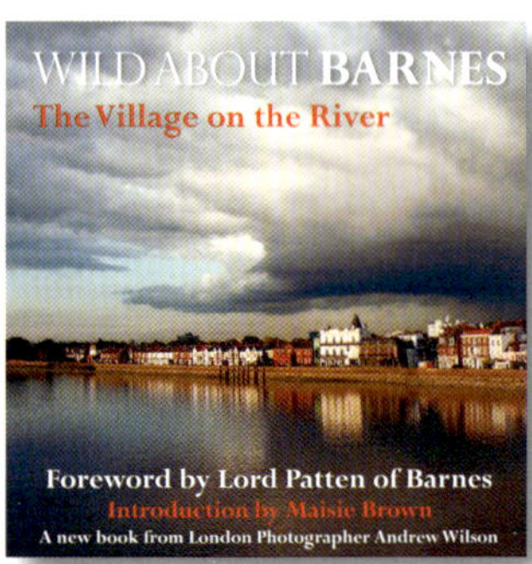

Wild in the City, Wild about the Thames and my latest book Wild about Barnes are available to buy at all good book stores, including Barnes, Kew and Sheen Bookshops.

Follow Andrew on Twitter @andrewpics and view a selection of pictures from all my books and much more plus have the opportunity to buy prints at www.wildinthecity.co.uk

Printed by ***Pensord*** www.pensord.co.uk, with thanks to Paul Mills and Marie Brown & bound by ***Green Street Bindery*** of Oxford with thanks to Garry Phipps www.maltbysbookbinders.com. Colour Management provided by Paul Sherfield of ***The Missing Horse Consultancy*** www.missinghorsecons.co.uk. Finishing advice provided by Steve Giddins of ***Perfect Bindery Solutions*** - www.binderysolutions.co.uk

The pictures from this book were taken using a **Canon** 450D

Published by Unity Print and Publishing Limited,
18 Dungarvan Avenue, London SW15 5QU
Tel: +44 (0)20 8487 2199 - www.unity-publishing.co.uk

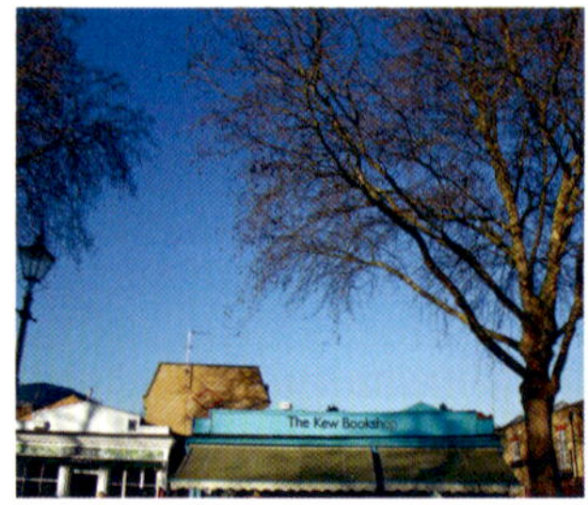

Thank you again to Mark Brighton and Isla Dawes of Kew Bookshop for their help and encouragement over the past year whilst producing this book.

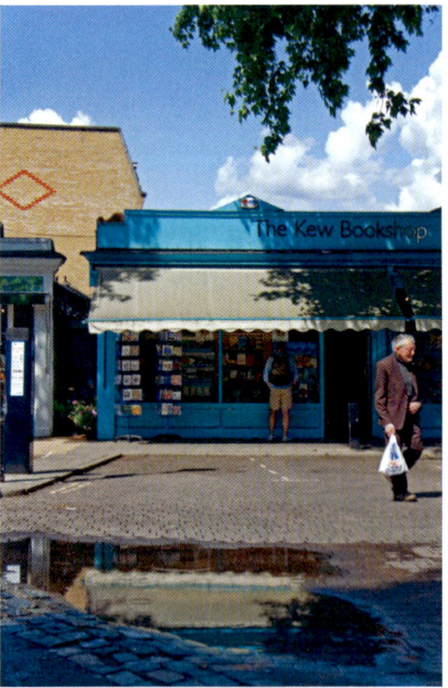